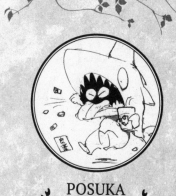

POSUKA DEMIZU

How is volume 16? Ayshe, who appears in this volume, is someone I've been looking forward to revealing.

And finally, the Japanese live-action movie was announced! I just received the production materials, and wow! The demons are super real!!

They've already built the 3D models, and even at this point the texture of the skin is creepy and amazing, but after some discussion they're going to polish the shapes and textures further.

They al... demons...

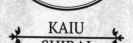

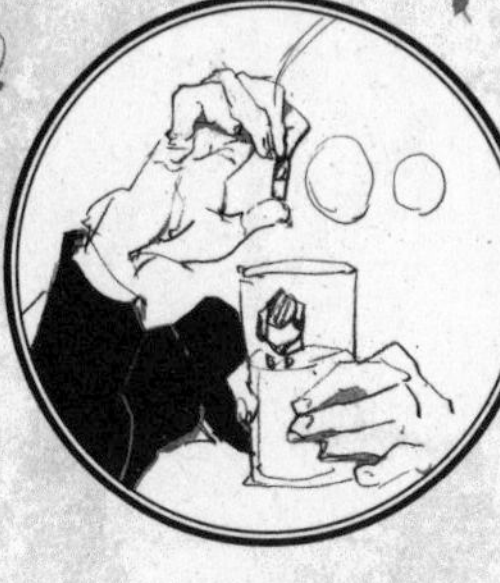

KAIU SHIRAI

Writer Shirai's personal highlights for *The Promised Neverland* fanatics, part 12!

1. They take home the trash! (expected behavior from Isabella's adorable children!)

2. Yukgaejang soup!! (is all I can see—again!)

There aren't very many demons who can speak the demon language anymore. Then why did that demon...?

Please enjoy this volume!

Posuka Demizu debuted as a manga artist with the 2013 *CoroCoro* series *Oreca Monster Bouken Retsuden*. A collection of illustrations, *The Art of Posuka Demizu*, was released in 2016 by PIE International.

Kaiu Shirai debuted in 2015 with *Ashley Gate no Yukue* on the *Shonen Jump+* website. Shirai first worked with Posuka Demizu on the two-shot *Poppy no Negai*, which was released in February 2016.

THE PROMISED NEVERLAND

VOLUME 16
SHONEN JUMP Manga Edition

STORY BY KAIU SHIRAI
ART BY POSUKA DEMIZU

Translation/Satsuki Yamashita
Touch-Up Art & Lettering/Mark McMurray
Design/Julian [JR] Robinson
Editor/Alexis Kirsch

YAKUSOKU NO NEVERLAND © 2016 by Kaiu Shirai, Posuka Demizu
All rights reserved.
First published in Japan in 2016 by SHUEISHA Inc., Tokyo.
English translation rights arranged by SHUEISHA Inc.

The stories, characters and incidents mentioned in this publication are
entirely fictional.

Printed in the U.S.A.

Published by VIZ Media, LLC
P.O. Box 77010
San Francisco, CA 94107

10 9 8 7 6 5 4 3 2 1
First printing, August 2020

PARENTAL ADVISORY
THE PROMISED NEVERLAND is rated T+
and is recommended for ages 16 and up.
This volume contains fantasy violence and
adult themes.

viz.com

shonenjump.com

CHARACTERS

The Children of Grace Field House

They aim to free all of the children who are trapped in Grace Field House within the next two months.

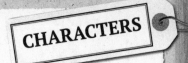

RAY

On the Run

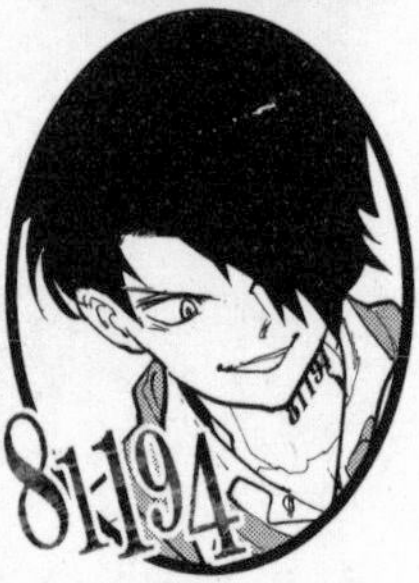
81194

The only one among the Grace Field House children who can match wits with Norman.

EMMA

On the Run

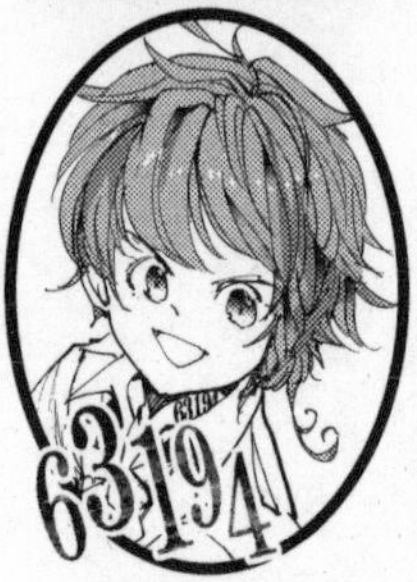
63194

An enthusiastic and optimistic girl with superb athletic and learning abilities.

NORMAN

On the Run

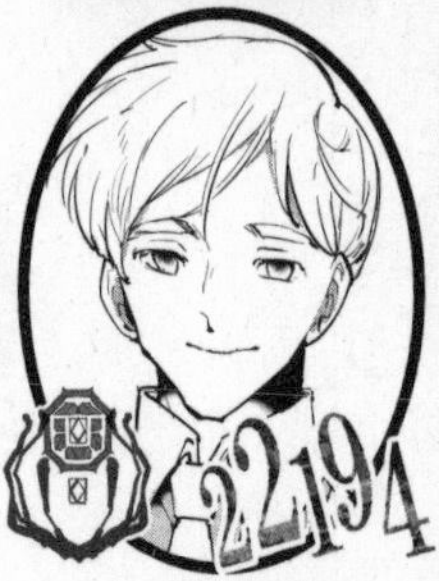
22194

A boy with excellent analytical and decision-making capabilities. He is the smartest of the children from Grace Field House.

CAROL

In Grace Field House

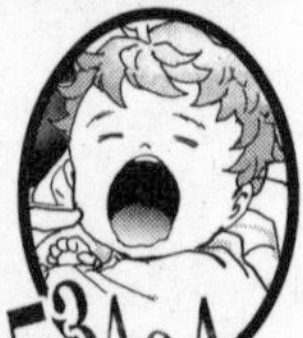
53494

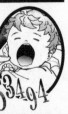

PHIL

In Grace Field House

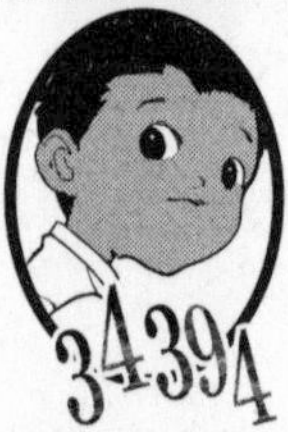
34394

GILDA

On the Run

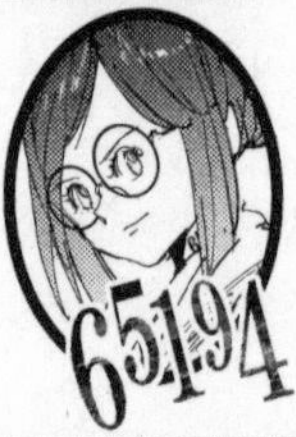
65194

DON

On the Run

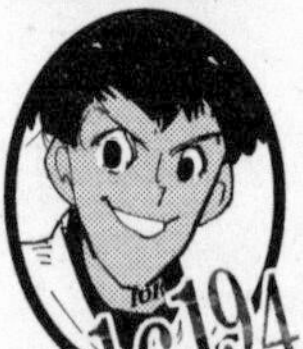
16194

The Escapees of Lambda 7214

They obtained superpowers from being repeatedly experimented on by the demons. They are devoted to Norman and have destroyed many farms with him.

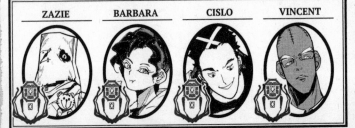

ZAZIE

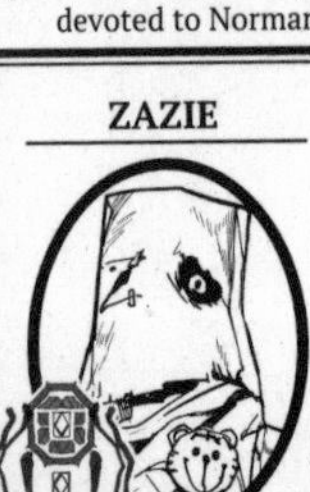

BARBARA

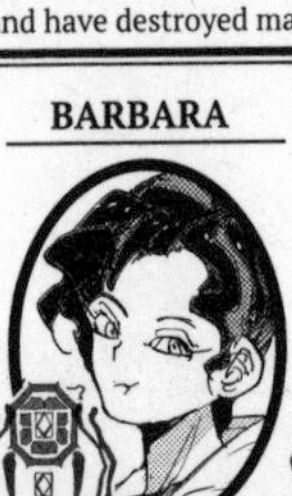

CISLO

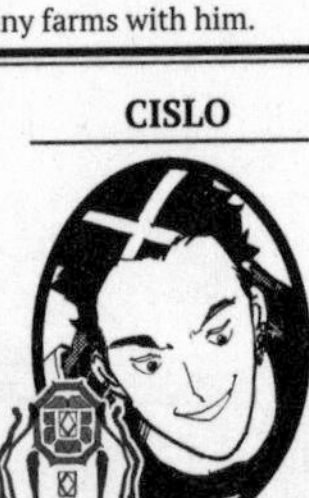

VINCENT

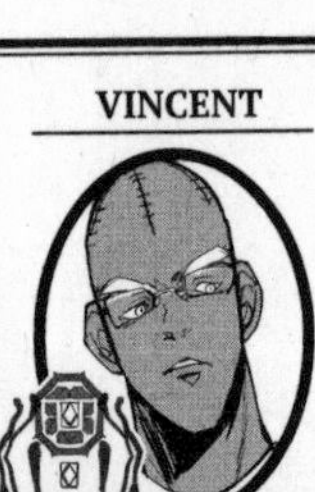

???
Said to be located in a mysterious space with a dragon.

???

Evil-Blooded Girl Group
Thought to have been killed by the royal family for her ability to maintain human form, but she has secretly survived.

MUJIKA   SONJU

Geelan Clan
Joined an alliance with Norman to get revenge on the royal family and the aristocrats.

GEELAN

Royal Family
The queen who rules the many subjects of the demon world.

LEGRAVALIMA

The Five Regent Houses
They govern the demon world with the royal family. They also operate the farms that raise humans.

LORD DOZZA   DUKE YVERK   LADY NOUM
LORD PUPO   LORD BAYON (CURRENT)

The Story So Far

Emma is living happily at Grace Field House with her foster siblings. One day, she realizes that they are being bred as food for demons and escapes with a group of other children. After meeting new friends and gaining further information, she decides to free all of the children raised in the farms. Her group researches the Seven Walls, the key to making a new promise, and after a lot of hard work they find a way. But just then, they are attacked and lose some friends in addition to their home. Despite the uncertainty, Emma keeps moving toward her goal. She is reunited with Norman, who is alive. But he plans to annihilate the demons, and Emma, who is against the plan, decides to resolve the situation by searching for the Seven Walls with Ray. The two arrive at a mysterious place that looks a lot like Grace Field House.

THE PROMISED NEVERLAND 16

Lost Boy

CHAPTER 134: LOST BOY

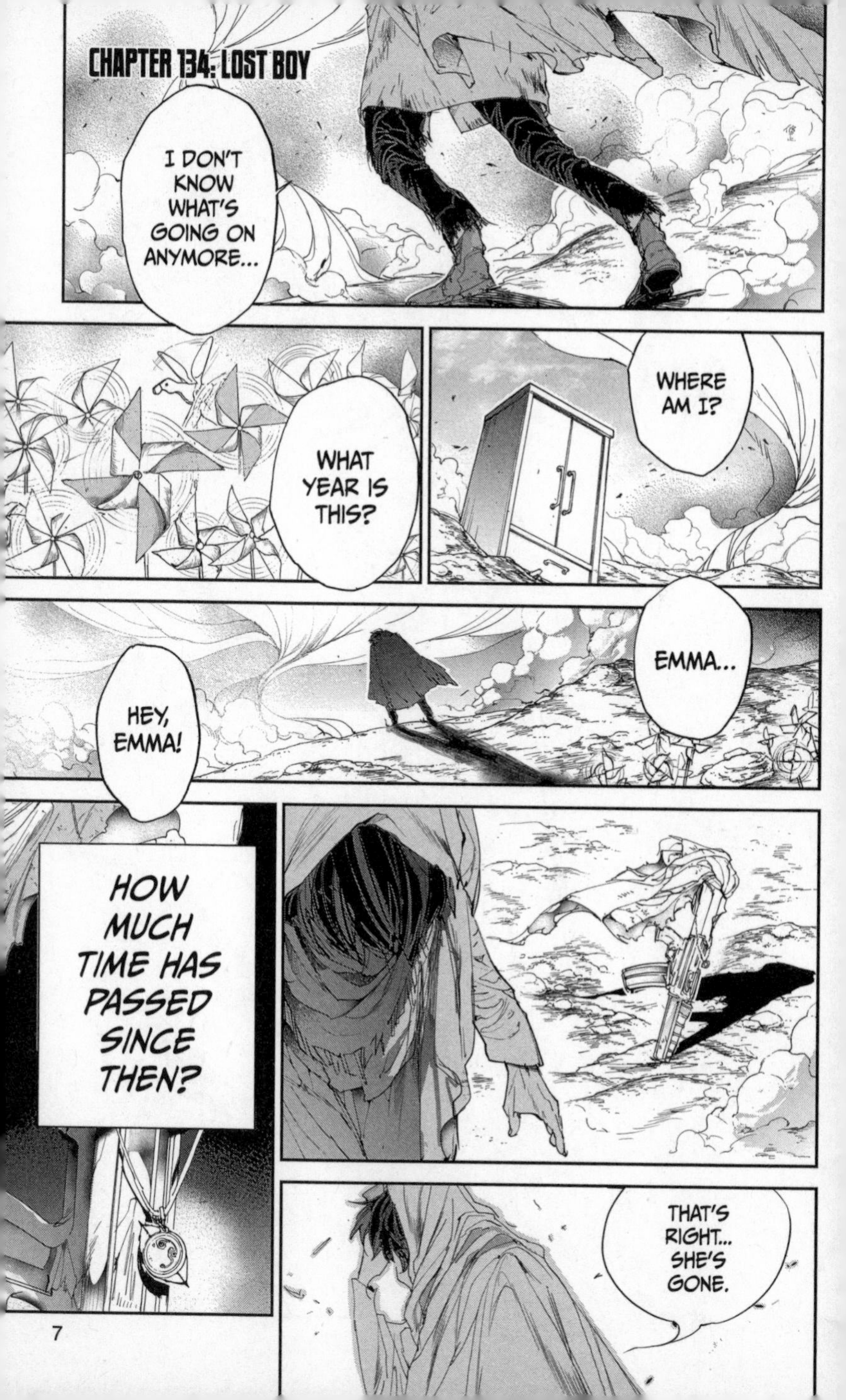
I DON'T KNOW WHAT'S GOING ON ANYMORE...
WHERE AM I?
WHAT YEAR IS THIS?
EMMA...
HEY, EMMA!
THAT'S RIGHT... SHE'S GONE.
HOW MUCH TIME HAS PASSED SINCE THEN?

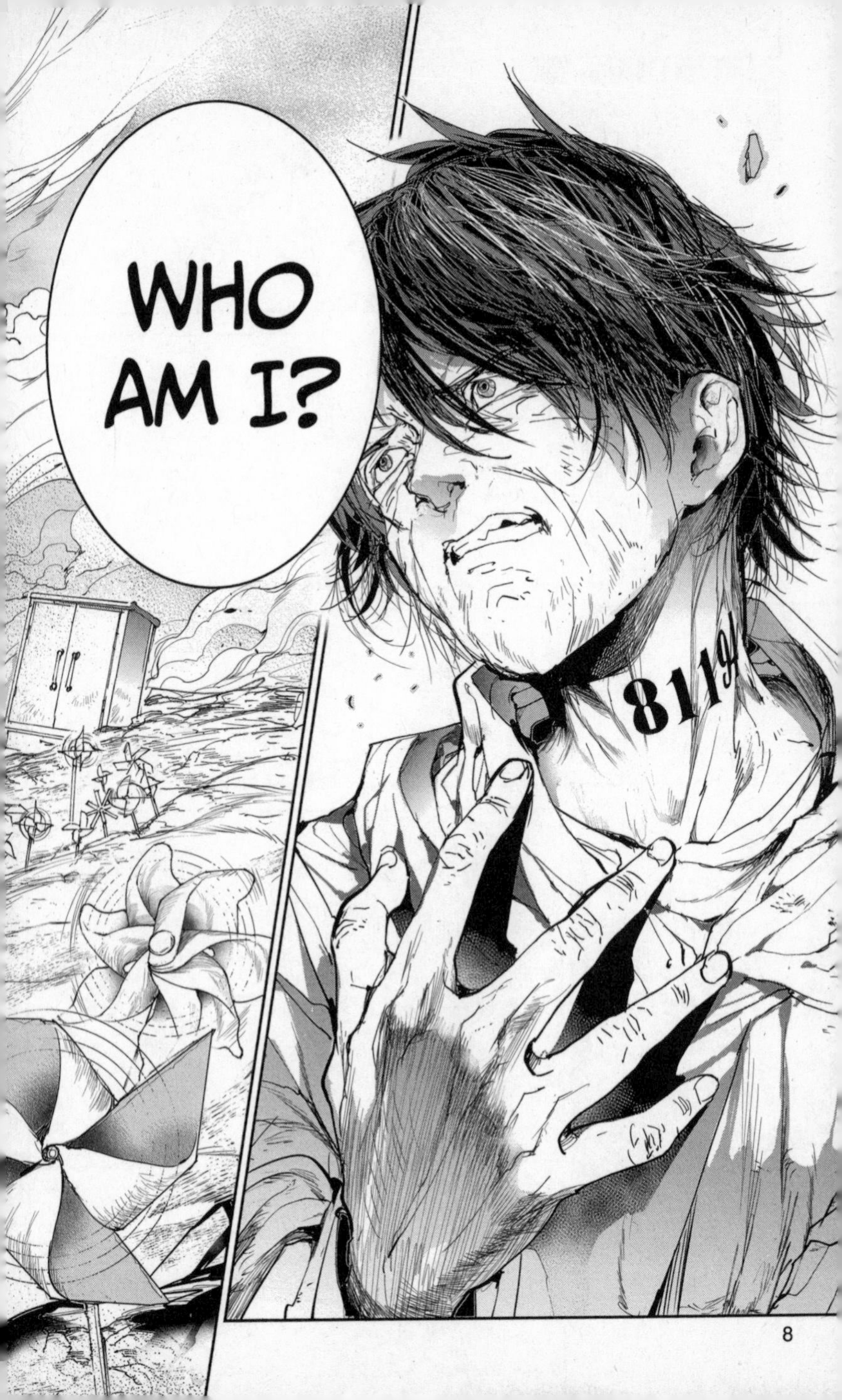
WHO AM I?

CHAPTER 134: LOST BOY

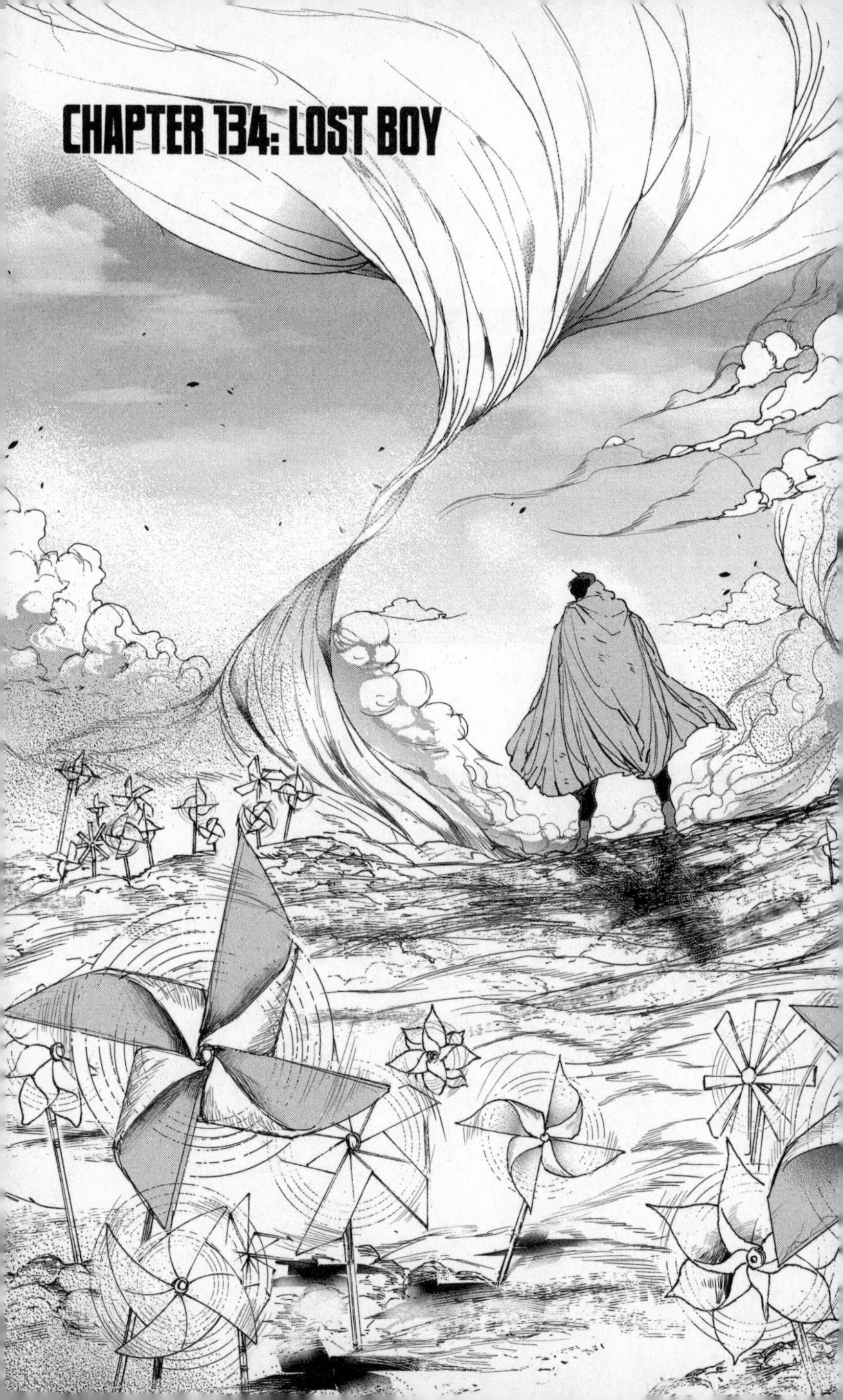

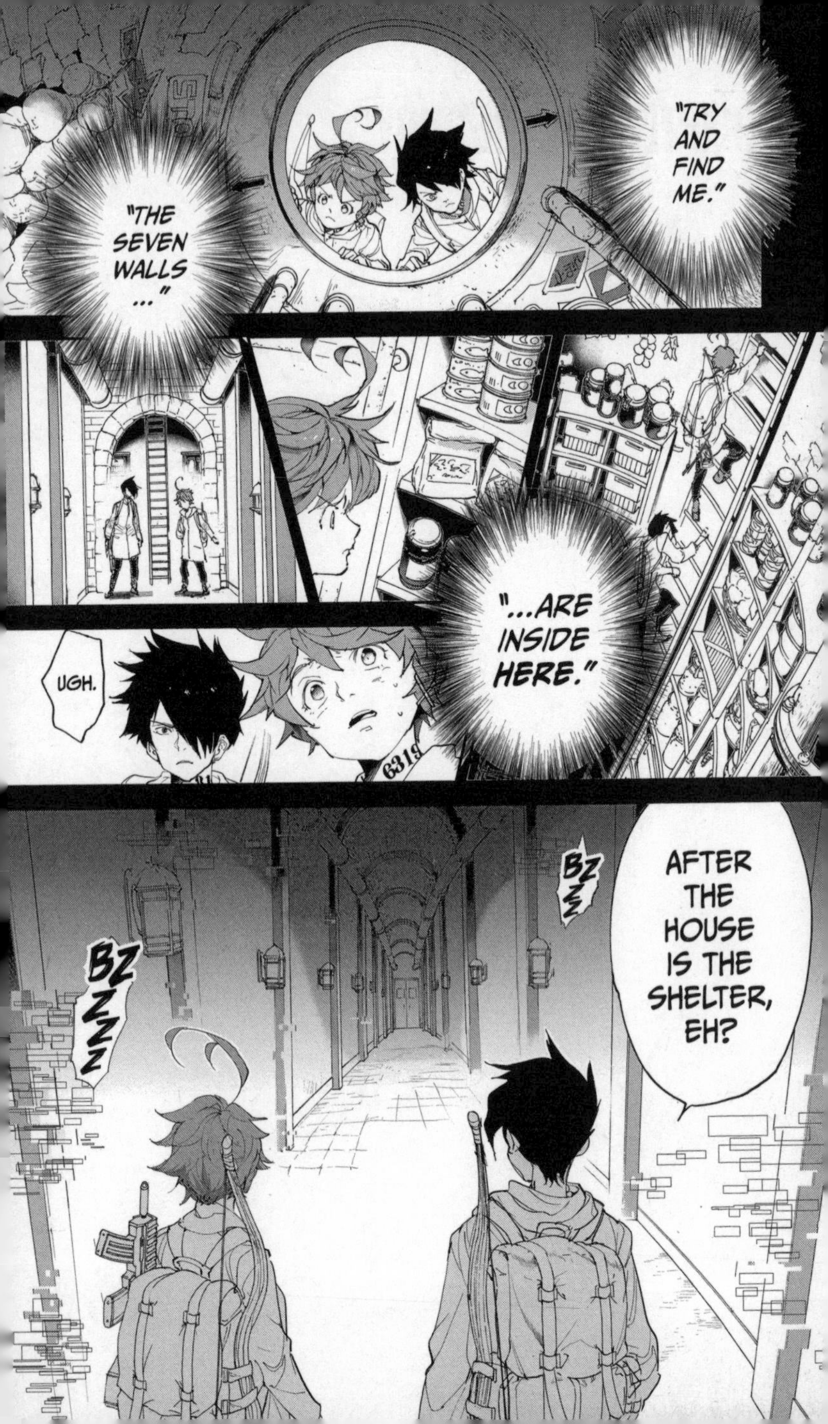
"TRY AND FIND ME."
"THE SEVEN WALLS ..."
"...ARE INSIDE HERE."
UGH.
AFTER THE HOUSE IS THE SHELTER, EH?
BZZZ
BZZZZ

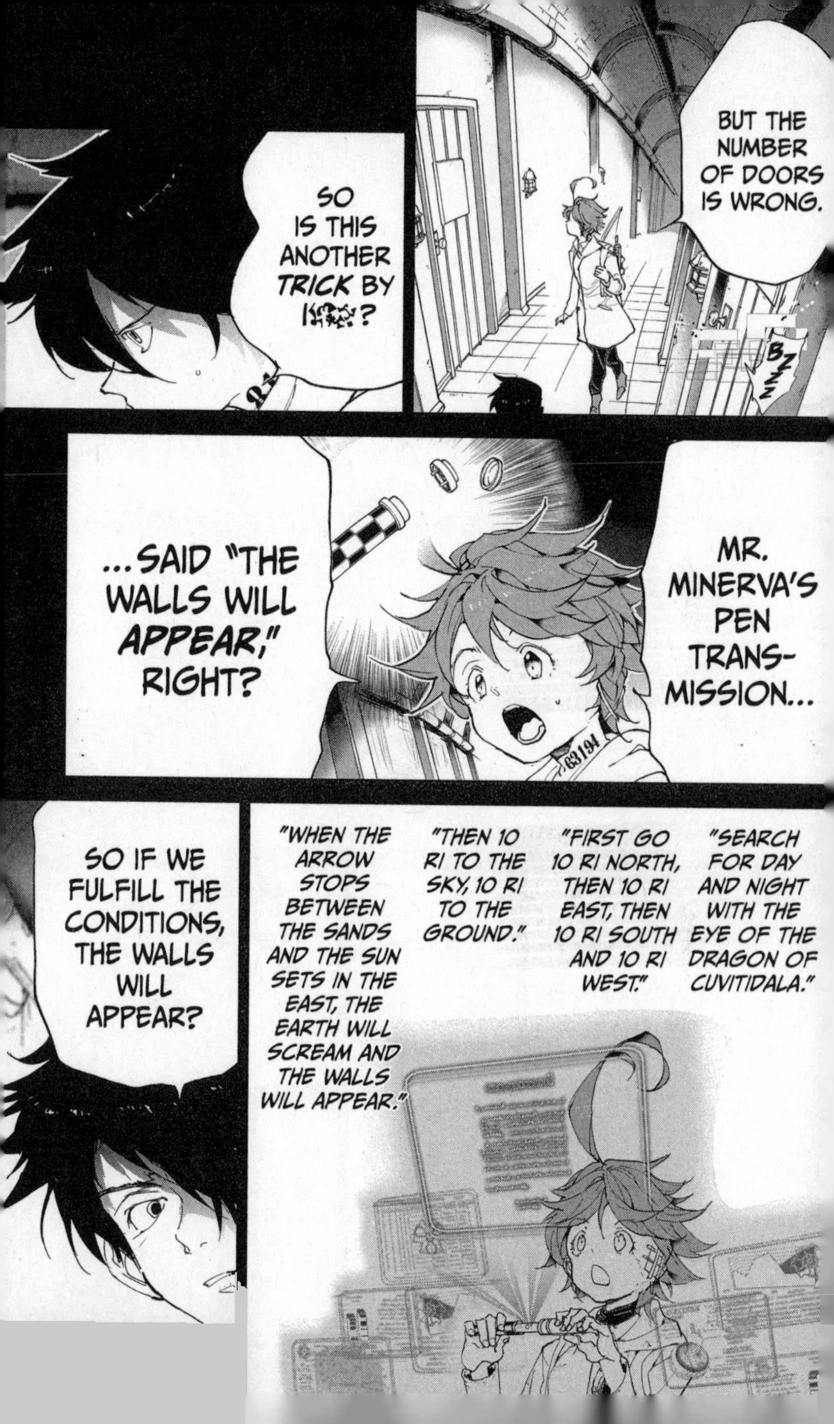
BUT THE NUMBER OF DOORS IS WRONG.
BZZZ
SO IS THIS ANOTHER TRICK BY ?
MR. MINERVA'S PEN TRANS-MISSION...
...SAID "THE WALLS WILL APPEAR," RIGHT?
"SEARCH FOR DAY AND NIGHT WITH THE EYE OF THE DRAGON OF CUVITIDALA."
"FIRST GO 10 RI NORTH, THEN 10 RI EAST, THEN 10 RI SOUTH AND 10 RI WEST."
"THEN 10 RI TO THE SKY, 10 RI TO THE GROUND."
"WHEN THE ARROW STOPS BETWEEN THE SANDS AND THE SUN SETS IN THE EAST, THE EARTH WILL SCREAM AND THE WALLS WILL APPEAR."
SO IF WE FULFILL THE CONDITIONS, THE WALLS WILL APPEAR?

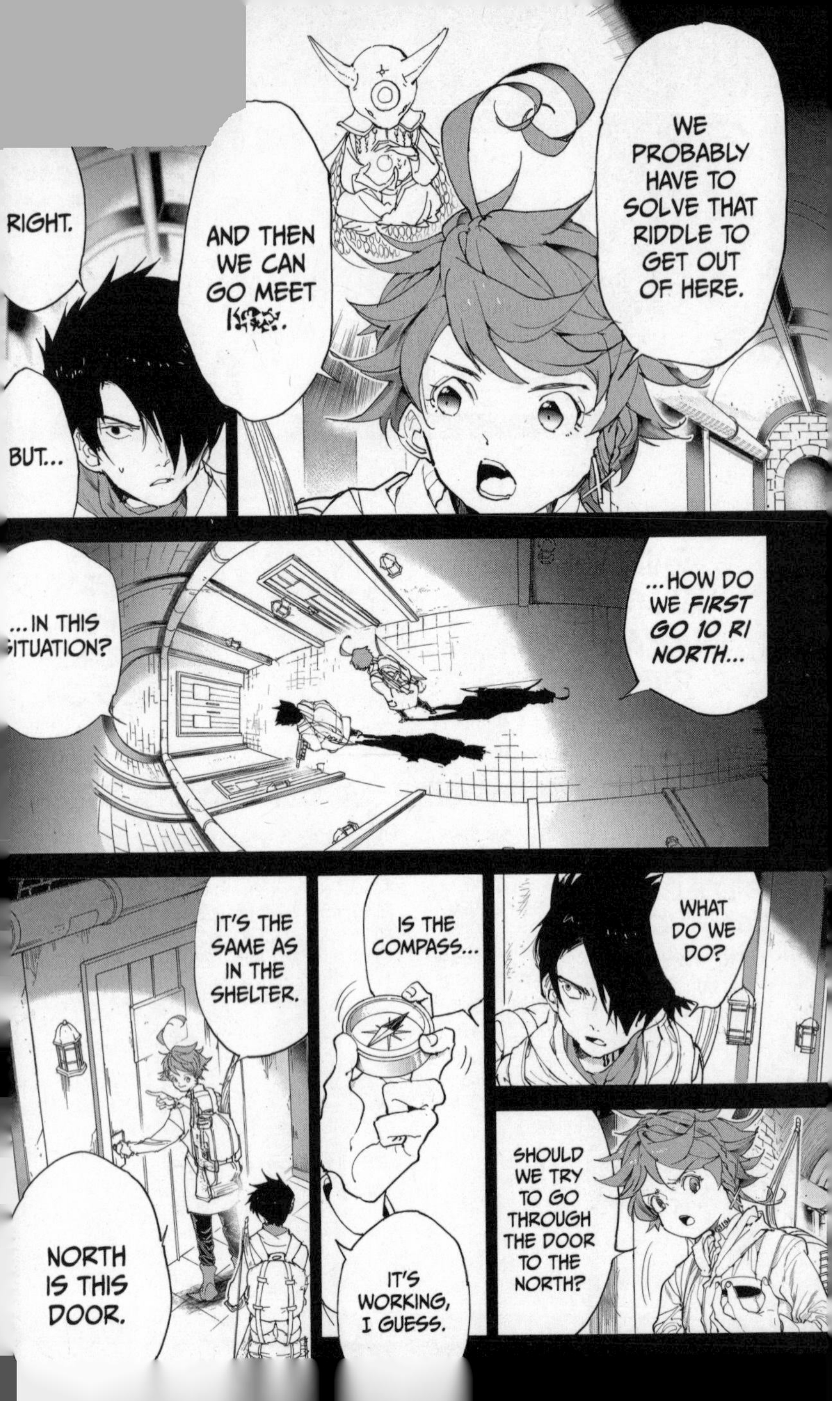
WE PROBABLY HAVE TO SOLVE THAT RIDDLE TO GET OUT OF HERE.
AND THEN WE CAN GO MEET
RIGHT.
BUT...
...HOW DO WE *FIRST GO 10 RI NORTH*...
...IN THIS SITUATION?
WHAT DO WE DO?
SHOULD WE TRY TO GO THROUGH THE DOOR TO THE NORTH?
IS THE COMPASS...
IT'S WORKING, I GUESS.
IT'S THE SAME AS IN THE SHELTER.
NORTH IS THIS DOOR.

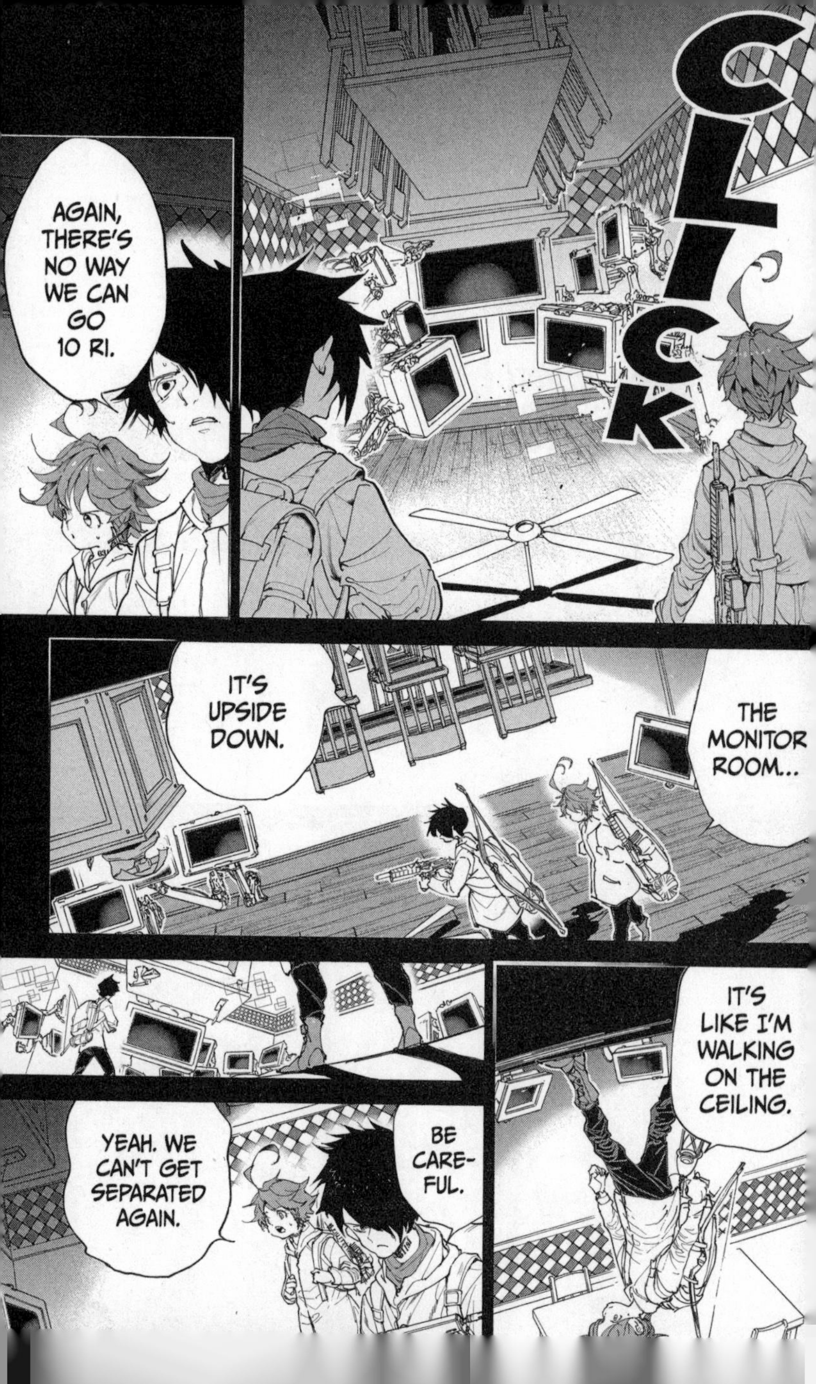
CLICK
AGAIN, THERE'S NO WAY WE CAN GO 10 RI.
THE MONITOR ROOM...
IT'S UPSIDE DOWN.
IT'S LIKE I'M WALKING ON THE CEILING.
BE CARE-FUL.
YEAH. WE CAN'T GET SEPARATED AGAIN.

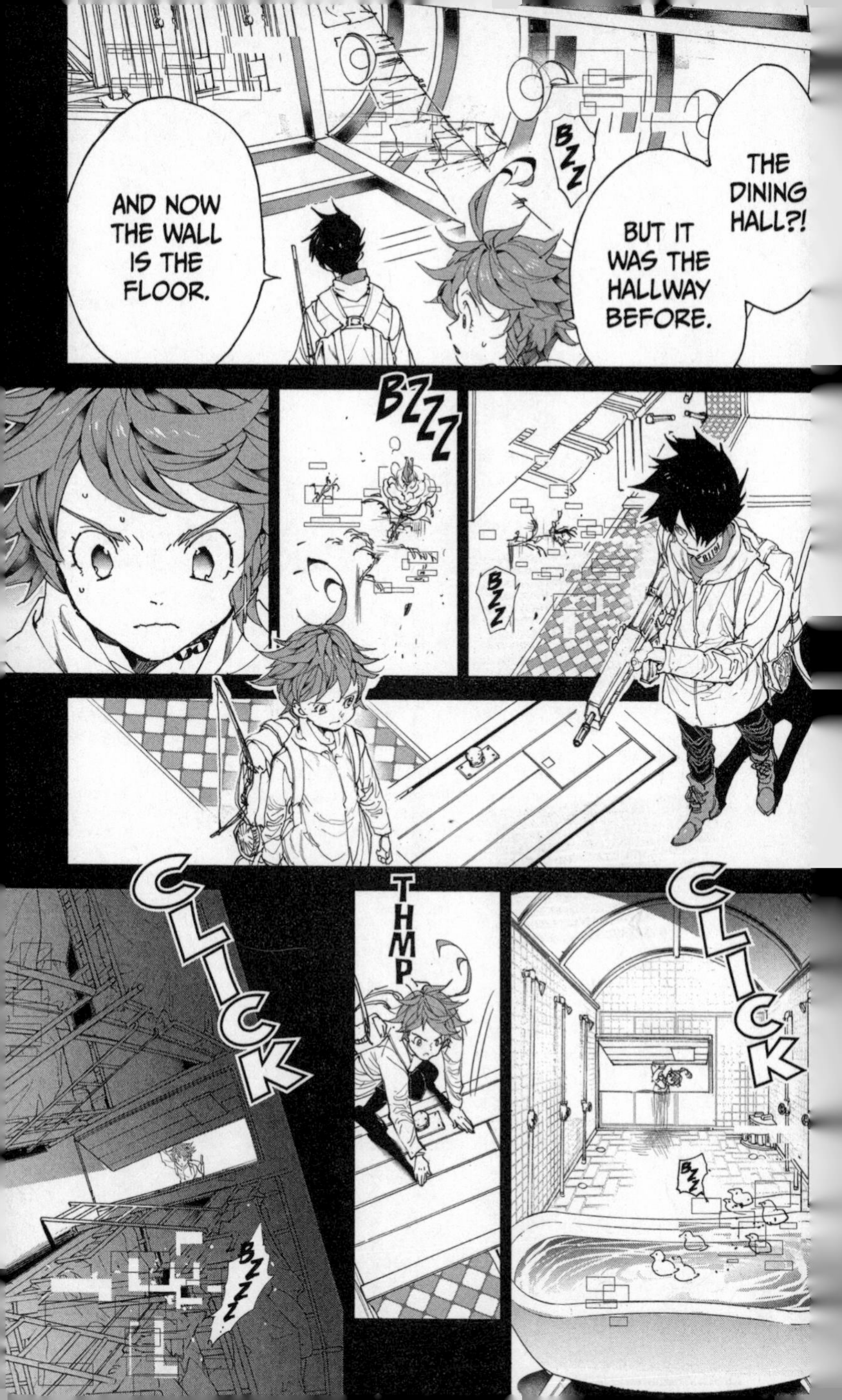
THE DINING HALL?!
BUT IT WAS THE HALLWAY BEFORE.
BZZ
AND NOW THE WALL IS THE FLOOR.
BZZ
BZZZ
CLICK
BZZ
THMP
CLICK
BZZZZ

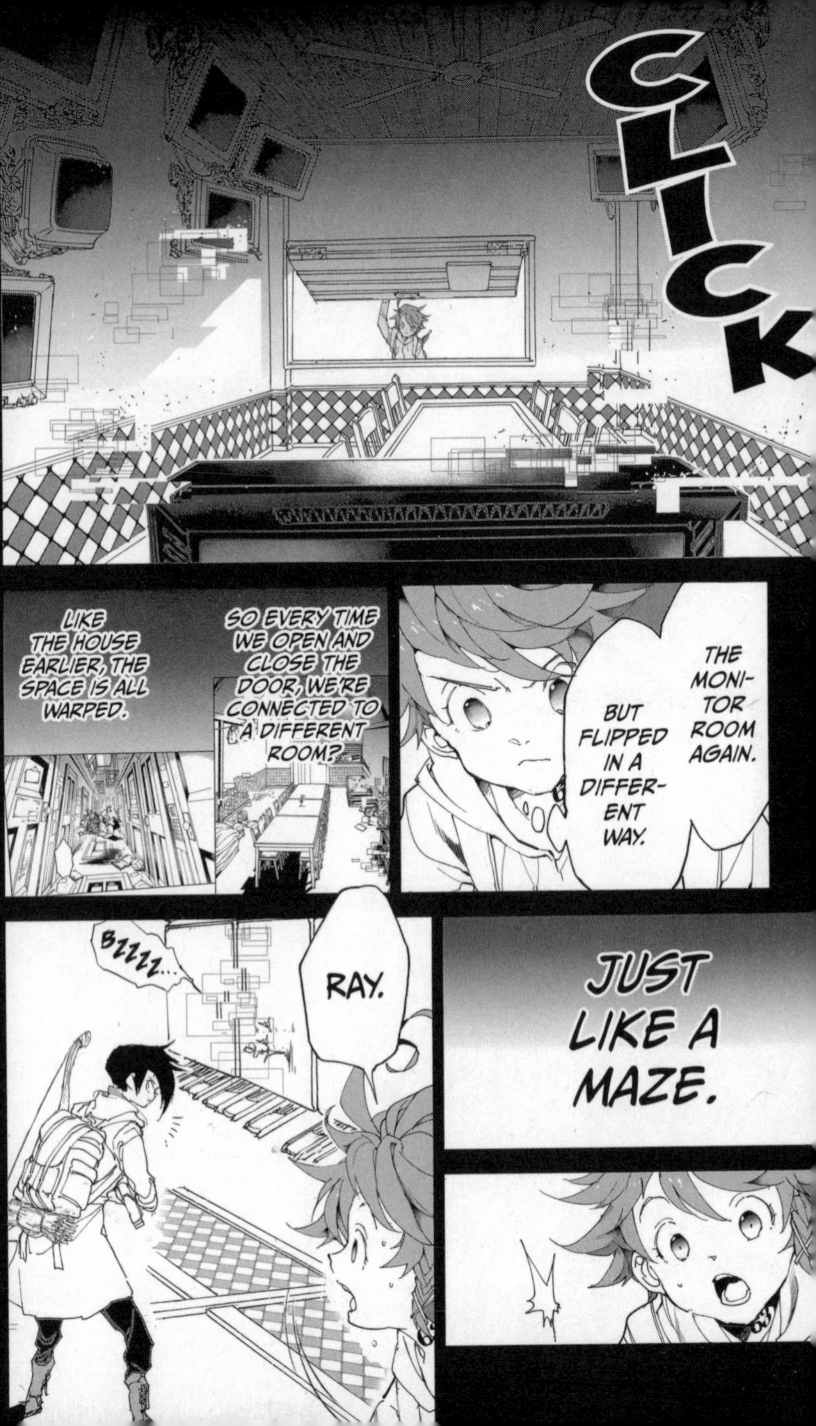
CLICK
THE MONI-TOR ROOM AGAIN.
BUT FLIPPED IN A DIFFER-ENT WAY.
SO EVERY TIME WE OPEN AND CLOSE THE DOOR, WE'RE CONNECTED TO A DIFFERENT ROOM?
LIKE THE HOUSE EARLIER, THE SPACE IS ALL WARPED.
JUST LIKE A MAZE.
RAY.
BZZZZ...

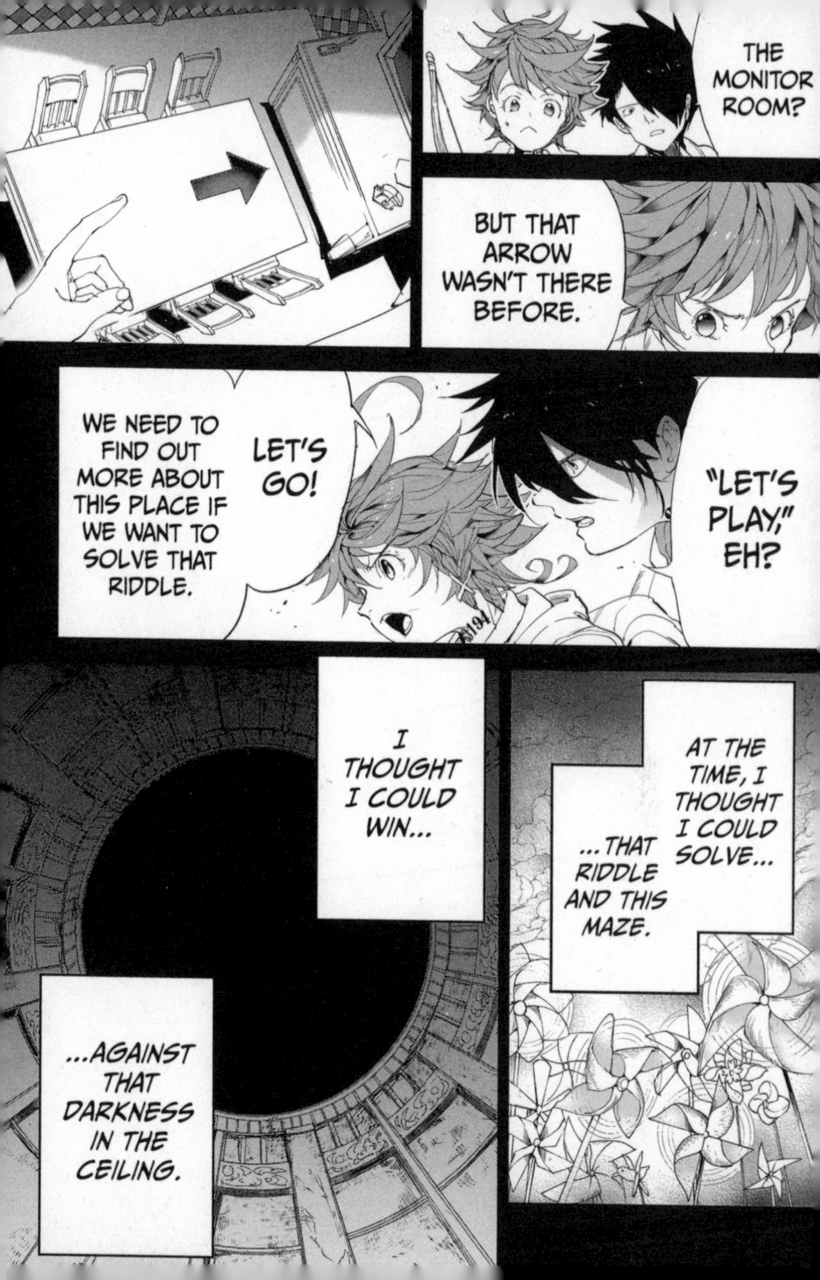
THE MONITOR ROOM?
BUT THAT ARROW WASN'T THERE BEFORE.
"LET'S PLAY," EH?
LET'S GO!
WE NEED TO FIND OUT MORE ABOUT THIS PLACE IF WE WANT TO SOLVE THAT RIDDLE.
AT THE TIME, I THOUGHT I COULD SOLVE...
...THAT RIDDLE AND THIS MAZE.
I THOUGHT I COULD WIN...
...AGAINST THAT DARKNESS IN THE CEILING.

CHAPTER 135: THE SEARCH

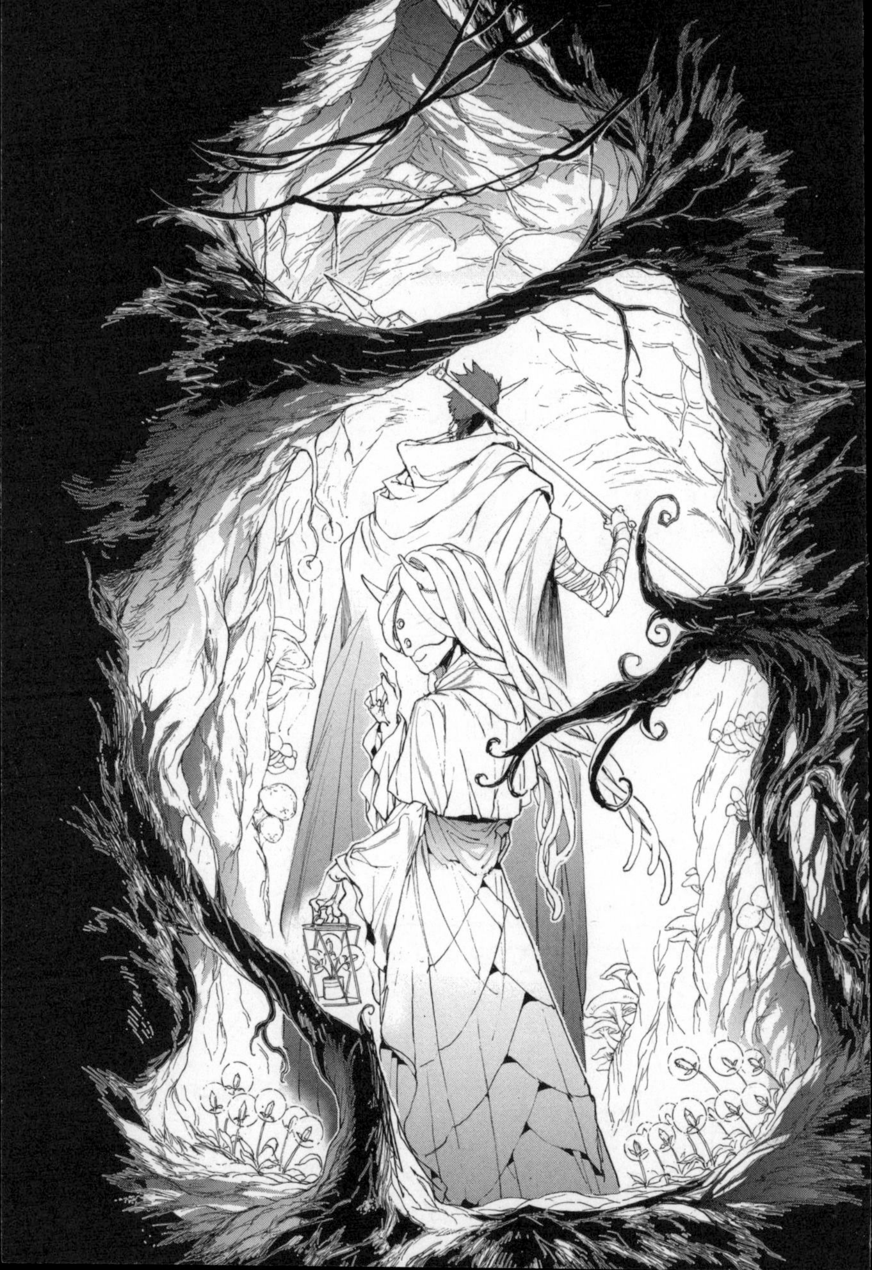

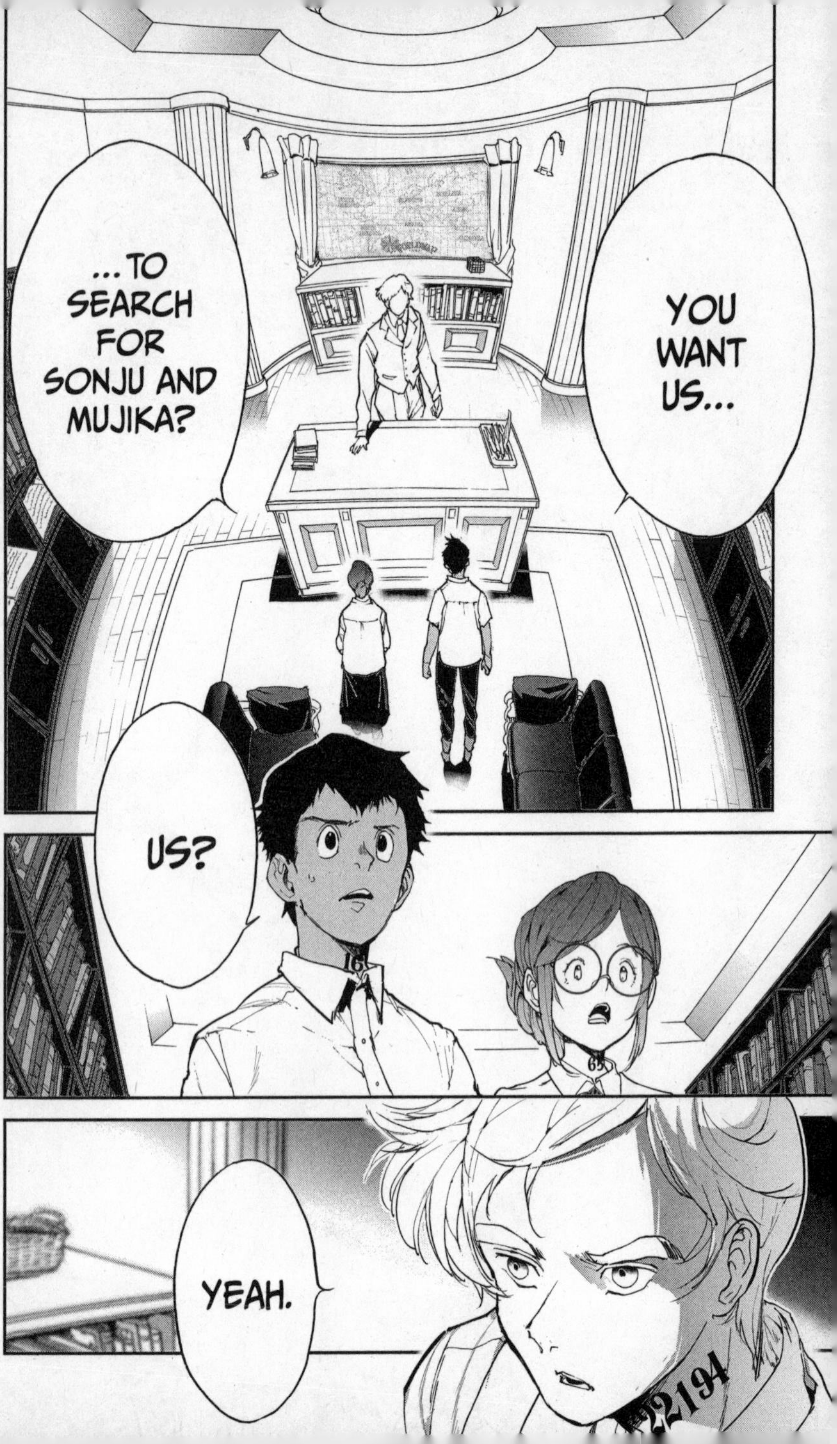
YOU WANT US...
...TO SEARCH FOR SONJU AND MUJIKA?
US?
YEAH.

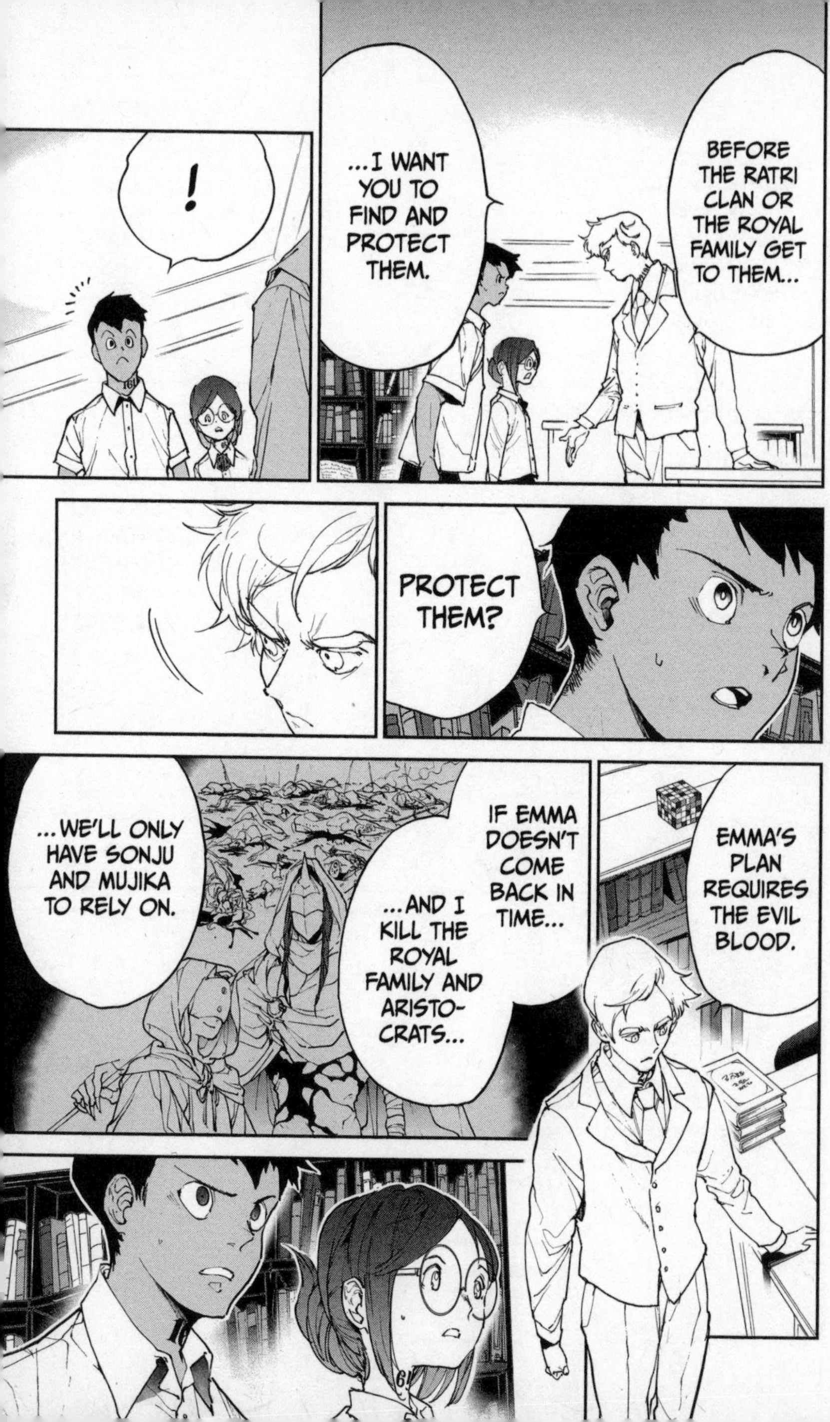
BEFORE THE RATRI CLAN OR THE ROYAL FAMILY GET TO THEM...
...I WANT YOU TO FIND AND PROTECT THEM.
!
PROTECT THEM?
EMMA'S PLAN REQUIRES THE EVIL BLOOD.
IF EMMA DOESN'T COME BACK IN TIME...
...AND I KILL THE ROYAL FAMILY AND ARISTO-CRATS...
...WE'LL ONLY HAVE SONJU AND MUJIKA TO RELY ON.

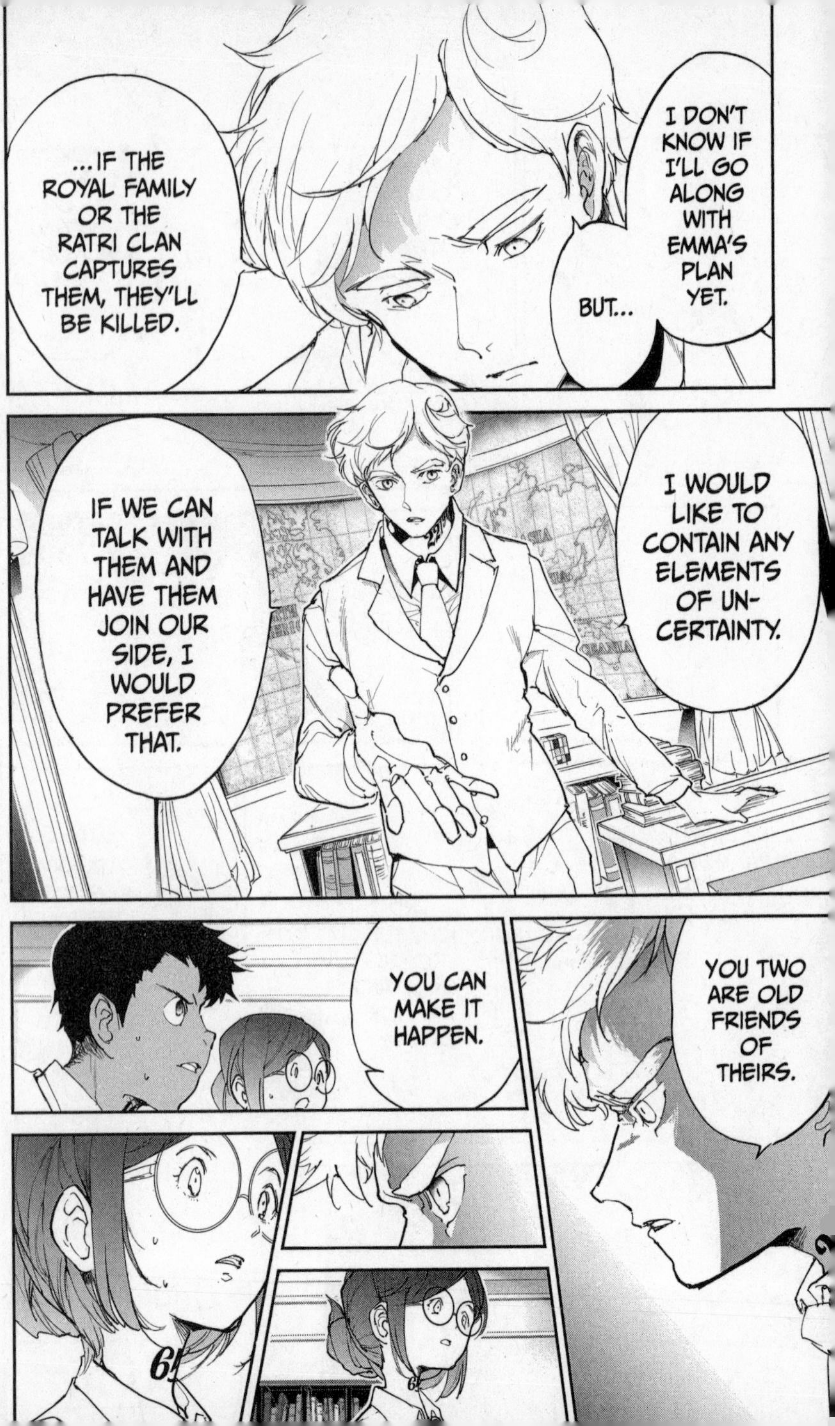
I DON'T KNOW IF I'LL GO ALONG WITH EMMA'S PLAN YET.
BUT...
...IF THE ROYAL FAMILY OR THE RATRI CLAN CAPTURES THEM, THEY'LL BE KILLED.
I WOULD LIKE TO CONTAIN ANY ELEMENTS OF UN-CERTAINTY.
IF WE CAN TALK WITH THEM AND HAVE THEM JOIN OUR SIDE, I WOULD PREFER THAT.
YOU TWO ARE OLD FRIENDS OF THEIRS.
YOU CAN MAKE IT HAPPEN.

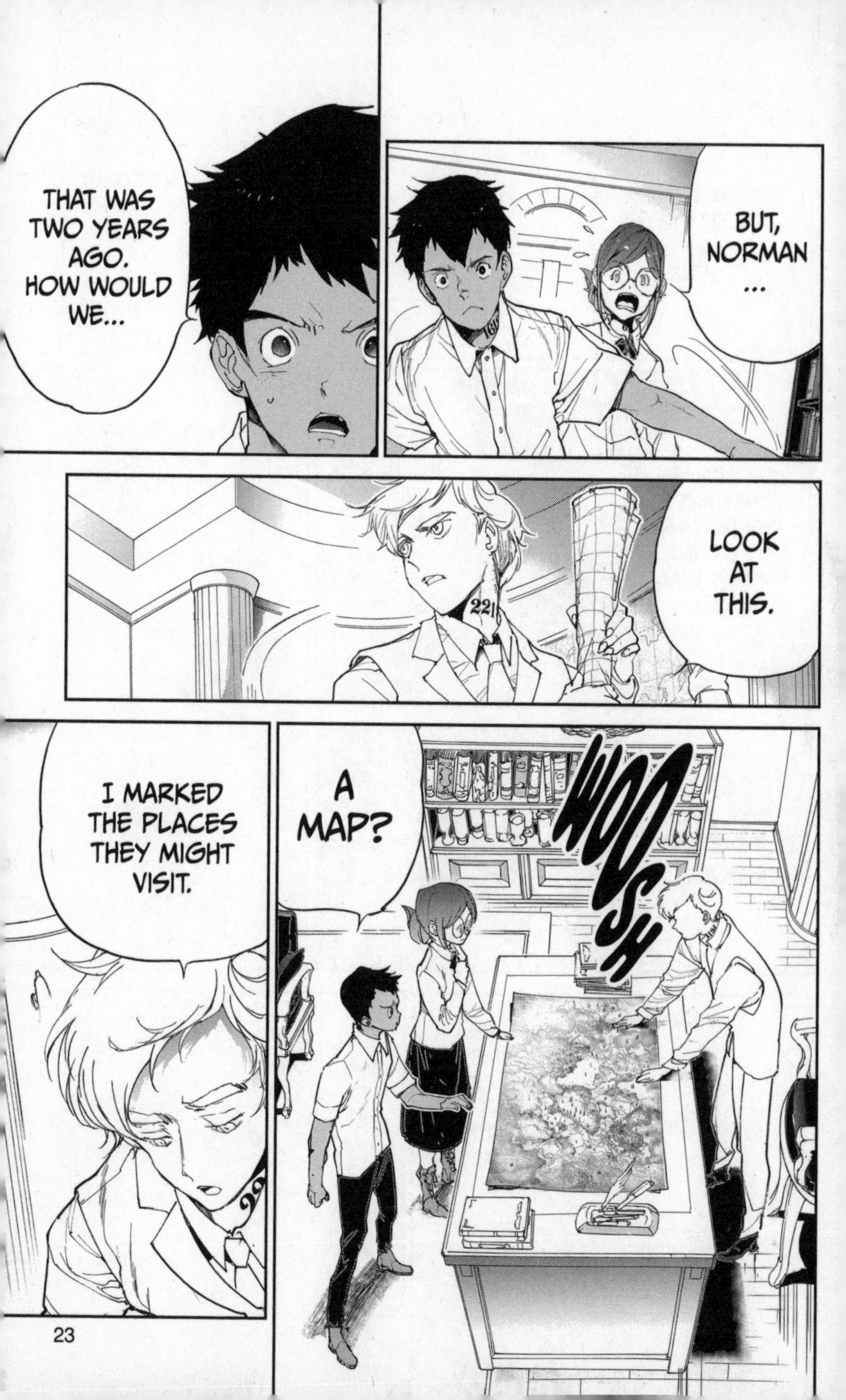
BUT, NORMAN ...
THAT WAS TWO YEARS AGO. HOW WOULD WE...
LOOK AT THIS.
WOOSH
A MAP?
I MARKED THE PLACES THEY MIGHT VISIT.

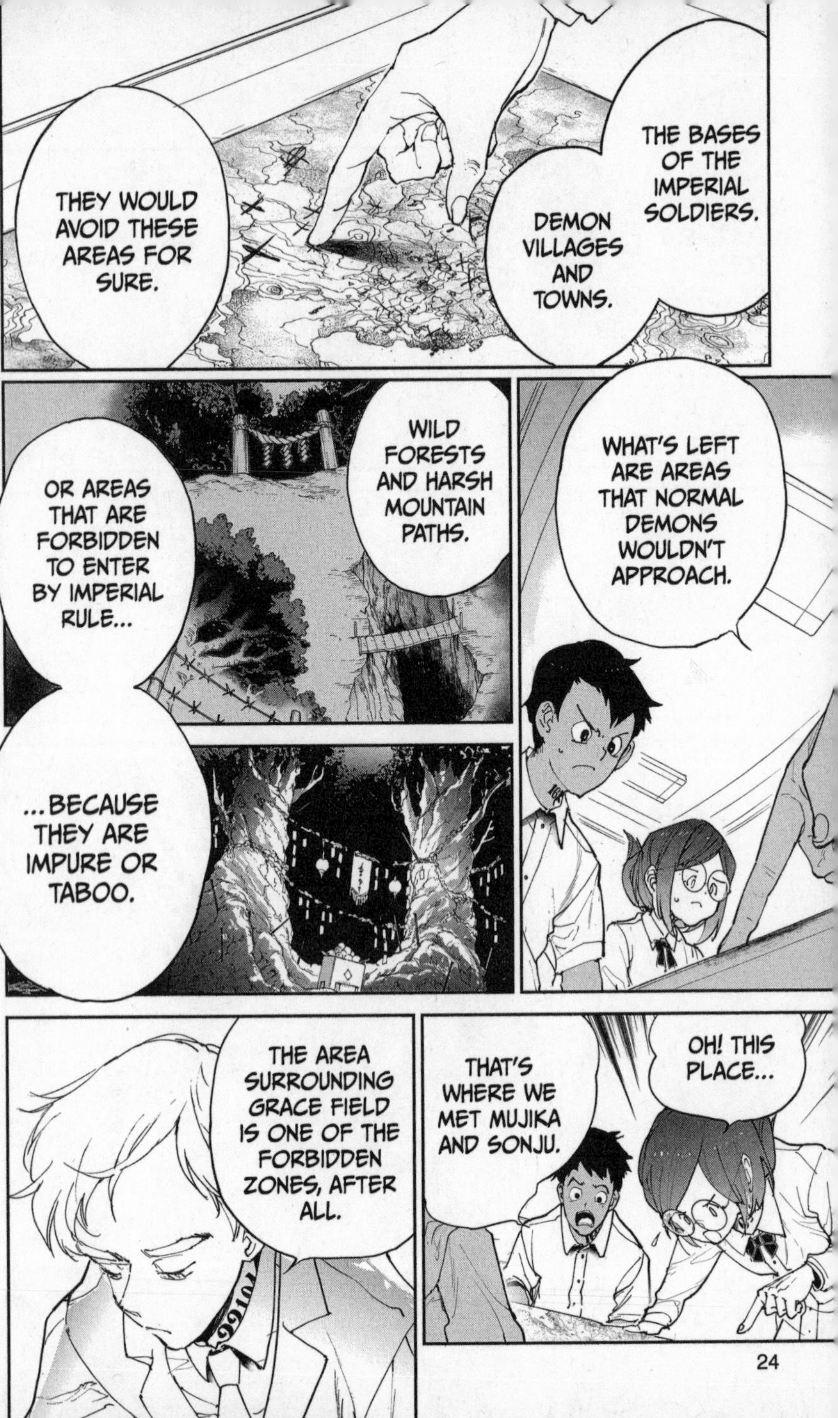
THE BASES OF THE IMPERIAL SOLDIERS.
DEMON VILLAGES AND TOWNS.
THEY WOULD AVOID THESE AREAS FOR SURE.
WHAT'S LEFT ARE AREAS THAT NORMAL DEMONS WOULDN'T APPROACH.
WILD FORESTS AND HARSH MOUNTAIN PATHS.
OR AREAS THAT ARE FORBIDDEN TO ENTER BY IMPERIAL RULE...
...BECAUSE THEY ARE IMPURE OR TABOO.
OH! THIS PLACE...
THAT'S WHERE WE MET MUJIKA AND SONJU.
THE AREA SURROUNDING GRACE FIELD IS ONE OF THE FORBIDDEN ZONES, AFTER ALL.

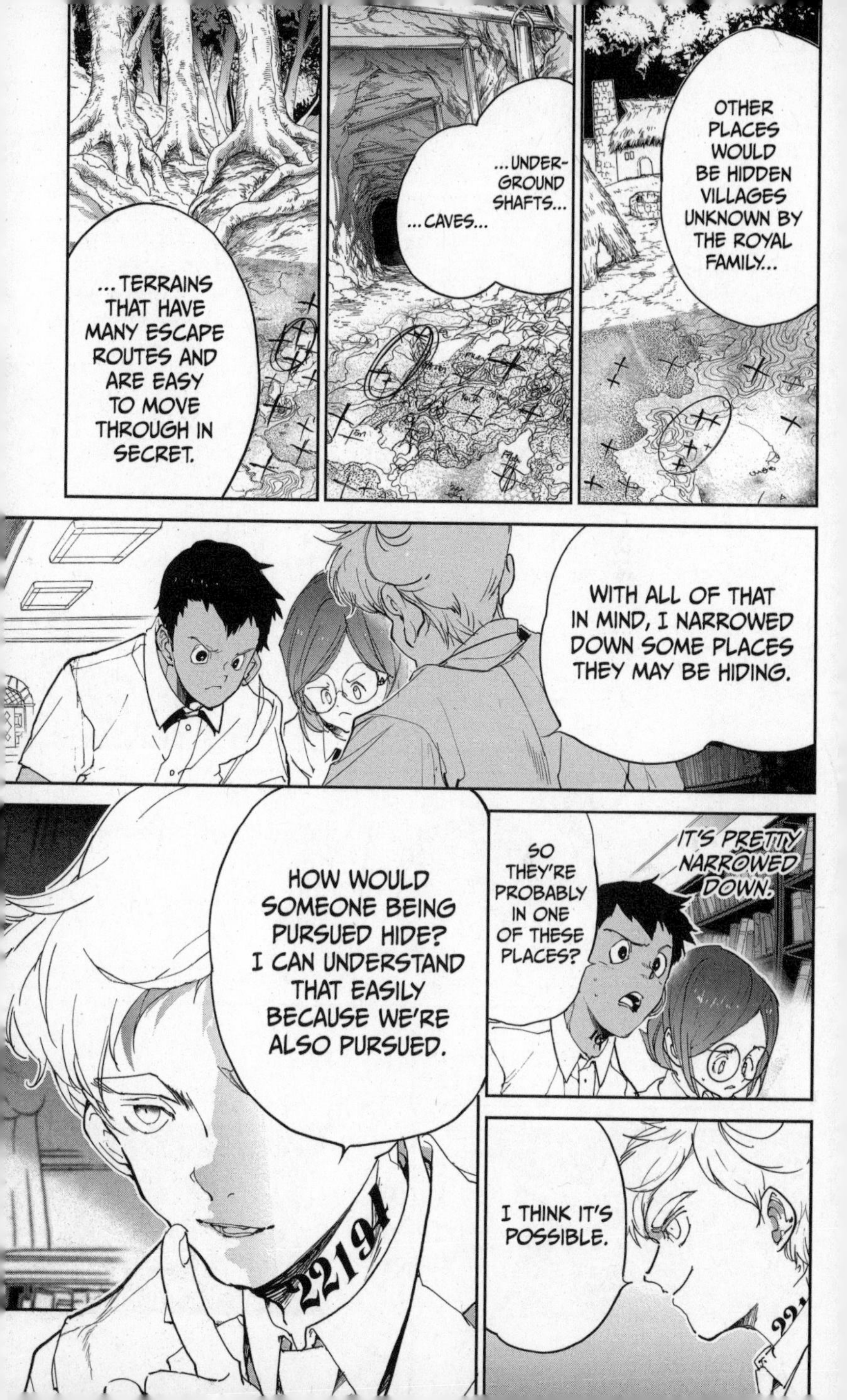
OTHER PLACES WOULD BE HIDDEN VILLAGES UNKNOWN BY THE ROYAL FAMILY...
...UNDER-GROUND SHAFTS...
...CAVES...
...TERRAINS THAT HAVE MANY ESCAPE ROUTES AND ARE EASY TO MOVE THROUGH IN SECRET.
WITH ALL OF THAT IN MIND, I NARROWED DOWN SOME PLACES THEY MAY BE HIDING.
IT'S PRETTY NARROWED DOWN.
SO THEY'RE PROBABLY IN ONE OF THESE PLACES?
I THINK IT'S POSSIBLE.
HOW WOULD SOMEONE BEING PURSUED HIDE? I CAN UNDERSTAND THAT EASILY BECAUSE WE'RE ALSO PURSUED.
22194

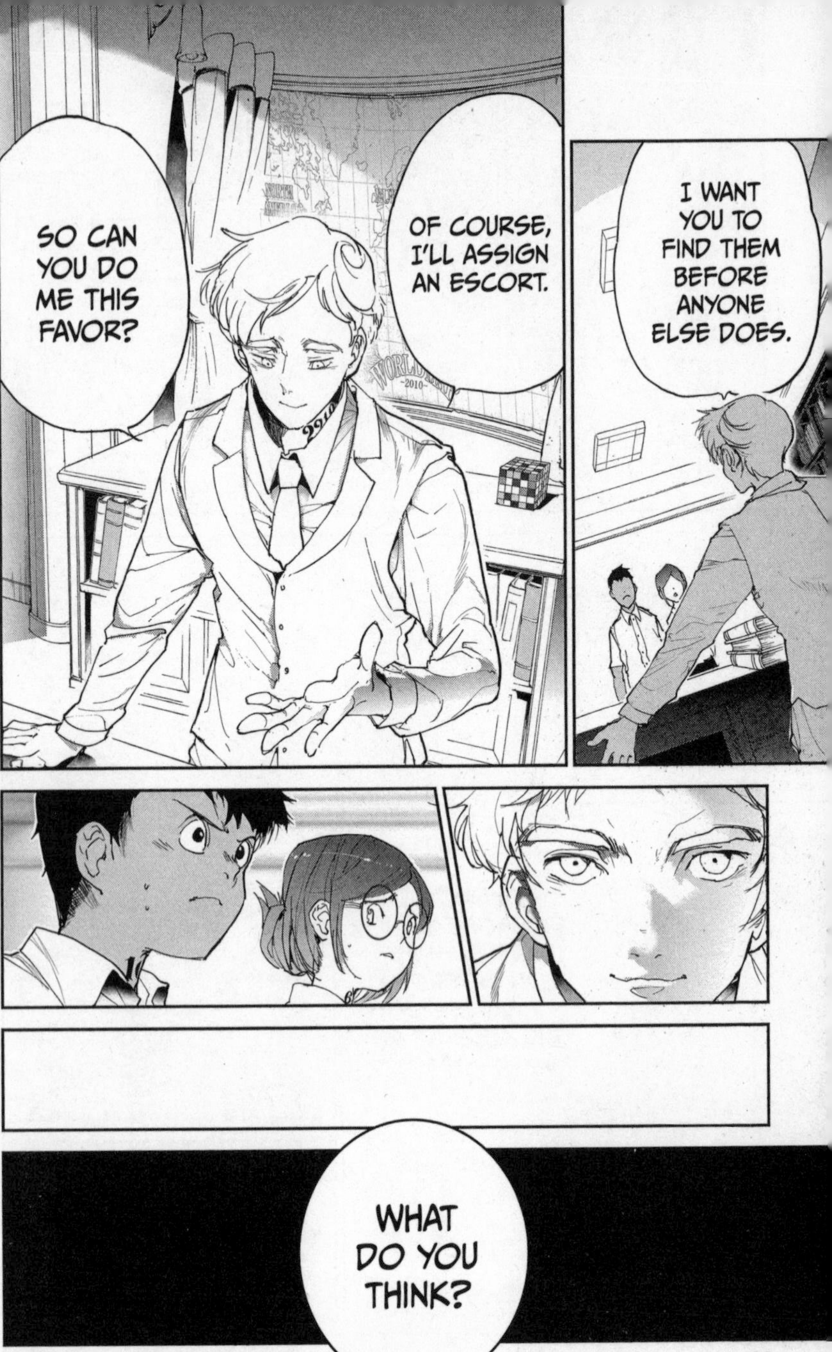
I WANT YOU TO FIND THEM BEFORE ANYONE ELSE DOES.
OF COURSE, I'LL ASSIGN AN ESCORT.
SO CAN YOU DO ME THIS FAVOR?
WHAT DO YOU THINK?

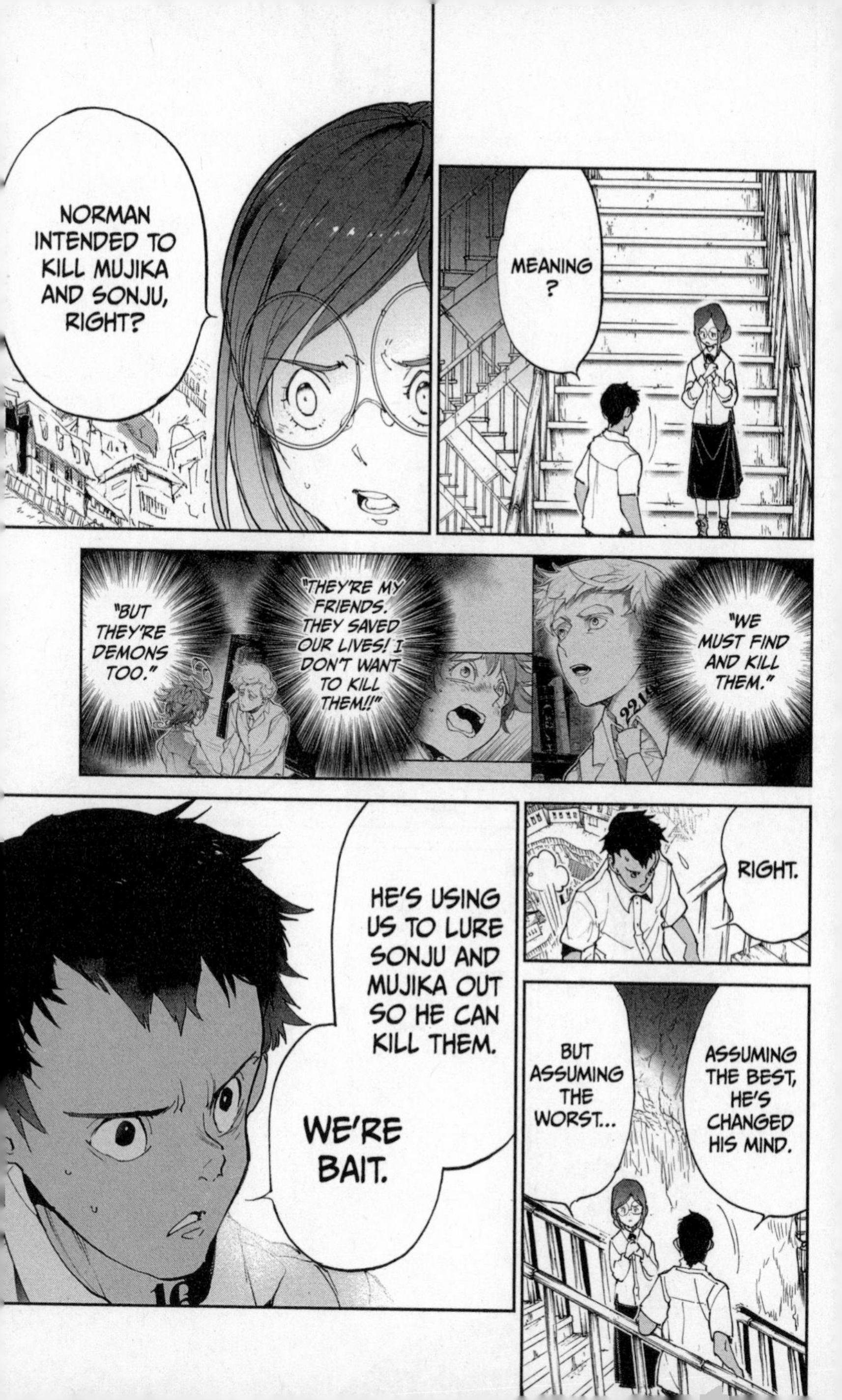
MEANING?
NORMAN INTENDED TO KILL MUJIKA AND SONJU, RIGHT?
"WE MUST FIND AND KILL THEM."
22194
"THEY'RE MY FRIENDS. THEY SAVED OUR LIVES! I DON'T WANT TO KILL THEM!!"
"BUT THEY'RE DEMONS TOO."
RIGHT.
ASSUMING THE BEST, HE'S CHANGED HIS MIND.
BUT ASSUMING THE WORST...
HE'S USING US TO LURE SONJU AND MUJIKA OUT SO HE CAN KILL THEM.
WE'RE BAIT.

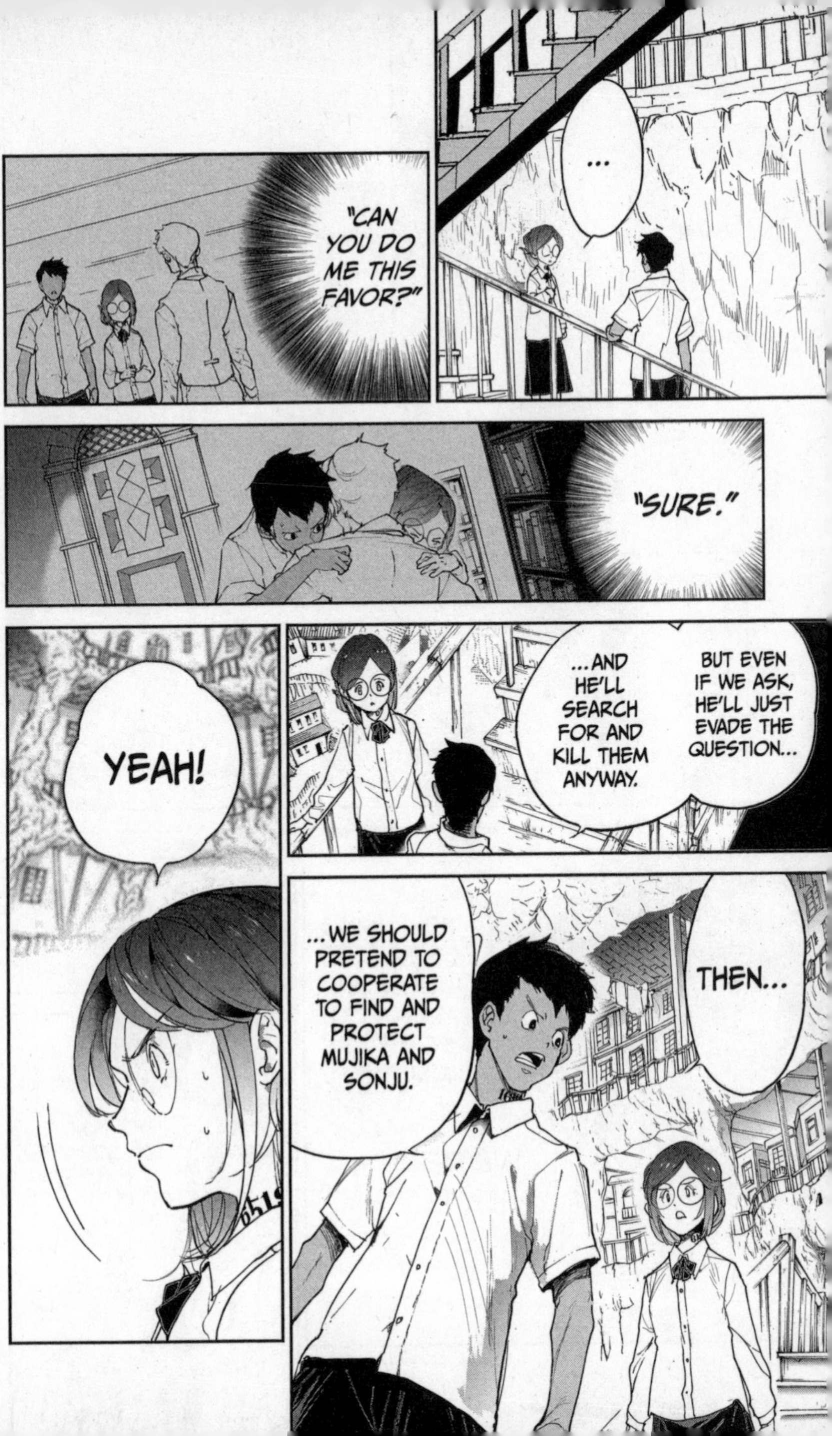
...
"CAN YOU DO ME THIS FAVOR?"
"SURE."
BUT EVEN IF WE ASK, HE'LL JUST EVADE THE QUESTION...
...AND HE'LL SEARCH FOR AND KILL THEM ANYWAY.
THEN...
...WE SHOULD PRETEND TO COOPERATE TO FIND AND PROTECT MUJIKA AND SONJU.
YEAH!

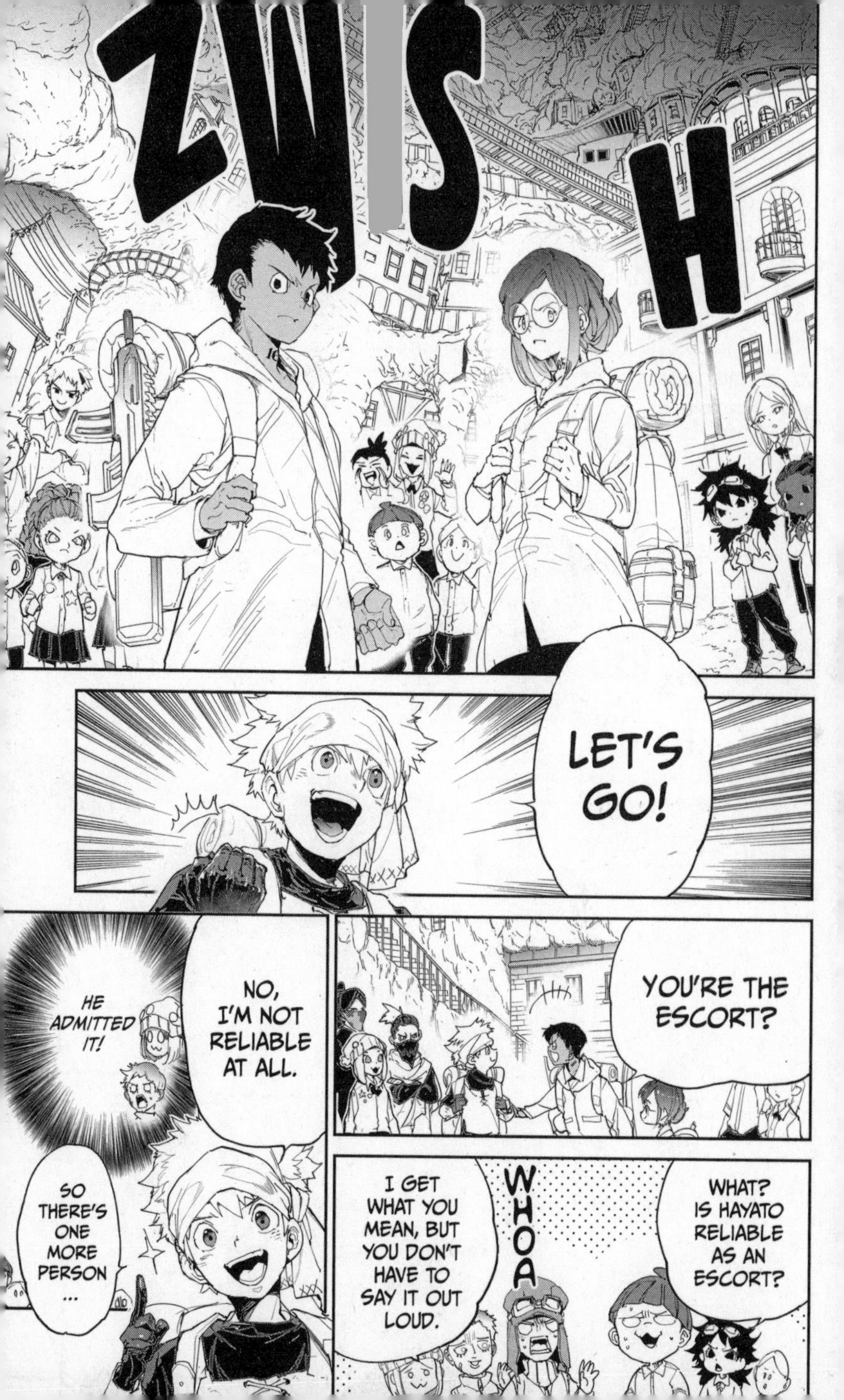
ZWISH
LET'S GO!
YOU'RE THE ESCORT?
WHAT? IS HAYATO RELIABLE AS AN ESCORT?
WHOA
I GET WHAT YOU MEAN, BUT YOU DON'T HAVE TO SAY IT OUT LOUD.
NO, I'M NOT RELIABLE AT ALL.
HE ADMITTED IT!
SO THERE'S ONE MORE PERSON ...

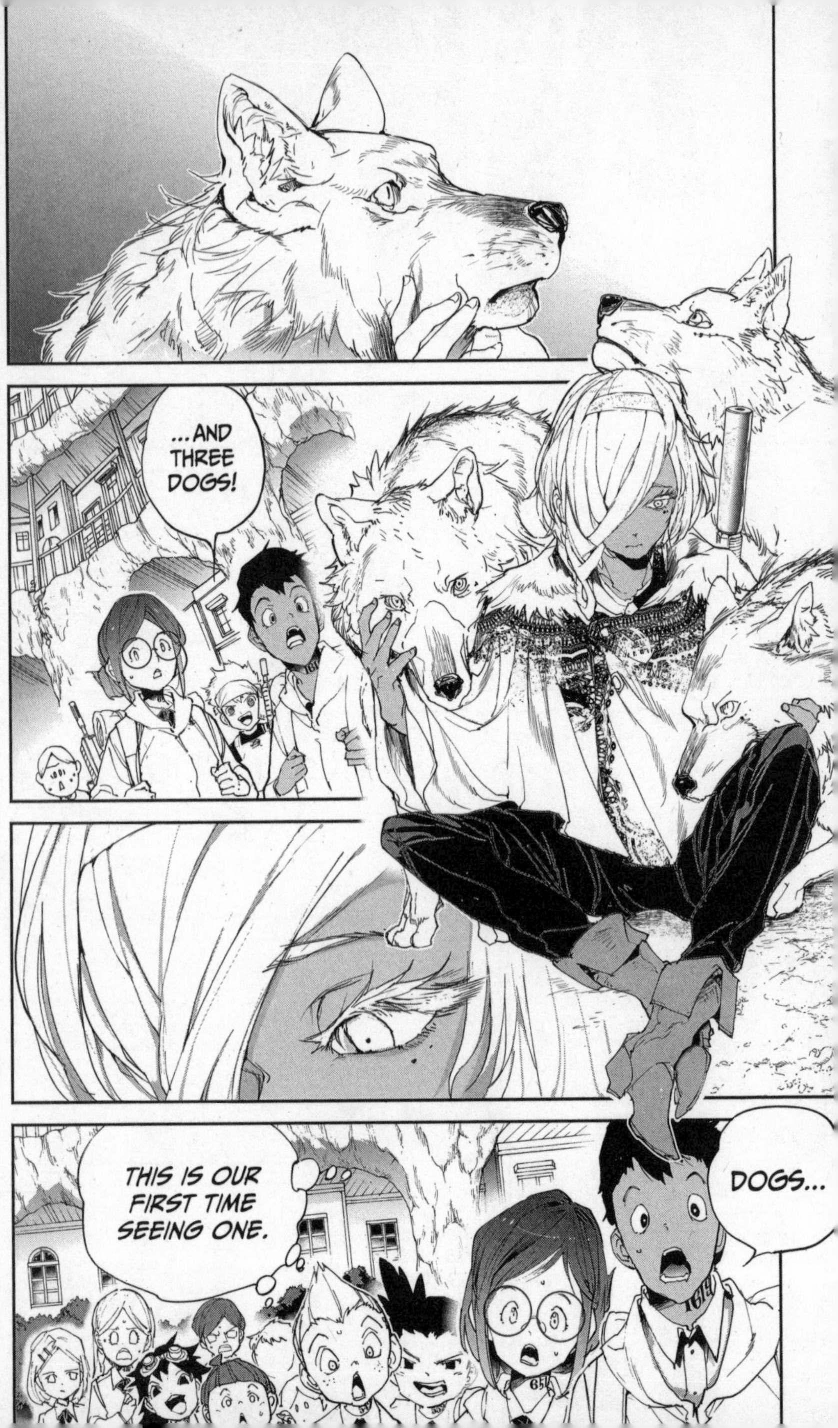
...AND THREE DOGS!
DOGS...
THIS IS OUR FIRST TIME SEEING ONE.

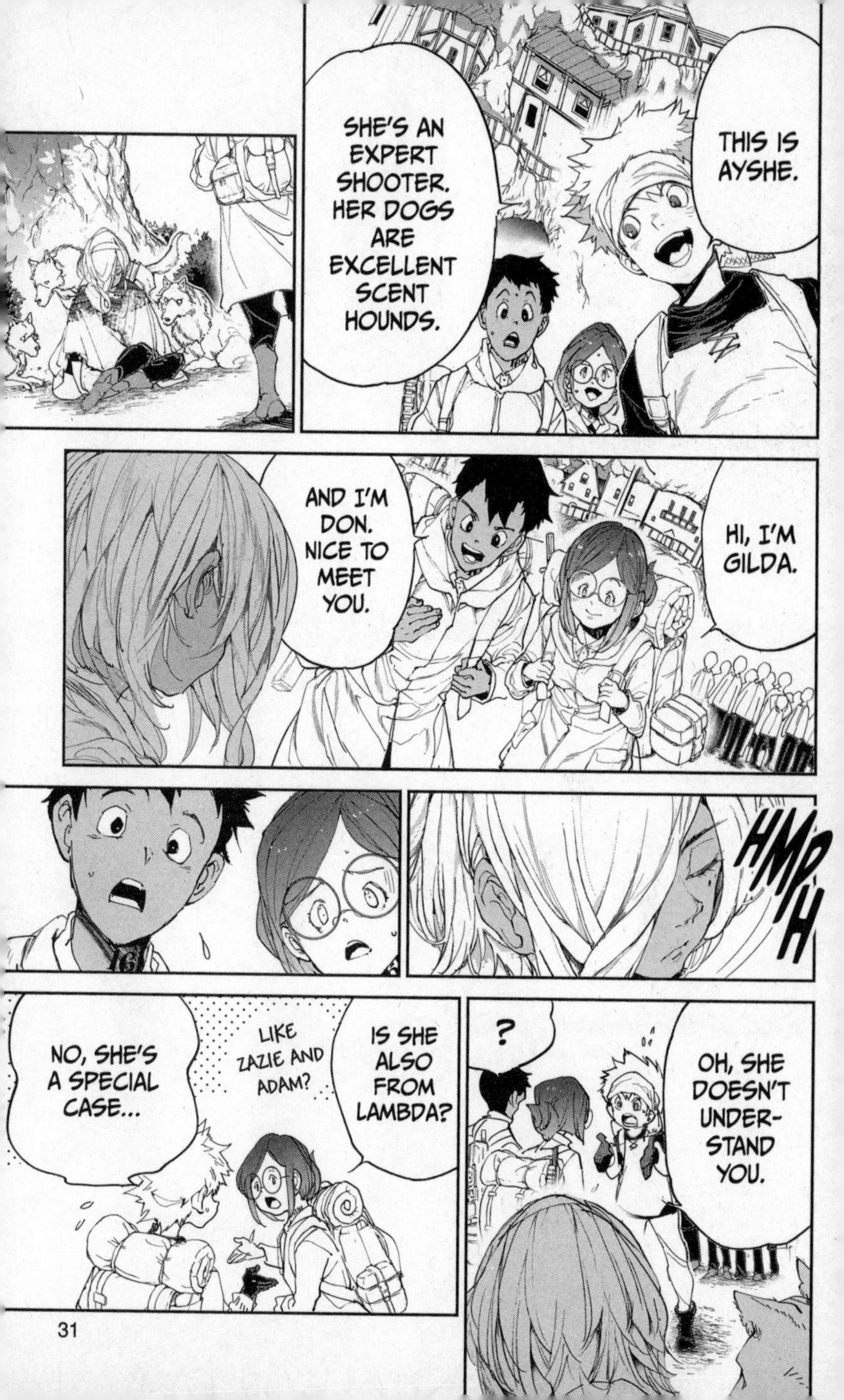
THIS IS AYSHE.
SHE'S AN EXPERT SHOOTER. HER DOGS ARE EXCELLENT SCENT HOUNDS.
HI, I'M GILDA.
AND I'M DON. NICE TO MEET YOU.
HMPH
OH, SHE DOESN'T UNDER-STAND YOU.
?
IS SHE ALSO FROM LAMBDA?
LIKE ZAZIE AND ADAM?
NO, SHE'S A SPECIAL CASE...

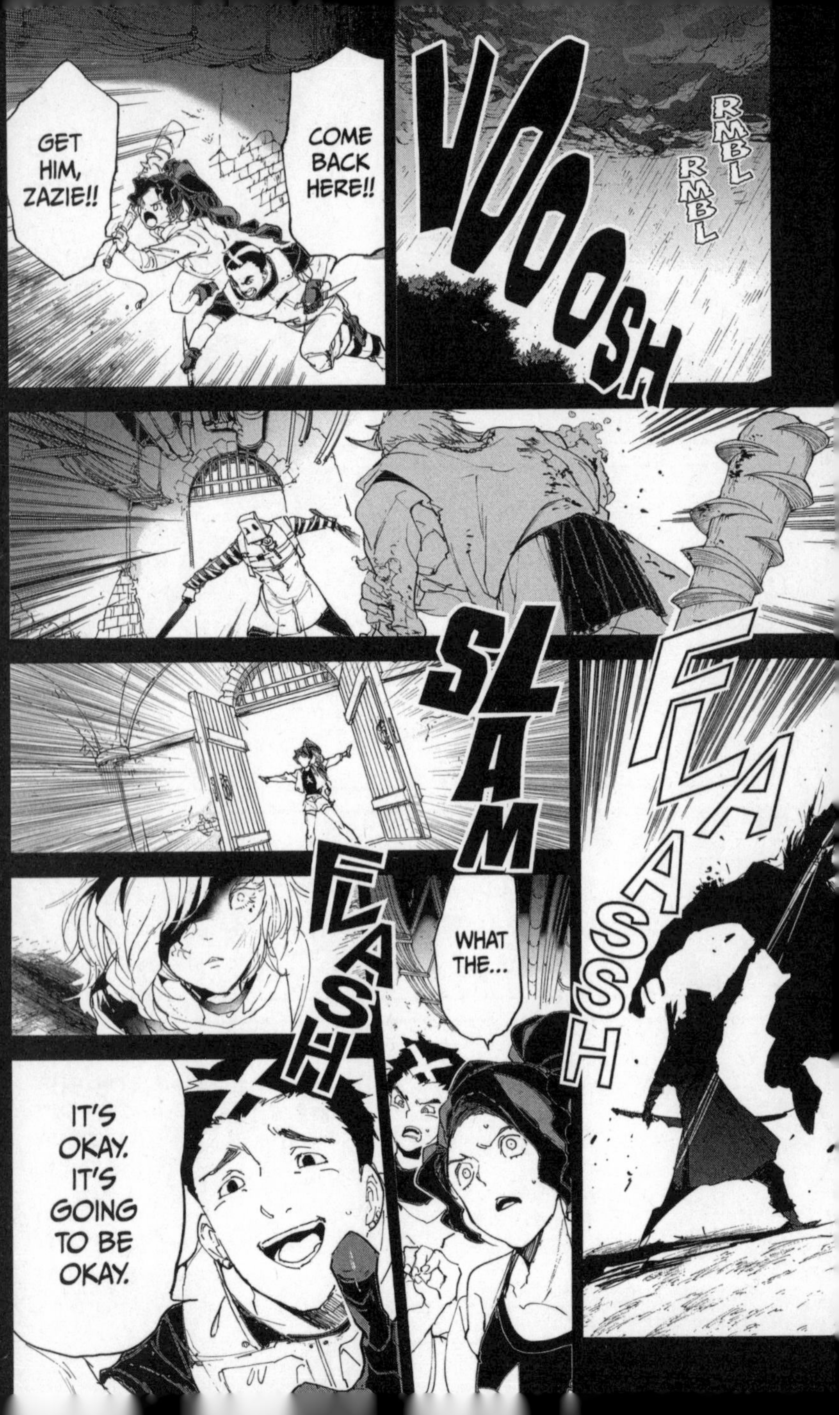
VOOOSH
RMBL
RMBL
COME BACK HERE!!
GET HIM, ZAZIE!!
FLAASH
SLAM
FLASH
WHAT THE...
IT'S OKAY. IT'S GOING TO BE OKAY.

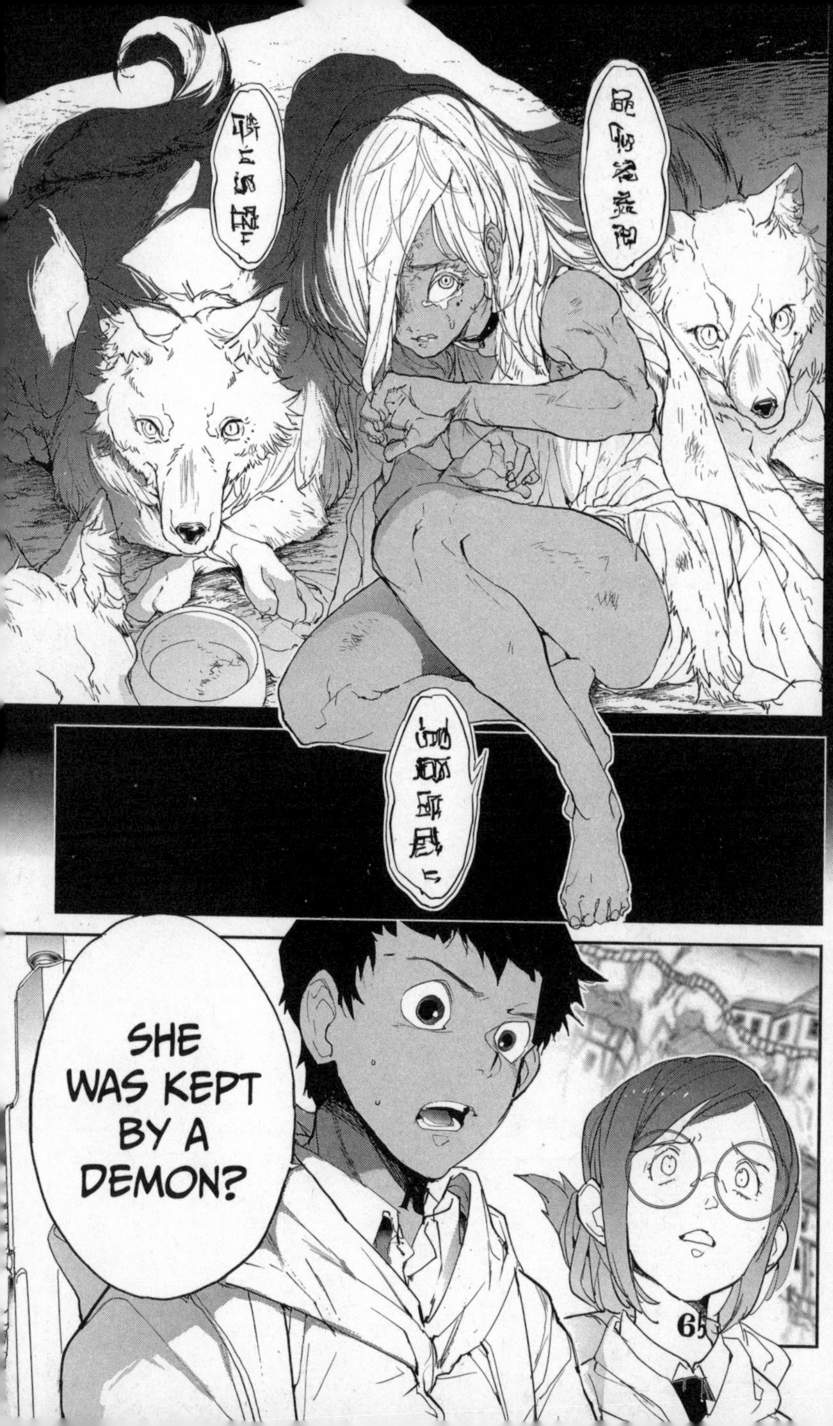
SHE WAS KEPT BY A DEMON?

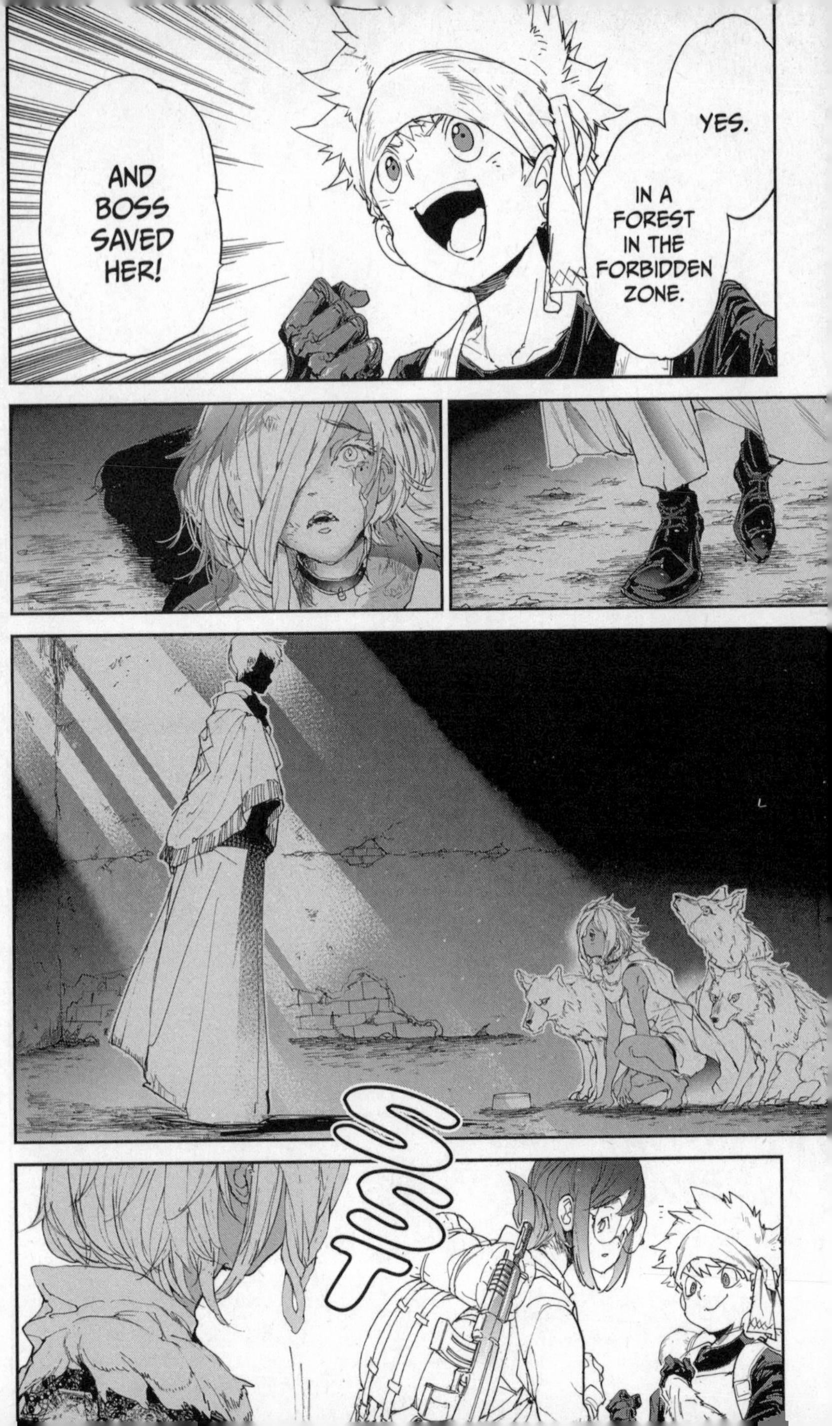
YES.
IN A FOREST IN THE FORBIDDEN ZONE.
AND BOSS SAVED HER!
SSST

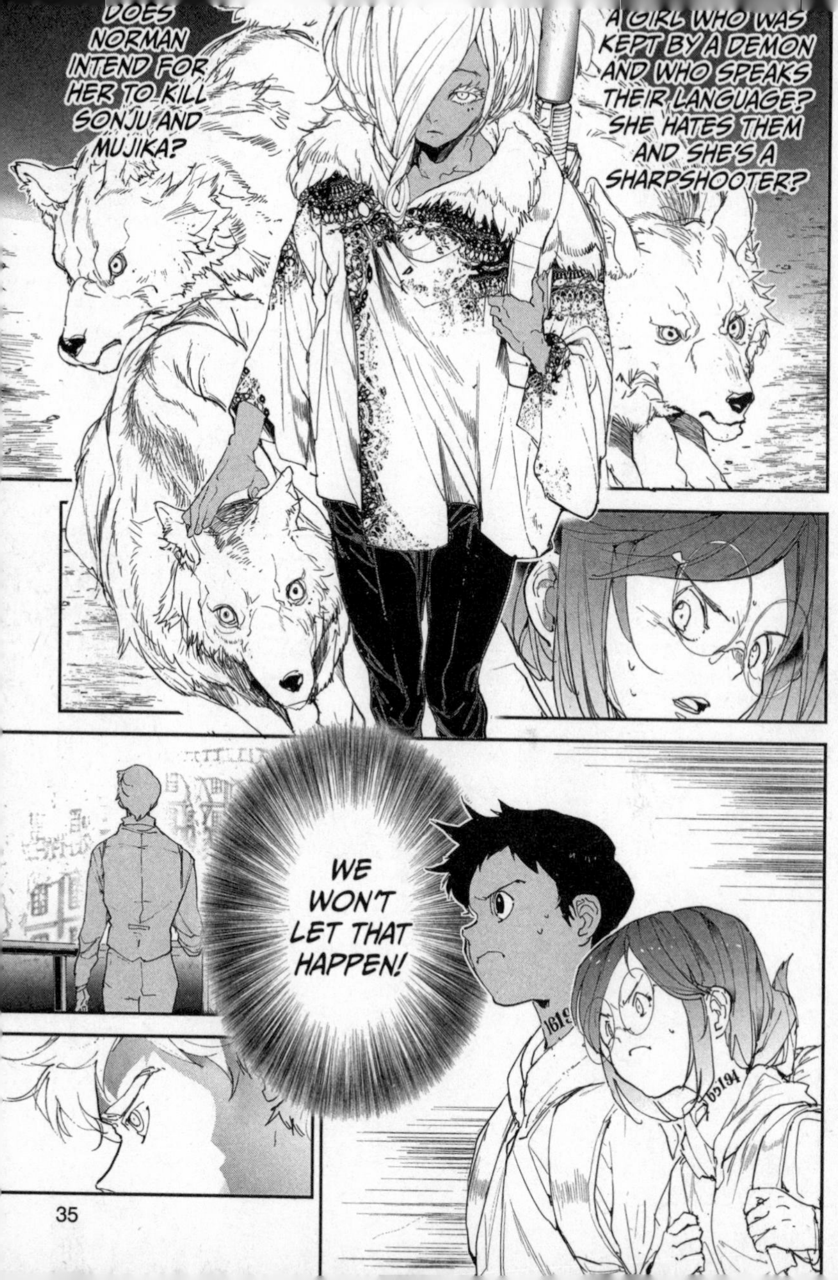
A GIRL WHO WAS KEPT BY A DEMON AND WHO SPEAKS THEIR LANGUAGE? SHE HATES THEM AND SHE'S A SHARPSHOOTER?
DOES NORMAN INTEND FOR HER TO KILL SONJU AND MUJIKA?
WE WON'T LET THAT HAPPEN!

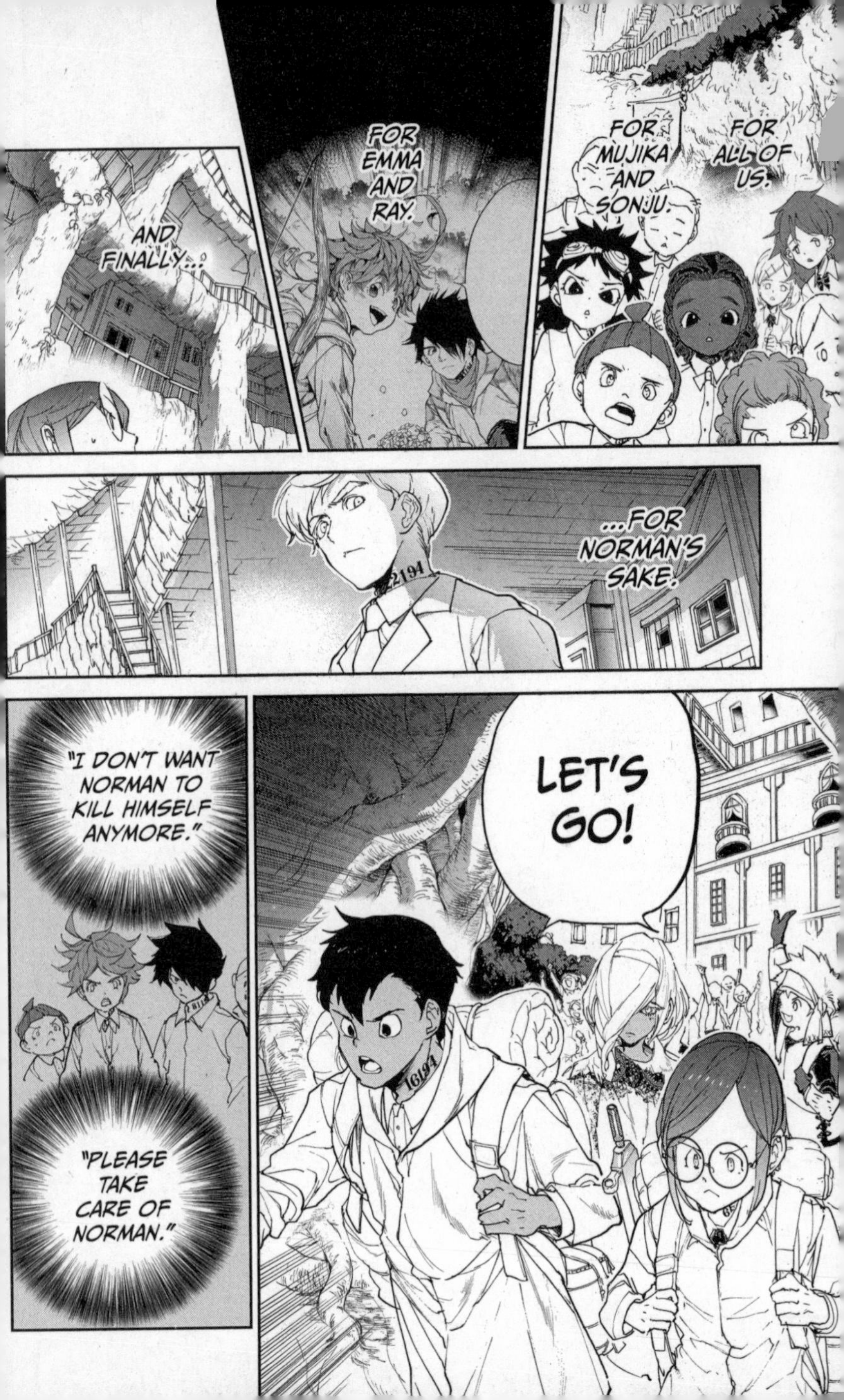
FOR ALL OF US.
FOR MUJIKA AND SONJU.
FOR EMMA AND RAY.
AND FINALLY...
...FOR NORMAN'S SAKE.
LET'S GO!
"I DON'T WANT NORMAN TO KILL HIMSELF ANYMORE."
"PLEASE TAKE CARE OF NORMAN."

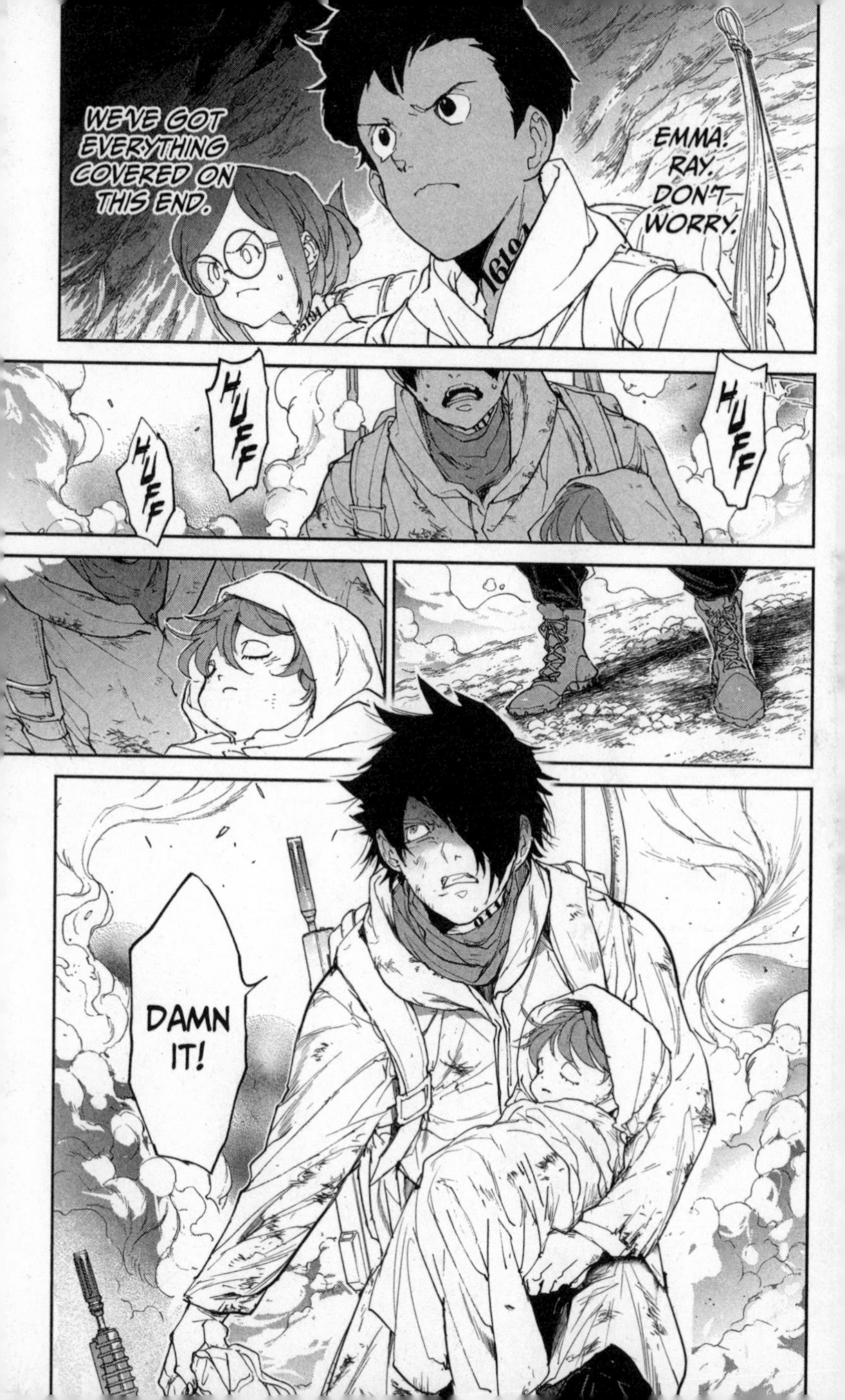
EMMA. RAY. DON'T WORRY.
WE'VE GOT EVERYTHING COVERED ON THIS END.
HUFF
HUFF
HUFF
DAMN IT!

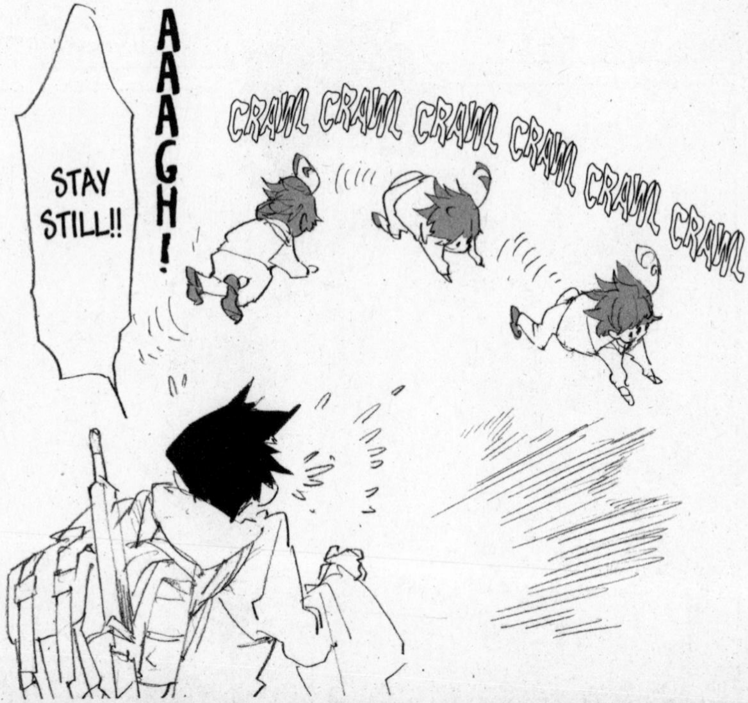
CRAWL CRAWL CRAWL CRAWL CRAWL CRAWL
AAAGH!
STAY STILL!!

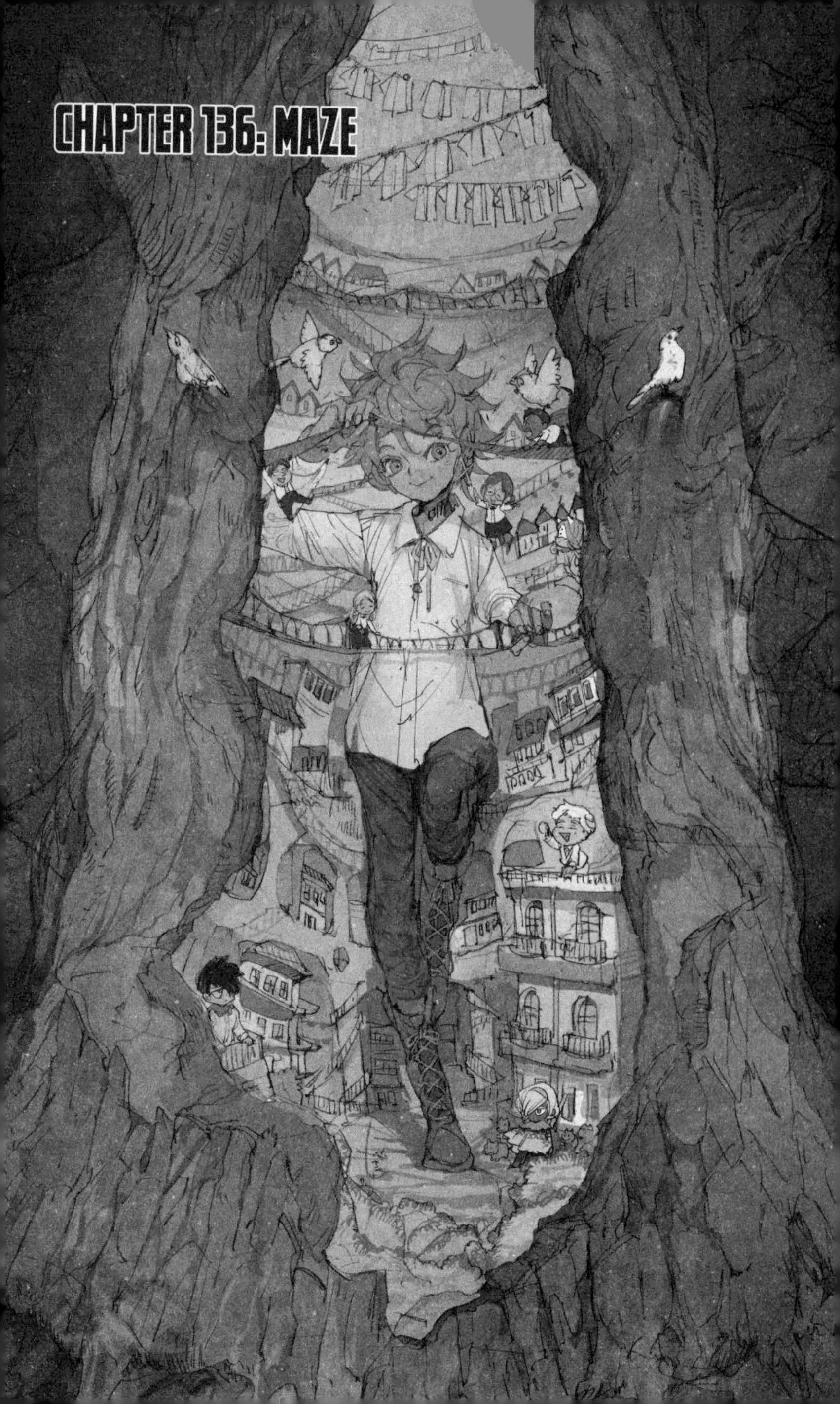
CHAPTER 136: MAZE

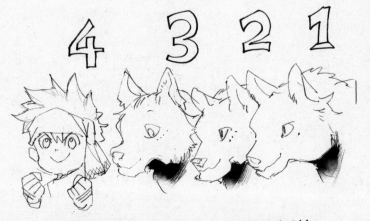

4 3 2 1

THE INTENSE FEELING OF HAYATO BEING A FOURTH DOGGY.

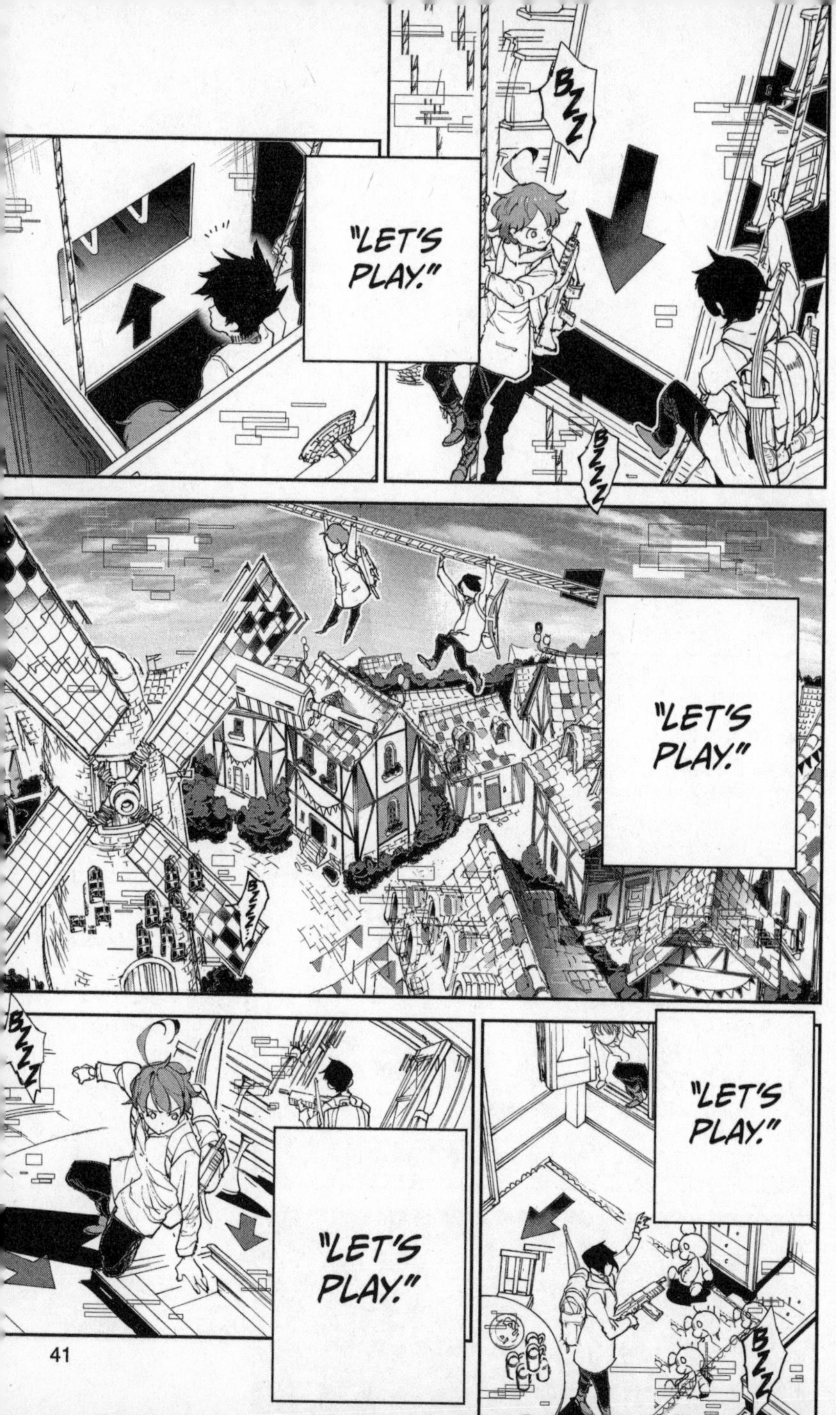
BZZ
"LET'S PLAY."
BZZZ
"LET'S PLAY."
BZZZZ...
"LET'S PLAY."
BZZ
BZZZ
"LET'S PLAY."

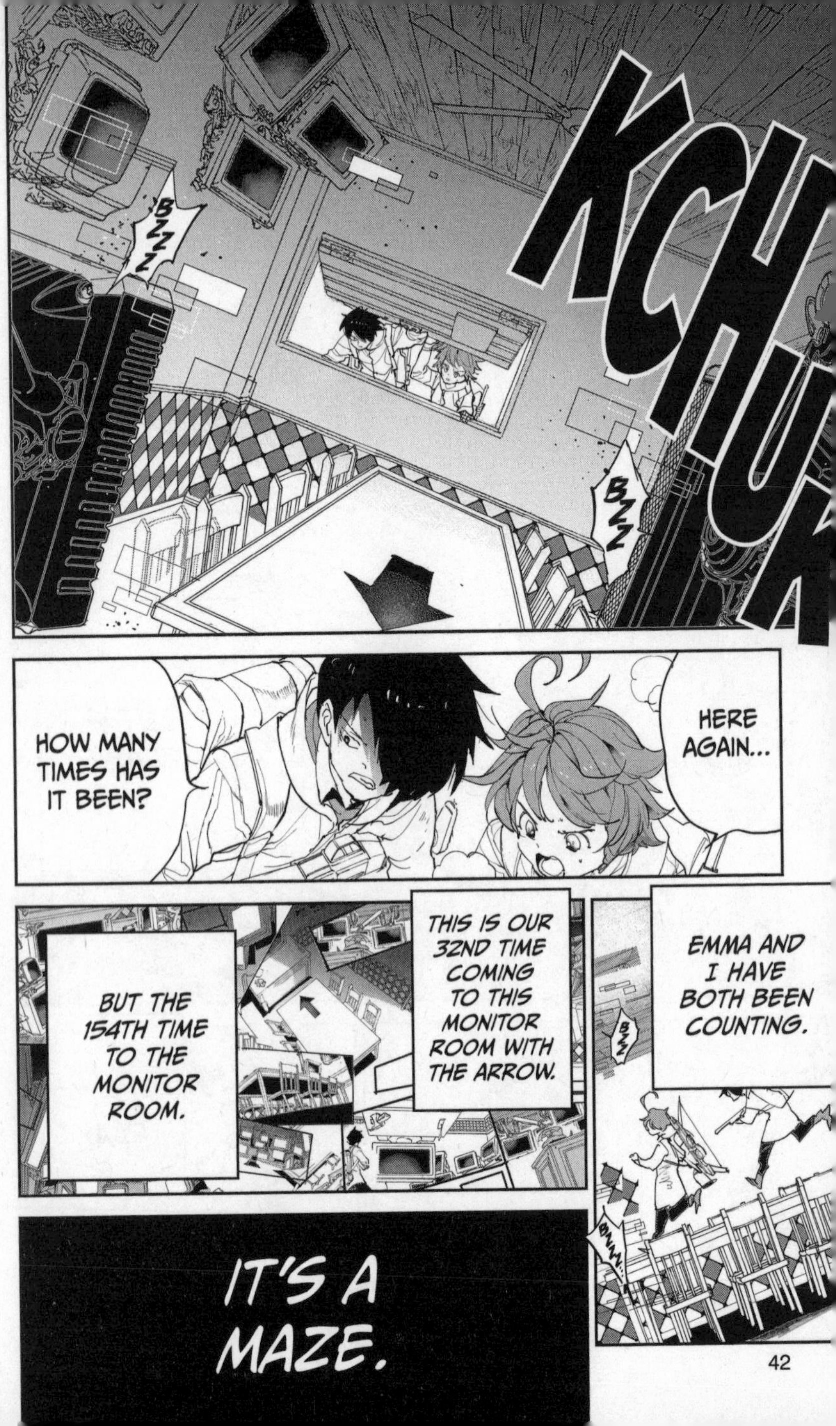
BZZZ
BZZZ
HERE AGAIN...
HOW MANY TIMES HAS IT BEEN?
EMMA AND I HAVE BOTH BEEN COUNTING.
BZZ
THIS IS OUR 32ND TIME COMING TO THIS MONITOR ROOM WITH THE ARROW.
BUT THE 154TH TIME TO THE MONITOR ROOM.
IT'S A MAZE.

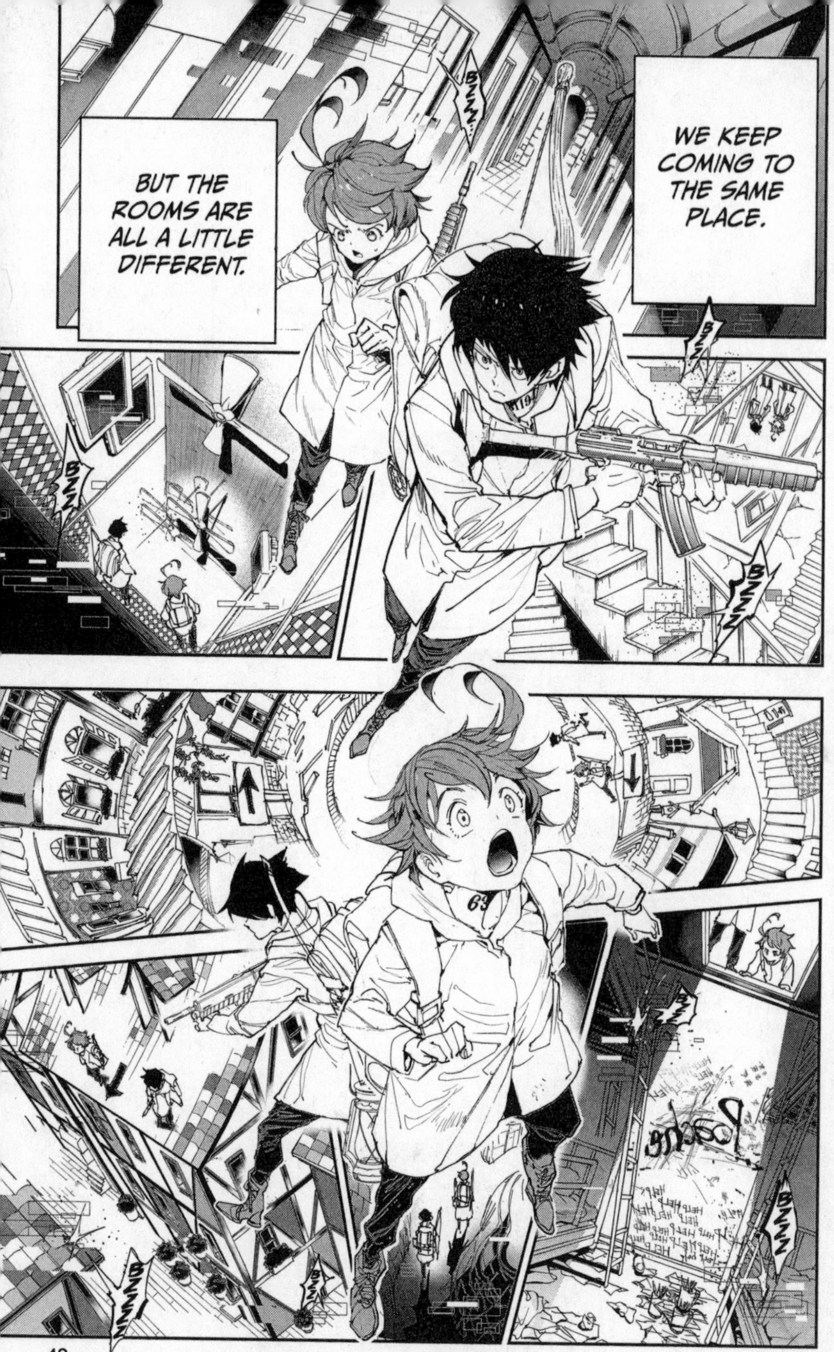
WE KEEP COMING TO THE SAME PLACE.
BZZZ...
BUT THE ROOMS ARE ALL A LITTLE DIFFERENT.
BZZZ
BZZZ
BZZZ
BZZZ
BZZZ
BZZZZZ
BZZ

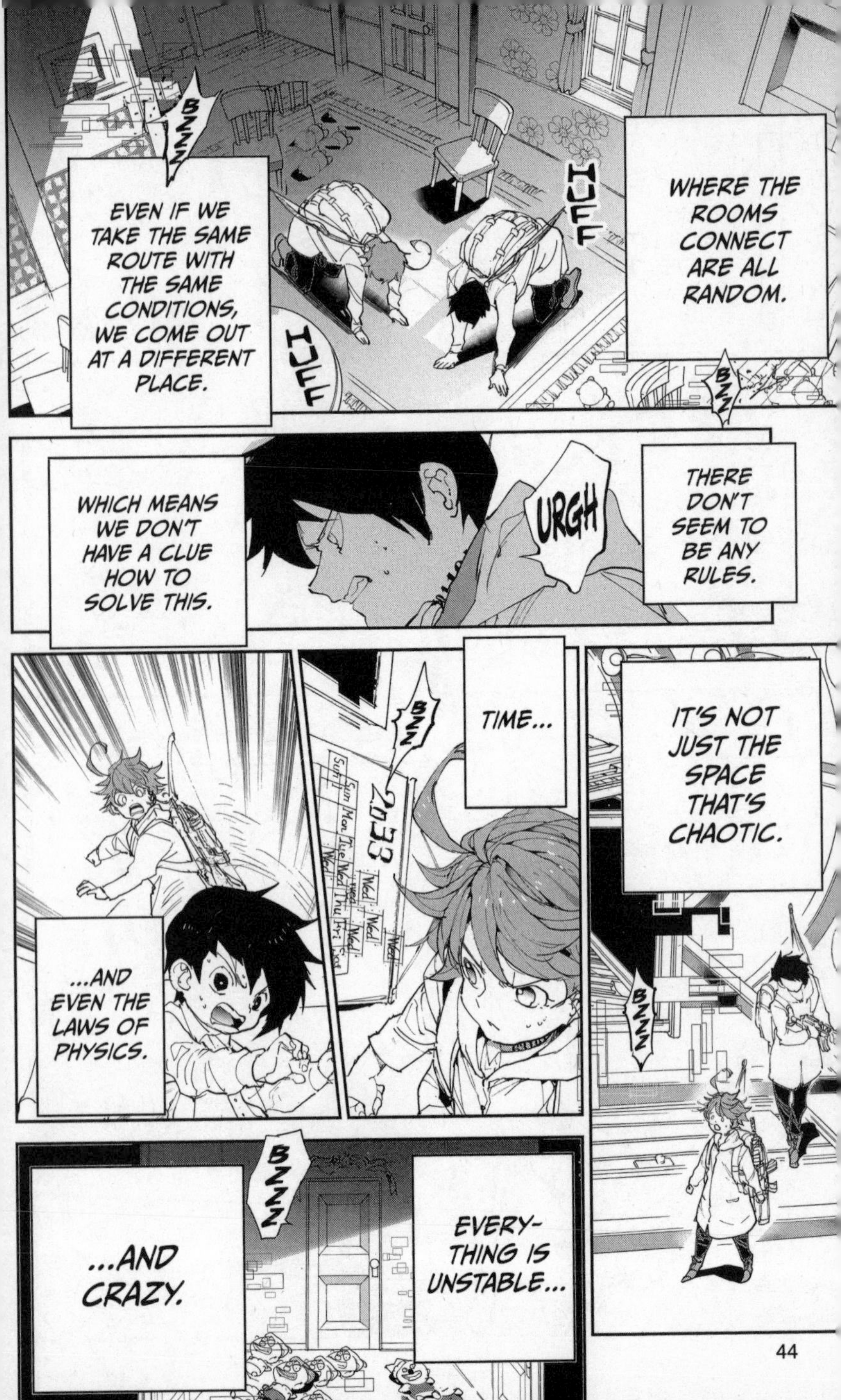
WHERE THE ROOMS CONNECT ARE ALL RANDOM.
BZZZ
HUFF
EVEN IF WE TAKE THE SAME ROUTE WITH THE SAME CONDITIONS, WE COME OUT AT A DIFFERENT PLACE.
HUFF
BZZ
THERE DON'T SEEM TO BE ANY RULES.
URGH
WHICH MEANS WE DON'T HAVE A CLUE HOW TO SOLVE THIS.
IT'S NOT JUST THE SPACE THAT'S CHAOTIC.
BZZZ
TIME...
BZZ
...AND EVEN THE LAWS OF PHYSICS.
EVERY-THING IS UNSTABLE...
BZZZ
...AND CRAZY.

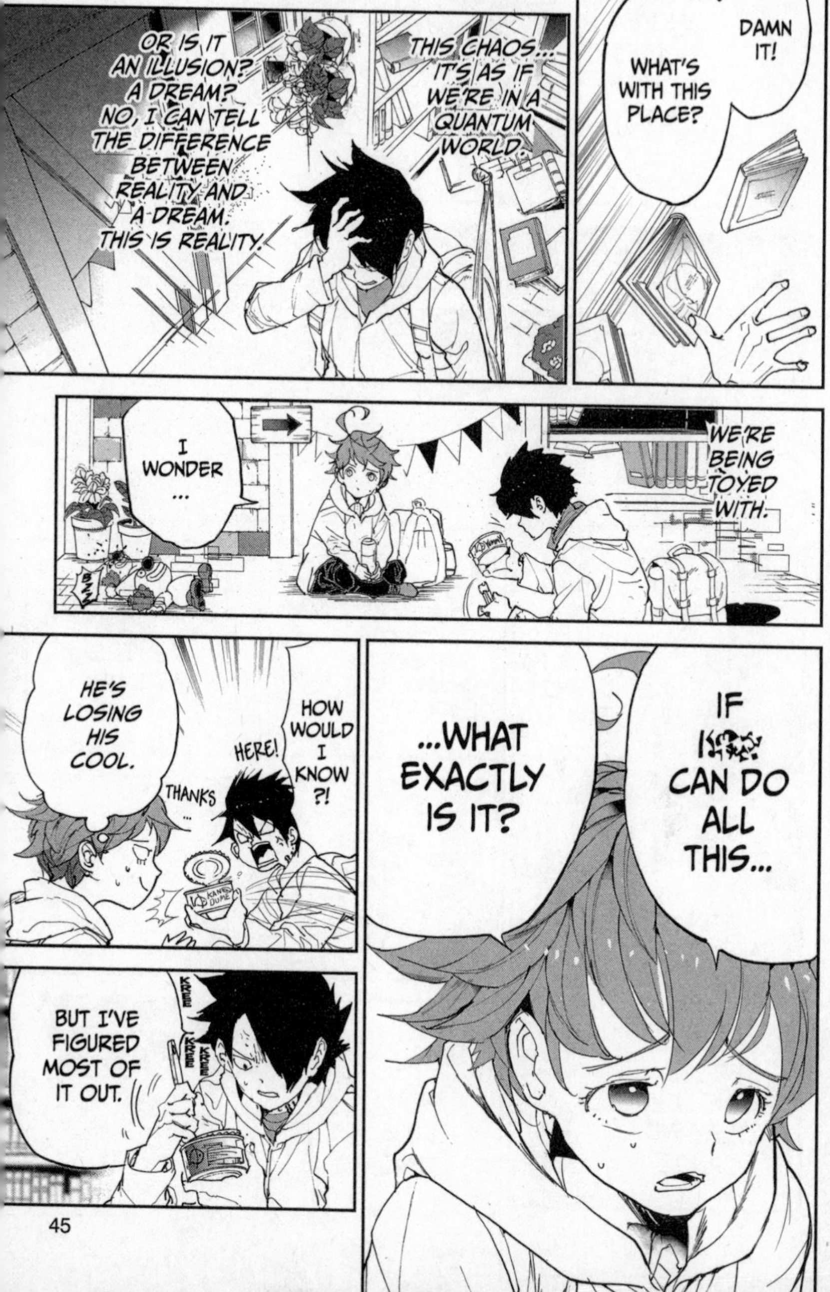
DAMN IT!
WHAT'S WITH THIS PLACE?
THIS CHAOS... IT'S AS IF WE'RE IN A QUANTUM WORLD.
OR IS IT AN ILLUSION? A DREAM? NO, I CAN TELL THE DIFFERENCE BETWEEN REALITY AND A DREAM. THIS IS REALITY.
WE'RE BEING TOYED WITH.
I WONDER...
BZZ
IF
CAN DO ALL THIS...
...WHAT EXACTLY IS IT?
HOW WOULD I KNOW?!
HERE!
HE'S LOSING HIS COOL.
THANKS...
KANDUME
KREE
KREE
KREE
BUT I'VE FIGURED MOST OF IT OUT.

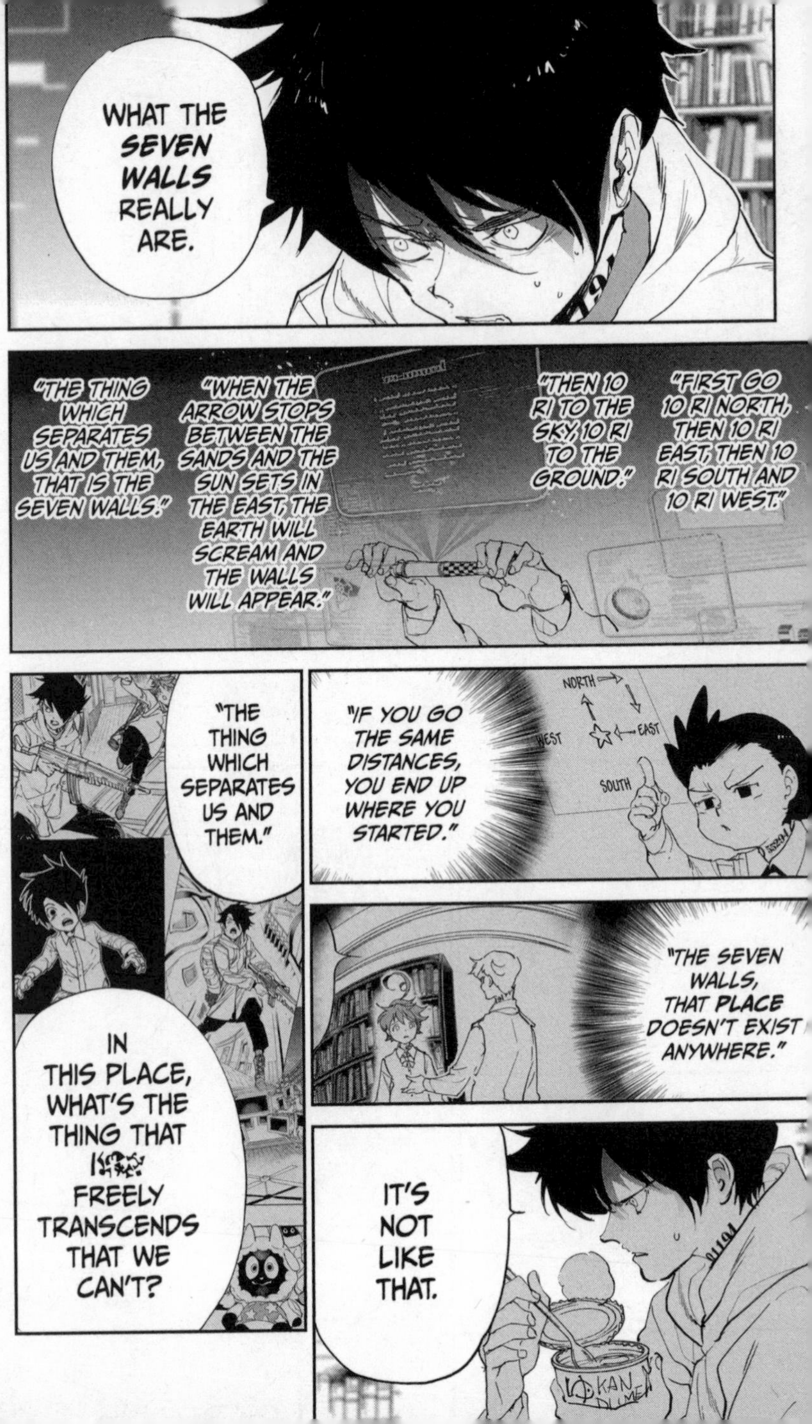
WHAT THE SEVEN WALLS REALLY ARE.
"FIRST GO 10 RI NORTH, THEN 10 RI EAST, THEN 10 RI SOUTH AND 10 RI WEST."
"THEN 10 RI TO THE SKY, 10 RI TO THE GROUND."
"WHEN THE ARROW STOPS BETWEEN THE SANDS AND THE SUN SETS IN THE EAST, THE EARTH WILL SCREAM AND THE WALLS WILL APPEAR."
"THE THING WHICH SEPARATES US AND THEM, THAT IS THE SEVEN WALLS."
NORTH
EAST
SOUTH
WEST
"IF YOU GO THE SAME DISTANCES, YOU END UP WHERE YOU STARTED."
"THE SEVEN WALLS, THAT PLACE DOESN'T EXIST ANYWHERE."
IT'S NOT LIKE THAT.
"THE THING WHICH SEPARATES US AND THEM."
IN THIS PLACE, WHAT'S THE THING THAT FREELY TRANSCENDS THAT WE CAN'T?

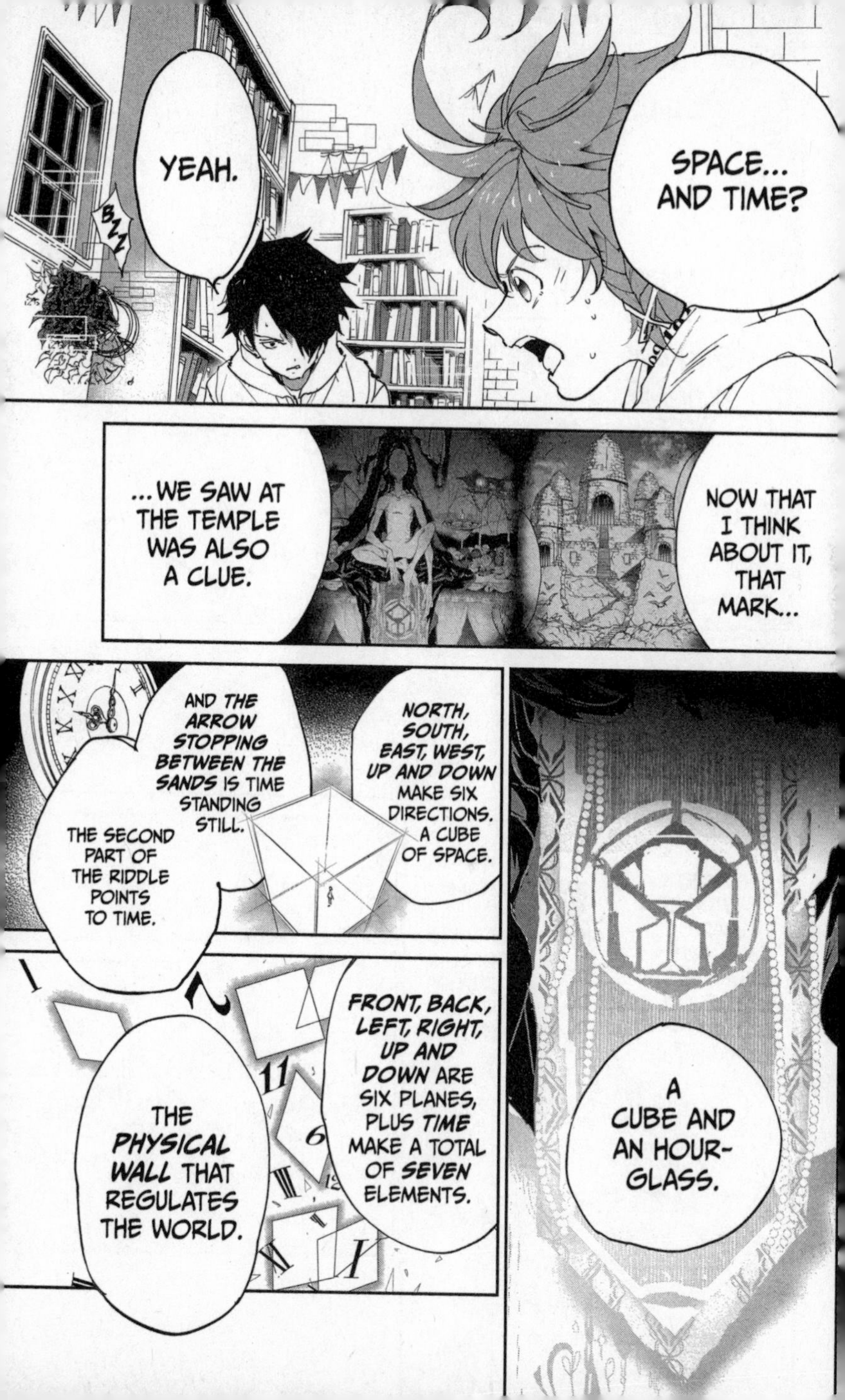

SPACE... AND TIME?
YEAH.
BZZ
NOW THAT I THINK ABOUT IT, THAT MARK...
...WE SAW AT THE TEMPLE WAS ALSO A CLUE.
A CUBE AND AN HOUR-GLASS.
NORTH, SOUTH, EAST, WEST, UP AND DOWN MAKE SIX DIRECTIONS. A CUBE OF SPACE.
AND THE ARROW STOPPING BETWEEN THE SANDS IS TIME STANDING STILL.
THE SECOND PART OF THE RIDDLE POINTS TO TIME.
FRONT, BACK, LEFT, RIGHT, UP AND DOWN ARE SIX PLANES, PLUS TIME MAKE A TOTAL OF SEVEN ELEMENTS.
THE PHYSICAL WALL THAT REGULATES THE WORLD.

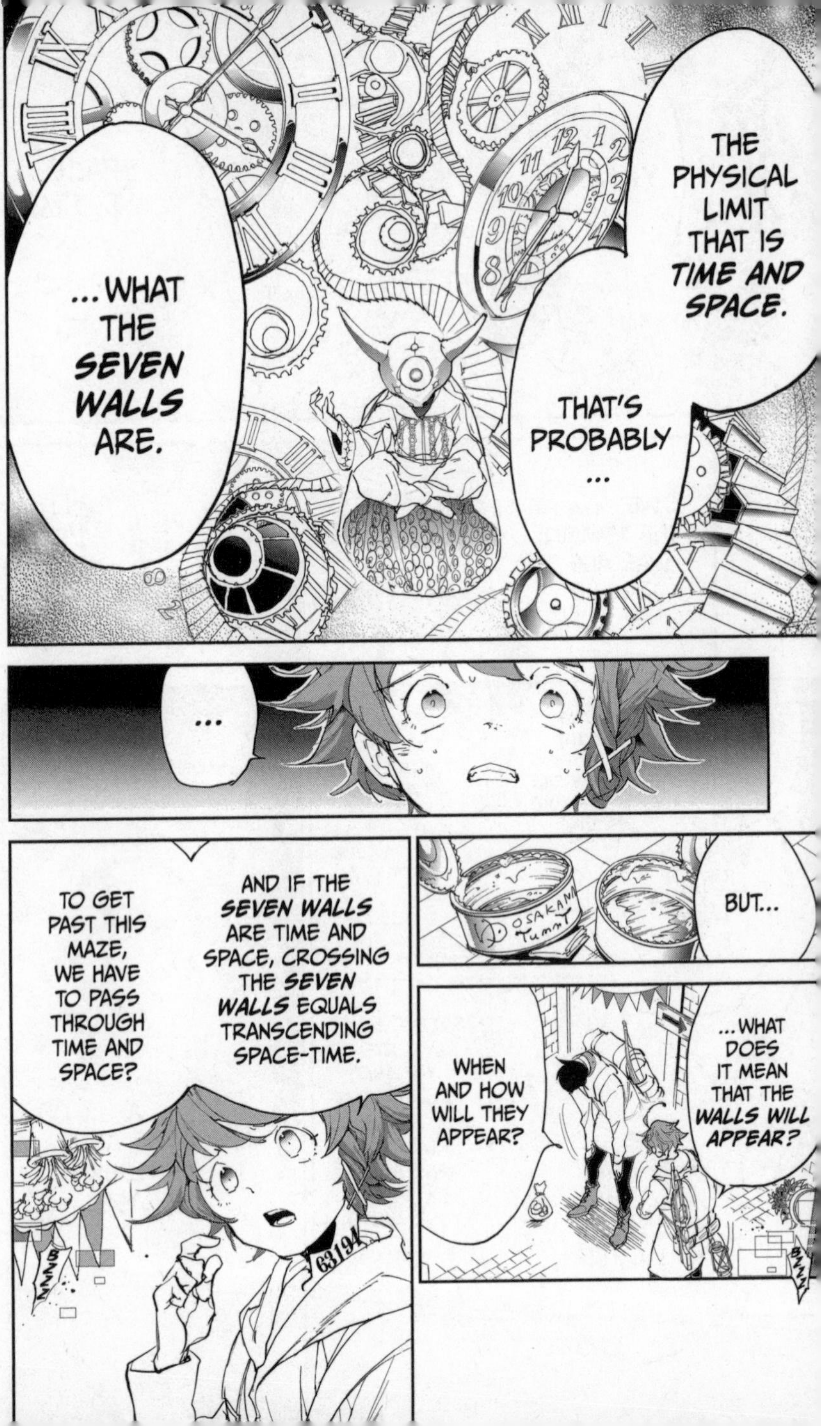
...WHAT THE SEVEN WALLS ARE.
THAT'S PROBABLY ...
THE PHYSICAL LIMIT THAT IS TIME AND SPACE.
...
BUT...
...WHAT DOES IT MEAN THAT THE WALLS WILL APPEAR?
WHEN AND HOW WILL THEY APPEAR?
BZZZ
AND IF THE SEVEN WALLS ARE TIME AND SPACE, CROSSING THE SEVEN WALLS EQUALS TRANSCENDING SPACE-TIME.
TO GET PAST THIS MAZE, WE HAVE TO PASS THROUGH TIME AND SPACE?
BZZZ

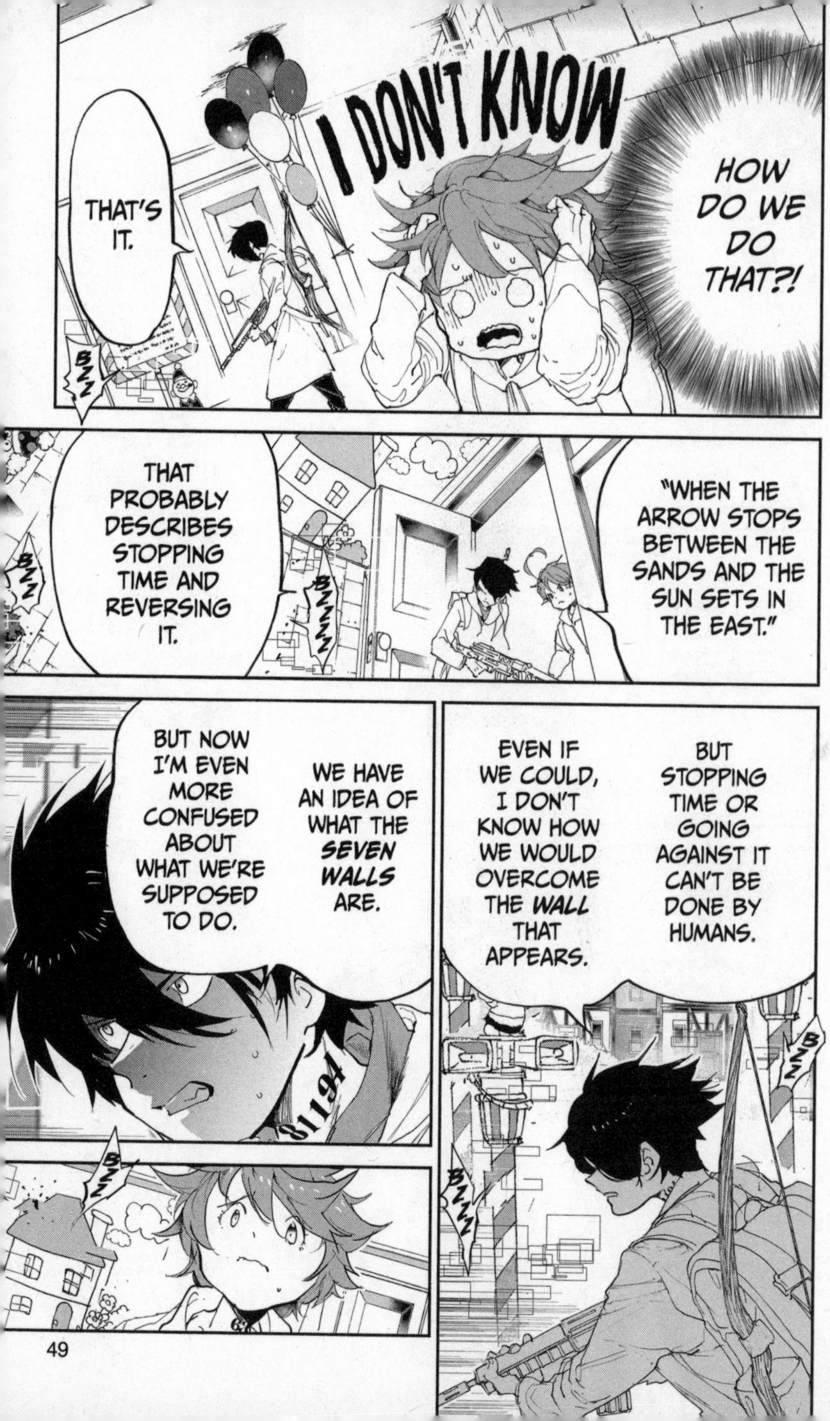
I DON'T KNOW
HOW DO WE DO THAT?!
THAT'S IT.
BZZ
"WHEN THE ARROW STOPS BETWEEN THE SANDS AND THE SUN SETS IN THE EAST."
BZZZZ
THAT PROBABLY DESCRIBES STOPPING TIME AND REVERSING IT.
BZZ
BUT STOPPING TIME OR GOING AGAINST IT CAN'T BE DONE BY HUMANS.
EVEN IF WE COULD, I DON'T KNOW HOW WE WOULD OVERCOME THE WALL THAT APPEARS.
BZZ
BZZZ
WE HAVE AN IDEA OF WHAT THE SEVEN WALLS ARE.
BUT NOW I'M EVEN MORE CONFUSED ABOUT WHAT WE'RE SUPPOSED TO DO.
81194
BZZ
63

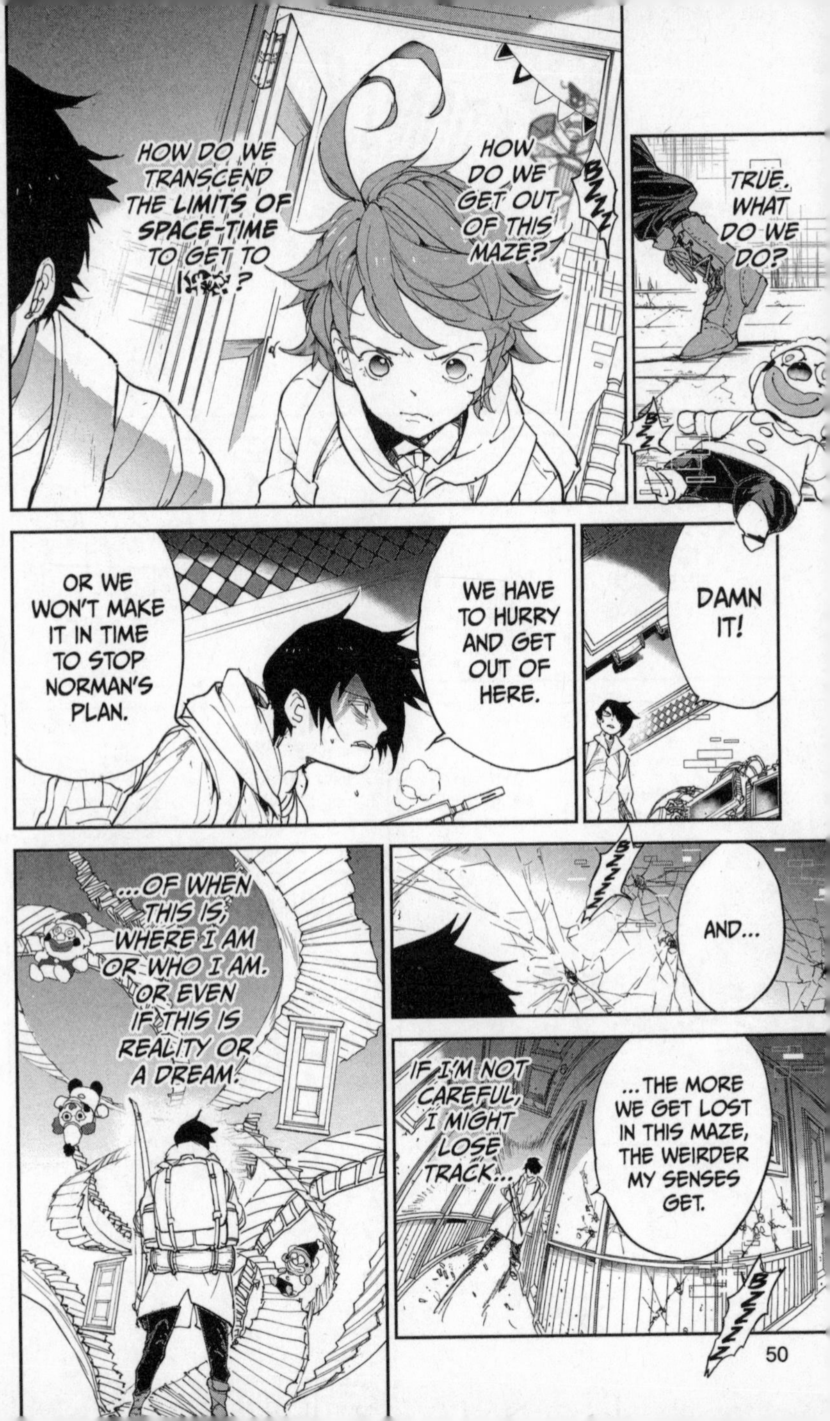
TRUE. WHAT DO WE DO?
BZZ
BZZZ
HOW DO WE GET OUT OF THIS MAZE?
HOW DO WE TRANSCEND THE LIMITS OF SPACE-TIME TO GET TO ?
DAMN IT!
WE HAVE TO HURRY AND GET OUT OF HERE.
OR WE WON'T MAKE IT IN TIME TO STOP NORMAN'S PLAN.
BZZZZ
AND...
...THE MORE WE GET LOST IN THIS MAZE, THE WEIRDER MY SENSES GET.
IF I'M NOT CAREFUL, I MIGHT LOSE TRACK...
BZZZZ
...OF WHEN THIS IS, WHERE I AM OR WHO I AM. OR EVEN IF THIS IS REALITY OR A DREAM.

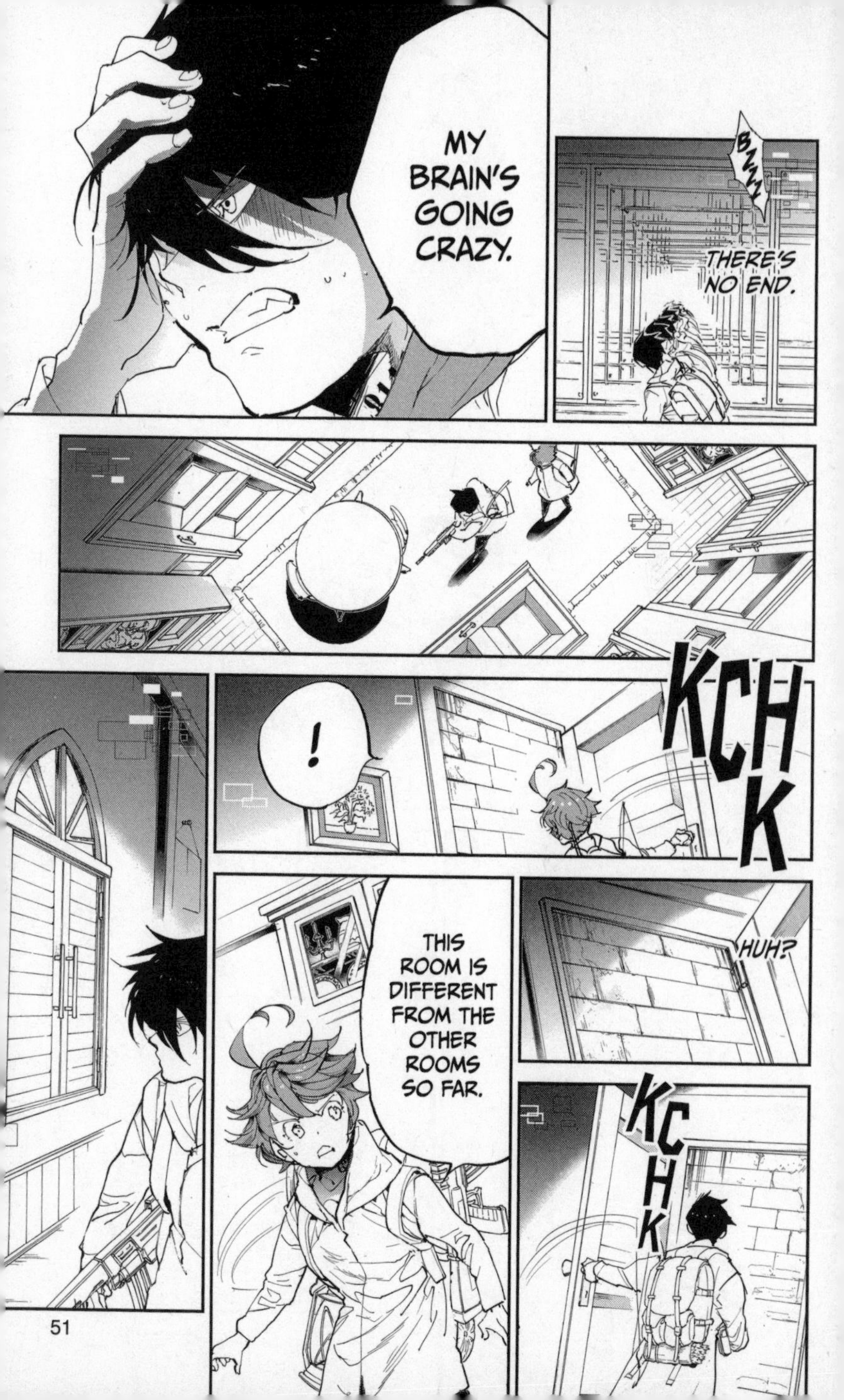
BZZZ
THERE'S NO END.
MY BRAIN'S GOING CRAZY.
!
KCHK
HUH?
KCHK
THIS ROOM IS DIFFERENT FROM THE OTHER ROOMS SO FAR.

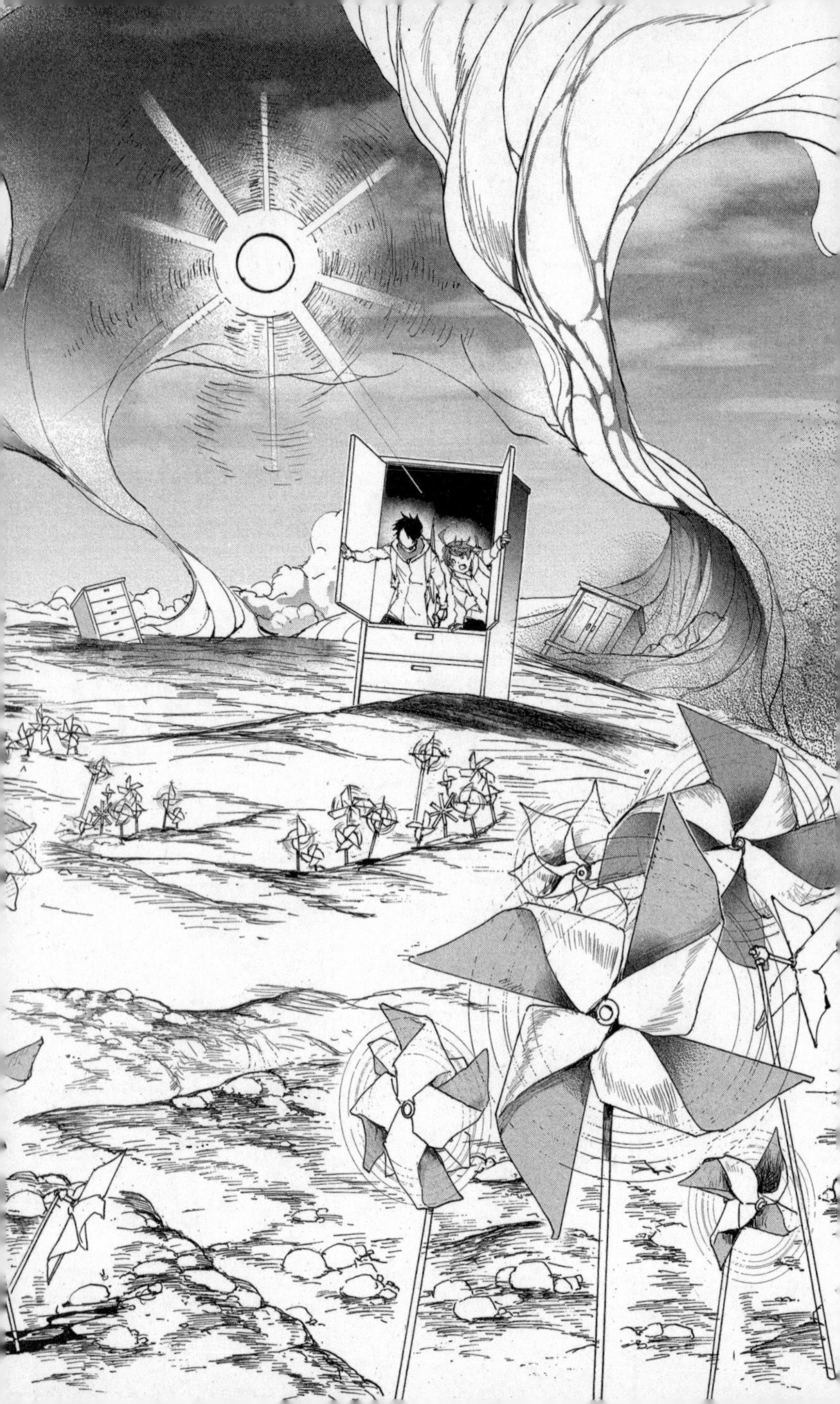

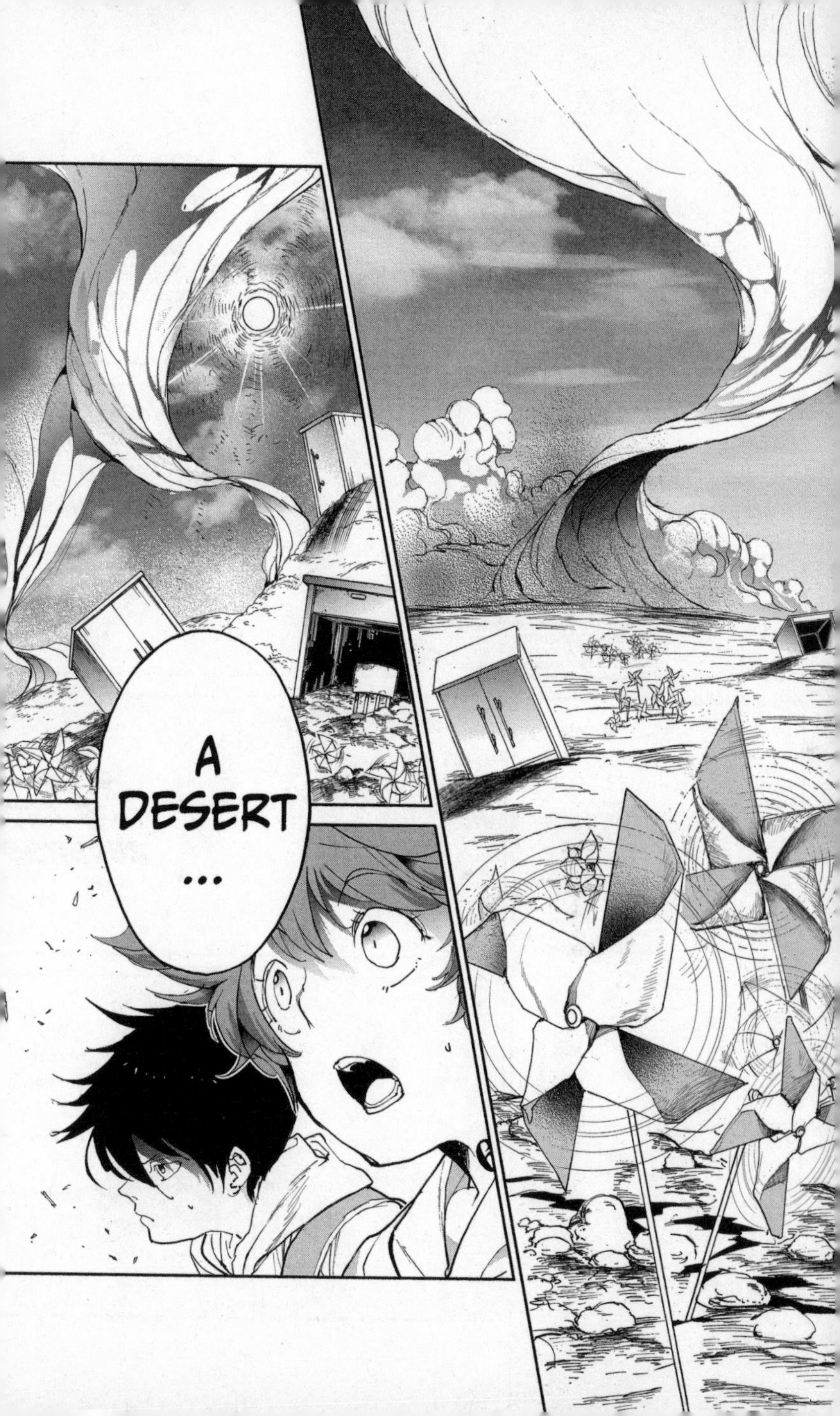
A DESERT ...

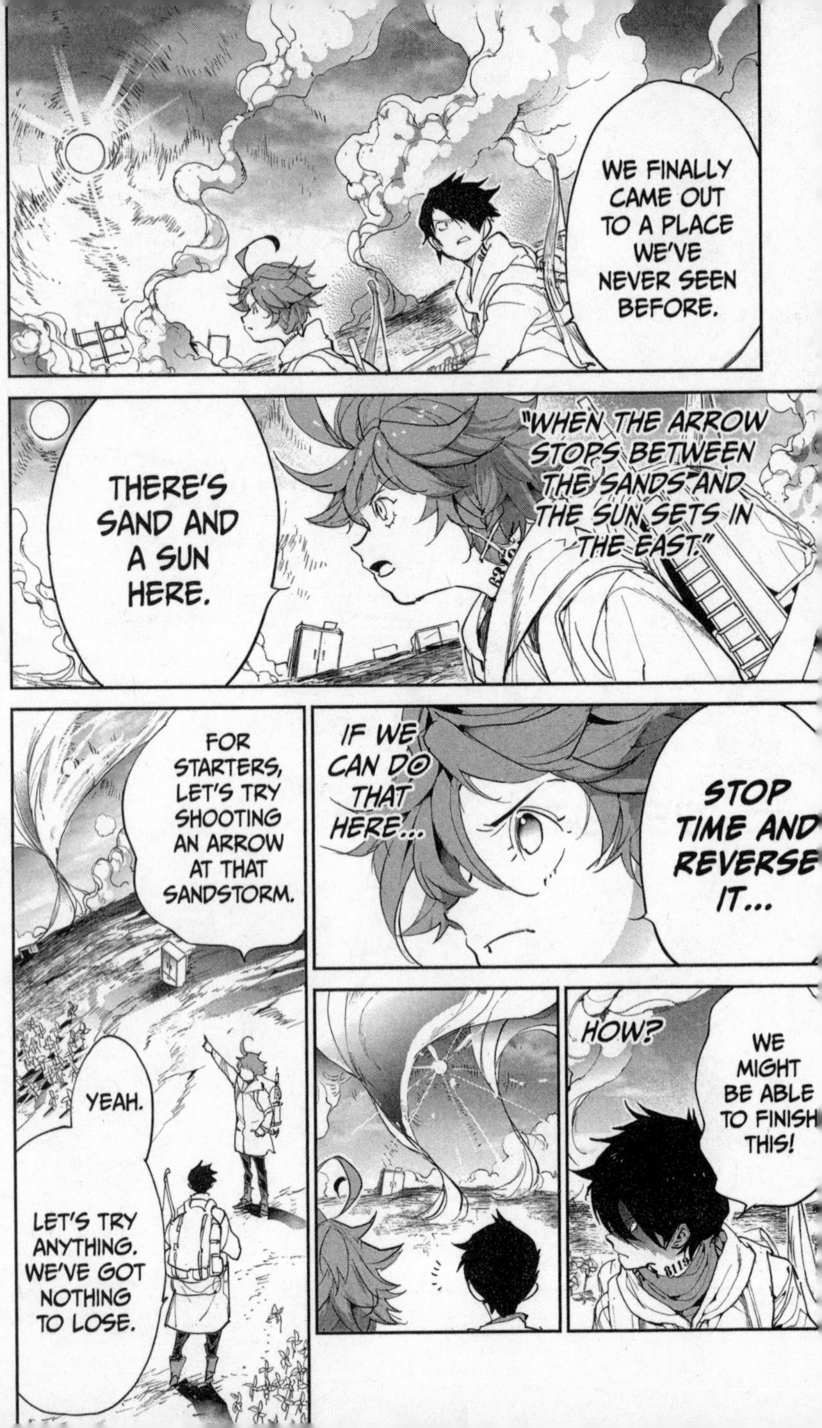
WE FINALLY CAME OUT TO A PLACE WE'VE NEVER SEEN BEFORE.
"WHEN THE ARROW STOPS BETWEEN THE SANDS AND THE SUN SETS IN THE EAST."
THERE'S SAND AND A SUN HERE.
STOP TIME AND REVERSE IT...
IF WE CAN DO THAT HERE...
WE MIGHT BE ABLE TO FINISH THIS!
HOW?
FOR STARTERS, LET'S TRY SHOOTING AN ARROW AT THAT SANDSTORM.
YEAH.
LET'S TRY ANYTHING. WE'VE GOT NOTHING TO LOSE.

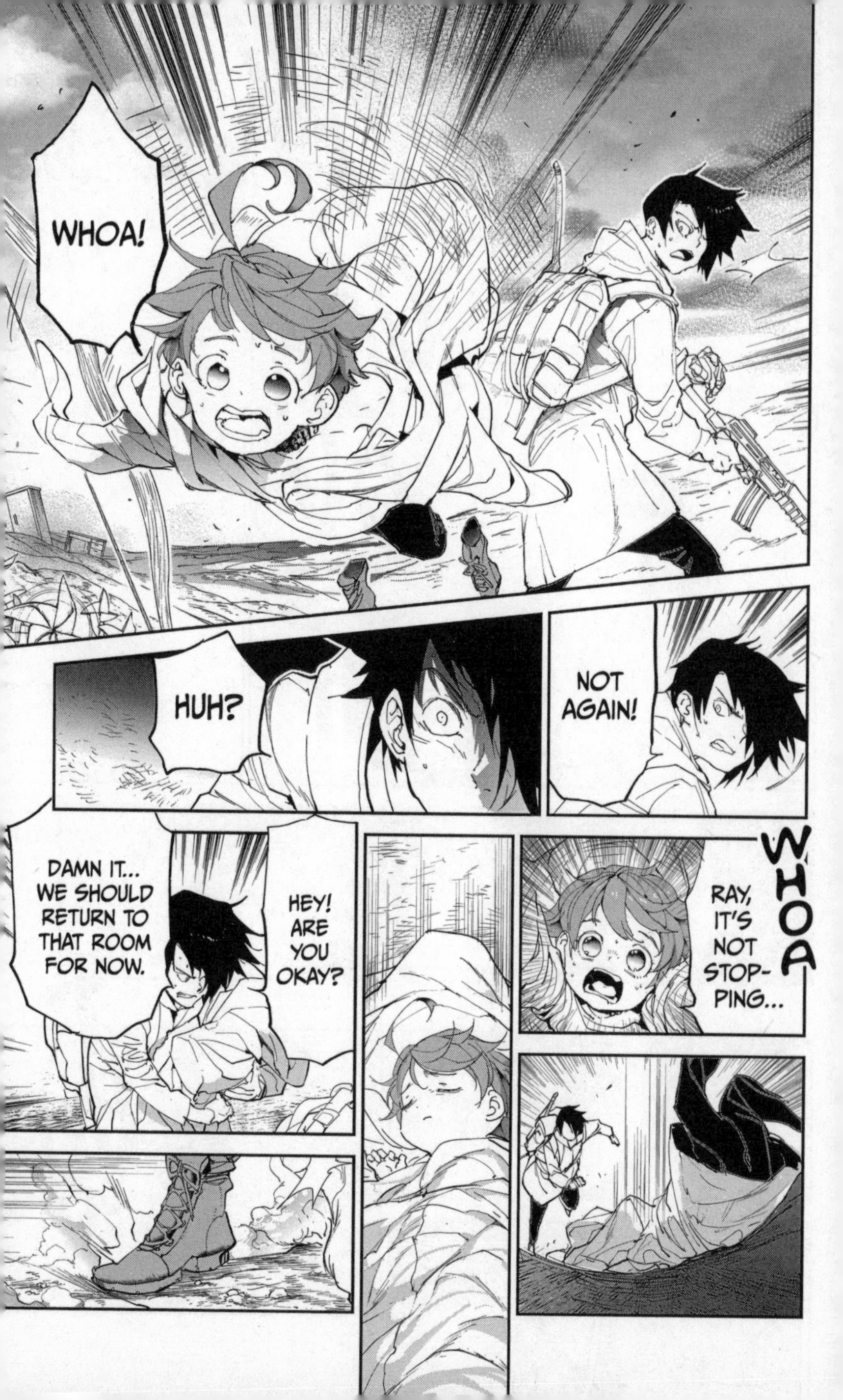
WHOA!
NOT AGAIN!
HUH?
WHOA
RAY, IT'S NOT STOPPING...
HEY! ARE YOU OKAY?
DAMN IT... WE SHOULD RETURN TO THAT ROOM FOR NOW.

VWOOOOSHH

KRAK

!

EMMA?

HUH?

...

...I CAN'T FIND IT.

NO MATTER HOW MUCH I SEARCH...

THUD

I CAN'T ANYMORE.

AH.

56

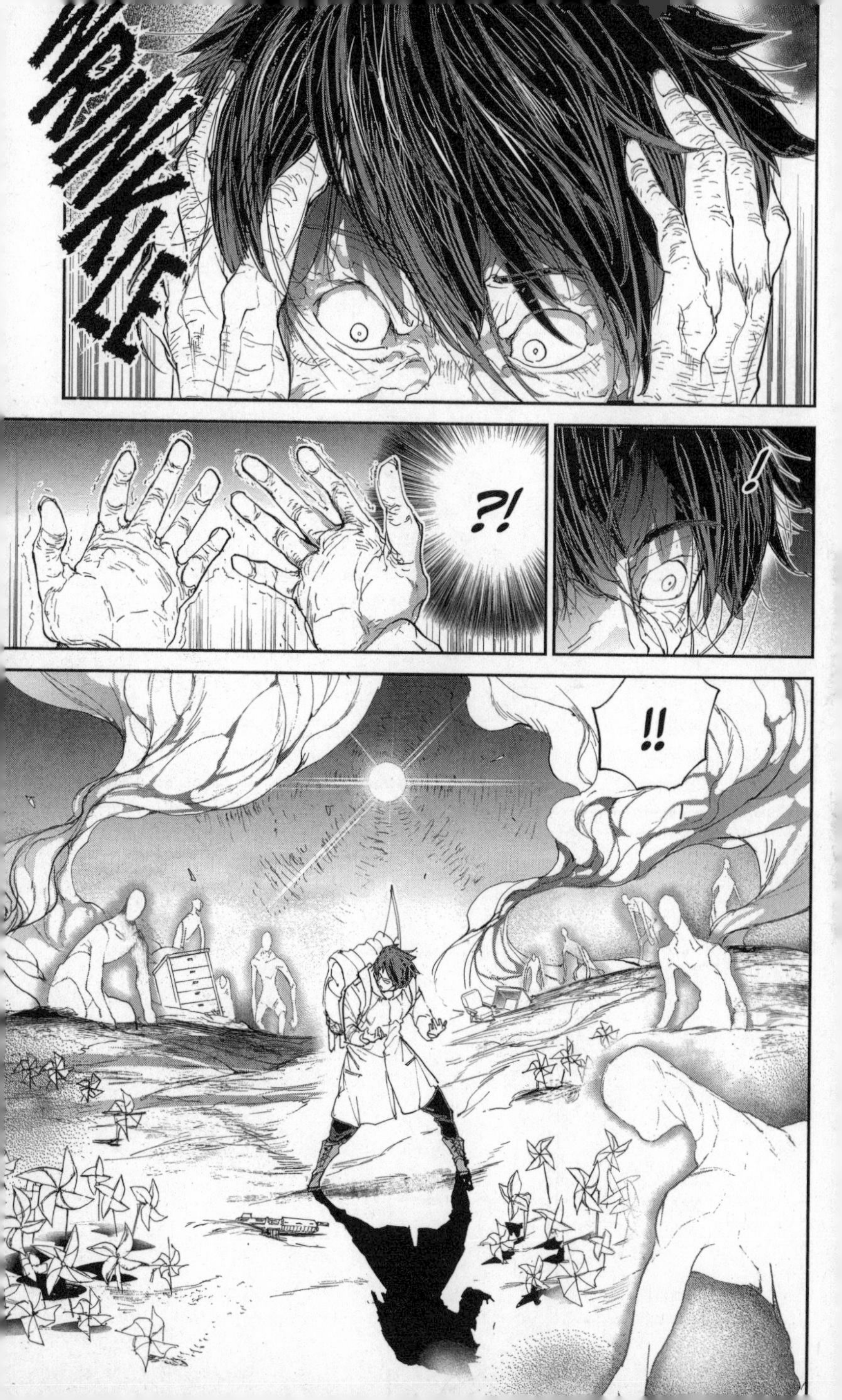
WRINKLE
!
?!
!!

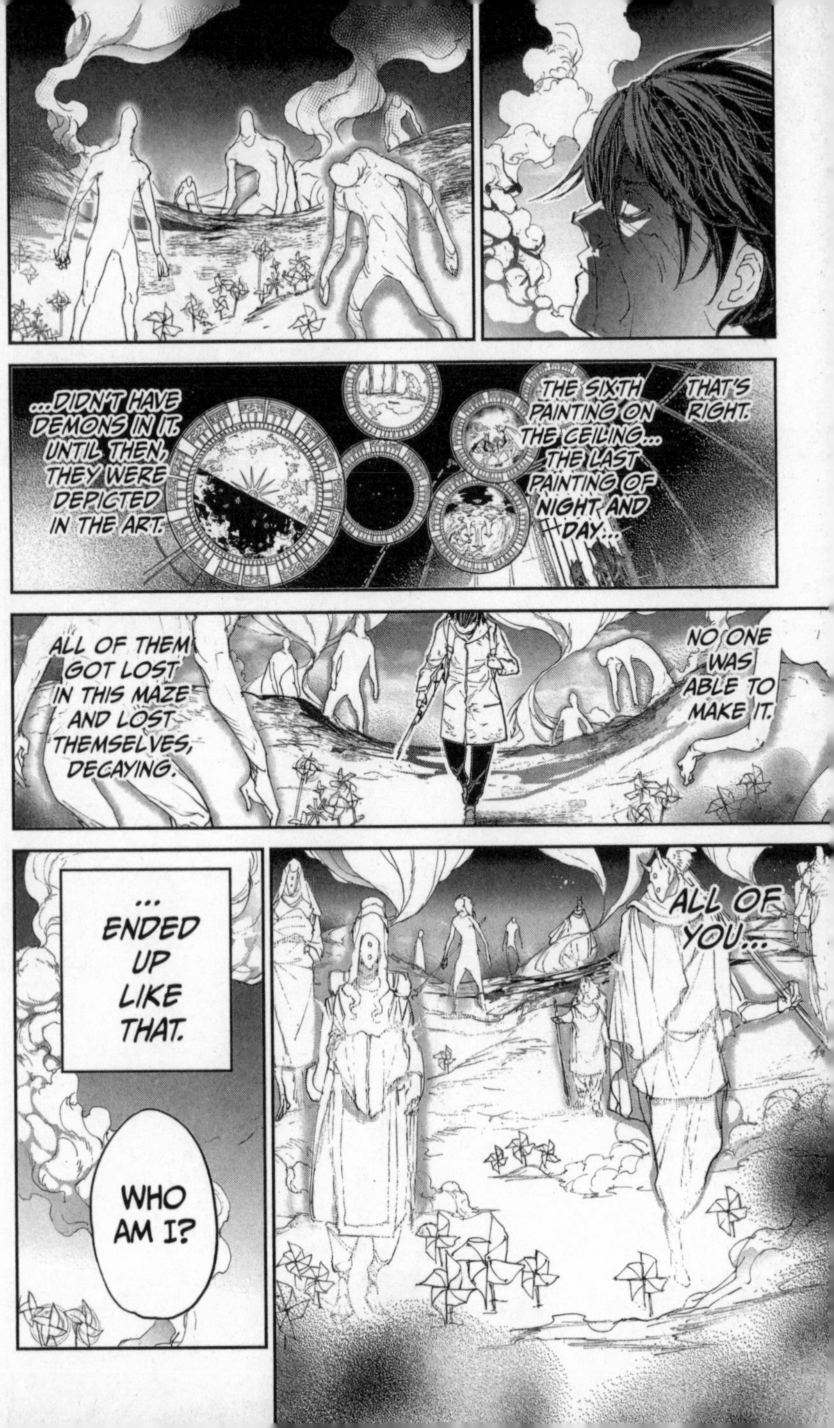
THAT'S RIGHT.
THE SIXTH PAINTING ON THE CEILING... THE LAST PAINTING OF NIGHT AND DAY...
...DIDN'T HAVE DEMONS IN IT. UNTIL THEN, THEY WERE DEPICTED IN THE ART.
NO ONE WAS ABLE TO MAKE IT.
ALL OF THEM GOT LOST IN THIS MAZE AND LOST THEMSELVES, DECAYING.
ALL OF YOU...
... ENDED UP LIKE THAT.
WHO AM I?

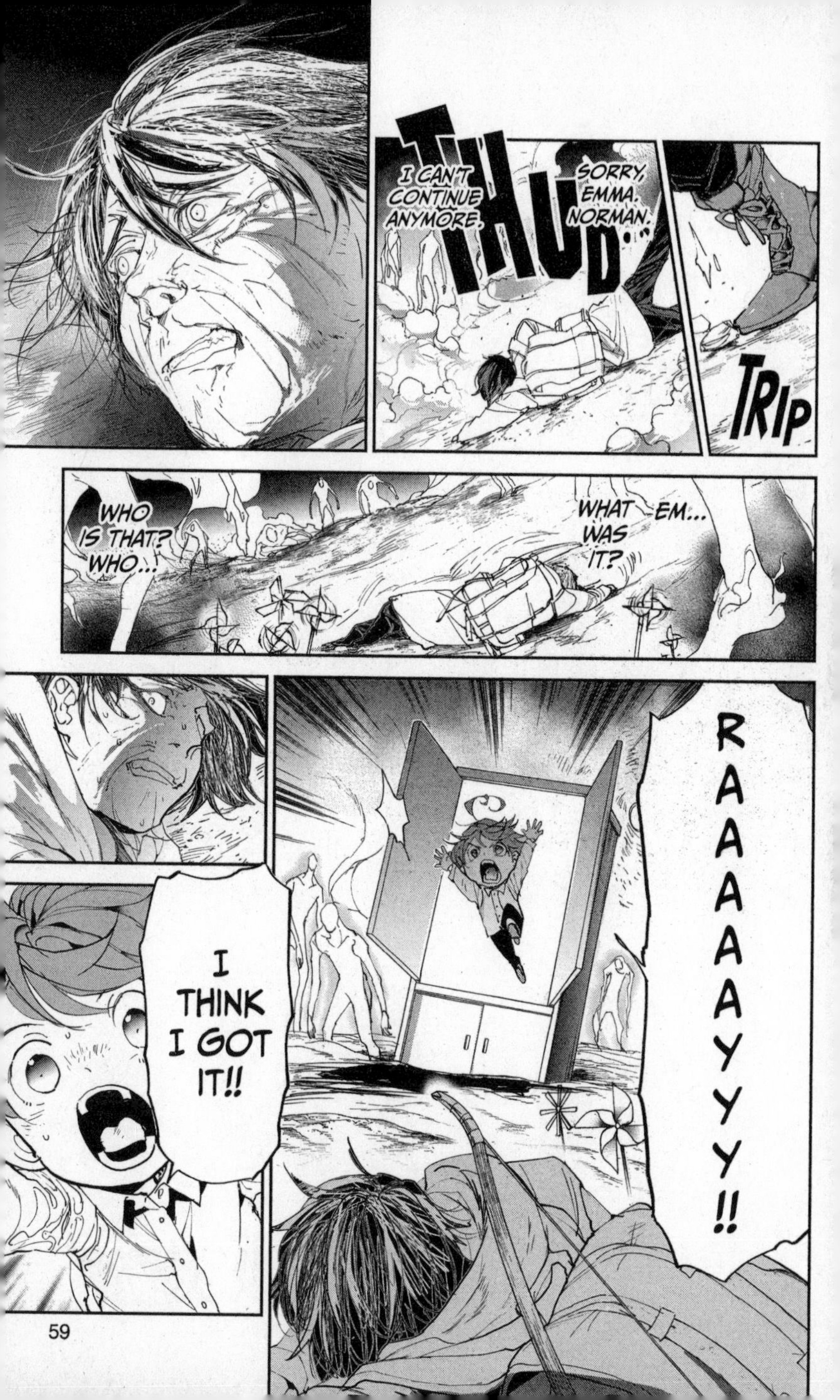
TRIP
THUD
SORRY, EMMA. NORMAN.
I CAN'T CONTINUE ANYMORE.
EM...
WHAT WAS IT?
WHO IS THAT? WHO...
RAAAAAYYY!!
I THINK I GOT IT!!

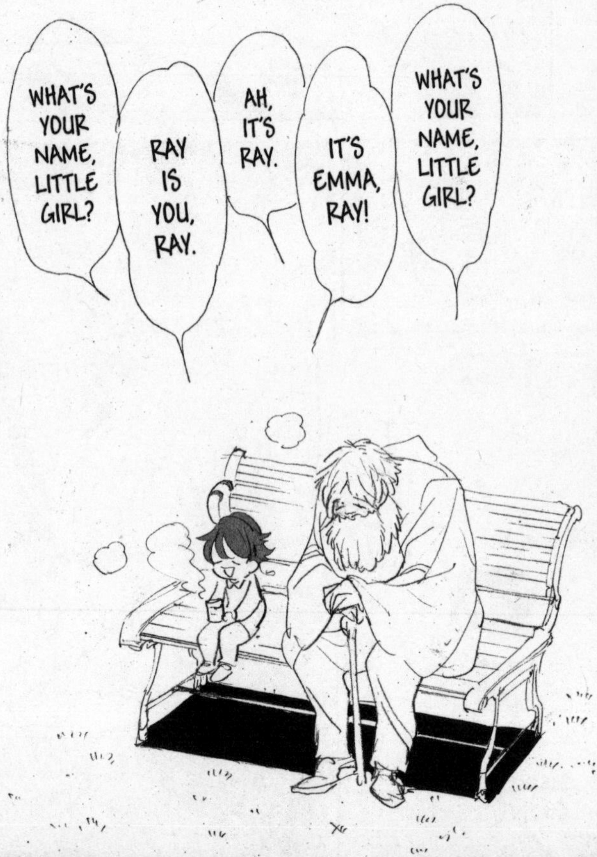
WHAT'S YOUR NAME, LITTLE GIRL?
IT'S EMMA, RAY!
AH, IT'S RAY.
RAY IS YOU, RAY.
WHAT'S YOUR NAME, LITTLE GIRL?

I CAN'T
CONTINUE
ANYMORE.

WHAT?

SORRY,
EMMA.
NORMAN.

WHO...

CHAPTER 137: CONVERSION

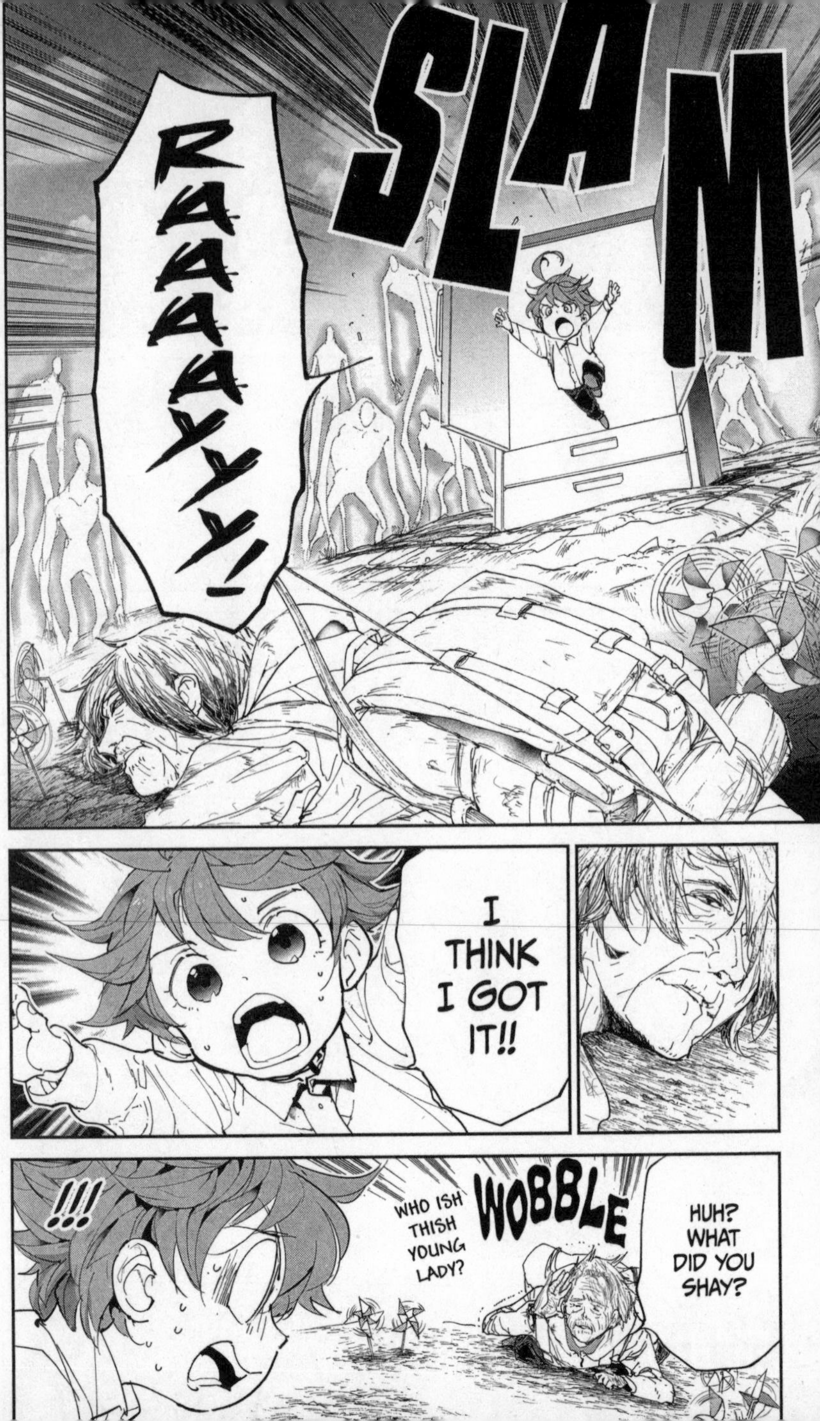
SLAM
RAAAAYYY!
I THINK I GOT IT!!
HUH? WHAT DID YOU SHAY?
WOBBLE
WHO ISH THISH YOUNG LADY?
!!!

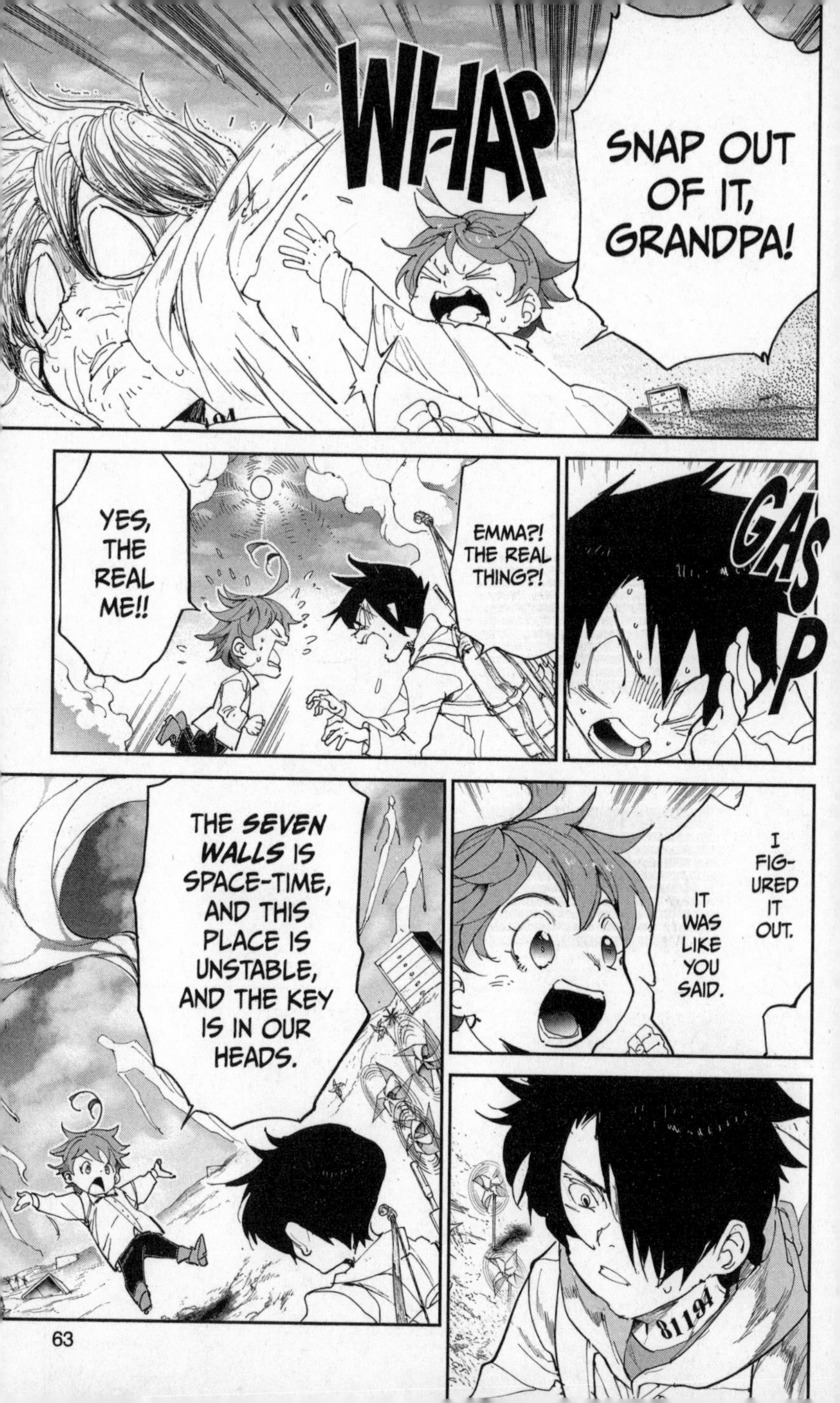
WHAP
SNAP OUT OF IT, GRANDPA!
GASP
EMMA?! THE REAL THING?!
YES, THE REAL ME!!
I FIGURED IT OUT.
IT WAS LIKE YOU SAID.
THE *SEVEN WALLS* IS SPACE-TIME, AND THIS PLACE IS UNSTABLE, AND THE KEY IS IN OUR HEADS.
81194

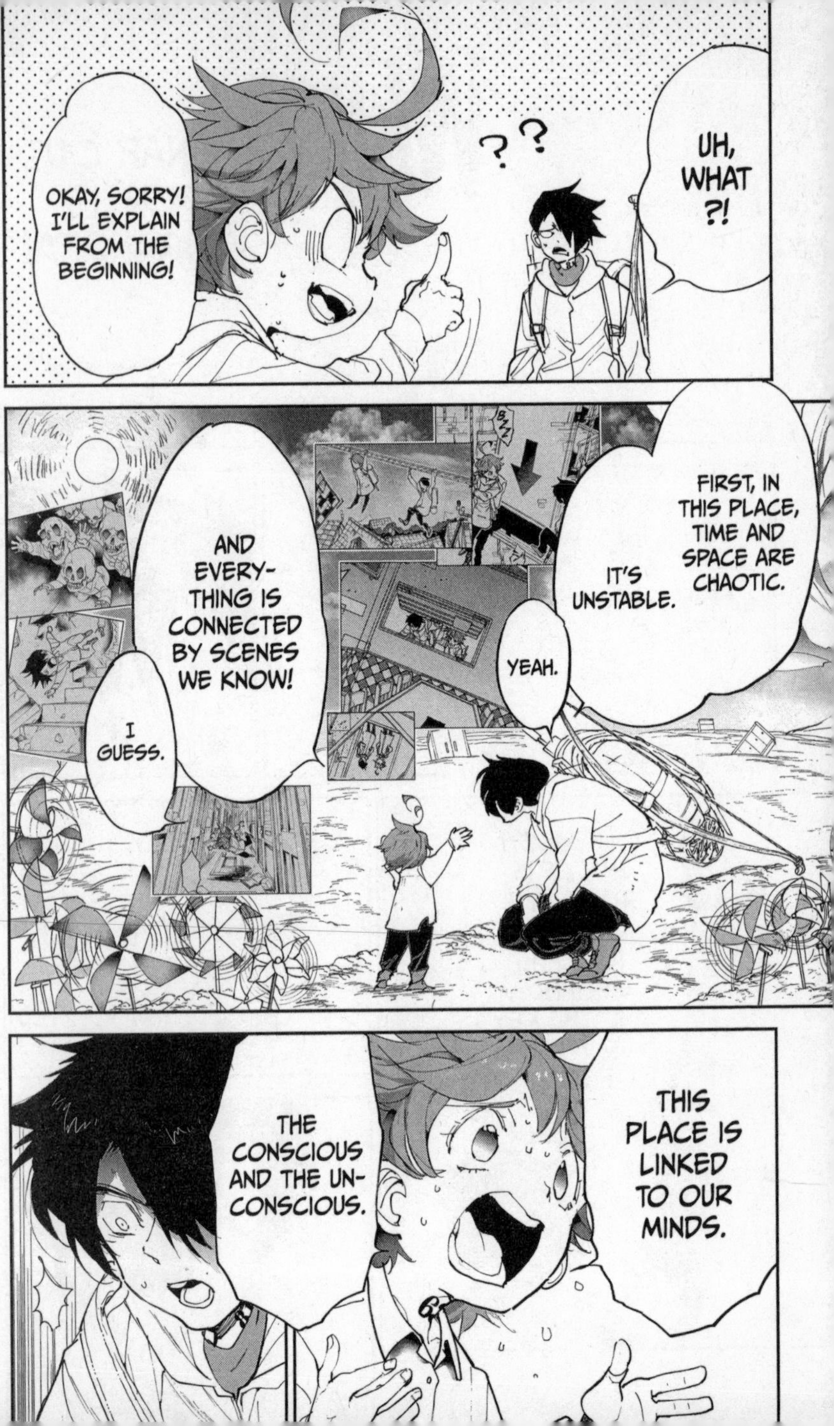
UH, WHAT ?!
OKAY, SORRY! I'LL EXPLAIN FROM THE BEGINNING!
BZZ
FIRST, IN THIS PLACE, TIME AND SPACE ARE CHAOTIC.
IT'S UNSTABLE.
YEAH.
AND EVERY-THING IS CONNECTED BY SCENES WE KNOW!
I GUESS.
THIS PLACE IS LINKED TO OUR MINDS.
THE CONSCIOUS AND THE UN-CONSCIOUS.

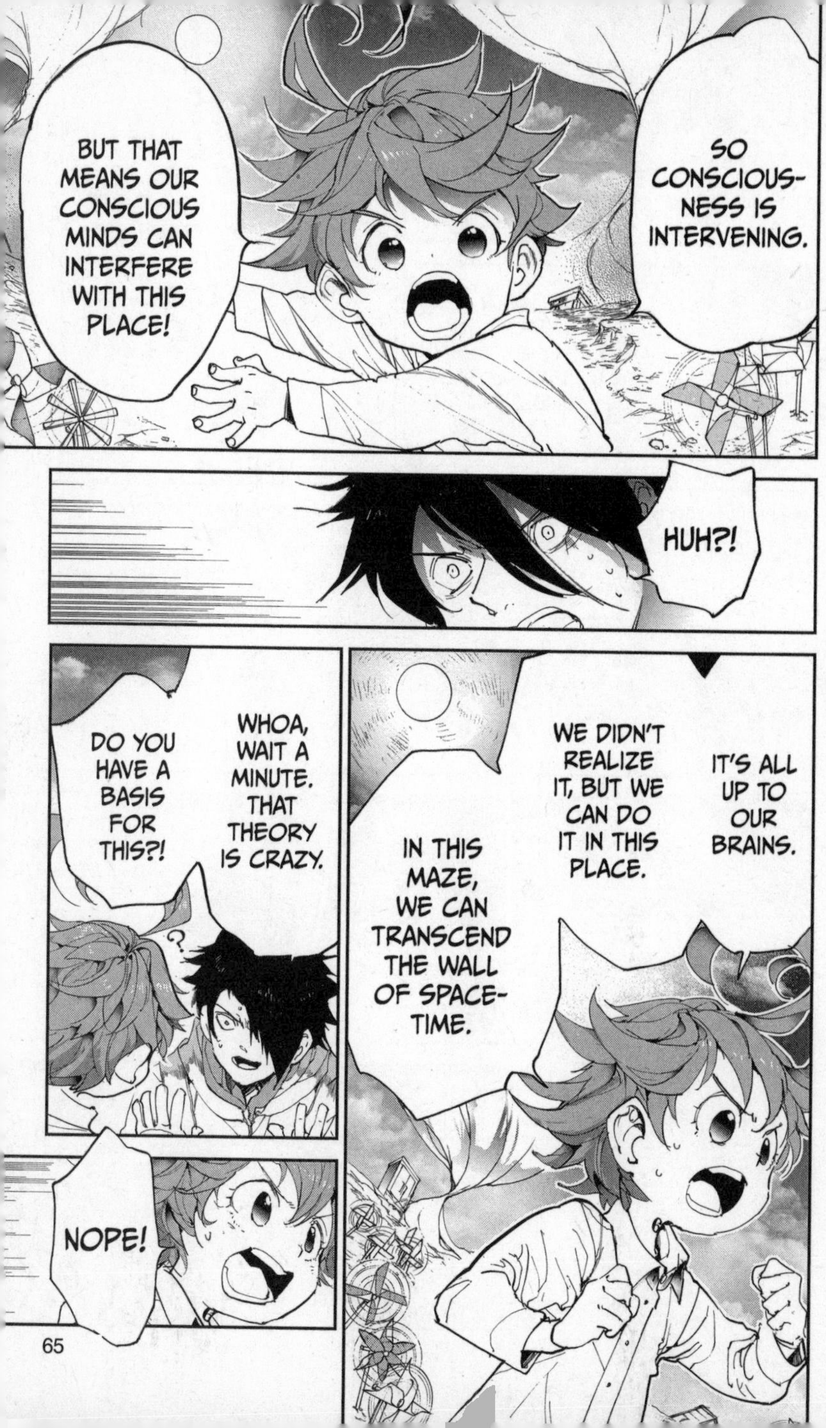
SO CONSCIOUS-NESS IS INTERVENING.
BUT THAT MEANS OUR CONSCIOUS MINDS CAN INTERFERE WITH THIS PLACE!
HUH?!
IT'S ALL UP TO OUR BRAINS.
WE DIDN'T REALIZE IT, BUT WE CAN DO IT IN THIS PLACE.
IN THIS MAZE, WE CAN TRANSCEND THE WALL OF SPACE-TIME.
WHOA, WAIT A MINUTE. THAT THEORY IS CRAZY.
DO YOU HAVE A BASIS FOR THIS?!
NOPE!

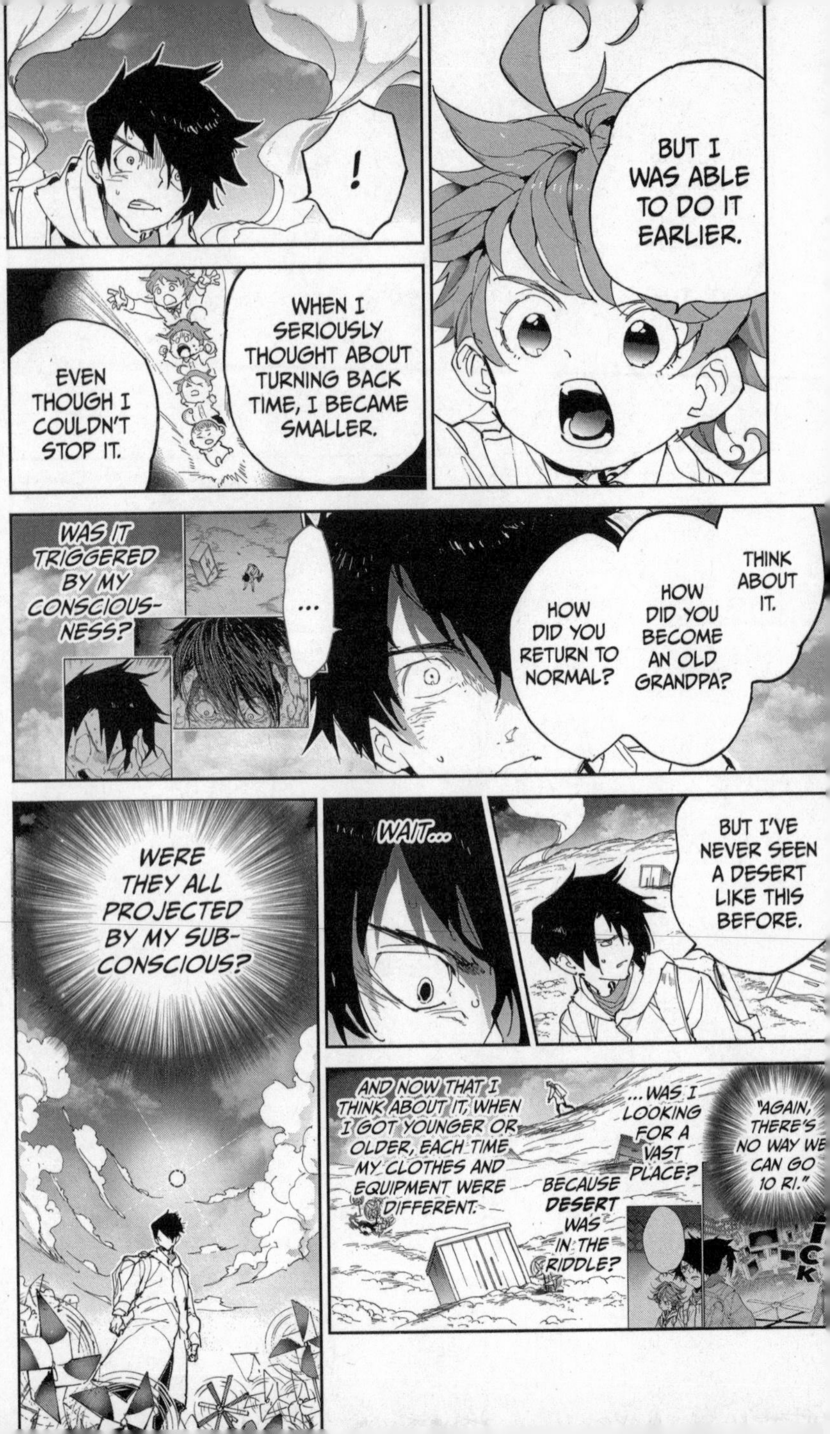
BUT I WAS ABLE TO DO IT EARLIER.
!
WHEN I SERIOUSLY THOUGHT ABOUT TURNING BACK TIME, I BECAME SMALLER.
EVEN THOUGH I COULDN'T STOP IT.
THINK ABOUT IT.
HOW DID YOU BECOME AN OLD GRANDPA?
HOW DID YOU RETURN TO NORMAL?
...
WAS IT TRIGGERED BY MY CONSCIOUS-NESS?
BUT I'VE NEVER SEEN A DESERT LIKE THIS BEFORE.
WAIT...
"AGAIN, THERE'S NO WAY WE CAN GO 10 RI."
ICK
...WAS I LOOKING FOR A VAST PLACE?
BECAUSE **DESERT** WAS IN THE RIDDLE?
AND NOW THAT I THINK ABOUT IT, WHEN I GOT YOUNGER OR OLDER, EACH TIME MY CLOTHES AND EQUIPMENT WERE DIFFERENT.
WERE THEY ALL PROJECTED BY MY SUB-CONSCIOUS?

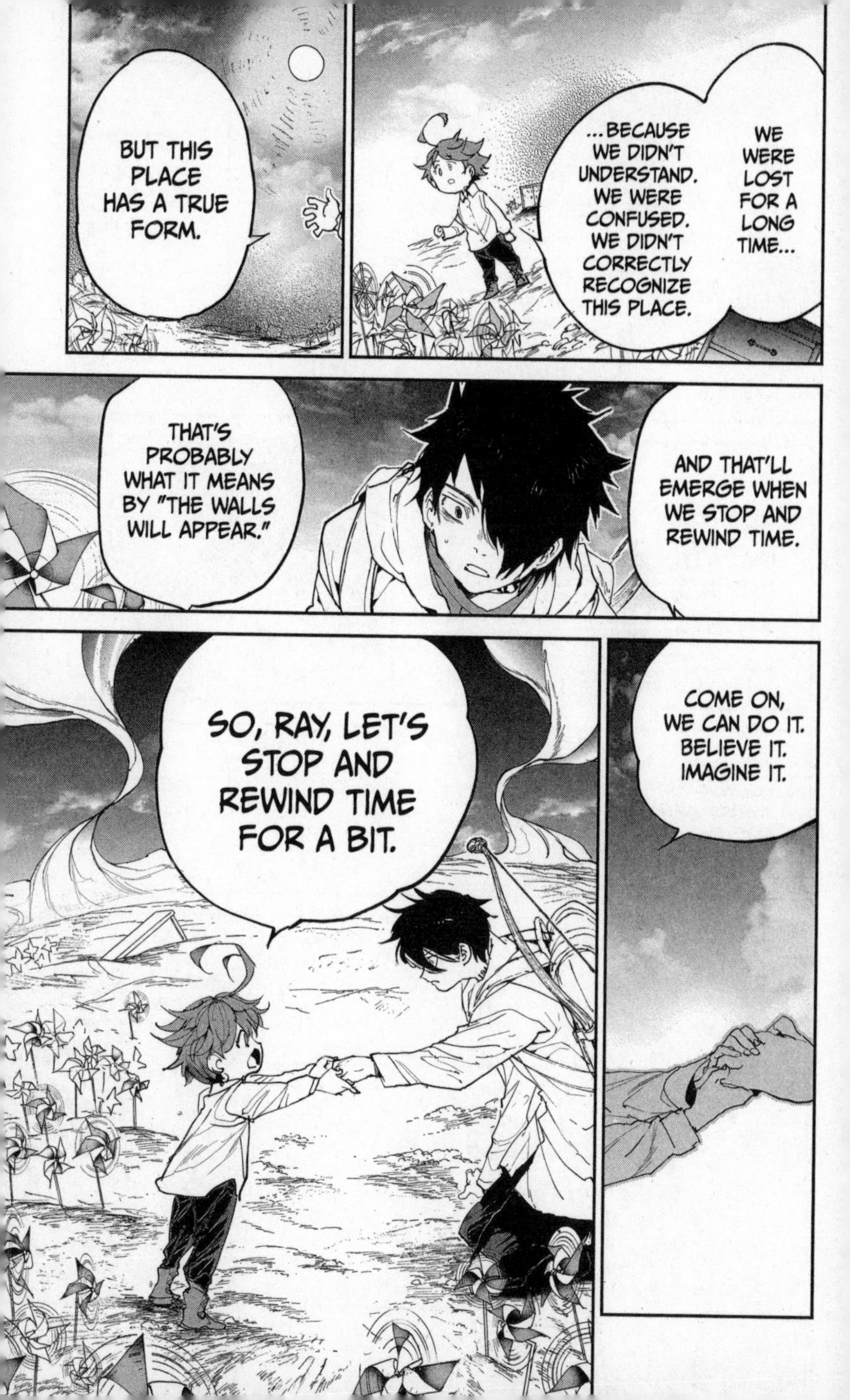
WE WERE LOST FOR A LONG TIME...
...BECAUSE WE DIDN'T UNDERSTAND. WE WERE CONFUSED. WE DIDN'T CORRECTLY RECOGNIZE THIS PLACE.
BUT THIS PLACE HAS A TRUE FORM.
AND THAT'LL EMERGE WHEN WE STOP AND REWIND TIME.
THAT'S PROBABLY WHAT IT MEANS BY "THE WALLS WILL APPEAR."
COME ON, WE CAN DO IT. BELIEVE IT. IMAGINE IT.
SO, RAY, LET'S STOP AND REWIND TIME FOR A BIT.

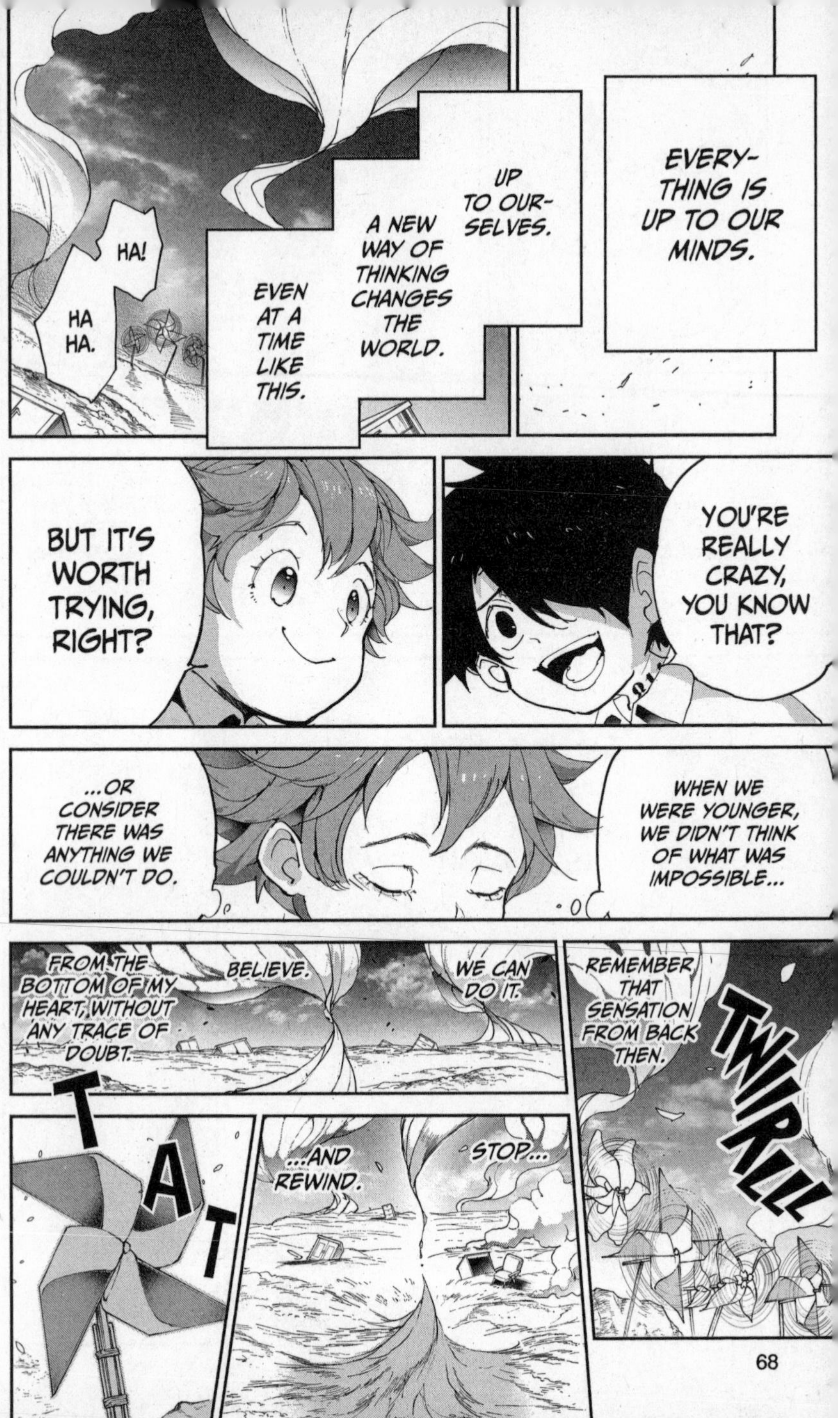
EVERYTHING IS UP TO OUR MINDS.
UP TO OURSELVES.
A NEW WAY OF THINKING CHANGES THE WORLD.
EVEN AT A TIME LIKE THIS.
HA!
HA HA.
YOU'RE REALLY CRAZY, YOU KNOW THAT?
BUT IT'S WORTH TRYING, RIGHT?
WHEN WE WERE YOUNGER, WE DIDN'T THINK OF WHAT WAS IMPOSSIBLE...
...OR CONSIDER THERE WAS ANYTHING WE COULDN'T DO.
REMEMBER THAT SENSATION FROM BACK THEN.
TWIRLL
WE CAN DO IT.
BELIEVE.
FROM THE BOTTOM OF MY HEART, WITHOUT ANY TRACE OF DOUBT.
STOP...
...AND REWIND.
TAT

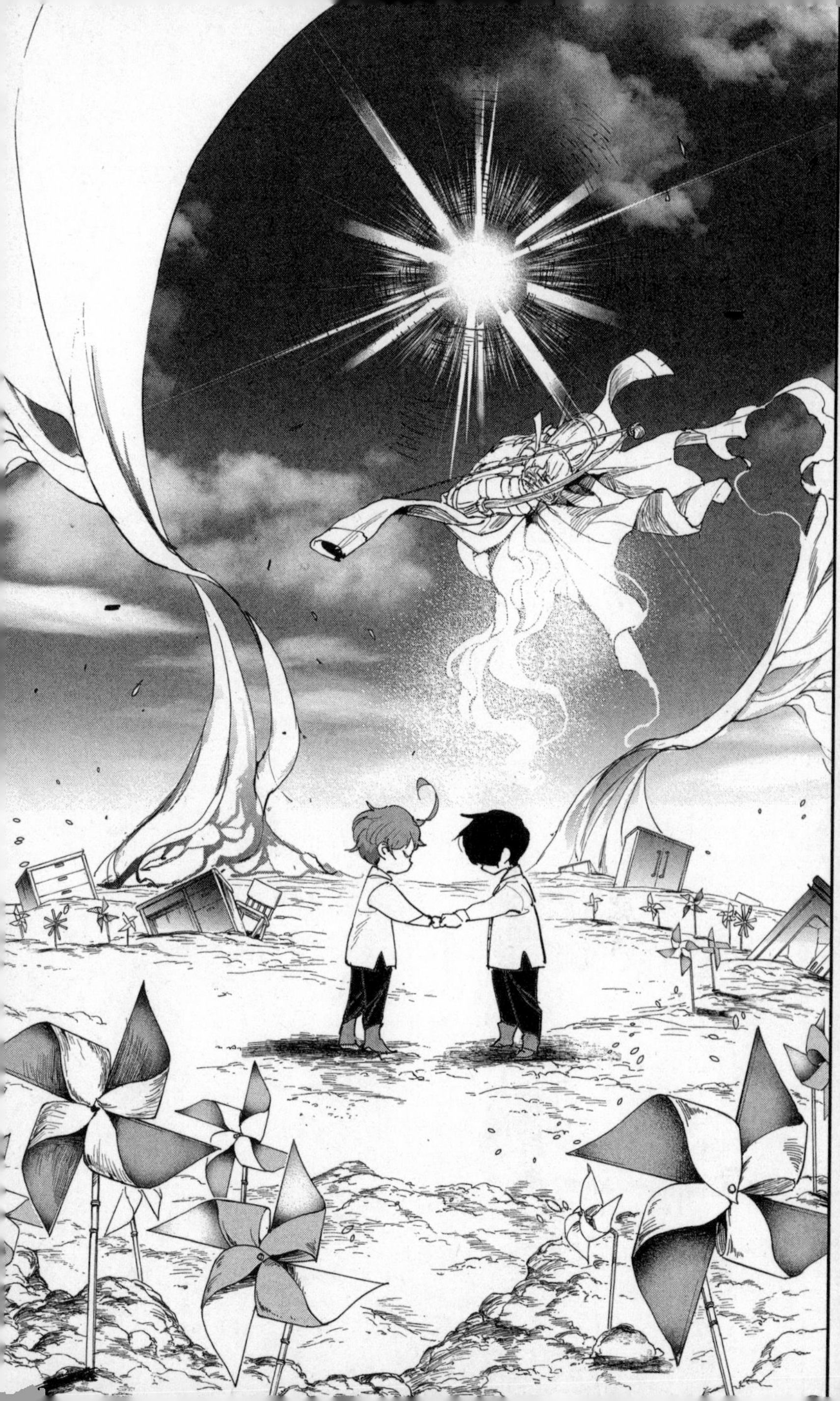

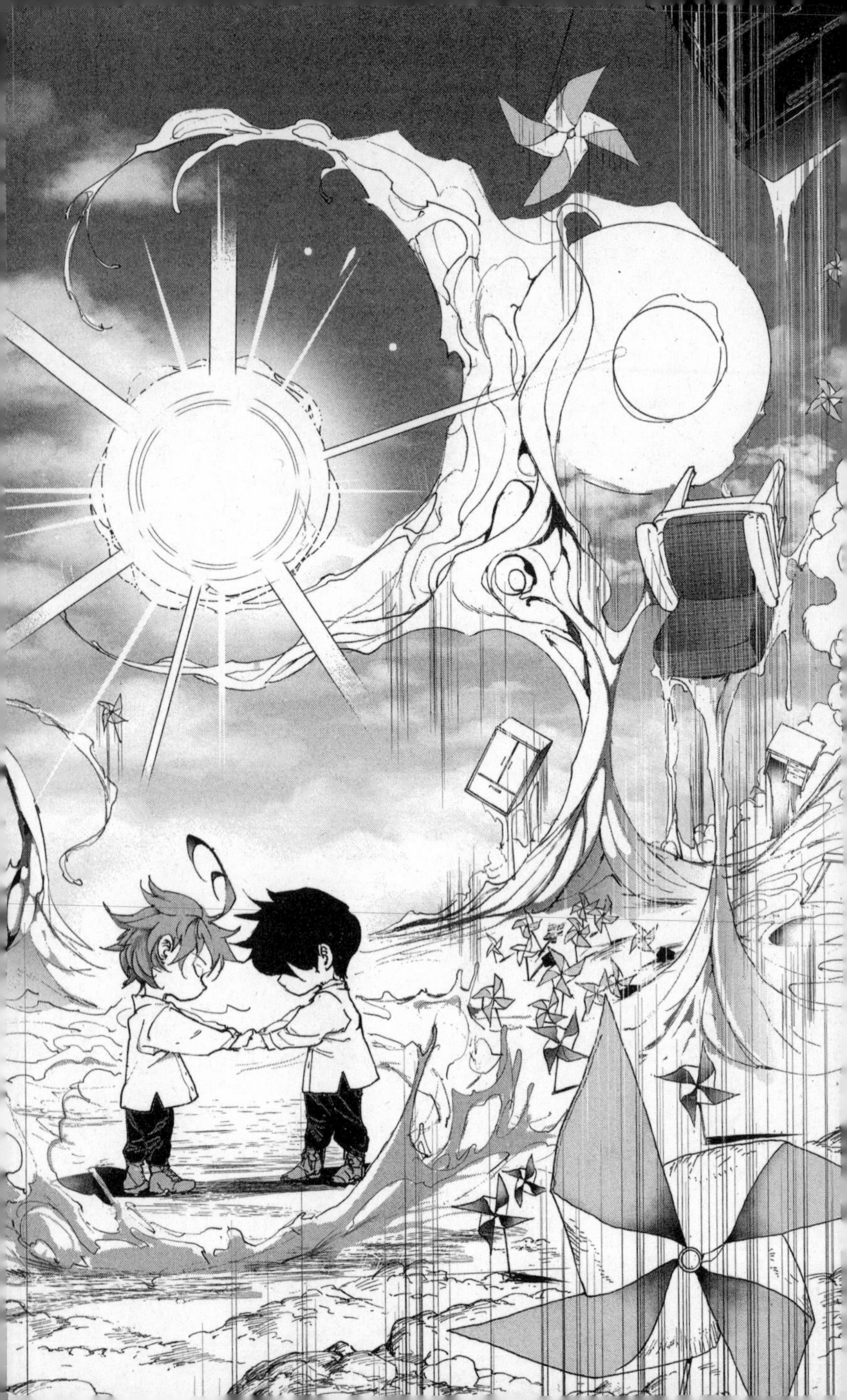

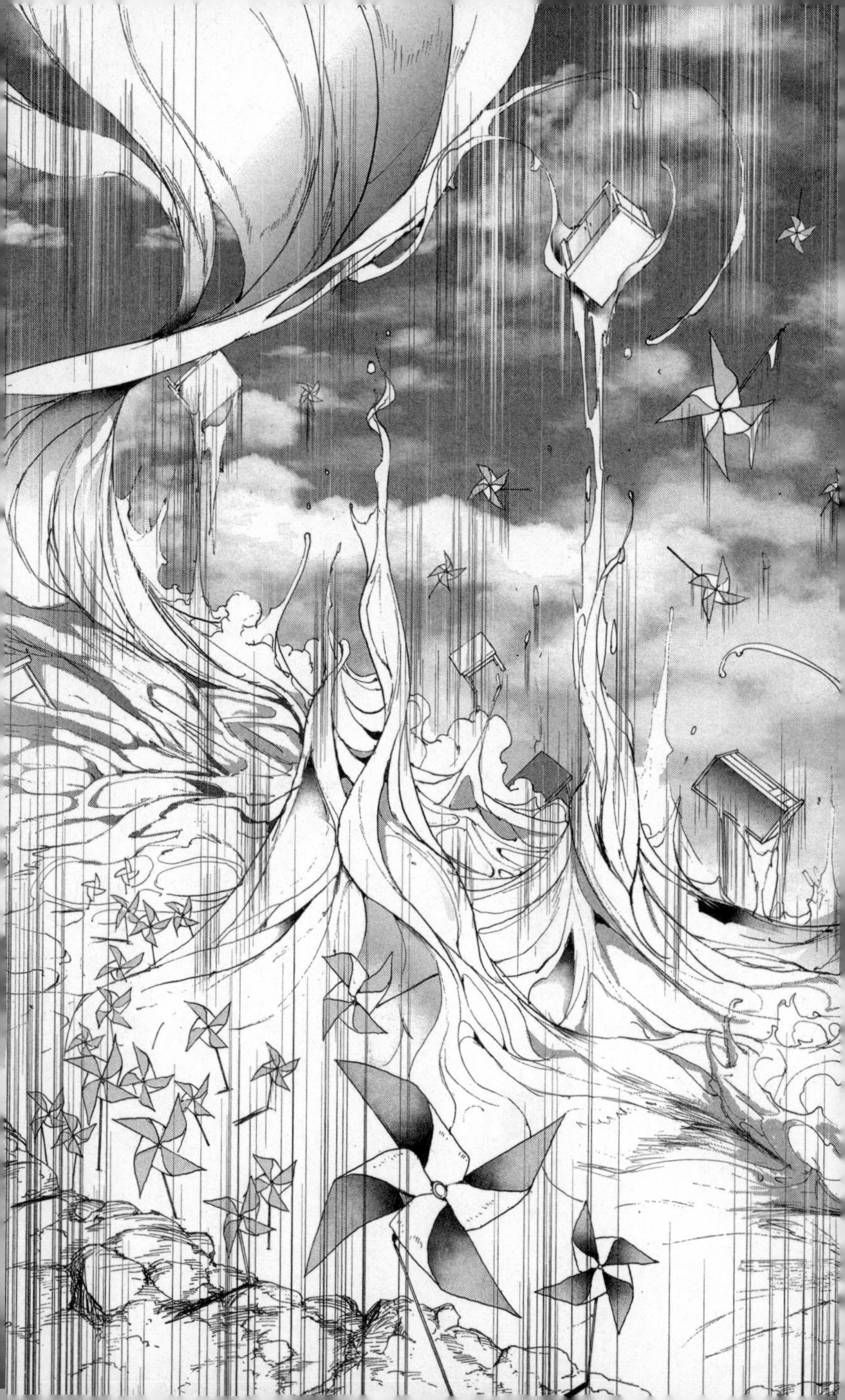

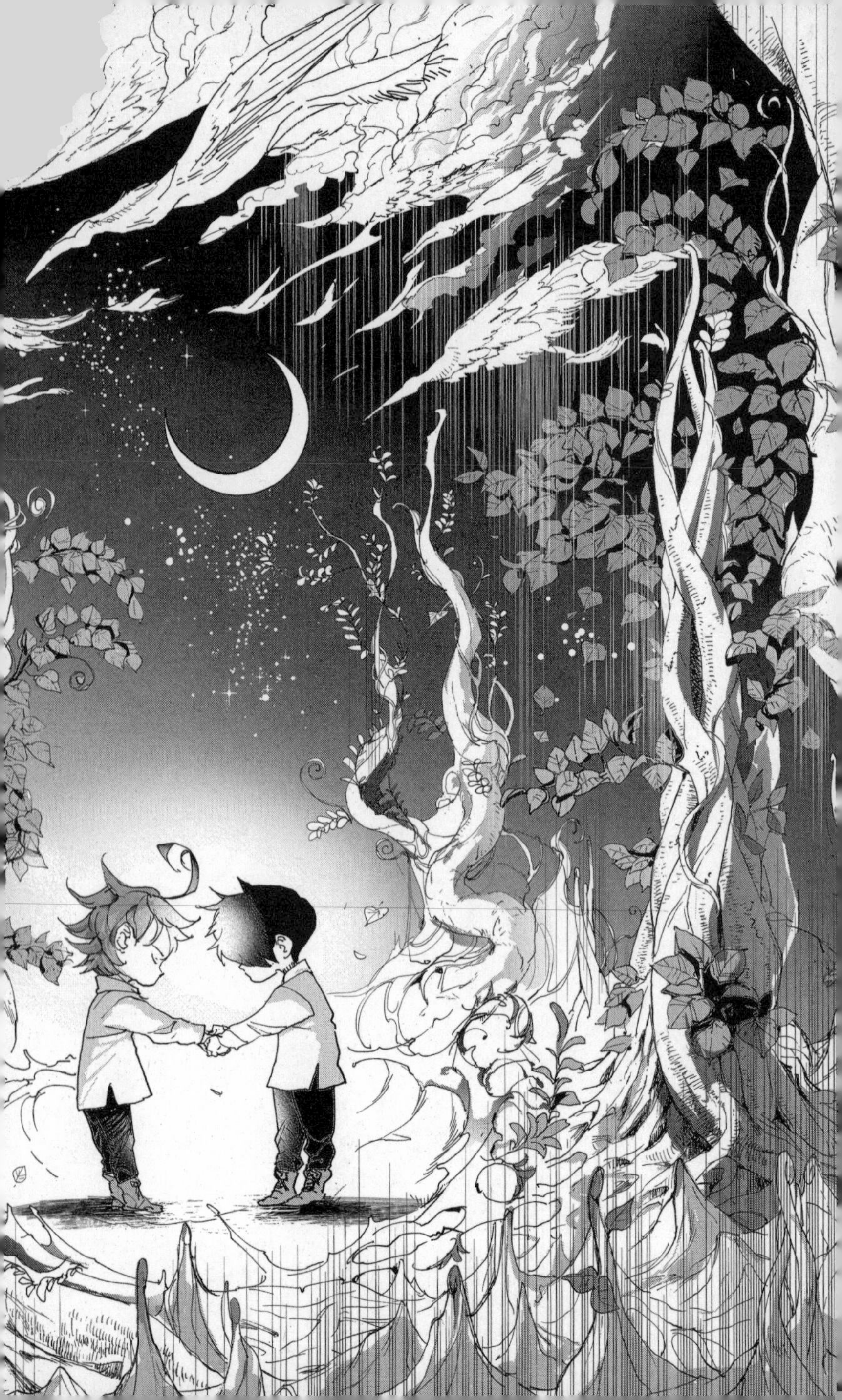

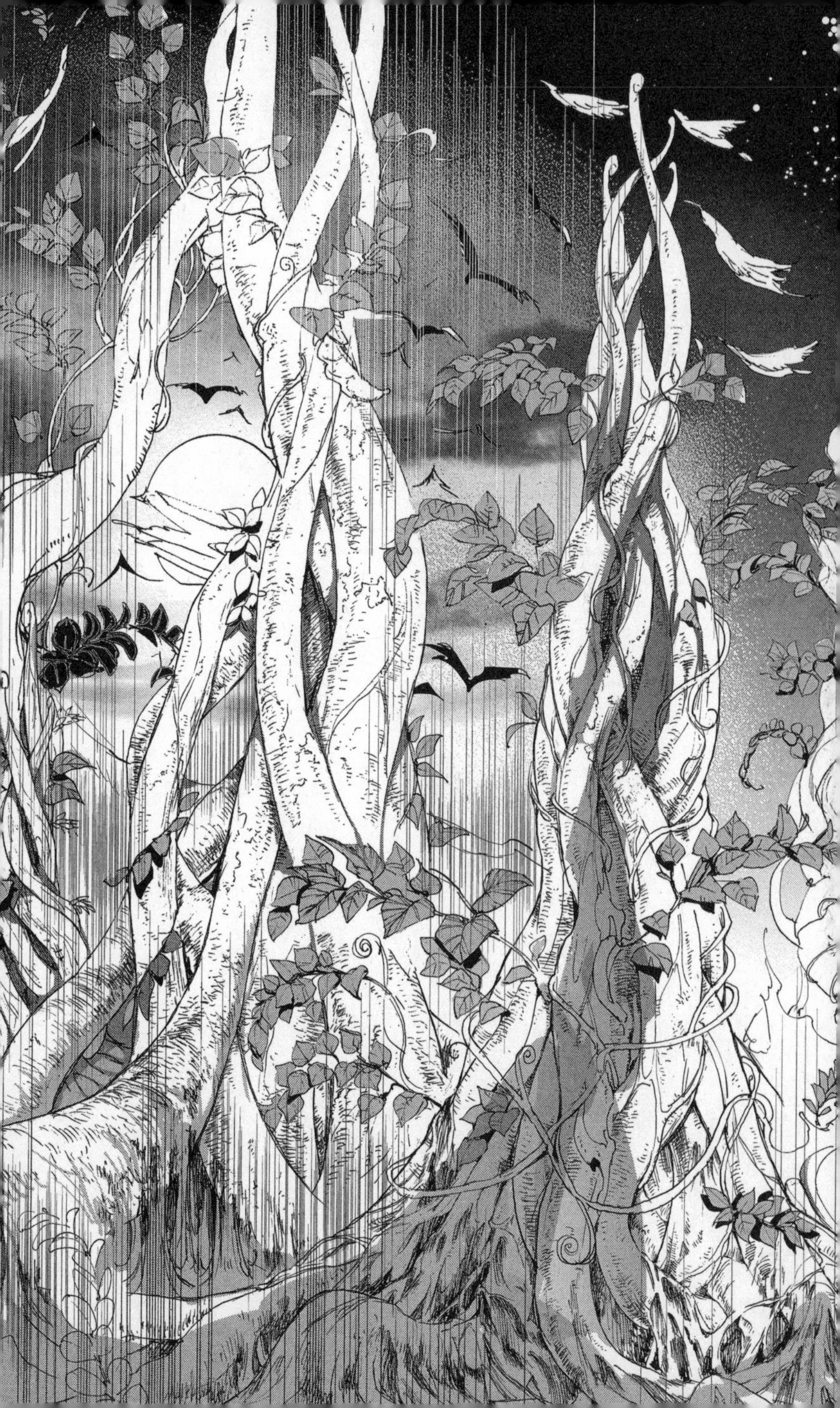

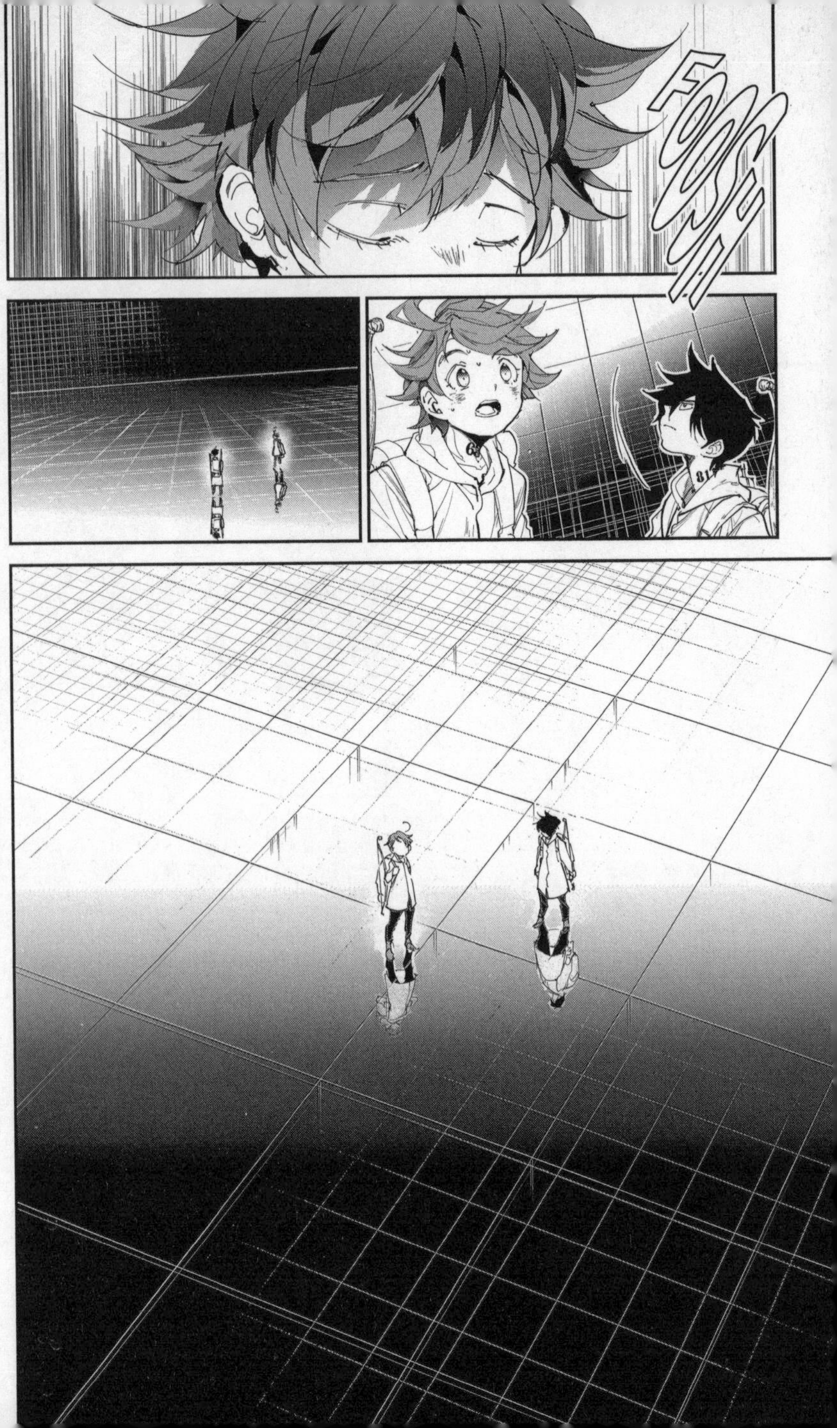
FOOSH!!

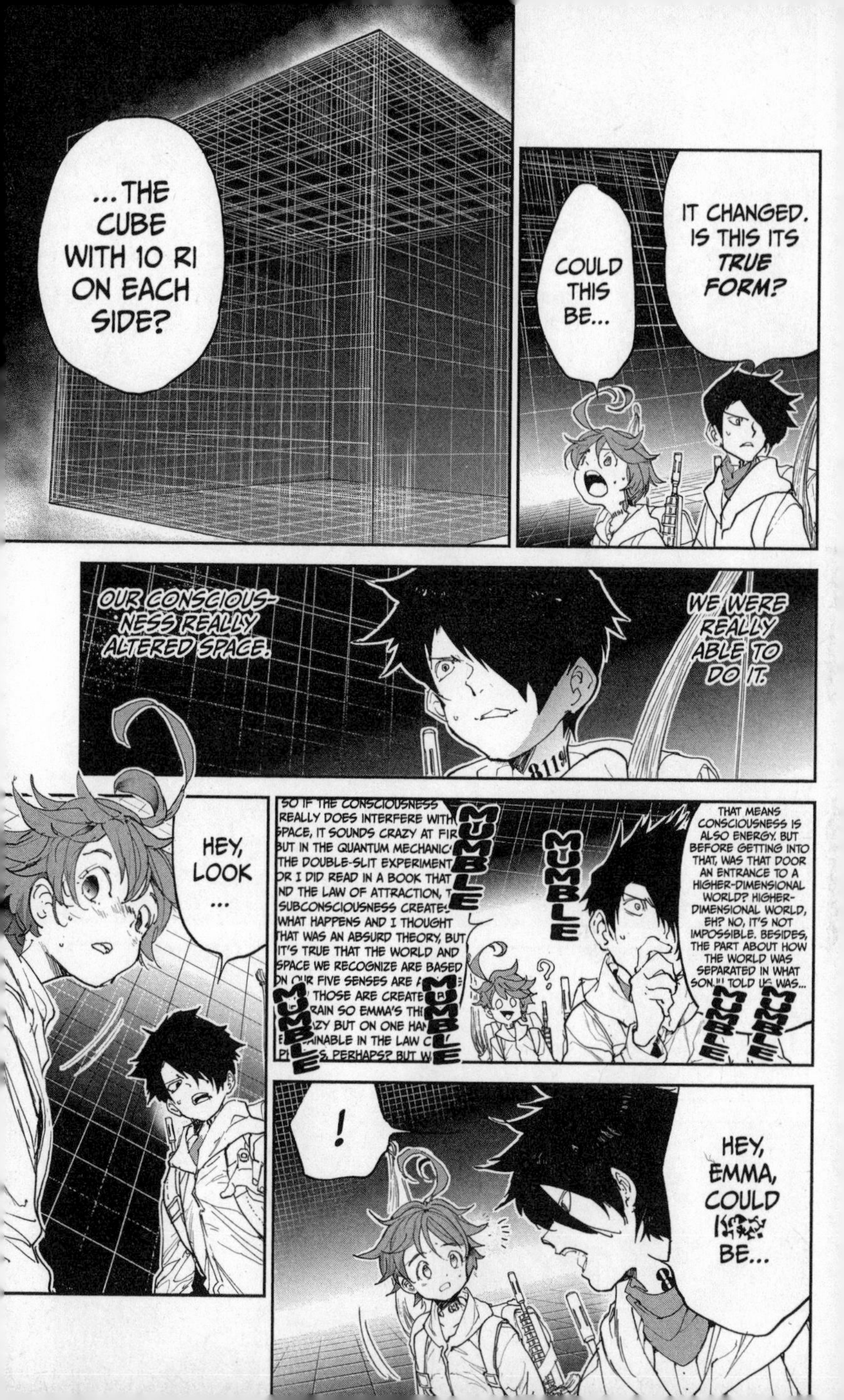
IT CHANGED. IS THIS ITS TRUE FORM?
COULD THIS BE...
...THE CUBE WITH 10 RI ON EACH SIDE?
WE WERE REALLY ABLE TO DO IT.
OUR CONSCIOUSNESS REALLY ALTERED SPACE.
THAT MEANS CONSCIOUSNESS IS ALSO ENERGY. BUT BEFORE GETTING INTO THAT, WAS THAT DOOR AN ENTRANCE TO A HIGHER-DIMENSIONAL WORLD? HIGHER-DIMENSIONAL WORLD, EH? NO, IT'S NOT IMPOSSIBLE. BESIDES, THE PART ABOUT HOW THE WORLD WAS SEPARATED IN WHAT SON... TOLD US WAS...
MUMBLE
MUMBLE
MUMBLE
MUMBLE
?
SO IF THE CONSCIOUSNESS REALLY DOES INTERFERE WITH SPACE, IT SOUNDS CRAZY AT FIR BUT IN THE QUANTUM MECHANIC THE DOUBLE-SLIT EXPERIMENT OR I DID READ IN A BOOK THAT ND THE LAW OF ATTRACTION, T SUBCONSCIOUSNESS CREATES WHAT HAPPENS AND I THOUGHT THAT WAS AN ABSURD THEORY, BUT IT'S TRUE THAT THE WORLD AND SPACE WE RECOGNIZE ARE BASED ON OUR FIVE SENSES ARE A THOSE ARE CREATE RAIN SO EMMA'S TH AZY BUT ON ONE HA AINABLE IN THE LAW C S, PERHAPS? BUT W
MUMBLE
MUMBLE
MUMBLE
HEY, EMMA, COULD
BE...
!
HEY, LOOK ...

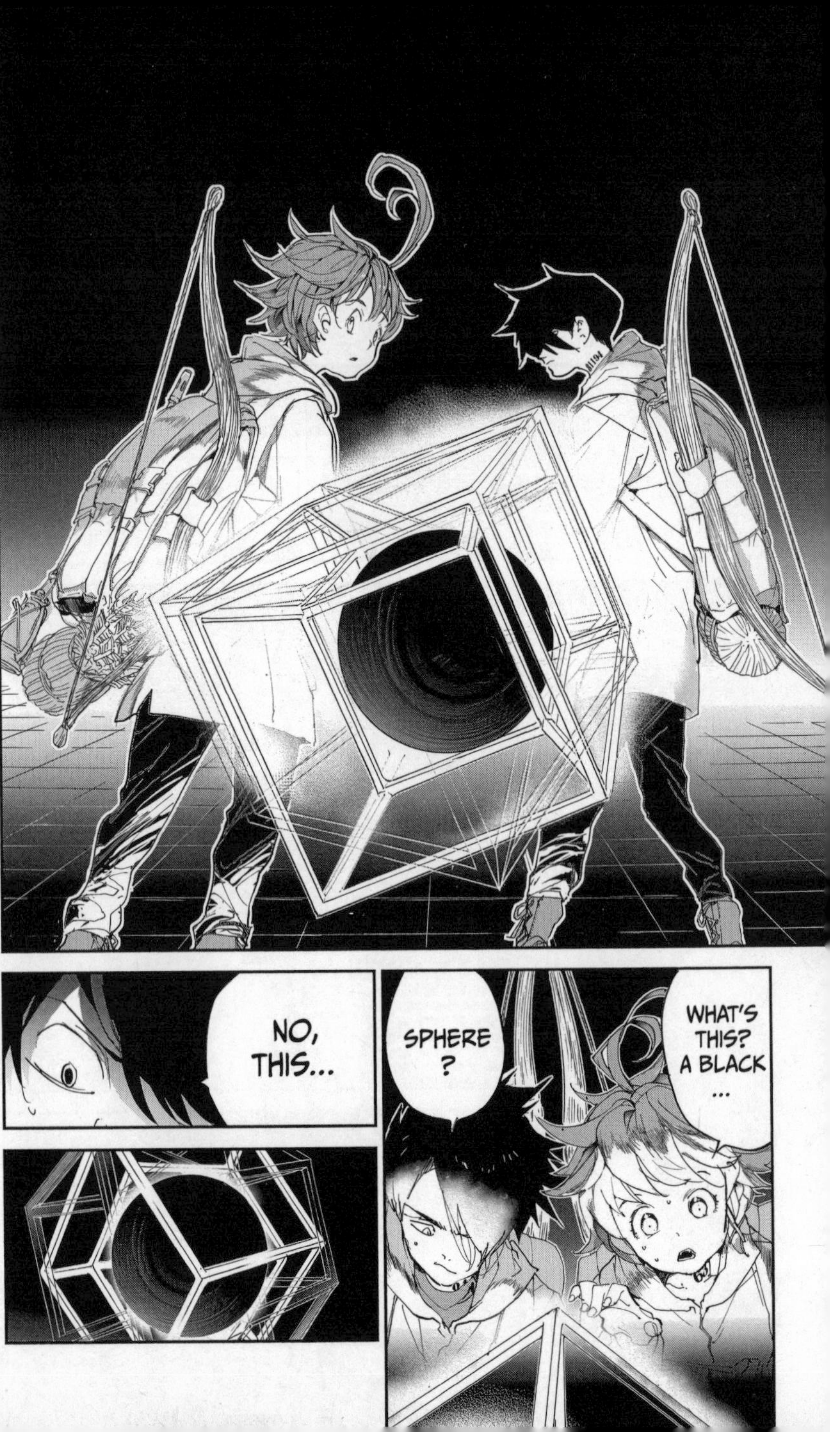
WHAT'S THIS? A BLACK ...
SPHERE?
NO, THIS...

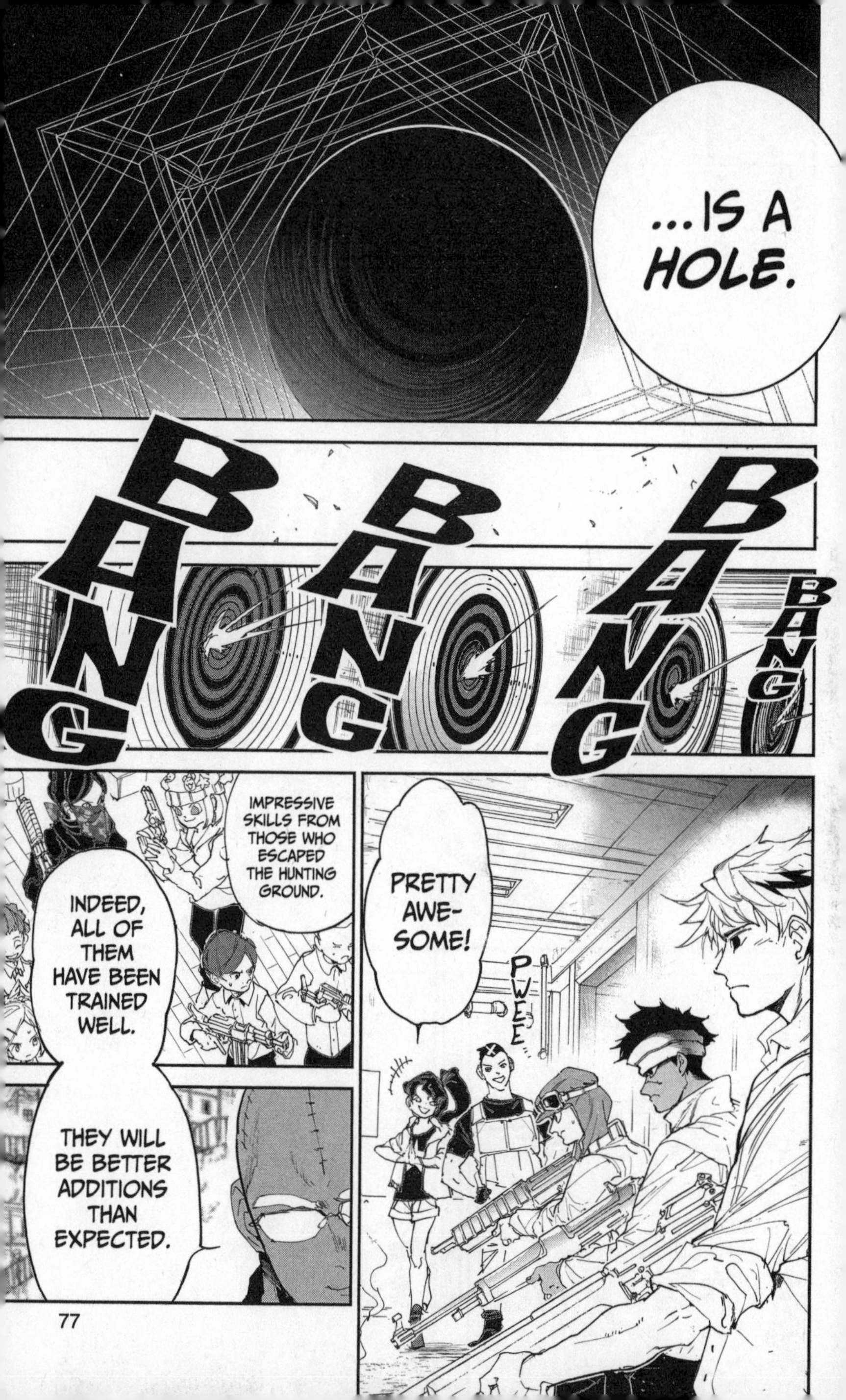
...IS A HOLE.
BANG
BANG
BANG
BANG
PRETTY AWE-SOME!
PWEE...
IMPRESSIVE SKILLS FROM THOSE WHO ESCAPED THE HUNTING GROUND.
INDEED, ALL OF THEM HAVE BEEN TRAINED WELL.
THEY WILL BE BETTER ADDITIONS THAN EXPECTED.

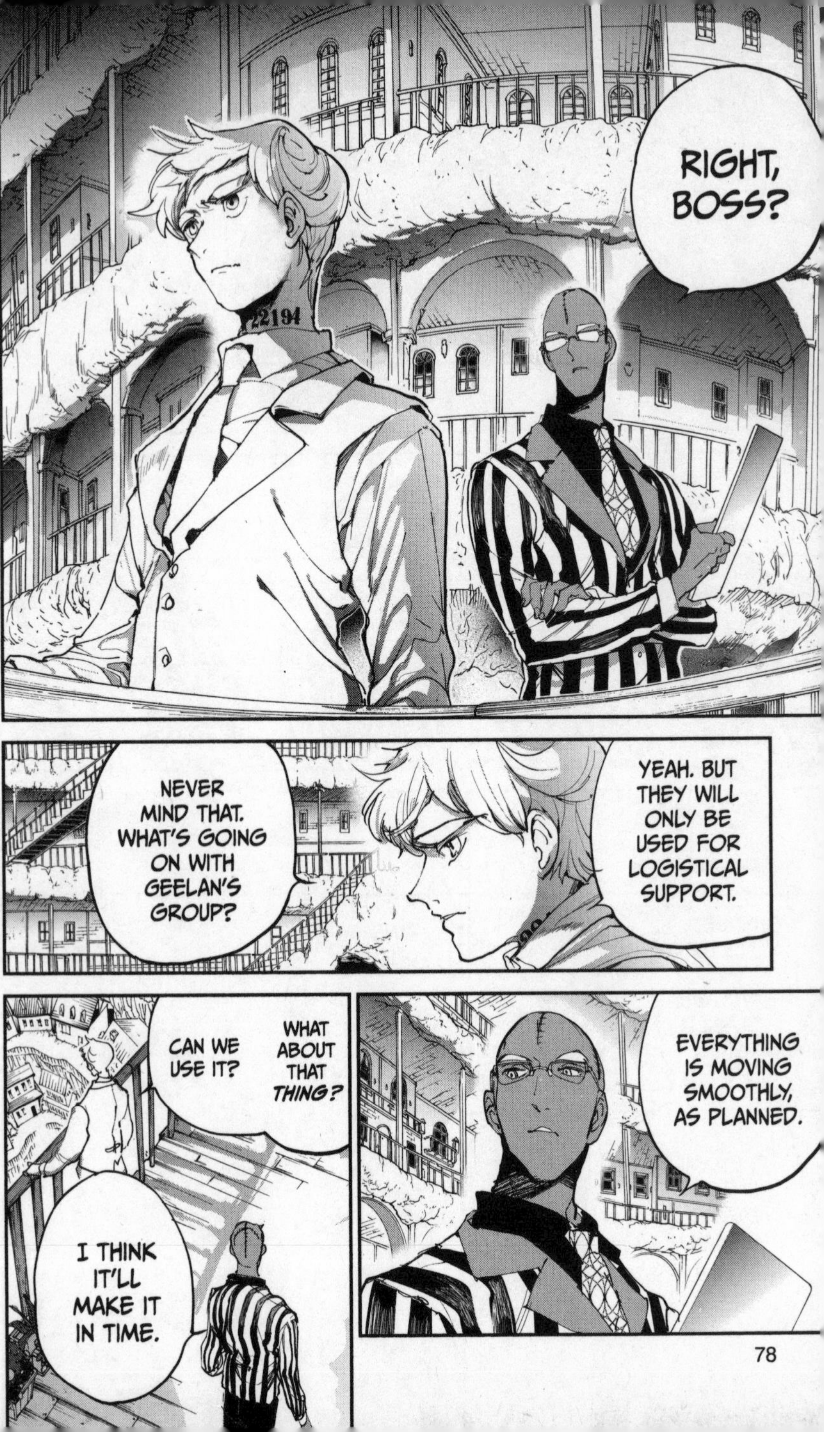
RIGHT, BOSS?
YEAH. BUT THEY WILL ONLY BE USED FOR LOGISTICAL SUPPORT.
NEVER MIND THAT. WHAT'S GOING ON WITH GEELAN'S GROUP?
EVERYTHING IS MOVING SMOOTHLY, AS PLANNED.
WHAT ABOUT THAT *THING?*
CAN WE USE IT?
I THINK IT'LL MAKE IT IN TIME.

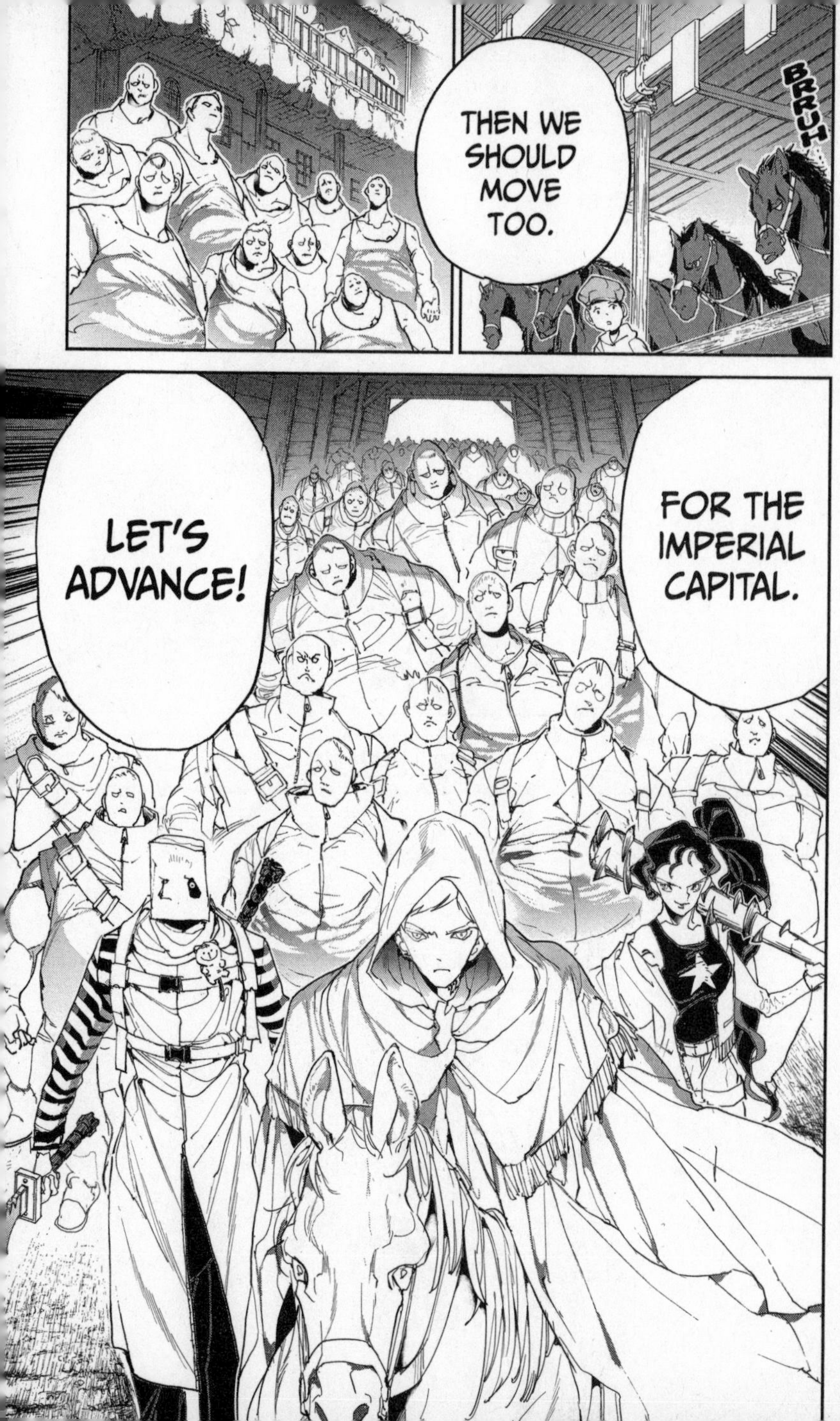
BRRUH
THEN WE SHOULD MOVE TOO.
FOR THE IMPERIAL CAPITAL.
LET'S ADVANCE!

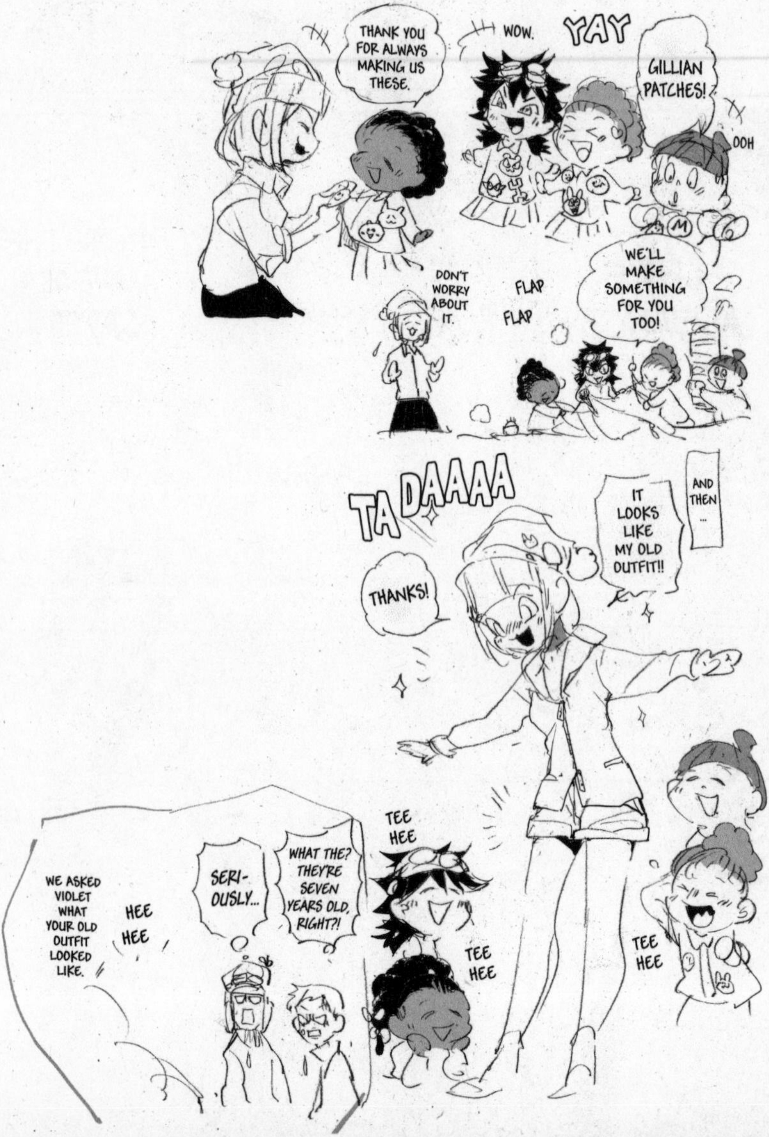
YAY
GILLIAN PATCHES!
OOH
WOW.
THANK YOU FOR ALWAYS MAKING US THESE.
WE'LL MAKE SOMETHING FOR YOU TOO!
FLAP
FLAP
DON'T WORRY ABOUT IT.
AND THEN...
IT LOOKS LIKE MY OLD OUTFIT!!
TA DAAAA
THANKS!
TEE HEE
TEE HEE
TEE HEE
WHAT THE? THEY'RE SEVEN YEARS OLD, RIGHT?!
SERI-OUSLY...
HEE HEE
WE ASKED VIOLET WHAT YOUR OLD OUTFIT LOOKED LIKE.

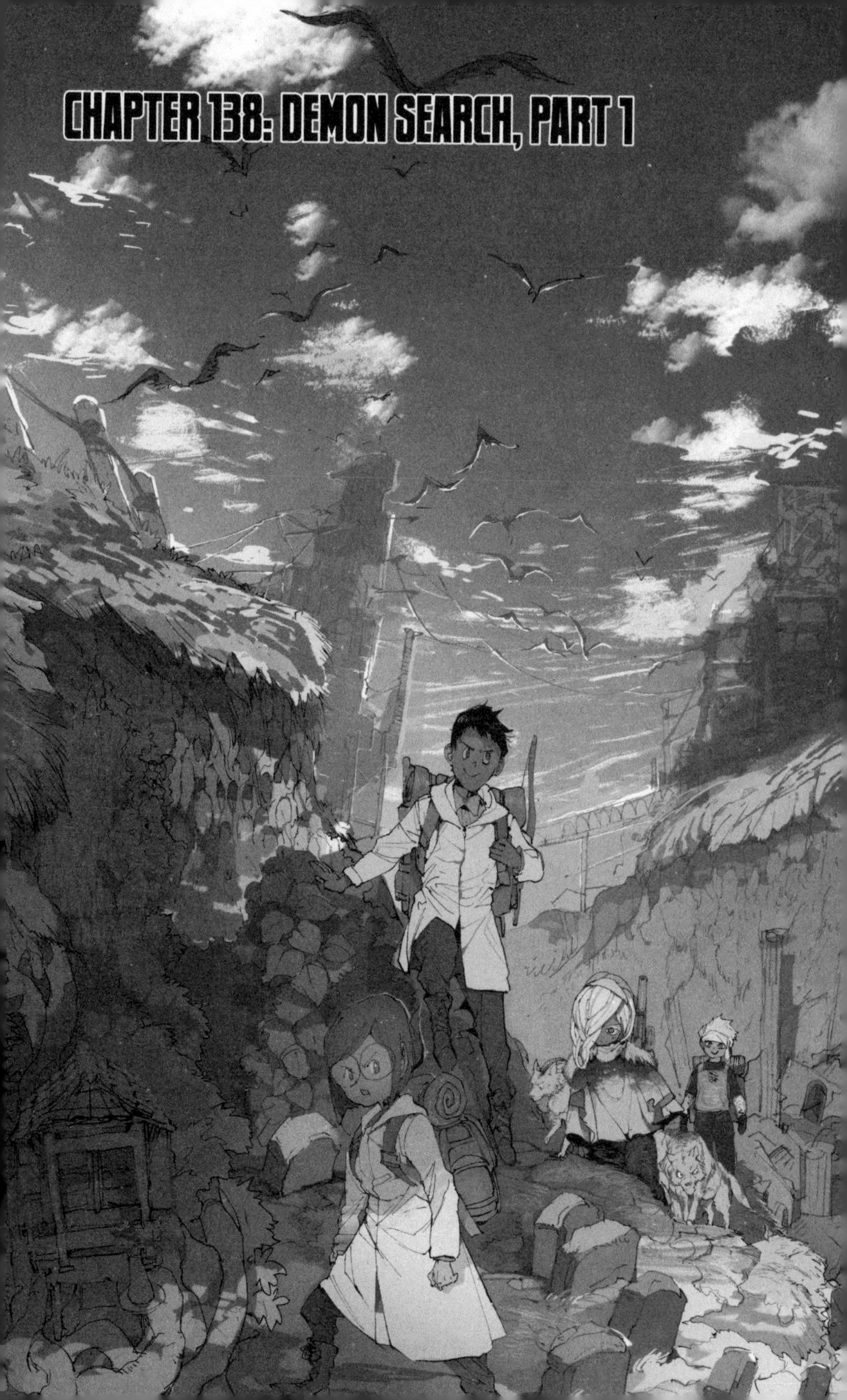
CHAPTER 138: DEMON SEARCH, PART 1

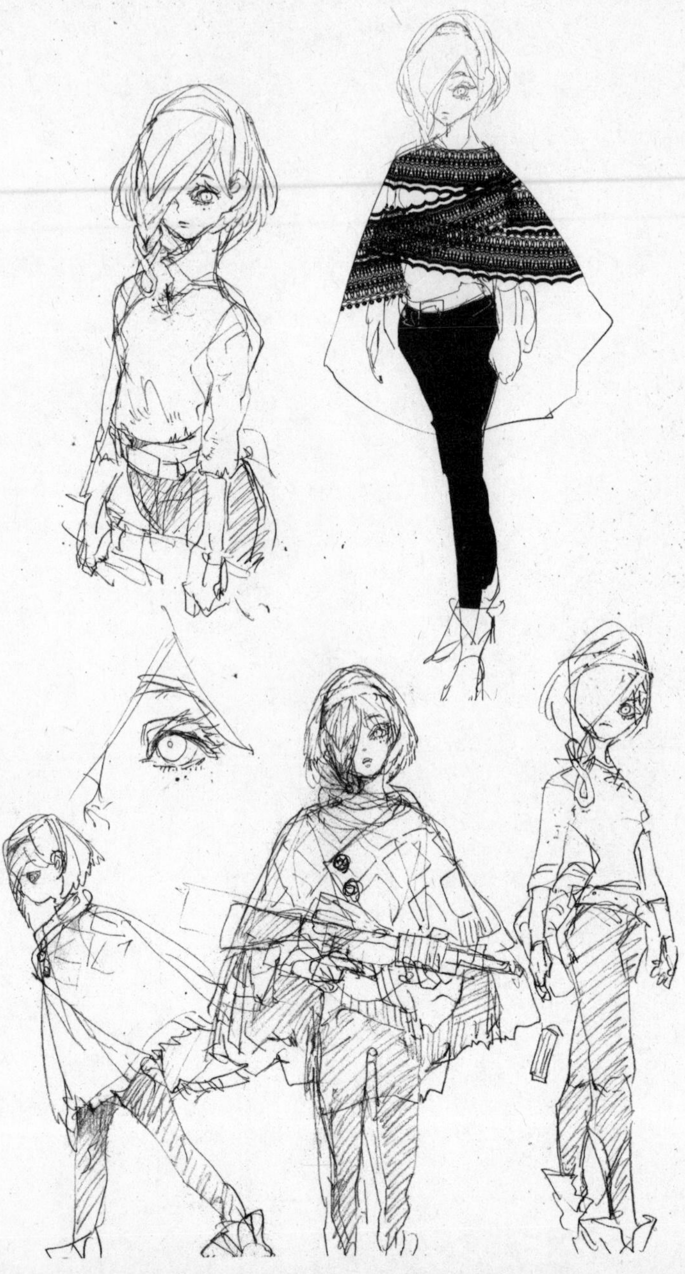

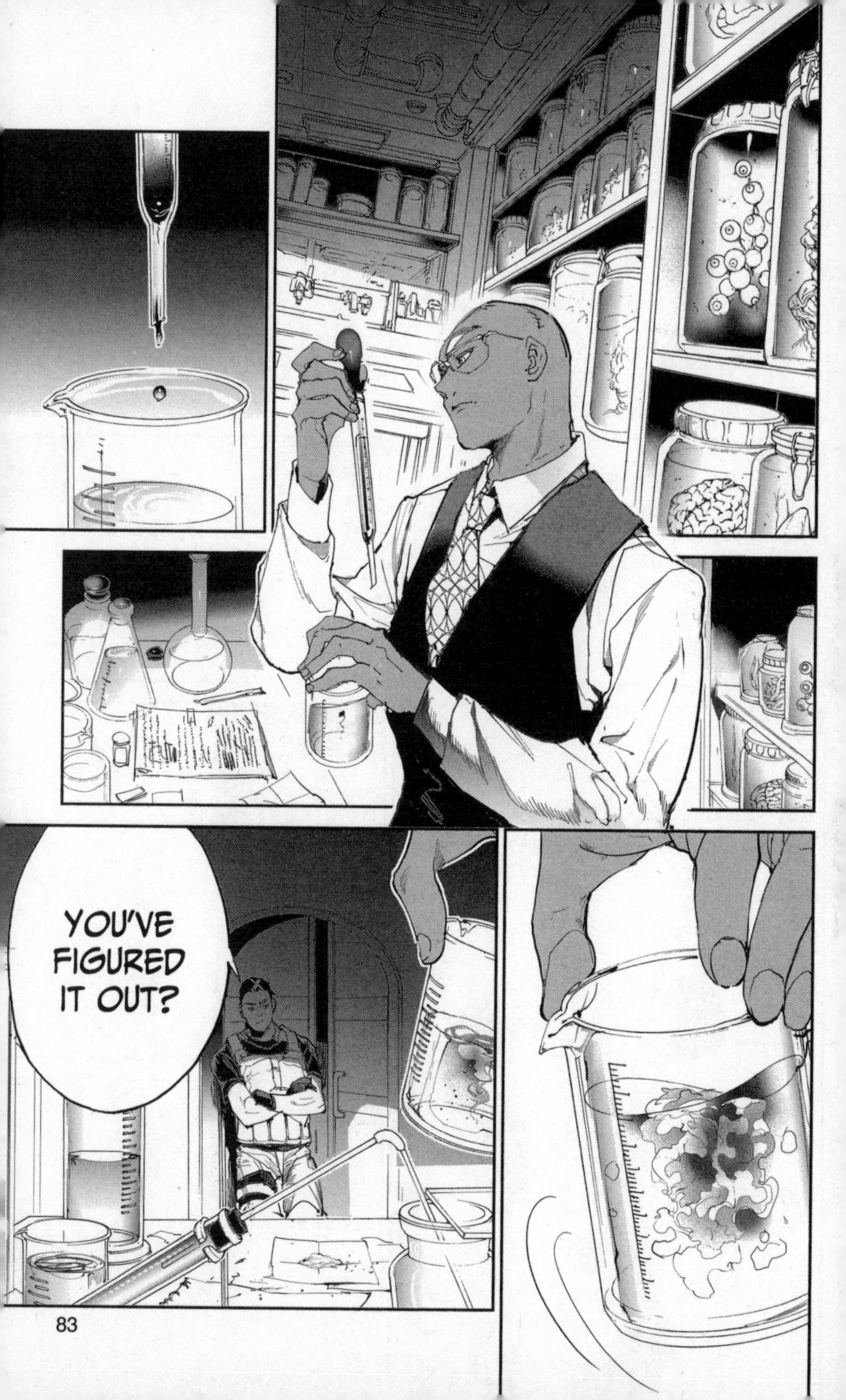
YOU'VE FIGURED IT OUT?

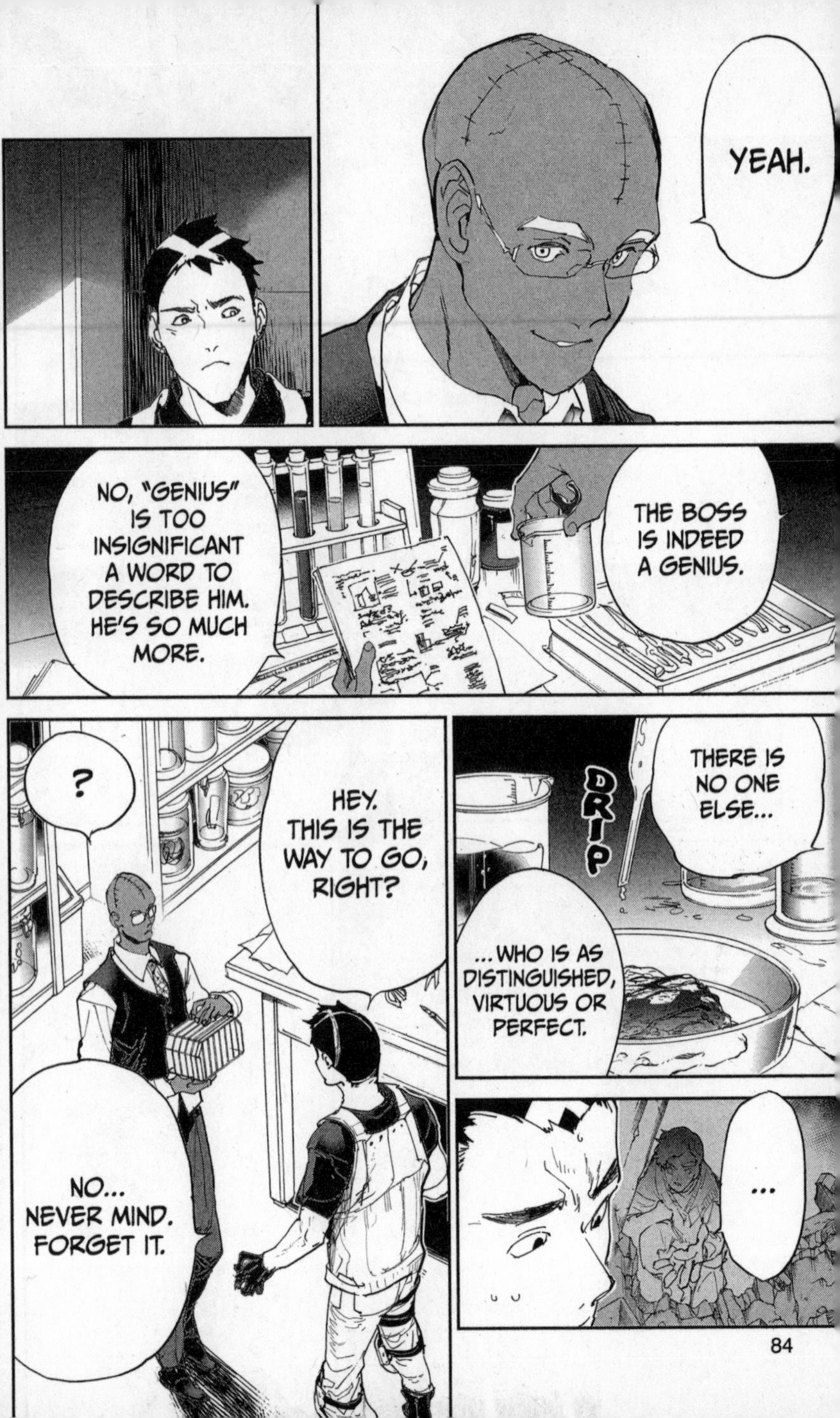
YEAH.
THE BOSS IS INDEED A GENIUS.
NO, "GENIUS" IS TOO INSIGNIFICANT A WORD TO DESCRIBE HIM. HE'S SO MUCH MORE.
THERE IS NO ONE ELSE...
DRIP
...WHO IS AS DISTINGUISHED, VIRTUOUS OR PERFECT.
...
HEY. THIS IS THE WAY TO GO, RIGHT?
?
NO... NEVER MIND. FORGET IT.

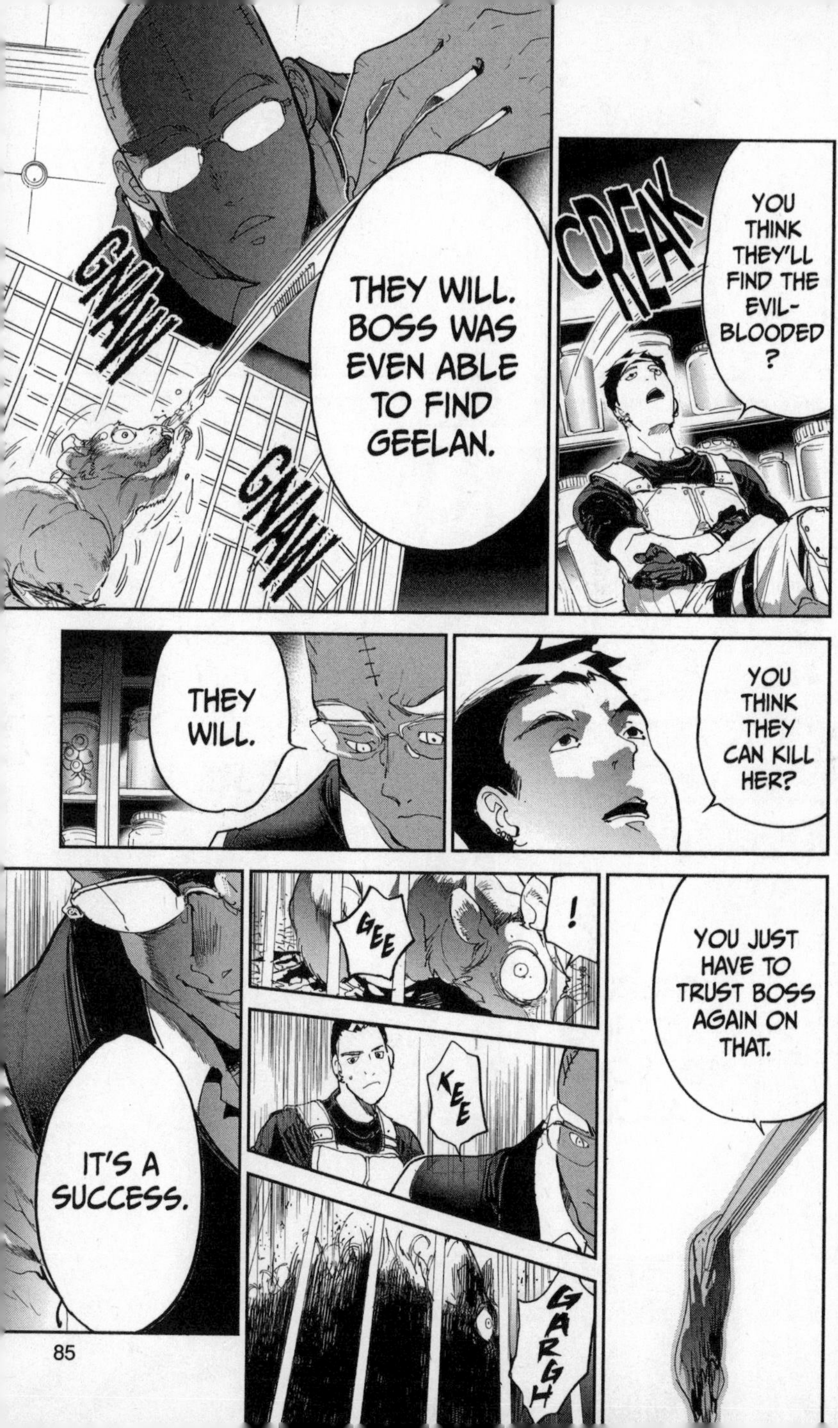
CREAK
YOU THINK THEY'LL FIND THE EVIL-BLOODED?
THEY WILL. BOSS WAS EVEN ABLE TO FIND GEELAN.
GNAW
GNAW
YOU THINK THEY CAN KILL HER?
THEY WILL.
YOU JUST HAVE TO TRUST BOSS AGAIN ON THAT.
!
GEE
KEE
GARGH
IT'S A SUCCESS.

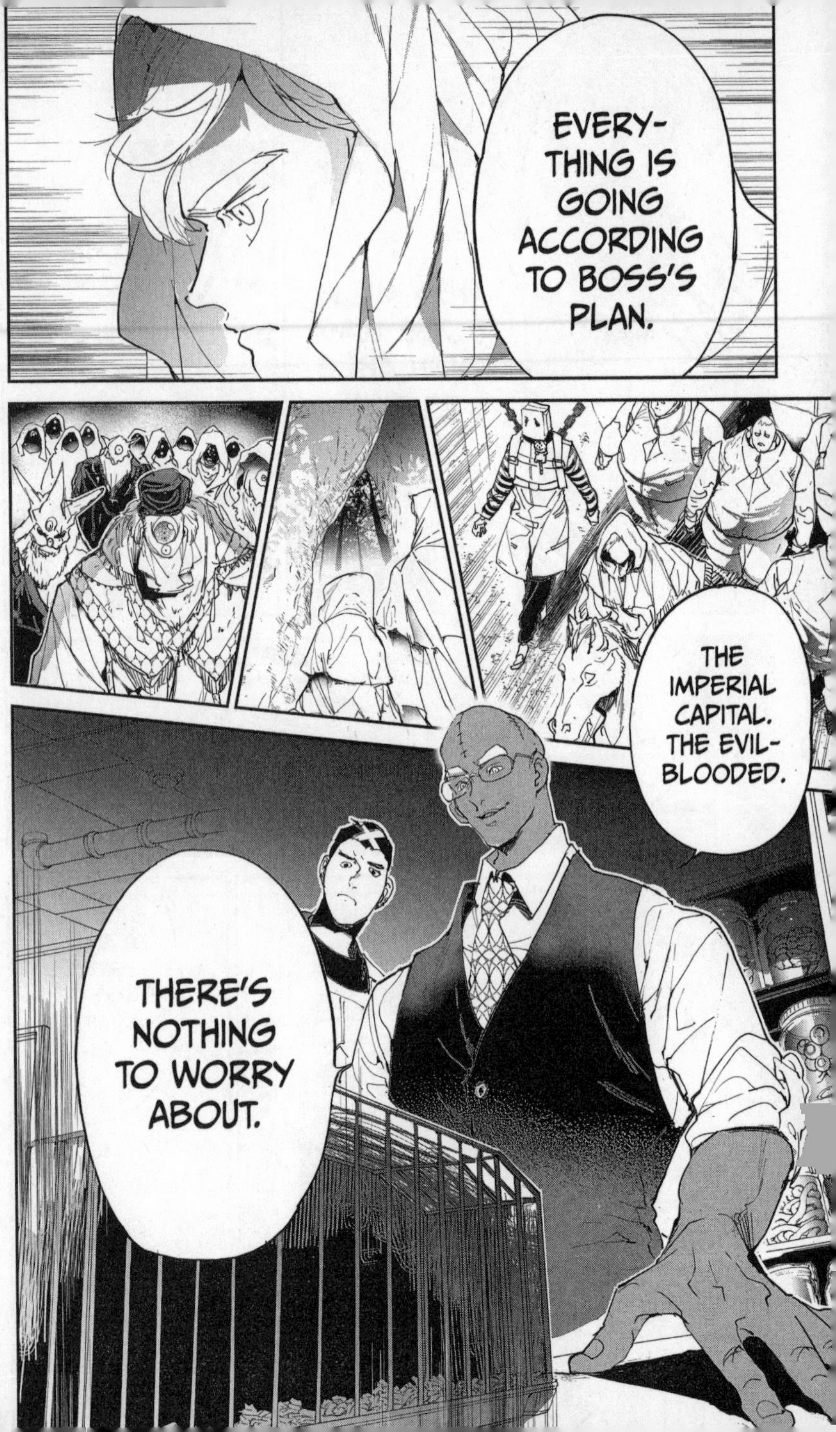
EVERY-THING IS GOING ACCORDING TO BOSS'S PLAN.
THE IMPERIAL CAPITAL. THE EVIL-BLOODED.
THERE'S NOTHING TO WORRY ABOUT.

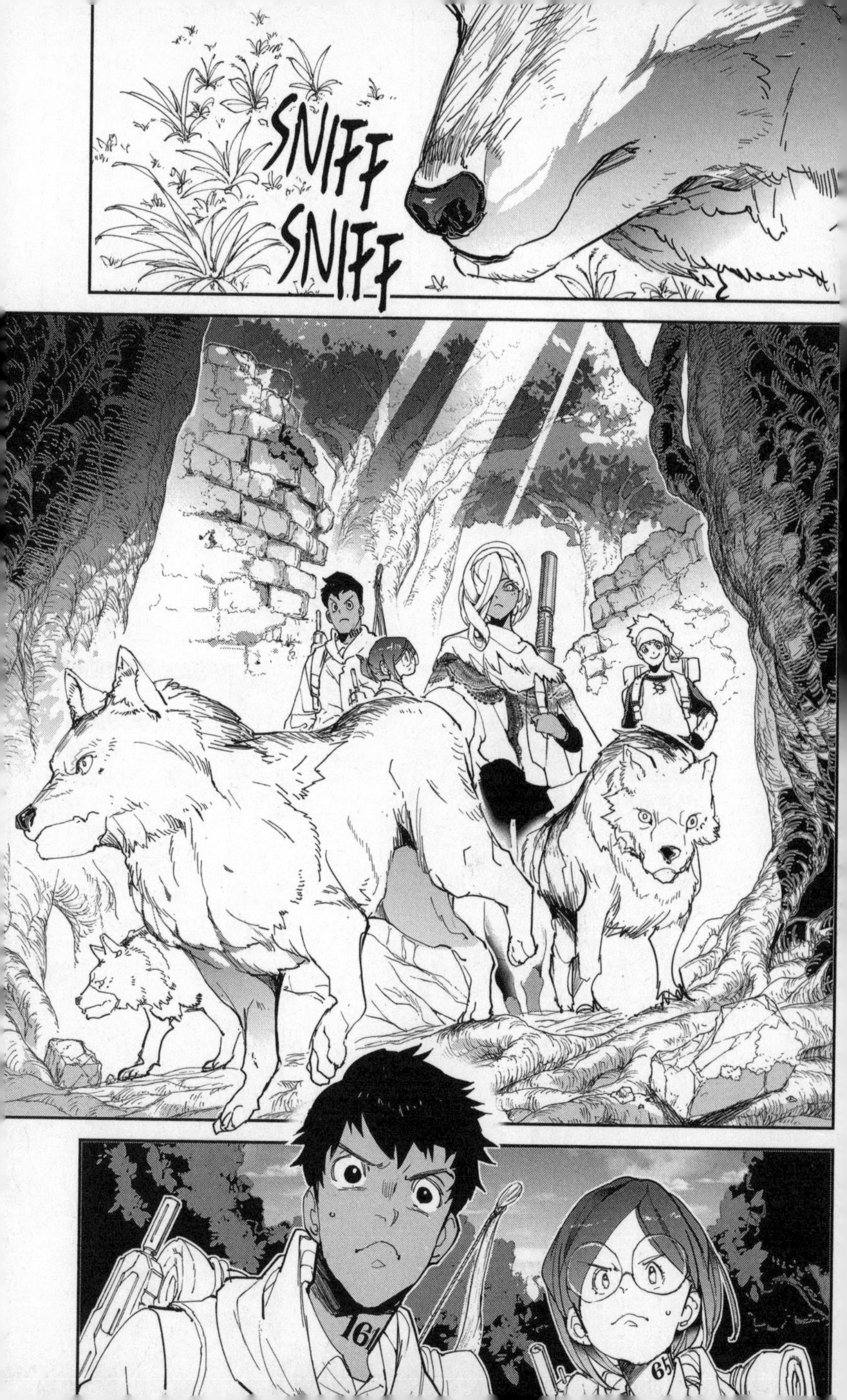
SNIFF
SNIFF

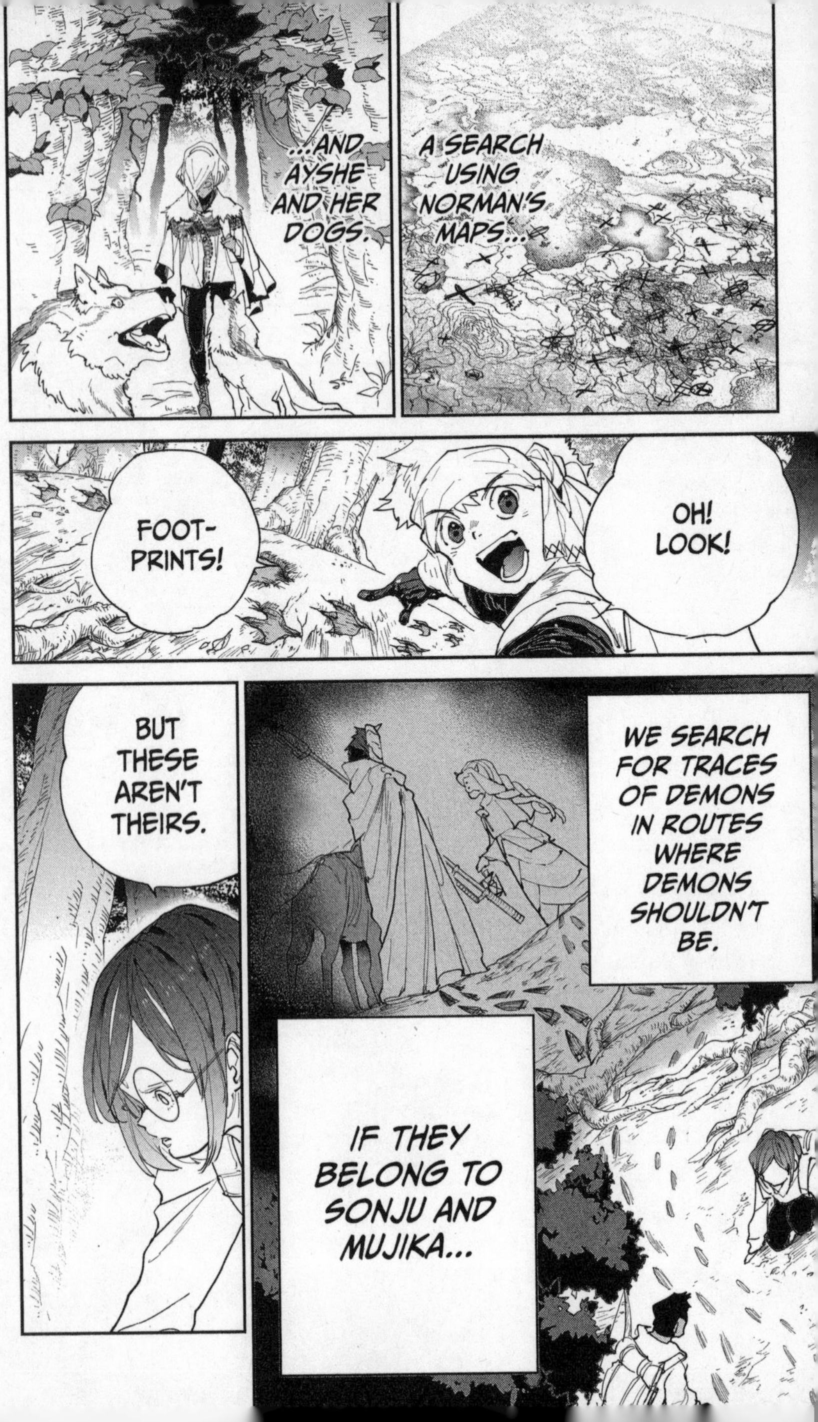
A SEARCH USING NORMAN'S MAPS...
...AND AYSHE AND HER DOGS.
OH! LOOK!
FOOT-PRINTS!
WE SEARCH FOR TRACES OF DEMONS IN ROUTES WHERE DEMONS SHOULDN'T BE.
IF THEY BELONG TO SONJU AND MUJIKA...
BUT THESE AREN'T THEIRS.

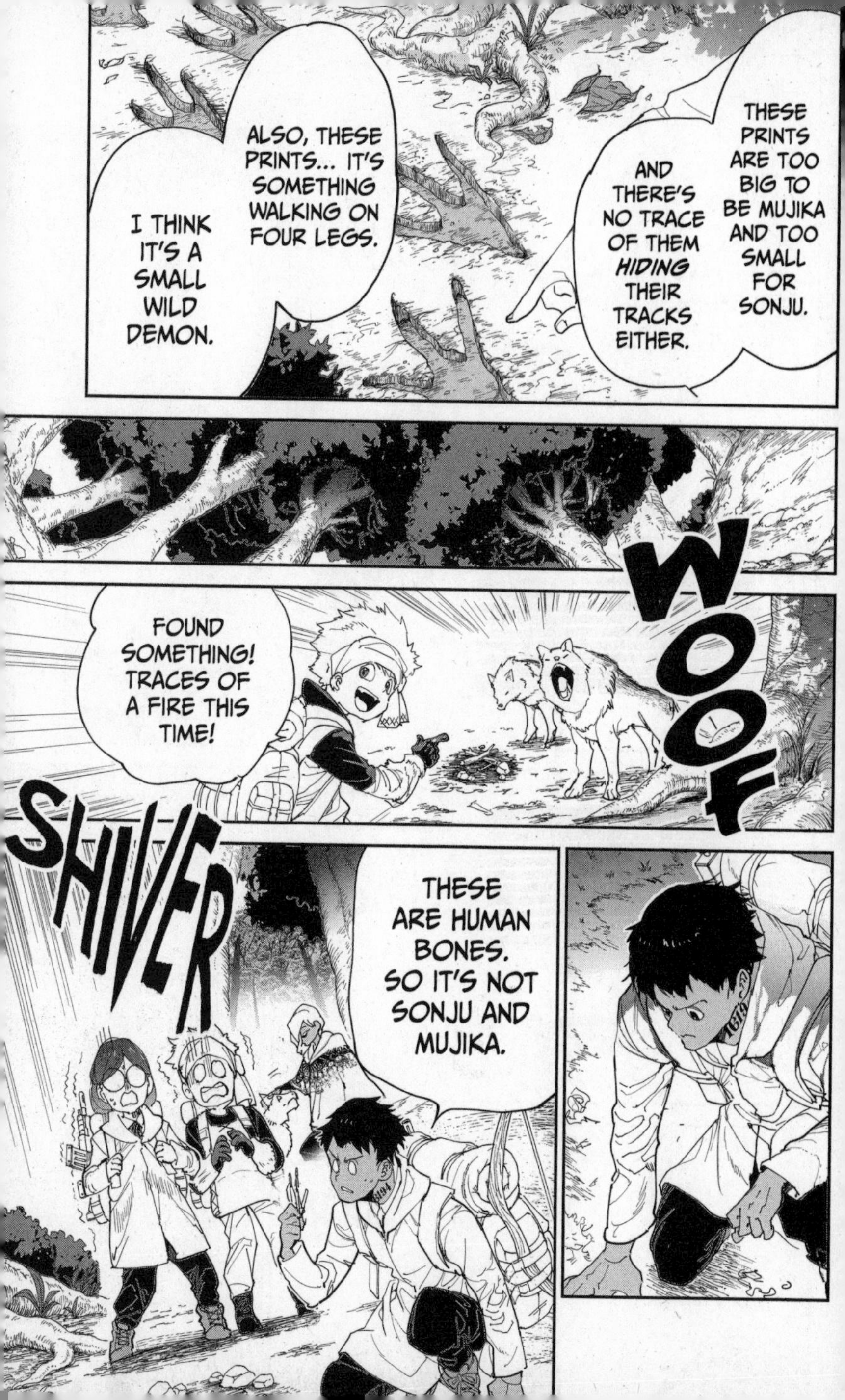
THESE PRINTS ARE TOO BIG TO BE MUJIKA AND TOO SMALL FOR SONJU.
AND THERE'S NO TRACE OF THEM *HIDING* THEIR TRACKS EITHER.
ALSO, THESE PRINTS... IT'S SOMETHING WALKING ON FOUR LEGS.
I THINK IT'S A SMALL WILD DEMON.
WOOF
FOUND SOMETHING! TRACES OF A FIRE THIS TIME!
THESE ARE HUMAN BONES. SO IT'S NOT SONJU AND MUJIKA.
SHIVER

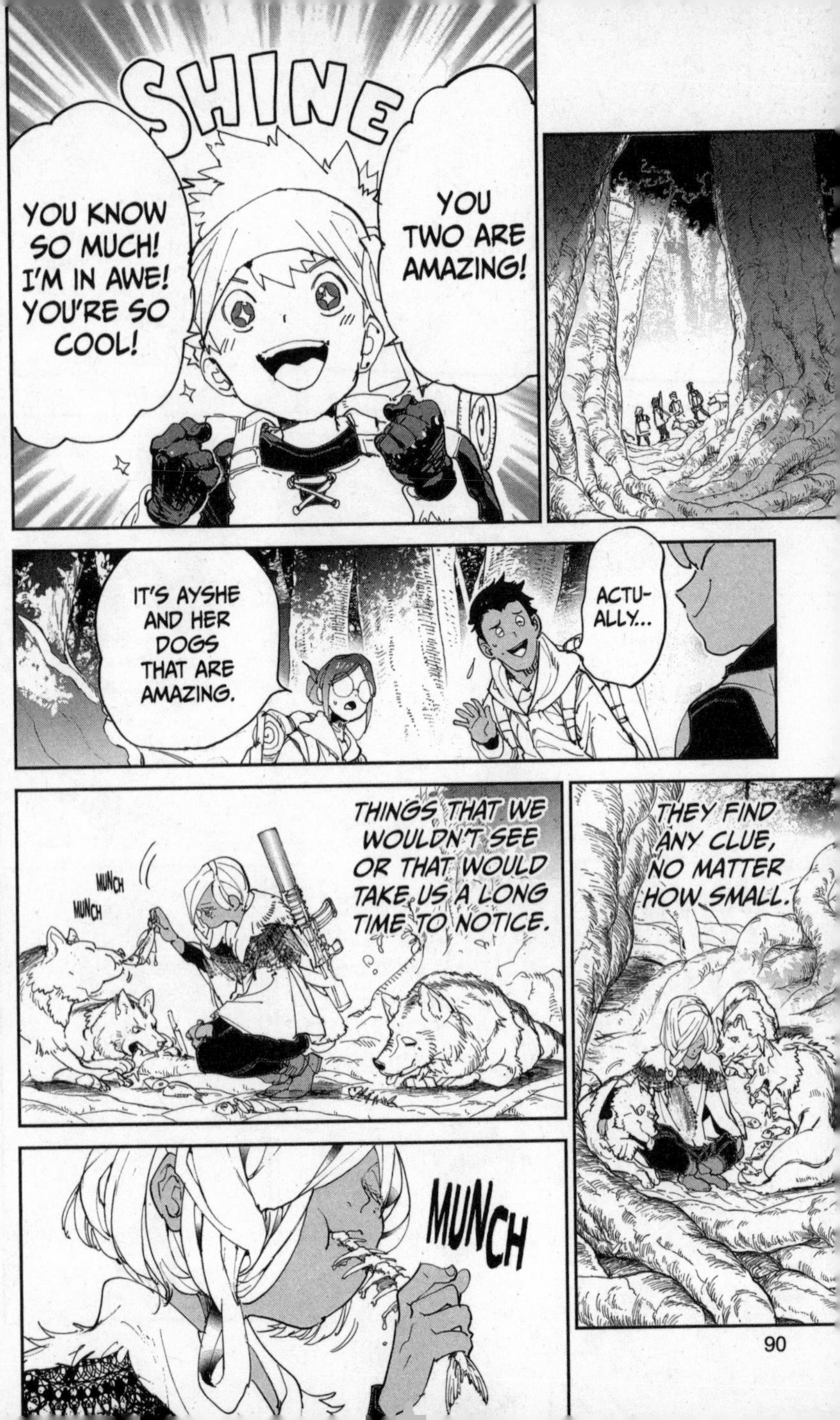

SHINE
YOU TWO ARE AMAZING!
YOU KNOW SO MUCH! I'M IN AWE! YOU'RE SO COOL!
ACTU-ALLY...
IT'S AYSHE AND HER DOGS THAT ARE AMAZING.
THEY FIND ANY CLUE, NO MATTER HOW SMALL.
THINGS THAT WE WOULDN'T SEE OR THAT WOULD TAKE US A LONG TIME TO NOTICE.
MUNCH
MUNCH
MUNCH

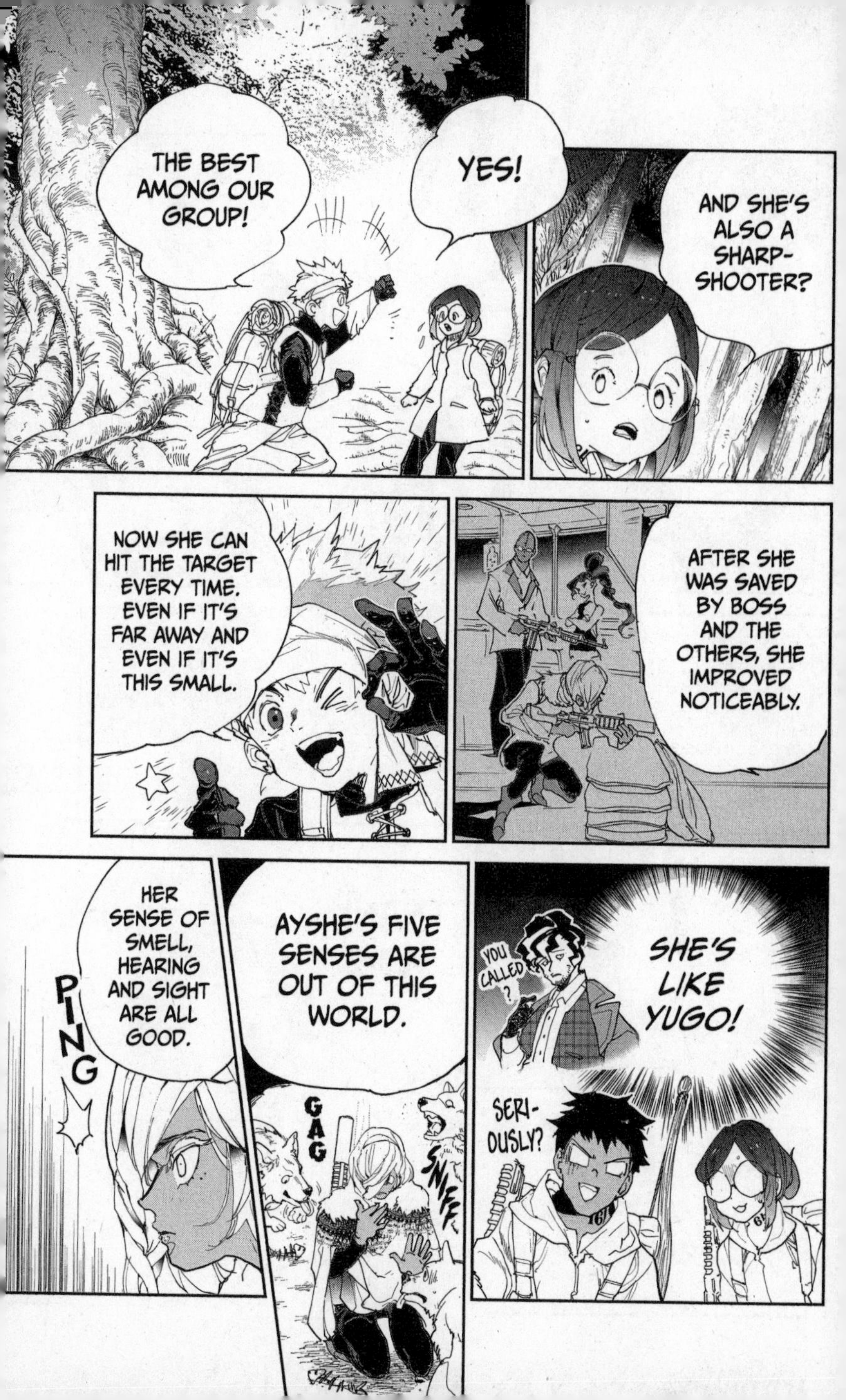
AND SHE'S ALSO A SHARP-SHOOTER?
YES!
THE BEST AMONG OUR GROUP!
AFTER SHE WAS SAVED BY BOSS AND THE OTHERS, SHE IMPROVED NOTICEABLY.
NOW SHE CAN HIT THE TARGET EVERY TIME. EVEN IF IT'S FAR AWAY AND EVEN IF IT'S THIS SMALL.
SHE'S LIKE YUGO!
YOU CALLED?
SERI-OUSLY?
AYSHE'S FIVE SENSES ARE OUT OF THIS WORLD.
SNIFF
GAG
HER SENSE OF SMELL, HEARING AND SIGHT ARE ALL GOOD.
PING

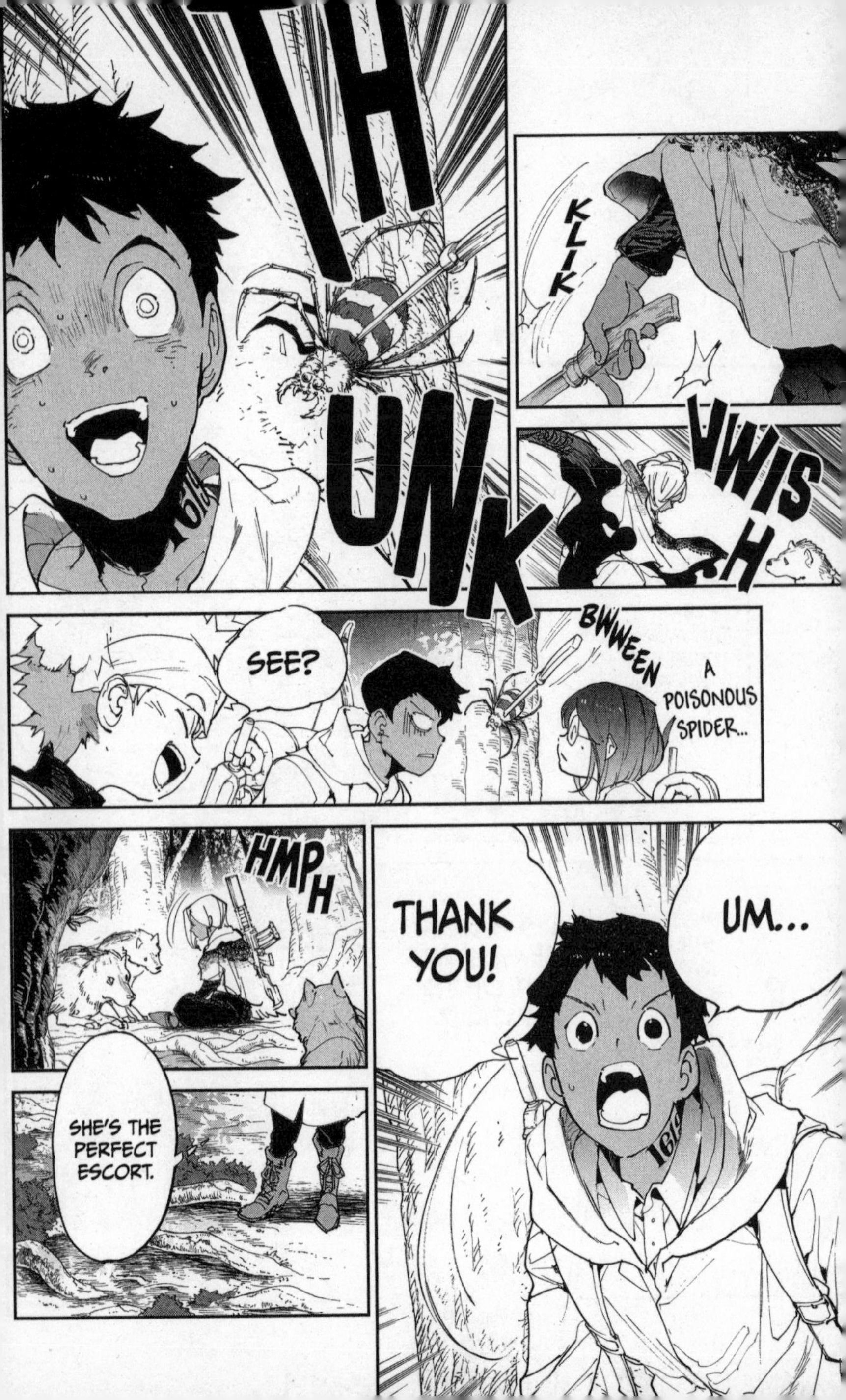
KLIK
WHISH
THUNK
A POISONOUS SPIDER...
BWWEEN
SEE?
UM...
THANK YOU!
HMPH
SHE'S THE PERFECT ESCORT.

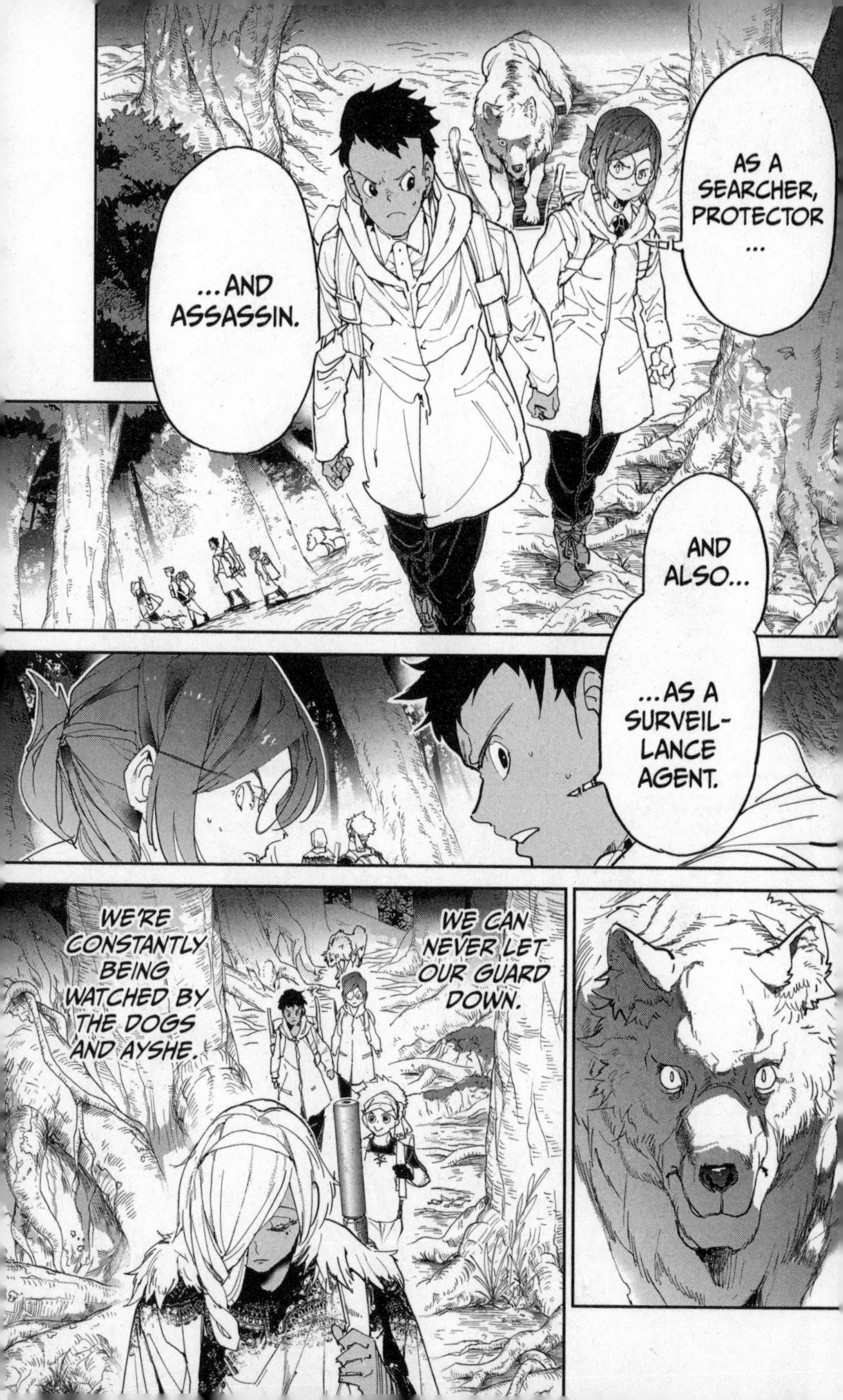
AS A SEARCHER, PROTECTOR...
...AND ASSASSIN.
AND ALSO...
...AS A SURVEILLANCE AGENT.
WE CAN NEVER LET OUR GUARD DOWN.
WE'RE CONSTANTLY BEING WATCHED BY THE DOGS AND AYSHE.

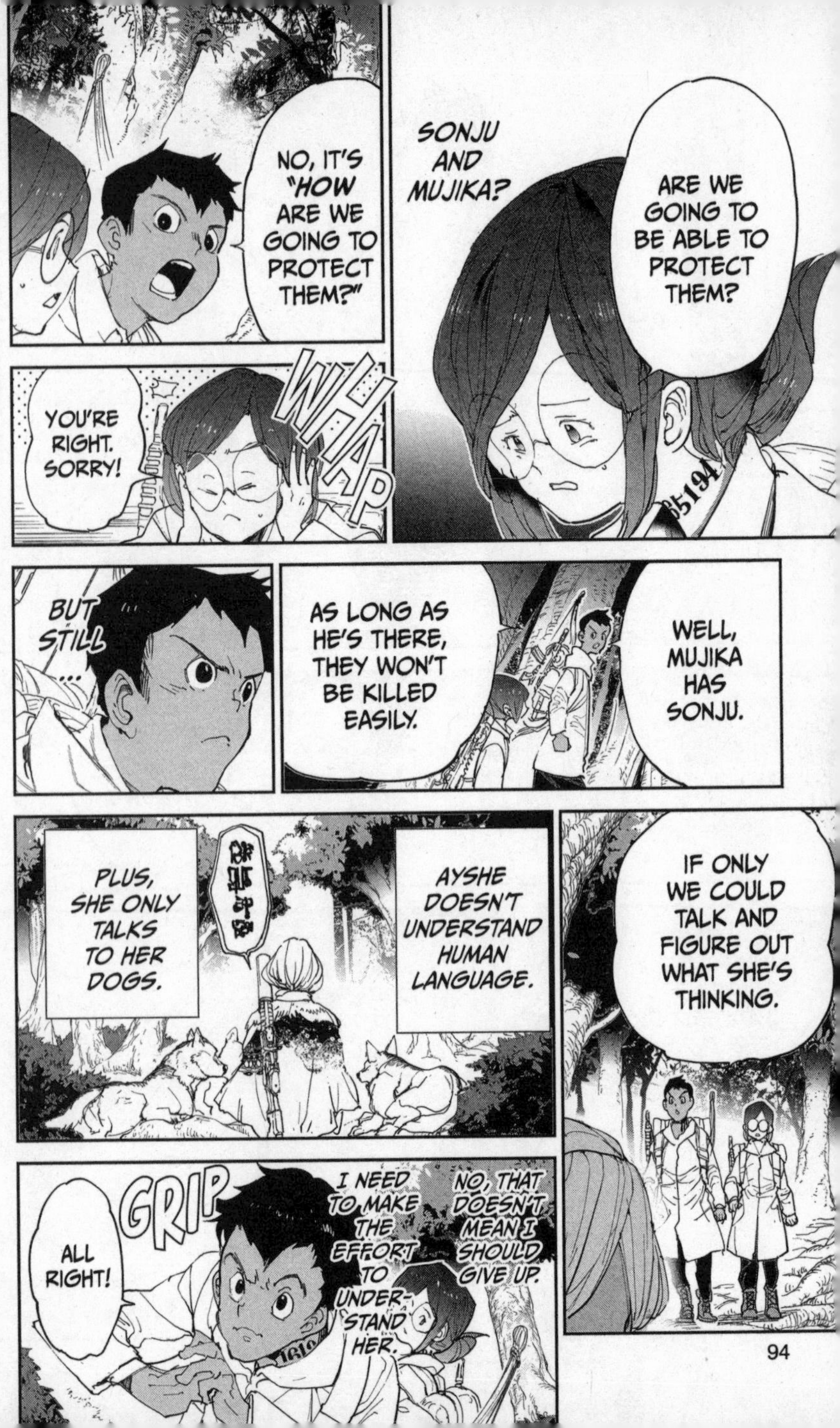
ARE WE GOING TO BE ABLE TO PROTECT THEM?
SONJU AND MUJIKA?
NO, IT'S "HOW ARE WE GOING TO PROTECT THEM?"
WHAP
YOU'RE RIGHT. SORRY!
WELL, MUJIKA HAS SONJU.
AS LONG AS HE'S THERE, THEY WON'T BE KILLED EASILY.
BUT STILL...
IF ONLY WE COULD TALK AND FIGURE OUT WHAT SHE'S THINKING.
AYSHE DOESN'T UNDERSTAND HUMAN LANGUAGE.
PLUS, SHE ONLY TALKS TO HER DOGS.
NO, THAT DOESN'T MEAN I SHOULD GIVE UP.
I NEED TO MAKE THE EFFORT TO UNDER-STAND HER.
GRIP
ALL RIGHT!

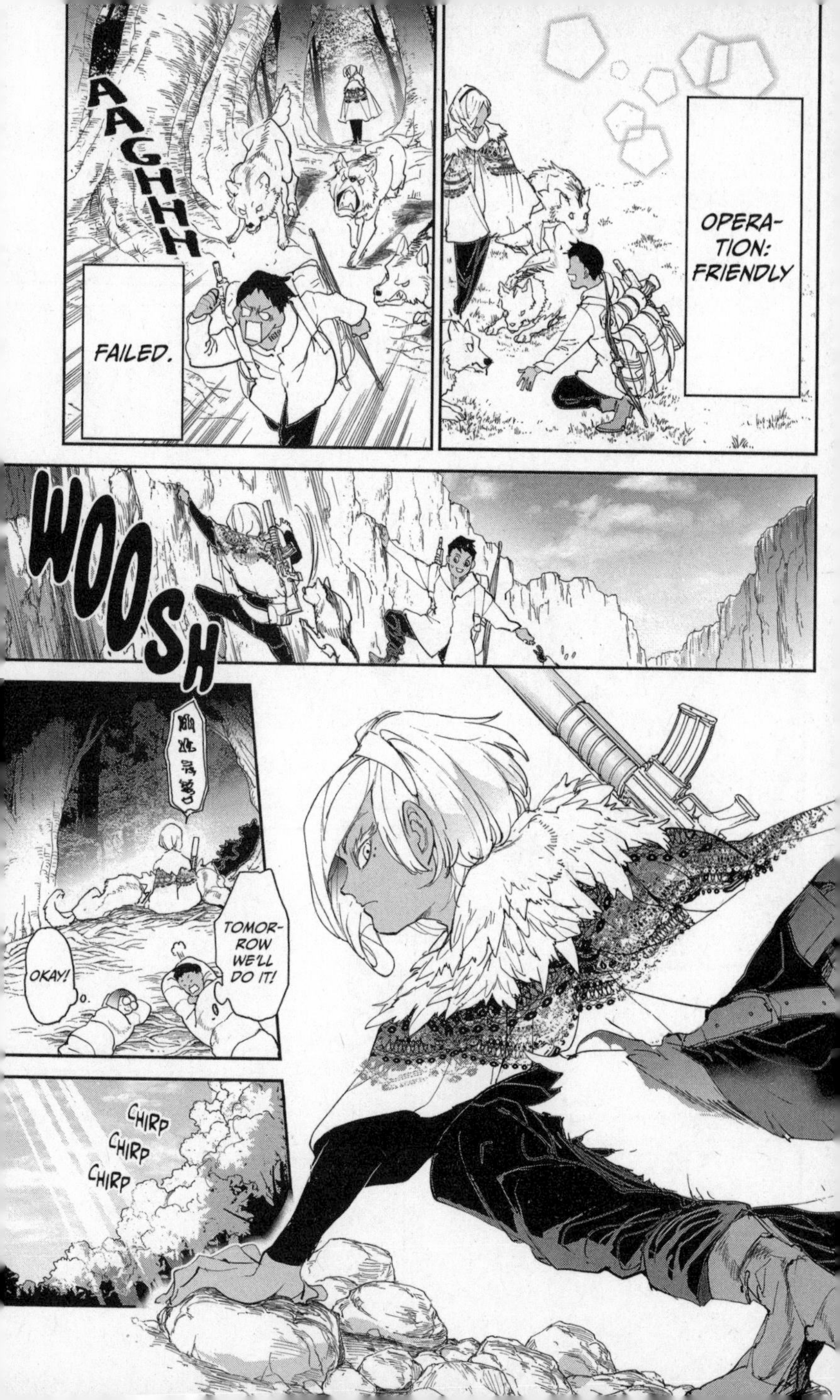
OPERATION: FRIENDLY
AAGHHH
FAILED.
WOOSH
TOMORROW WE'LL DO IT!
OKAY!
CHIRP
CHIRP
CHIRP

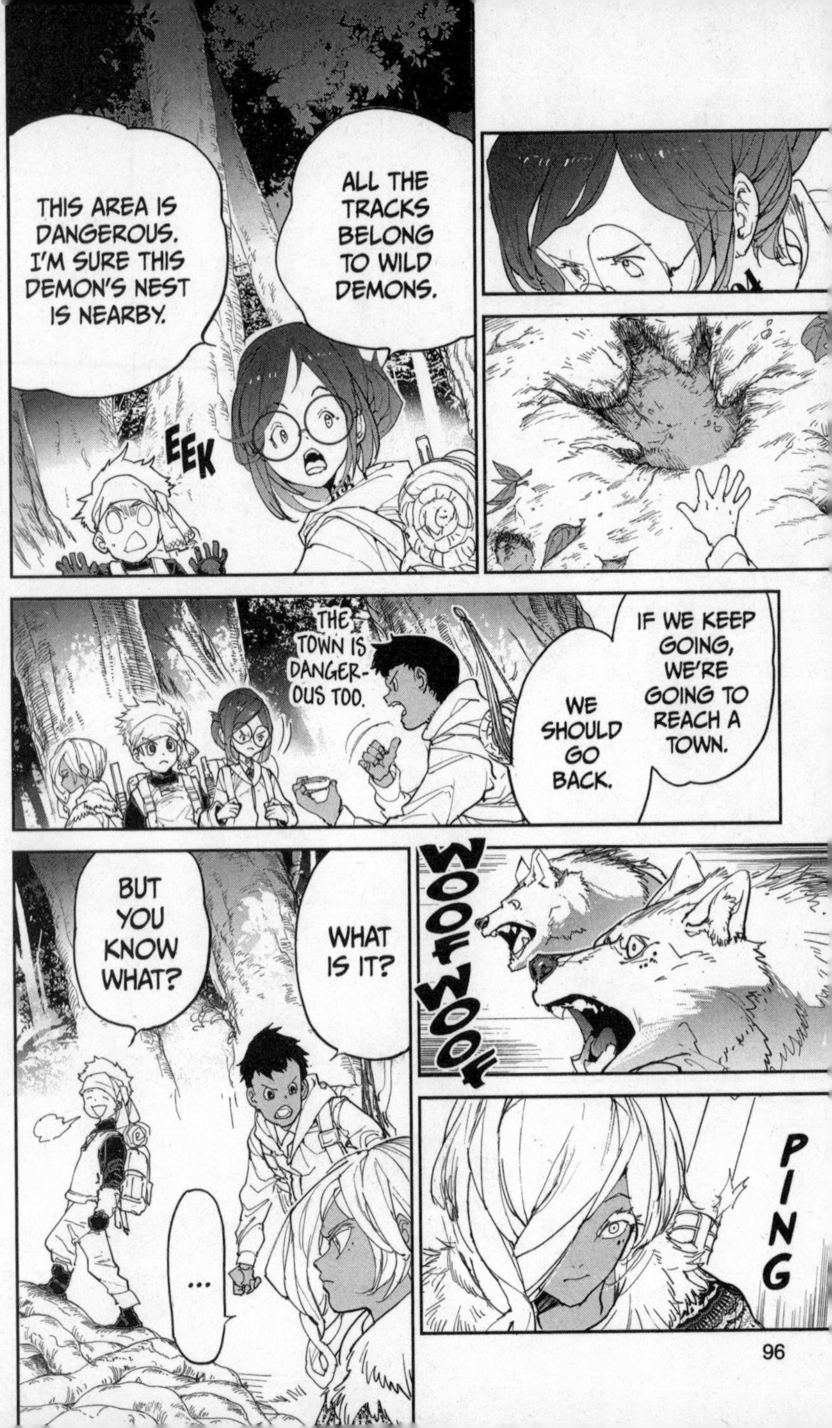
ALL THE TRACKS BELONG TO WILD DEMONS.
THIS AREA IS DANGEROUS. I'M SURE THIS DEMON'S NEST IS NEARBY.
EEK
IF WE KEEP GOING, WE'RE GOING TO REACH A TOWN.
WE SHOULD GO BACK.
THE TOWN IS DANGER-OUS TOO.
WOOF WOOF
PING
WHAT IS IT?
BUT YOU KNOW WHAT?
...

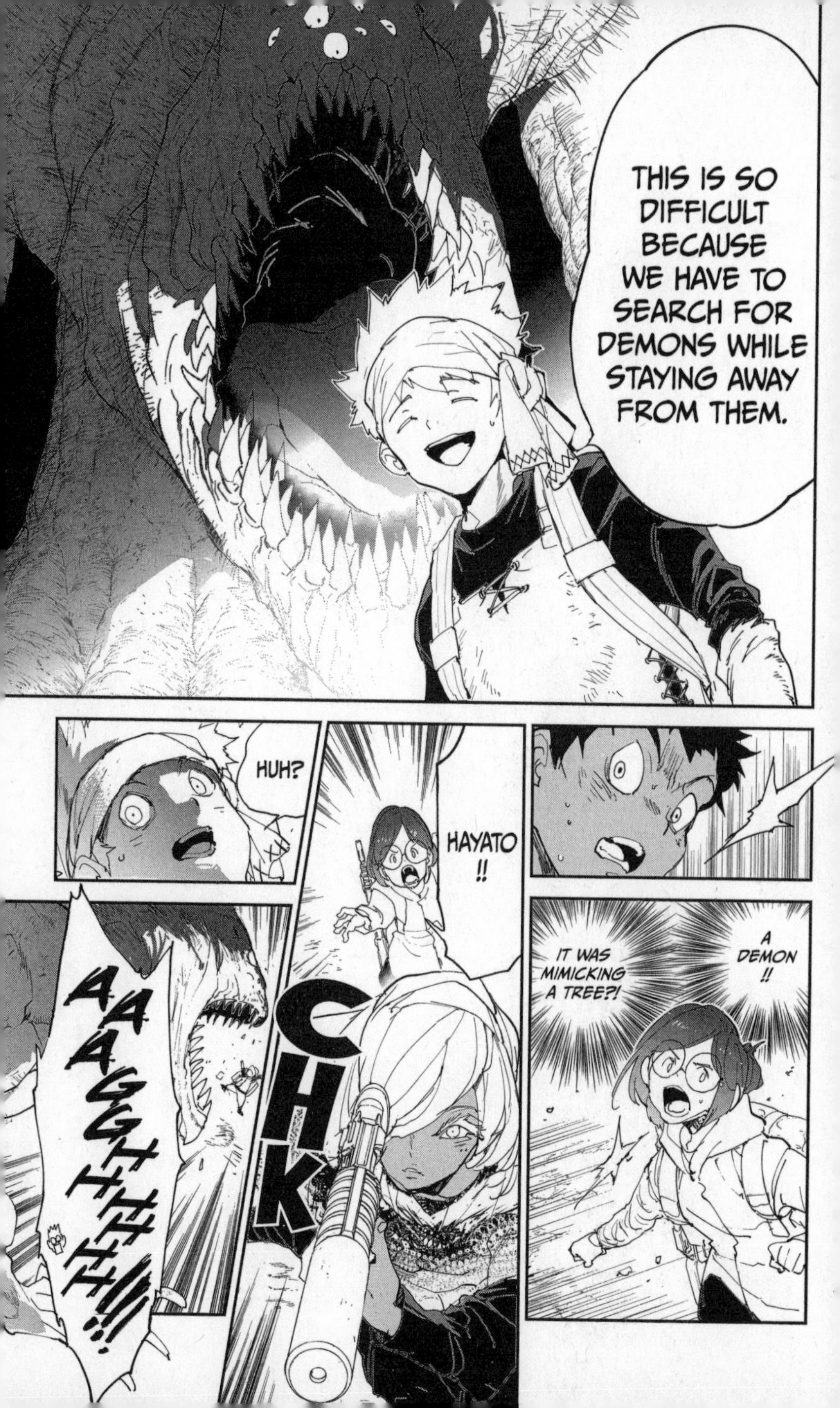
THIS IS SO DIFFICULT BECAUSE WE HAVE TO SEARCH FOR DEMONS WHILE STAYING AWAY FROM THEM.
HAYATO !!
HUH?
A DEMON !!
IT WAS MIMICKING A TREE?!
CHK
AAAGGHHHHHH!!!!

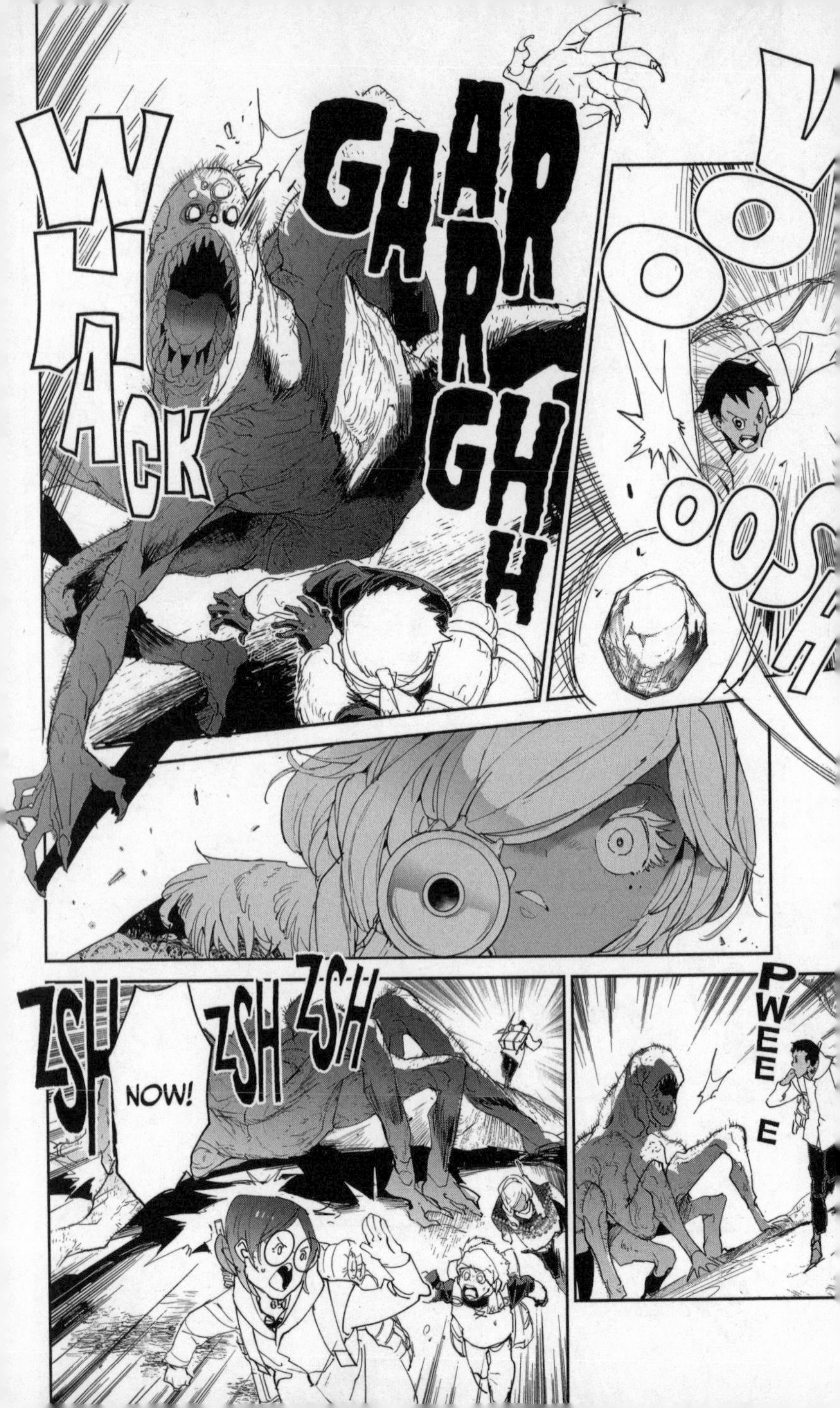
WOOOOOSH
WHACK
GAARRGHH
PWEEE
ZSH
NOW!
ZSH
ZSH

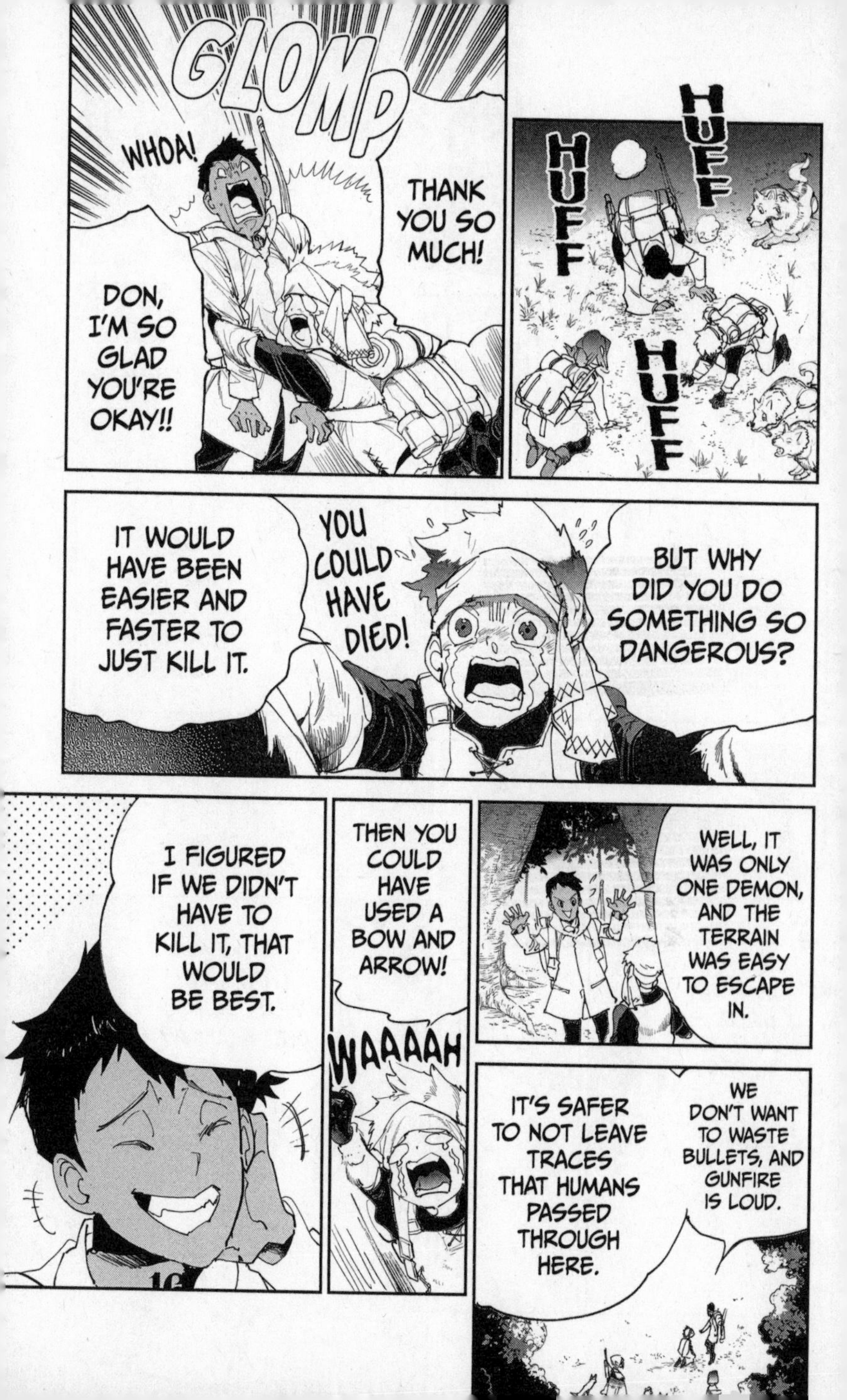
HUFF HUFF
HUFF HUFF
GLOMP
THANK YOU SO MUCH!
WHOA!
DON, I'M SO GLAD YOU'RE OKAY!!
BUT WHY DID YOU DO SOMETHING SO DANGEROUS?
YOU COULD HAVE DIED!
IT WOULD HAVE BEEN EASIER AND FASTER TO JUST KILL IT.
WELL, IT WAS ONLY ONE DEMON, AND THE TERRAIN WAS EASY TO ESCAPE IN.
WE DON'T WANT TO WASTE BULLETS, AND GUNFIRE IS LOUD.
IT'S SAFER TO NOT LEAVE TRACES THAT HUMANS PASSED THROUGH HERE.
THEN YOU COULD HAVE USED A BOW AND ARROW!
WAAAAH
I FIGURED IF WE DIDN'T HAVE TO KILL IT, THAT WOULD BE BEST.

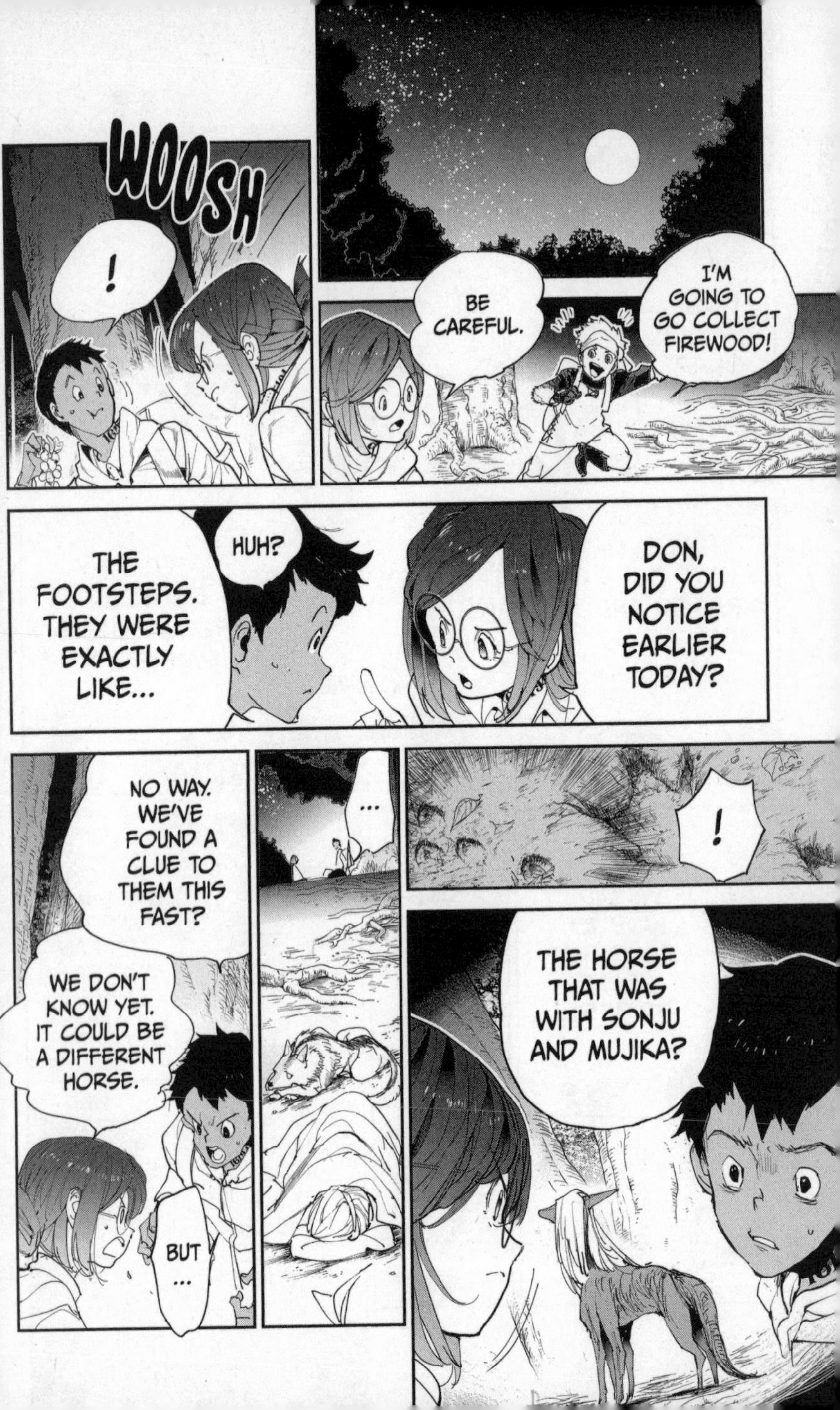
I'M GOING TO GO COLLECT FIREWOOD!
BE CAREFUL.
WOOSH
!
DON, DID YOU NOTICE EARLIER TODAY?
HUH?
THE FOOTSTEPS. THEY WERE EXACTLY LIKE...
!
THE HORSE THAT WAS WITH SONJU AND MUJIKA?
...
NO WAY. WE'VE FOUND A CLUE TO THEM THIS FAST?
WE DON'T KNOW YET. IT COULD BE A DIFFERENT HORSE.
BUT ...

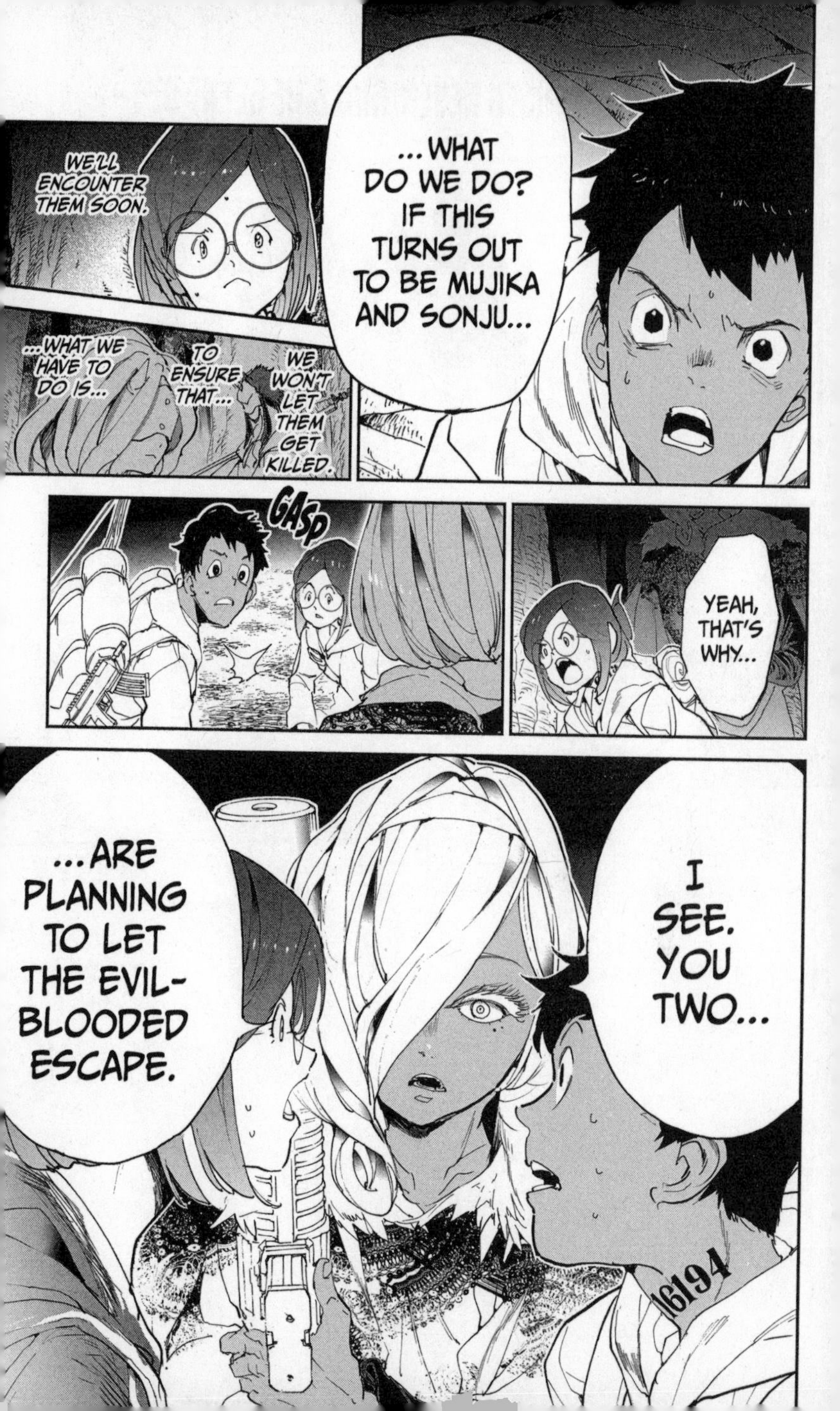
...WHAT DO WE DO? IF THIS TURNS OUT TO BE MUJIKA AND SONJU...
WE'LL ENCOUNTER THEM SOON.
WE WON'T LET THEM GET KILLED.
TO ENSURE THAT...
...WHAT WE HAVE TO DO IS...
YEAH, THAT'S WHY...
GASP
I SEE. YOU TWO...
...ARE PLANNING TO LET THE EVIL-BLOODED ESCAPE.
16194

THE PROMISED NEVERLAND SIDE SCENE 023

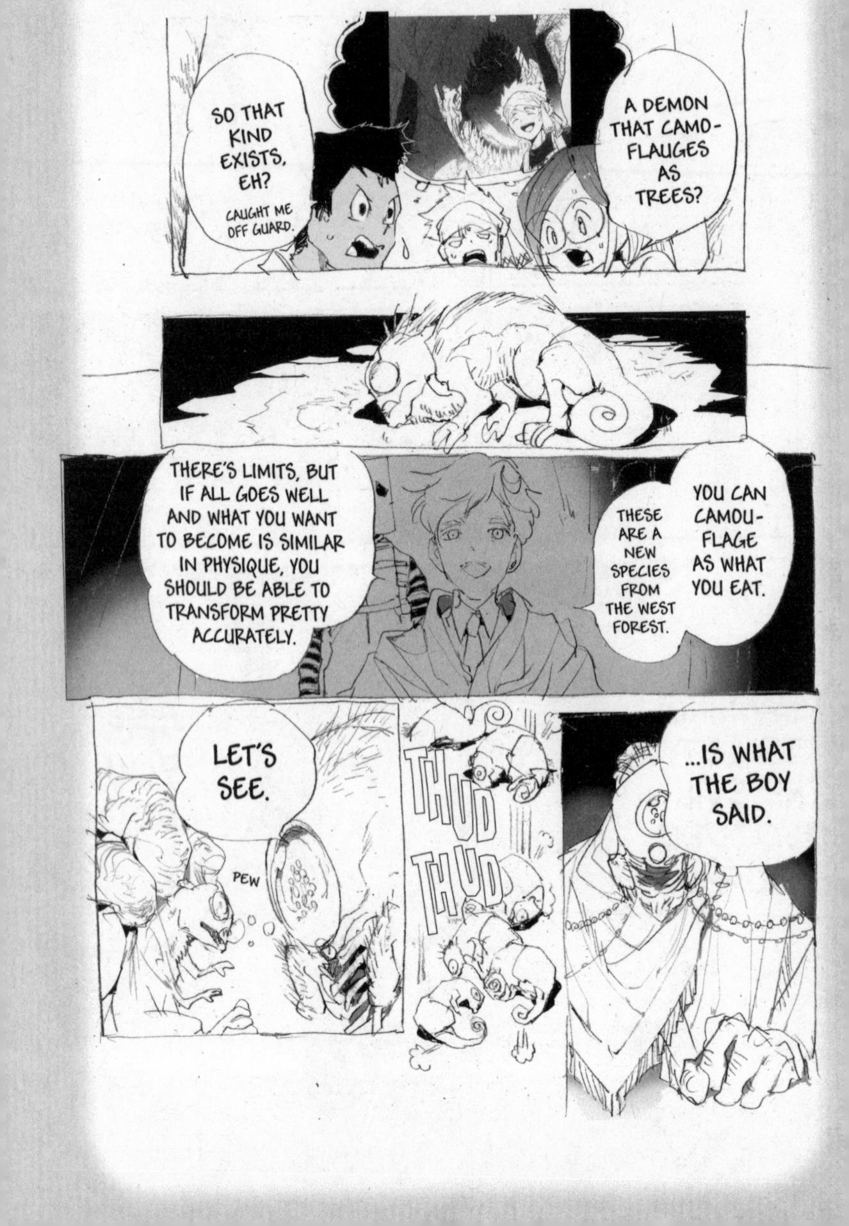

A DEMON THAT CAMOFLAUGES AS TREES?
SO THAT KIND EXISTS, EH?
CAUGHT ME OFF GUARD.
YOU CAN CAMOUFLAGE AS WHAT YOU EAT.
THESE ARE A NEW SPECIES FROM THE WEST FOREST.
THERE'S LIMITS, BUT IF ALL GOES WELL AND WHAT YOU WANT TO BECOME IS SIMILAR IN PHYSIQUE, YOU SHOULD BE ABLE TO TRANSFORM PRETTY ACCURATELY.
...IS WHAT THE BOY SAID.
THUD
THUD
LET'S SEE.
PEW

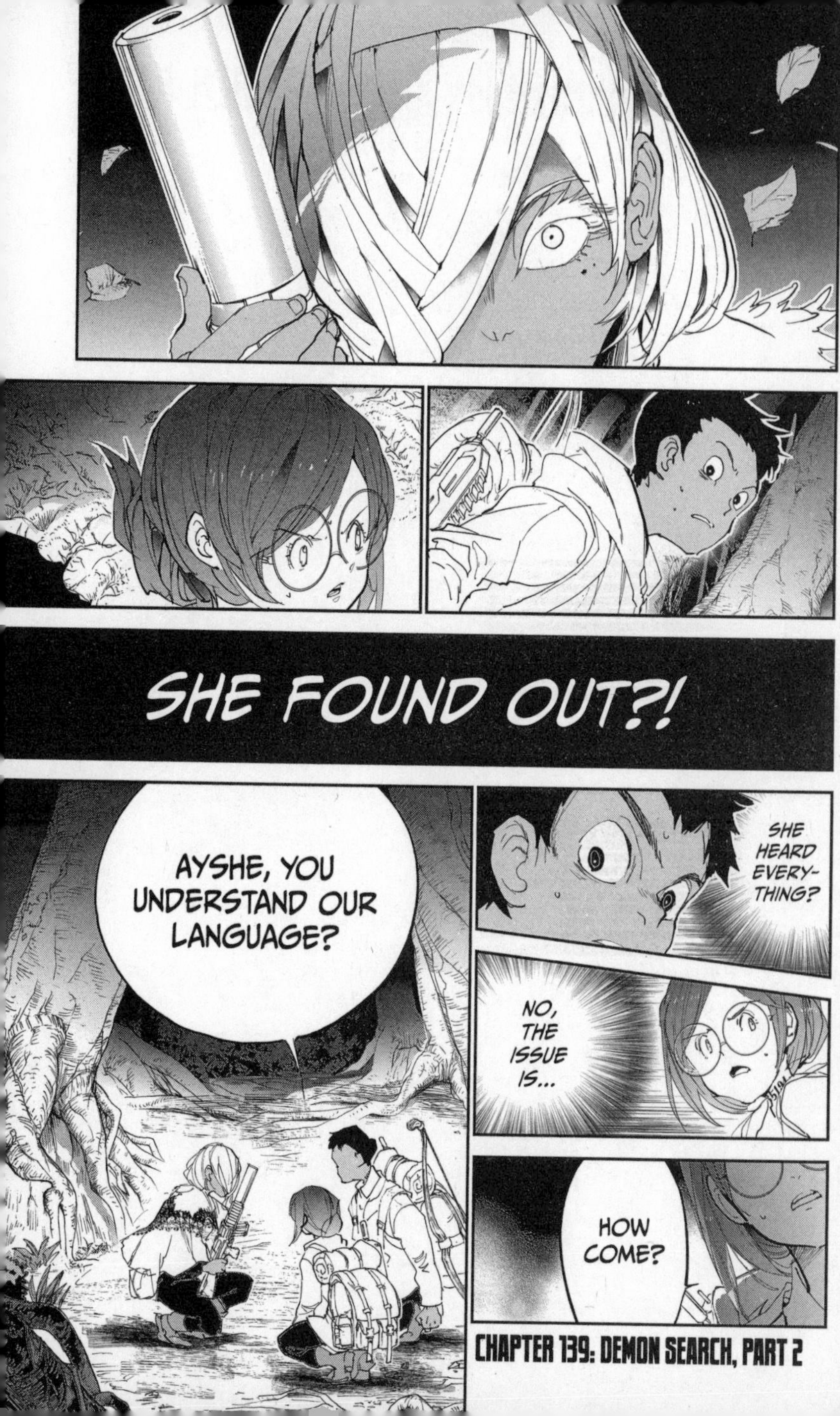
SHE FOUND OUT?!
SHE HEARD EVERY-THING?
NO, THE ISSUE IS...
HOW COME?
AYSHE, YOU UNDERSTAND OUR LANGUAGE?

CHAPTER 139: DEMON SEARCH, PART 2

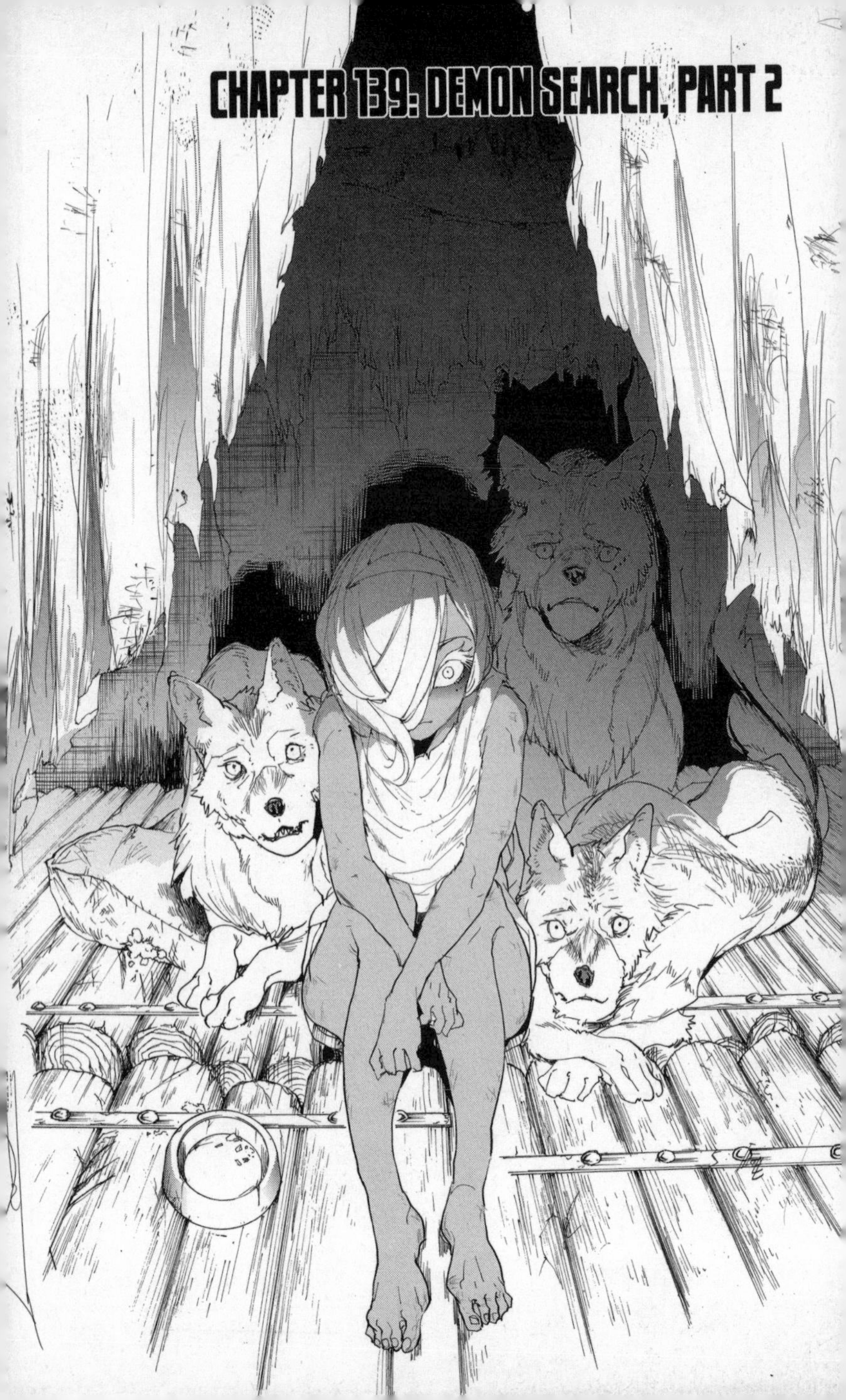
CHAPTER 139: DEMON SEARCH, PART 2

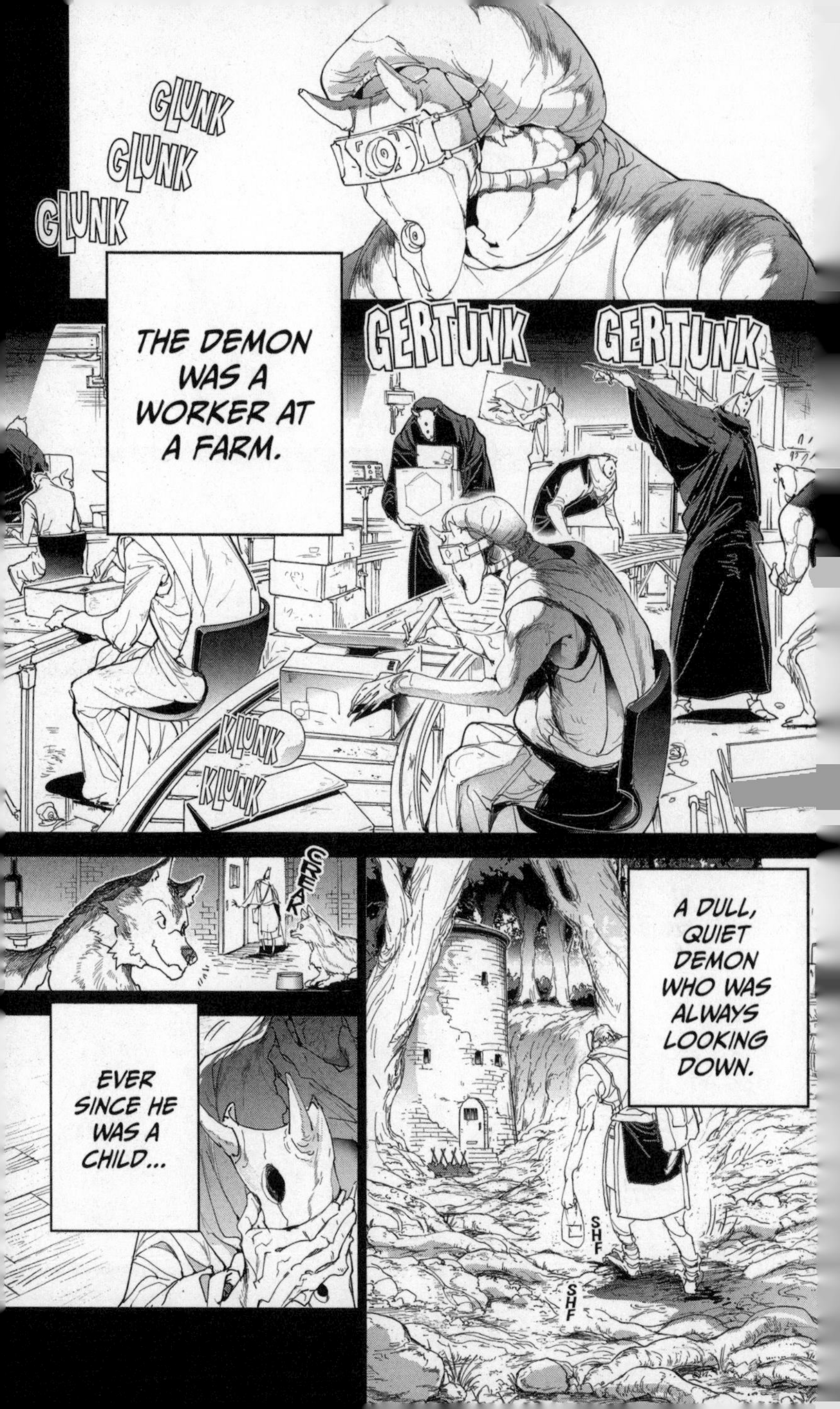
GLUNK
GLUNK
GLUNK
GERTUNK
GERTUNK
THE DEMON WAS A WORKER AT A FARM.
KLUNK
KLUNK
A DULL, QUIET DEMON WHO WAS ALWAYS LOOKING DOWN.
SHF
SHF
CREAK
EVER SINCE HE WAS A CHILD...

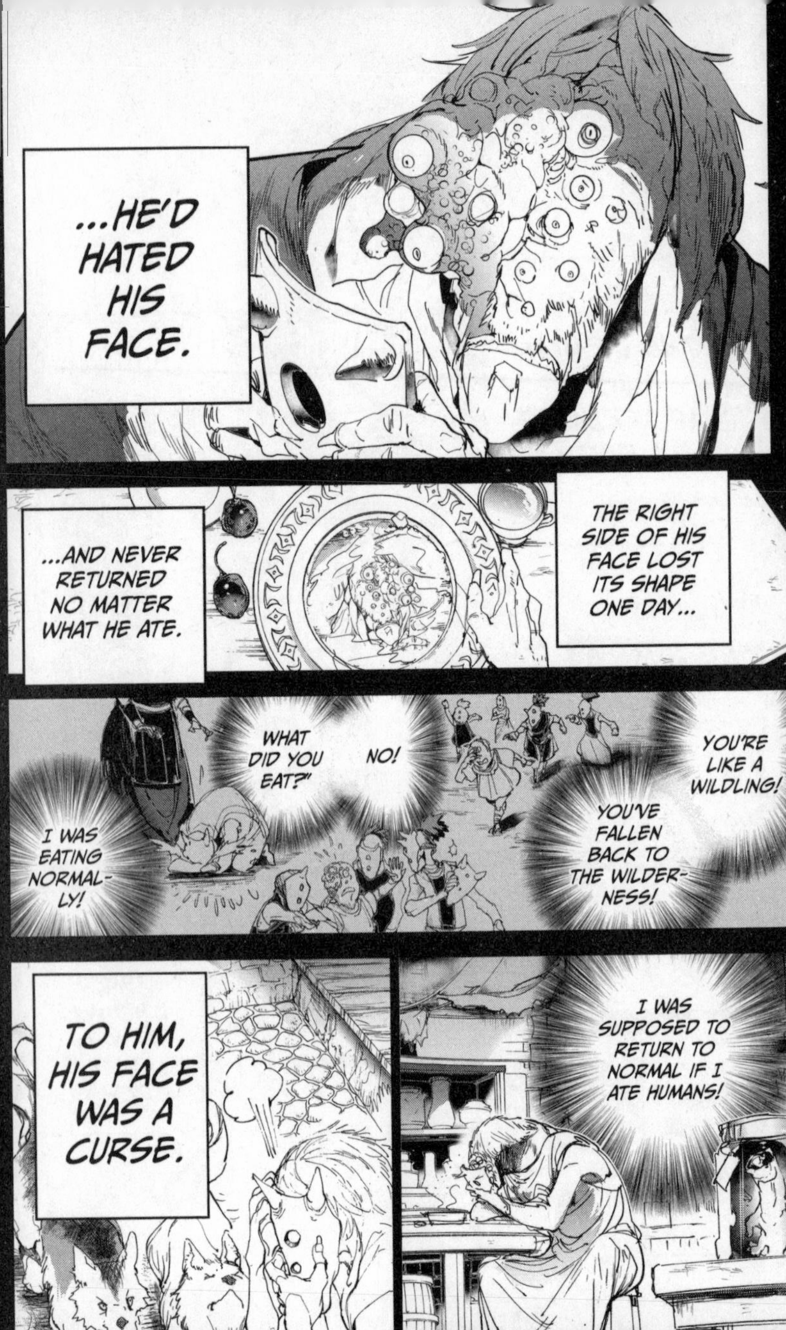
...HE'D HATED HIS FACE.
THE RIGHT SIDE OF HIS FACE LOST ITS SHAPE ONE DAY...
...AND NEVER RETURNED NO MATTER WHAT HE ATE.
YOU'RE LIKE A WILDLING!
NO!
WHAT DID YOU EAT?"
YOU'VE FALLEN BACK TO THE WILDERNESS!
I WAS EATING NORMALLY!
I WAS SUPPOSED TO RETURN TO NORMAL IF I ATE HUMANS!
TO HIM, HIS FACE WAS A CURSE.

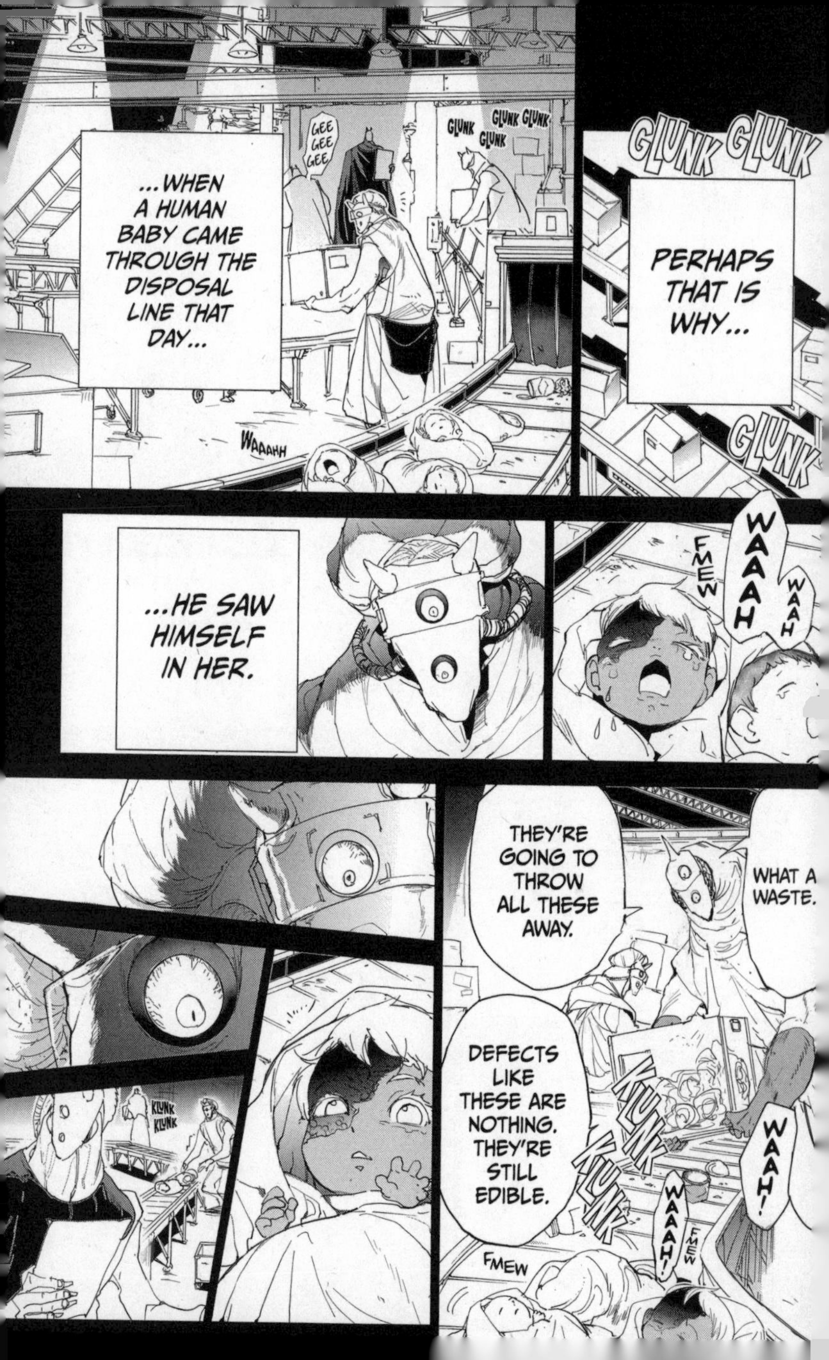
GLUNK GLUNK
PERHAPS THAT IS WHY...
GLUNK
GLUNK GLUNK
GLUNK GLUNK
GEE GEE GEE
...WHEN A HUMAN BABY CAME THROUGH THE DISPOSAL LINE THAT DAY...
WAAAHH
WAAAH
WAAAH
FMEW
...HE SAW HIMSELF IN HER.
WHAT A WASTE.
THEY'RE GOING TO THROW ALL THESE AWAY.
WAAAH!
KLUNK KLUNK
DEFECTS LIKE THESE ARE NOTHING. THEY'RE STILL EDIBLE.
FMEW
WAAAH!
FMEW
KLUNK KLUNK

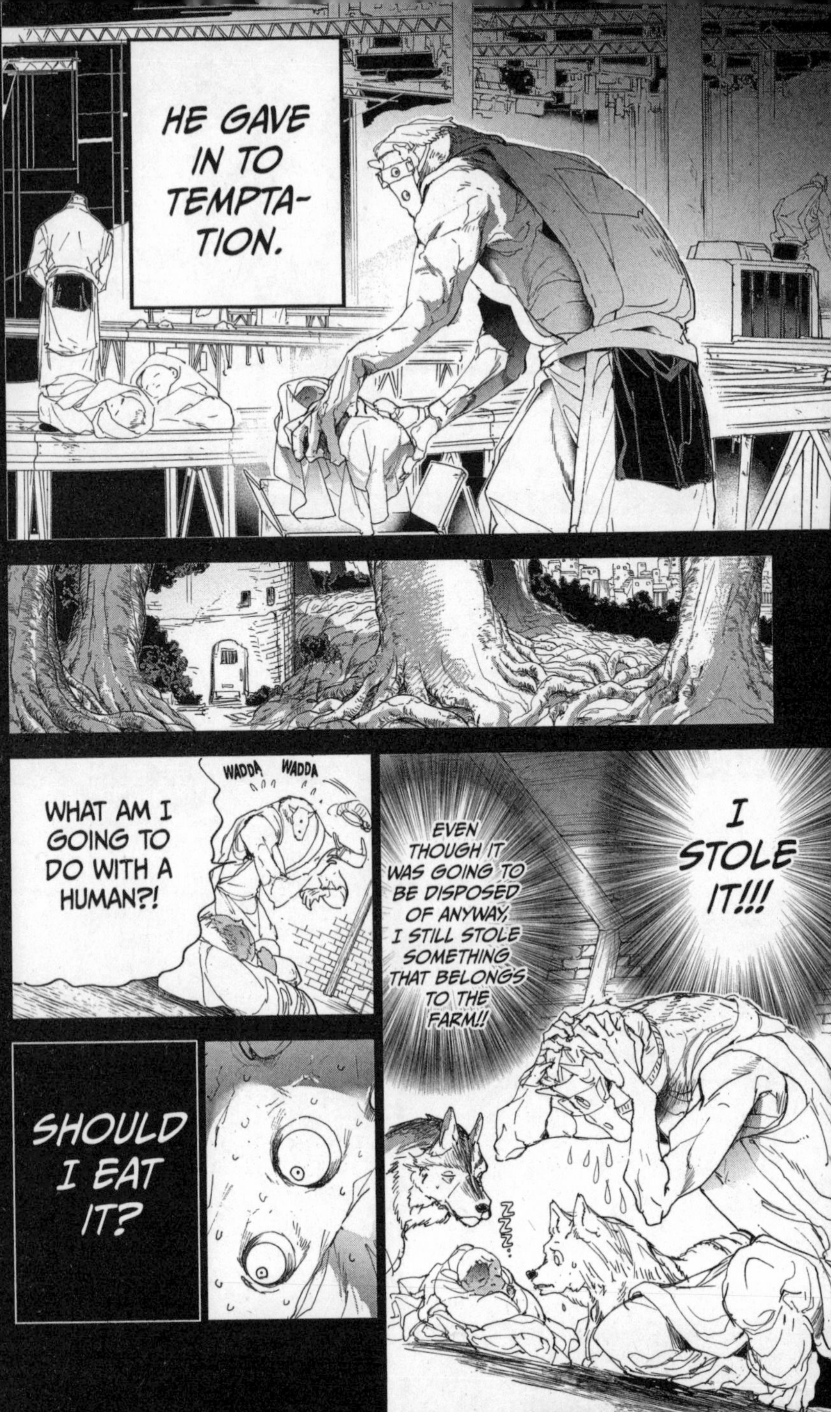
HE GAVE IN TO TEMPTATION.
I STOLE IT!!!
EVEN THOUGH IT WAS GOING TO BE DISPOSED OF ANYWAY, I STILL STOLE SOMETHING THAT BELONGS TO THE FARM!!
WADDA WADDA
WHAT AM I GOING TO DO WITH A HUMAN?!
ZZZ...
SHOULD I EAT IT?

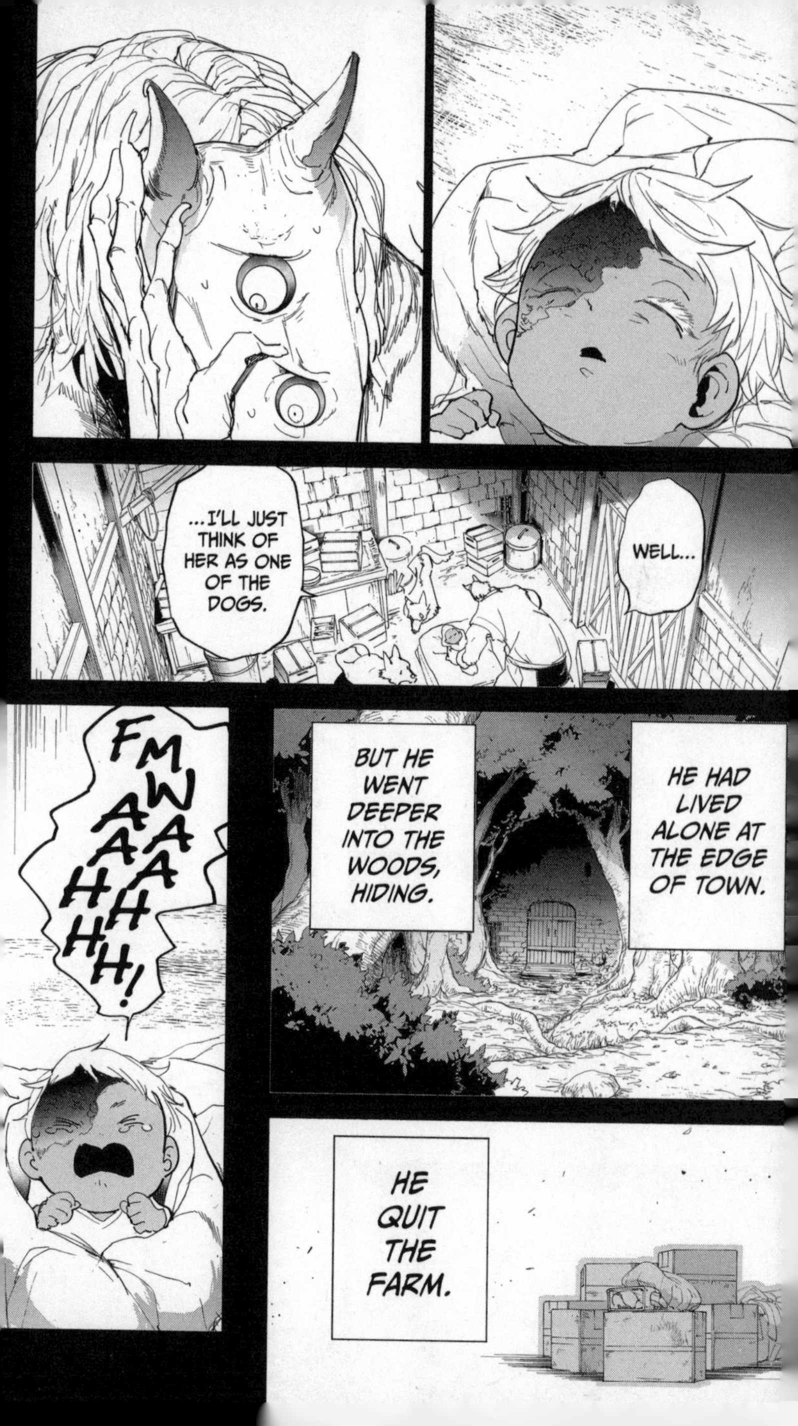
WELL...
...I'LL JUST THINK OF HER AS ONE OF THE DOGS.
HE HAD LIVED ALONE AT THE EDGE OF TOWN.
BUT HE WENT DEEPER INTO THE WOODS, HIDING.
HE QUIT THE FARM.
FMWAAAAHHHHH!

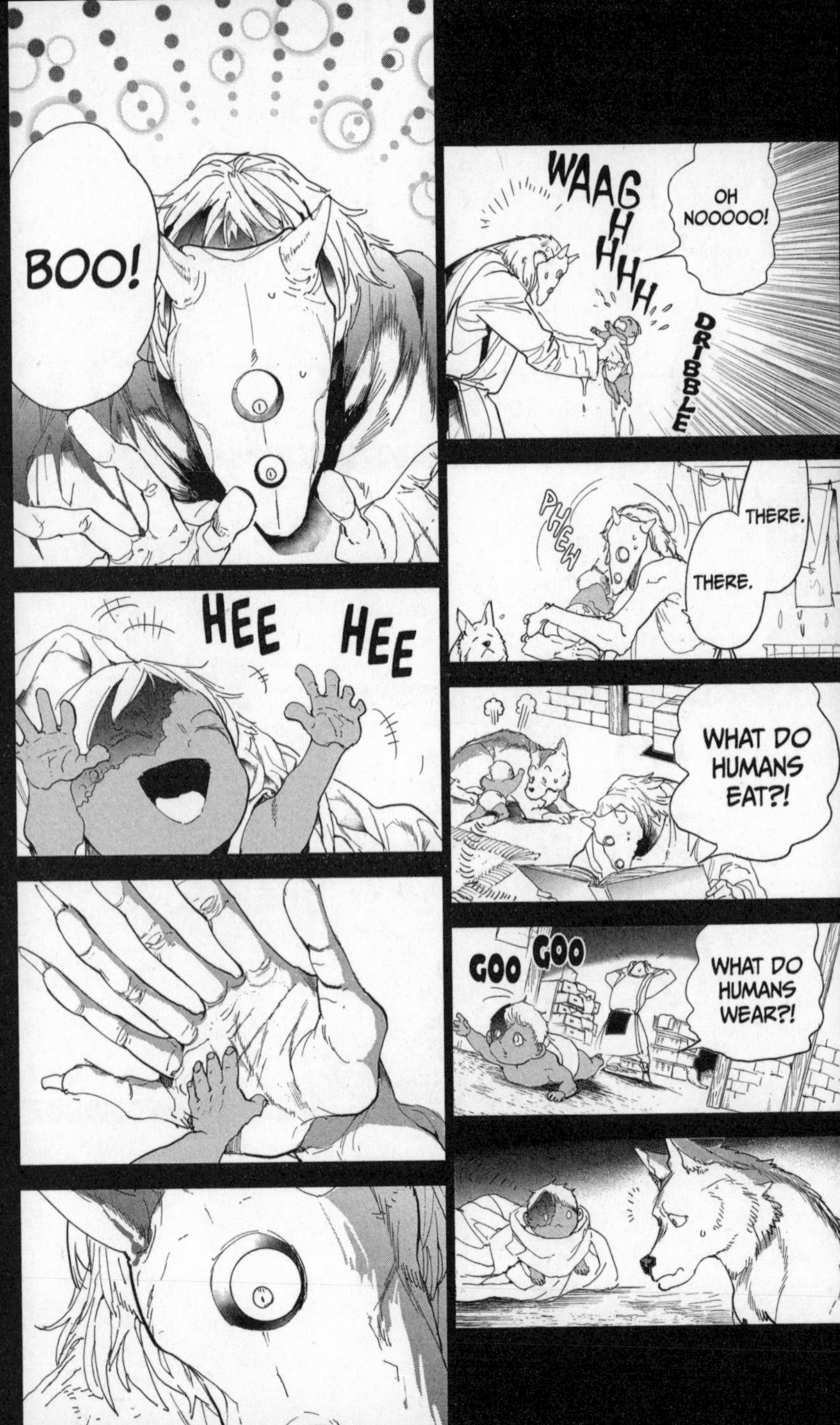
OH NOOOOO!
WAAGHHHHH
DRIBBLE
THERE.
THERE.
PHEW
WHAT DO HUMANS EAT?!
WHAT DO HUMANS WEAR?!
GOO
GOO
BOO!
HEE
HEE

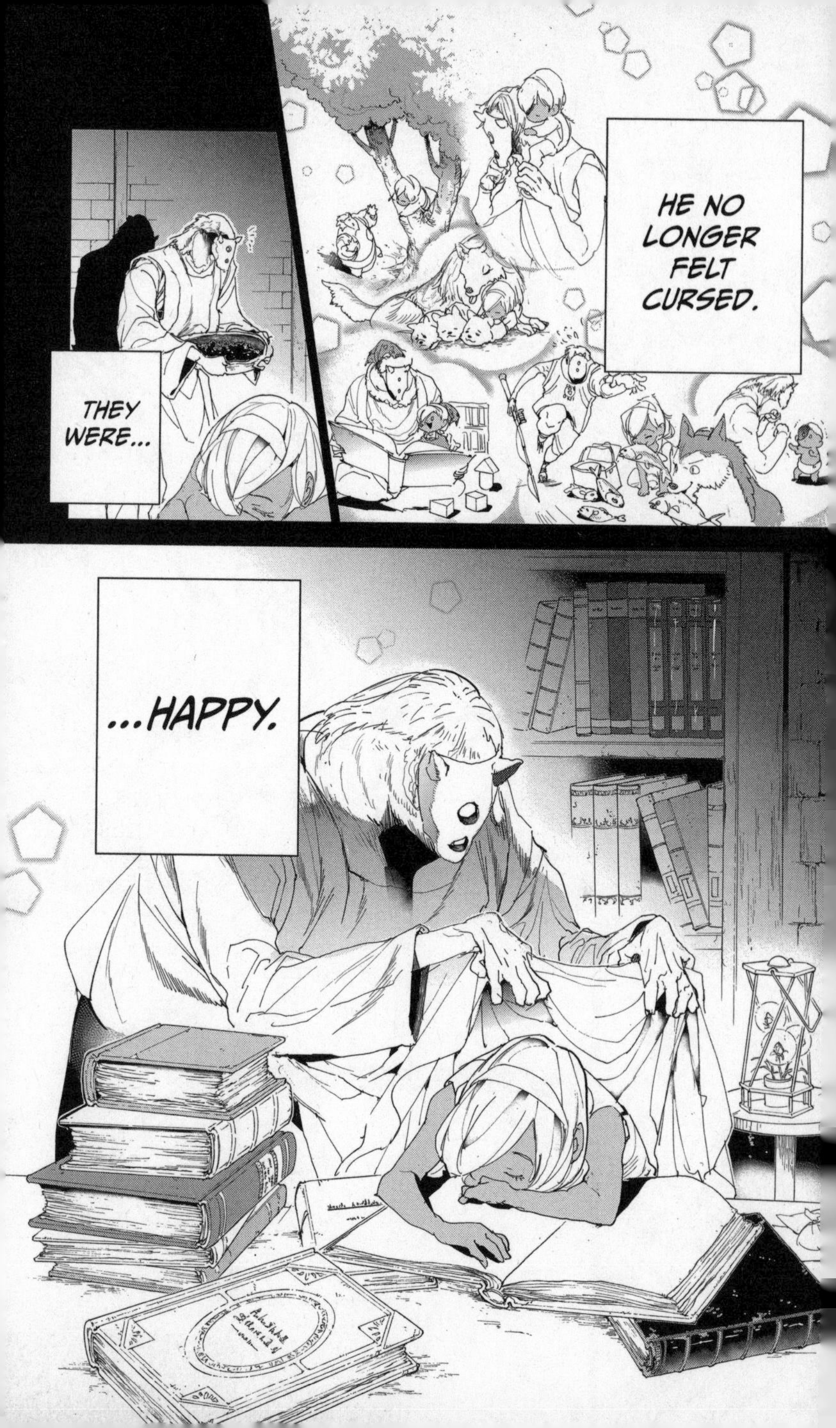
HE NO LONGER FELT CURSED.
THEY WERE...
...HAPPY.

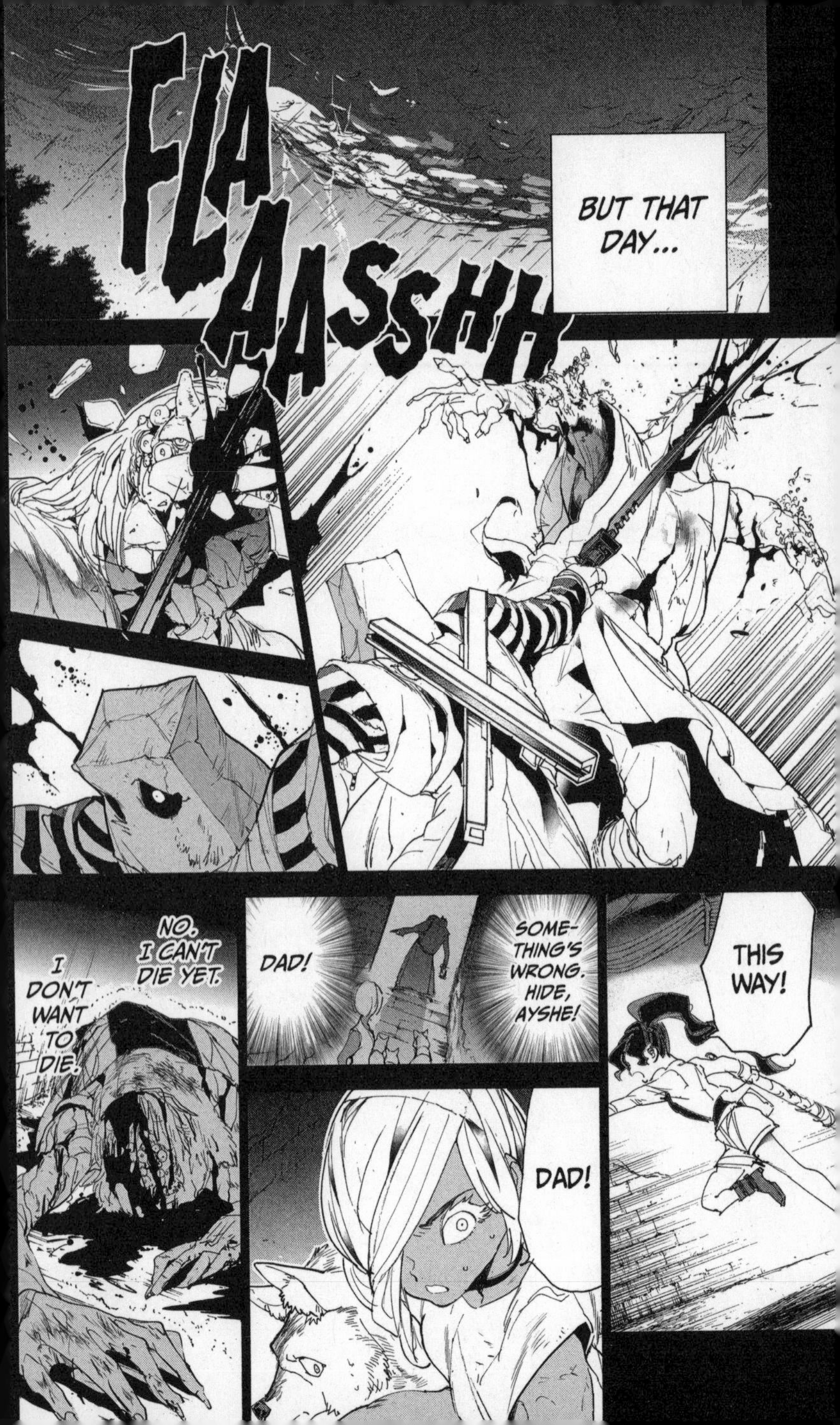
BUT THAT DAY...
FLAASHH
THIS WAY!
SOME-THING'S WRONG. HIDE, AYSHE!
DAD!
DAD!
NO. I CAN'T DIE YET.
I DON'T WANT TO DIE.

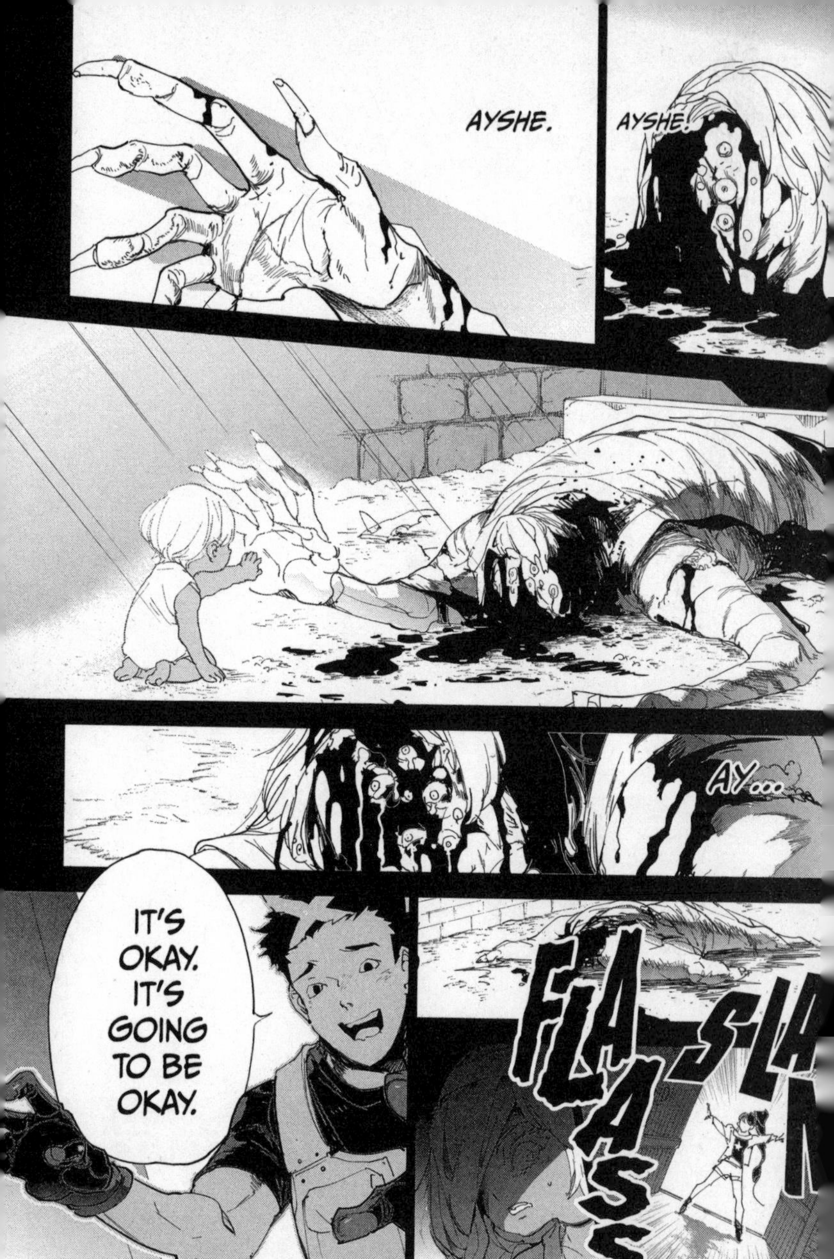
AYSHE!
AYSHE.
AY...
IT'S OKAY. IT'S GOING TO BE OKAY.

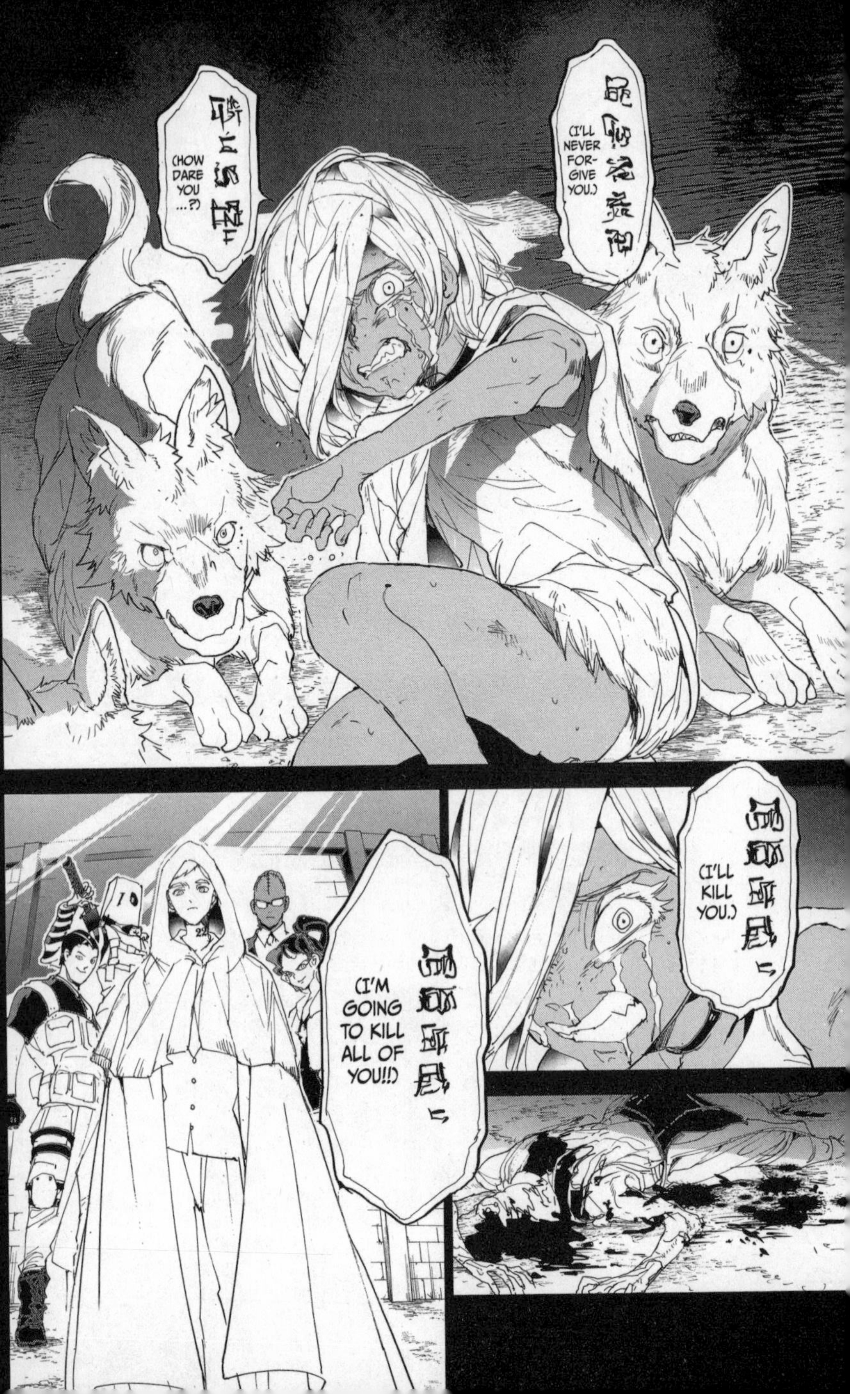
(I'LL NEVER FORGIVE YOU.)
(HOW DARE YOU ...?)
(I'LL KILL YOU.)
(I'M GOING TO KILL ALL OF YOU!!)

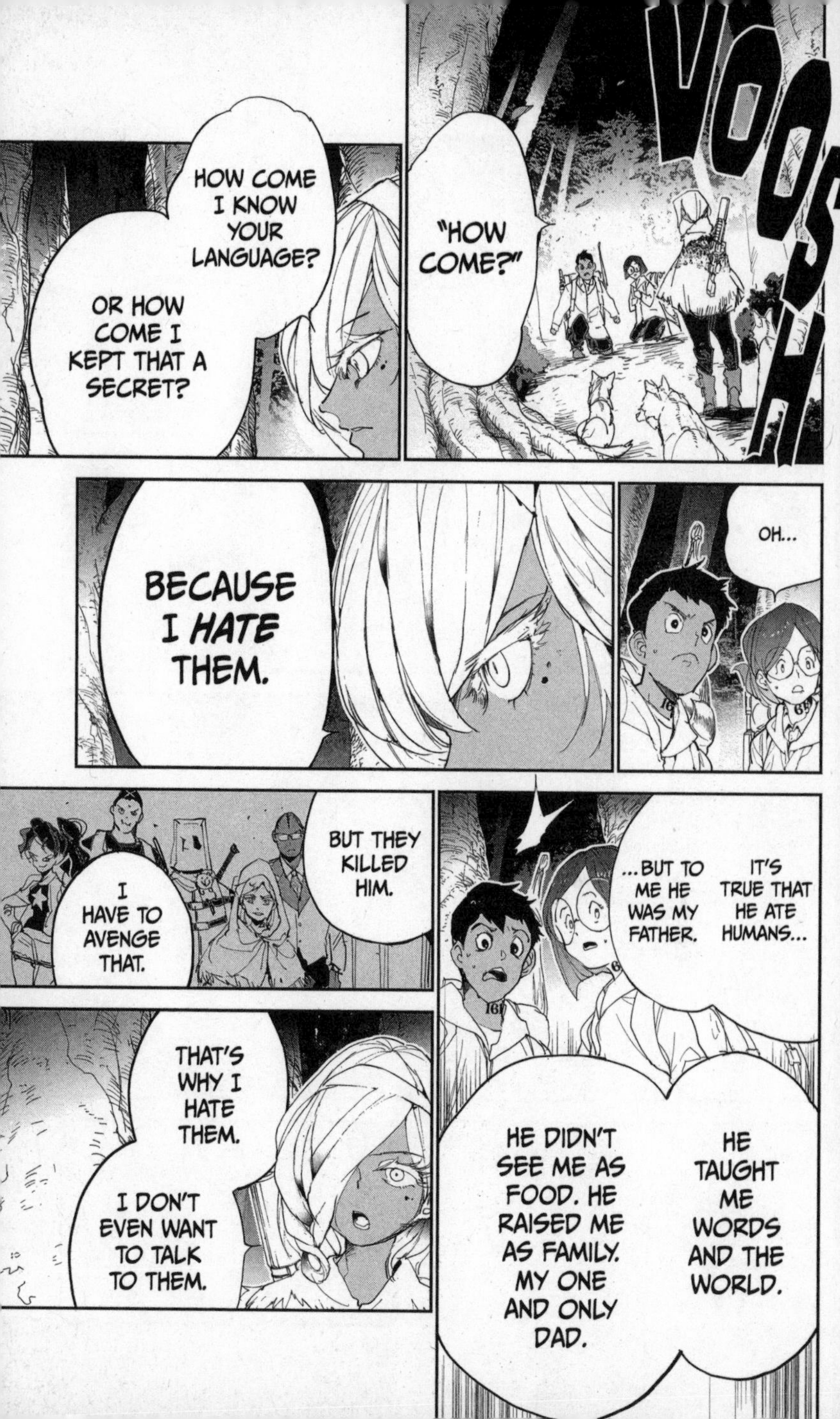
VOOSH
"HOW COME?"
HOW COME I KNOW YOUR LANGUAGE?
OR HOW COME I KEPT THAT A SECRET?
OH...
BECAUSE I *HATE* THEM.
IT'S TRUE THAT HE ATE HUMANS...
...BUT TO ME HE WAS MY FATHER.
HE TAUGHT ME WORDS AND THE WORLD.
HE DIDN'T SEE ME AS FOOD. HE RAISED ME AS FAMILY. MY ONE AND ONLY DAD.
BUT THEY KILLED HIM.
I HAVE TO AVENGE THAT.
THAT'S WHY I HATE THEM.
I DON'T EVEN WANT TO TALK TO THEM.

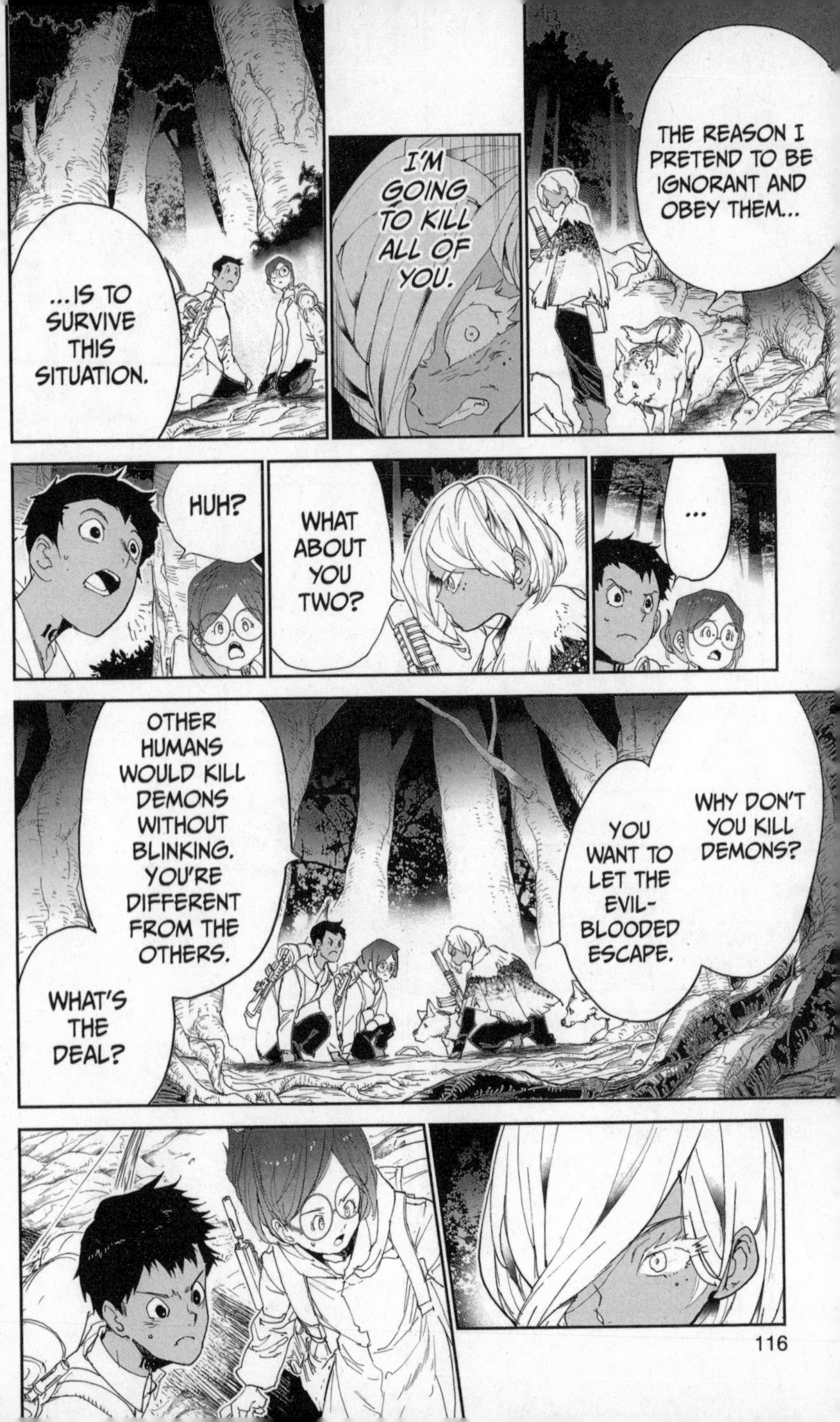
THE REASON I PRETEND TO BE IGNORANT AND OBEY THEM...
I'M GOING TO KILL ALL OF YOU.
...IS TO SURVIVE THIS SITUATION.
...
WHAT ABOUT YOU TWO?
HUH?
WHY DON'T YOU KILL DEMONS?
YOU WANT TO LET THE EVIL-BLOODED ESCAPE.
OTHER HUMANS WOULD KILL DEMONS WITHOUT BLINKING. YOU'RE DIFFERENT FROM THE OTHERS.
WHAT'S THE DEAL?

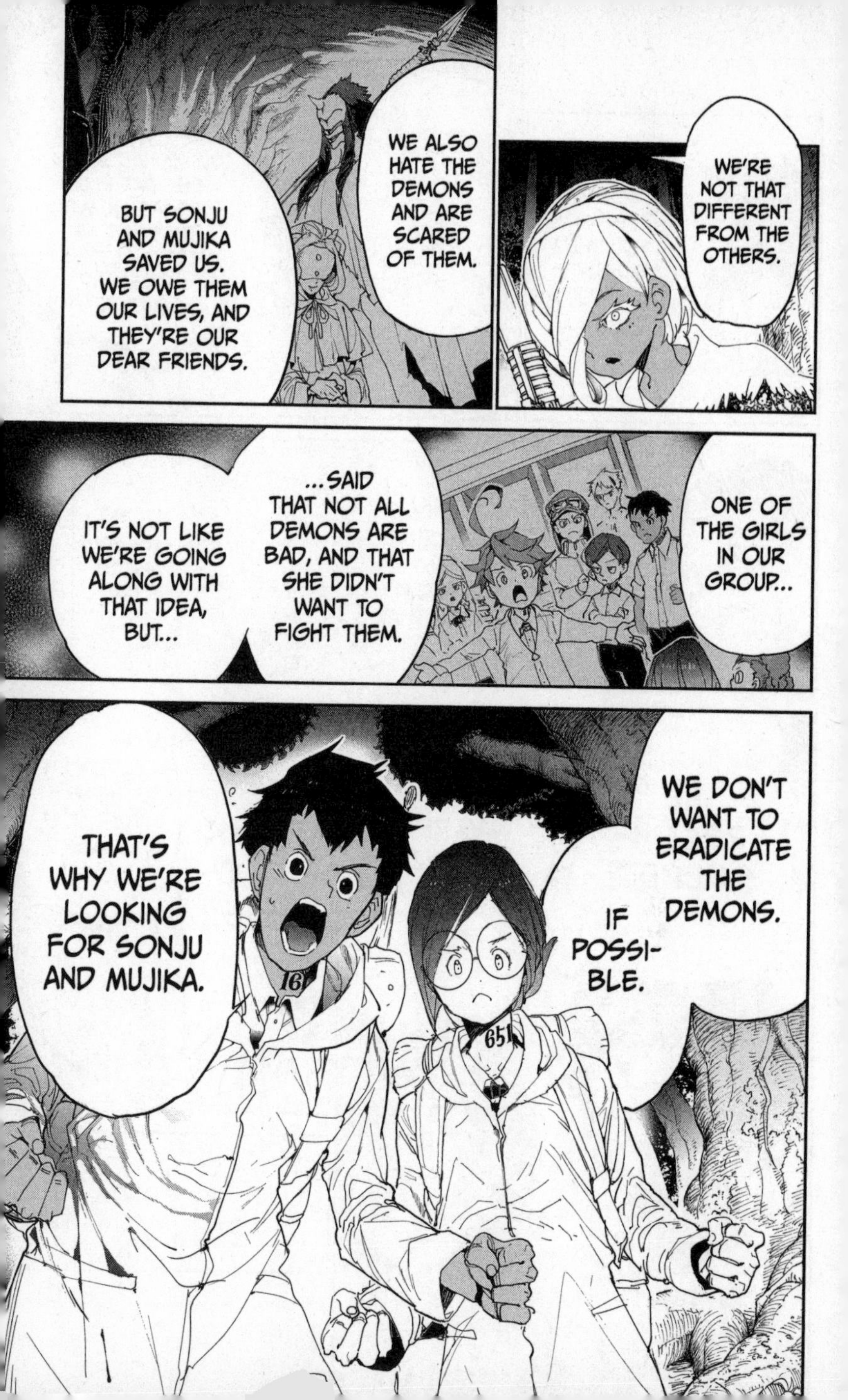
WE'RE NOT THAT DIFFERENT FROM THE OTHERS.
WE ALSO HATE THE DEMONS AND ARE SCARED OF THEM.
BUT SONJU AND MUJIKA SAVED US. WE OWE THEM OUR LIVES, AND THEY'RE OUR DEAR FRIENDS.
ONE OF THE GIRLS IN OUR GROUP...
...SAID THAT NOT ALL DEMONS ARE BAD, AND THAT SHE DIDN'T WANT TO FIGHT THEM.
IT'S NOT LIKE WE'RE GOING ALONG WITH THAT IDEA, BUT...
WE DON'T WANT TO ERADICATE THE DEMONS.
IF POSSI-BLE.
THAT'S WHY WE'RE LOOKING FOR SONJU AND MUJIKA.
16
65

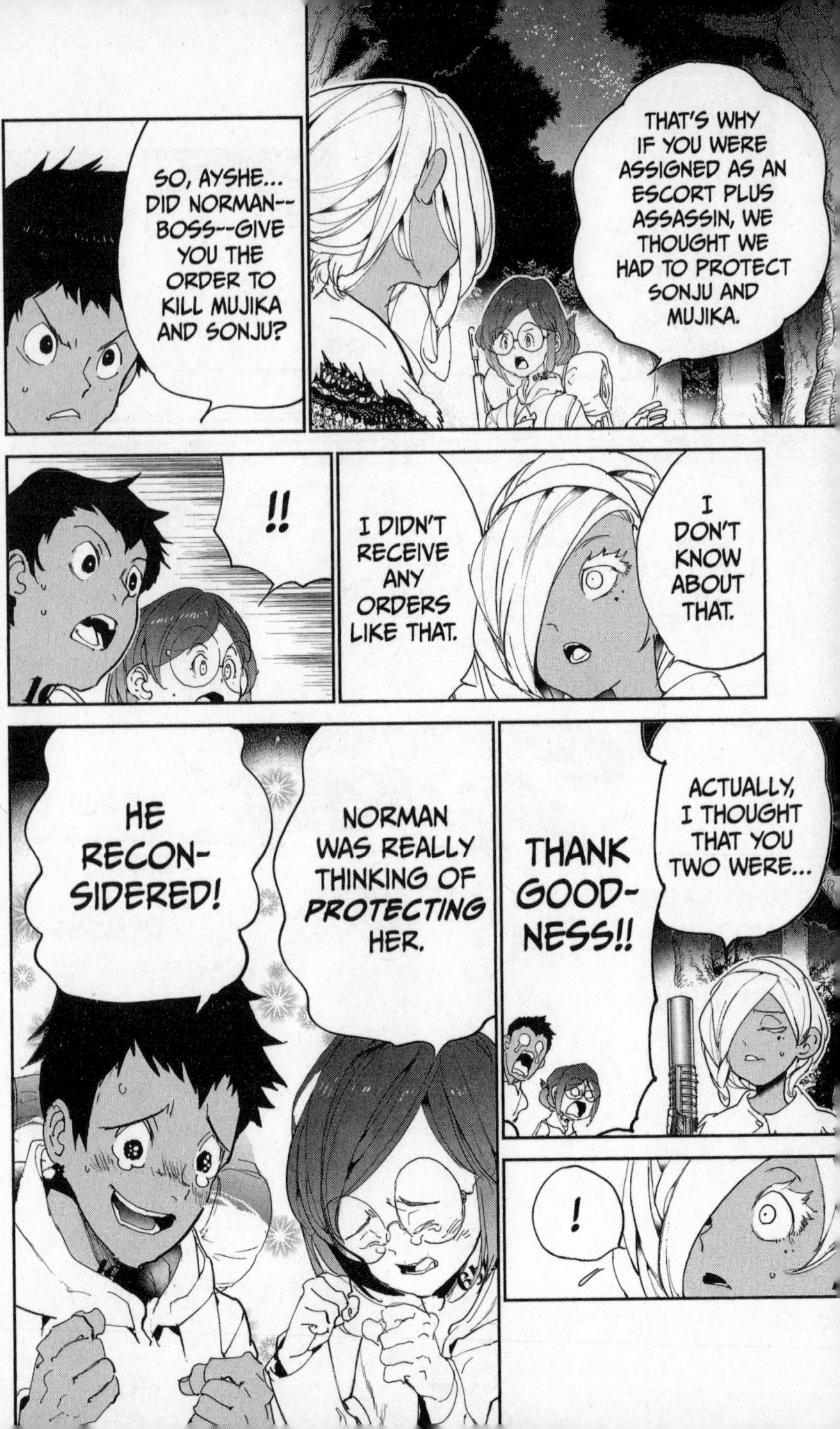
THAT'S WHY IF YOU WERE ASSIGNED AS AN ESCORT PLUS ASSASSIN, WE THOUGHT WE HAD TO PROTECT SONJU AND MUJIKA.
SO, AYSHE... DID NORMAN--BOSS--GIVE YOU THE ORDER TO KILL MUJIKA AND SONJU?
I DON'T KNOW ABOUT THAT.
I DIDN'T RECEIVE ANY ORDERS LIKE THAT.
!!
ACTUALLY, I THOUGHT THAT YOU TWO WERE...
THANK GOOD-NESS!!
!
NORMAN WAS REALLY THINKING OF *PROTECTING* HER.
HE RECON-SIDERED!

THEY'RE... CRYING...

SOB

SORRY FOR SUSPECTING YOU.

AND YOU AREN'T AN ASSASSIN. THANK GOODNESS.

...

DON AND GILDA, EH?

GOOD!

NOW WE CAN SEARCH FOR MUJIKA AND SONJU WITH EASE!!

...

WAIT! MAYBE NORMAN JUST WANTS TO BRING THEM BACK ONLY TO KILL THEM!

GASP

BUT THEY'LL STILL BE SAFE FOR A WHILE! AND THAT WOULD MEAN HE'S STILL LEAVING ROOM FOR NEGOTIATION. IT'S NOT THE MOST BRUTAL METHOD.

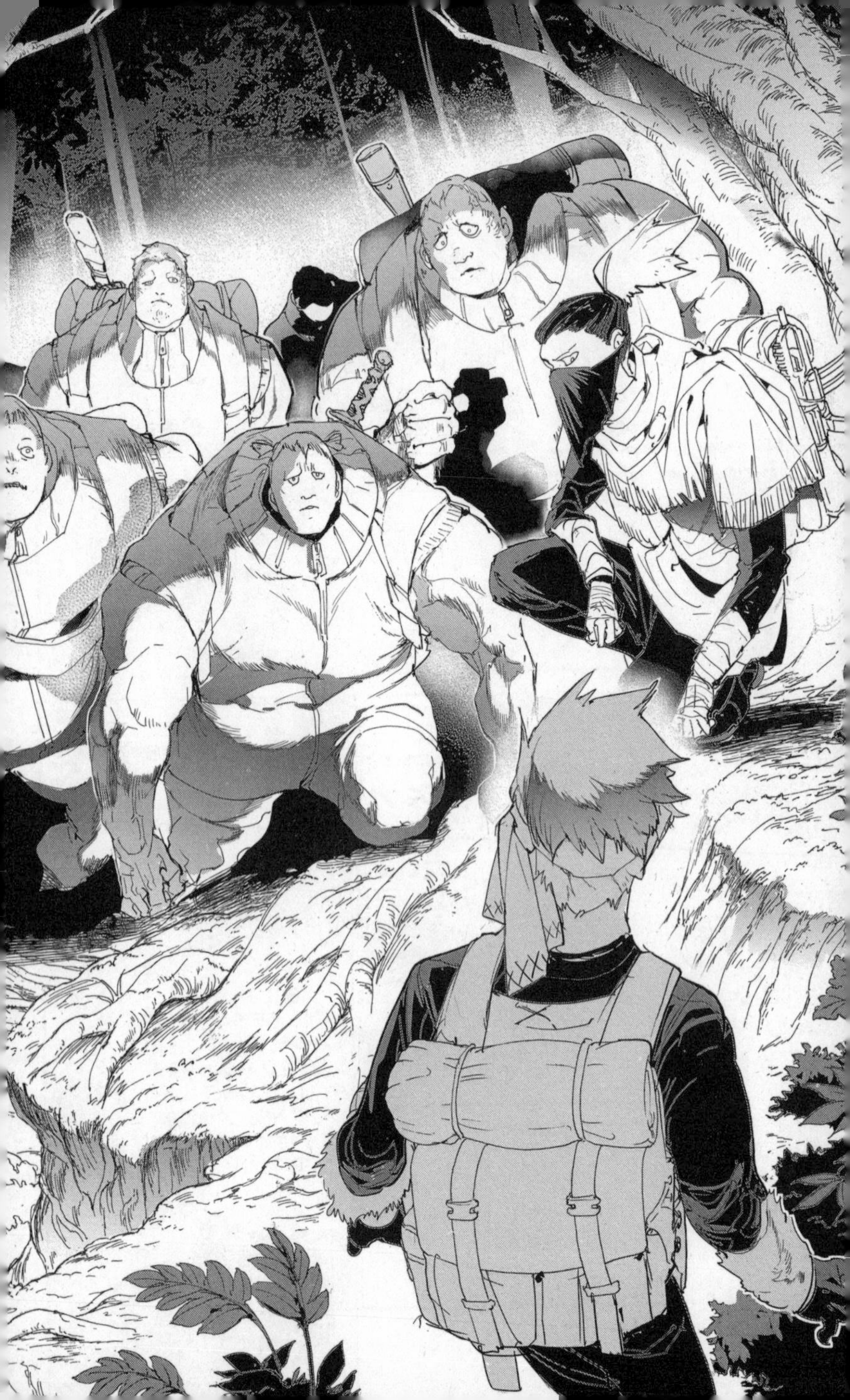

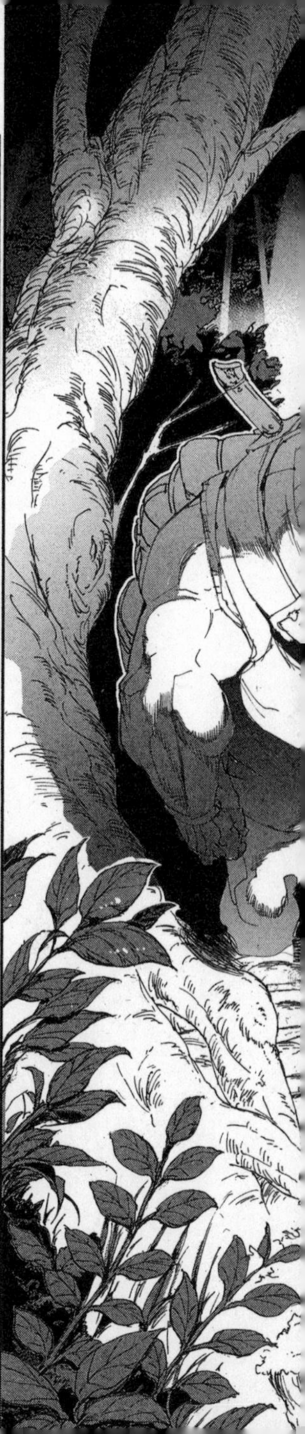

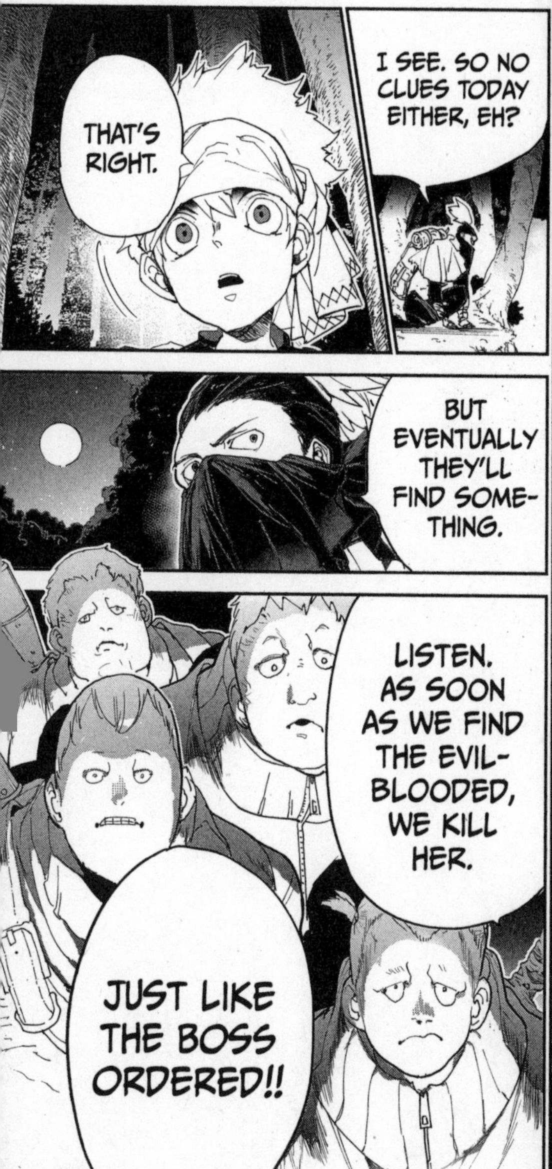

I SEE. SO NO CLUES TODAY EITHER, EH?
THAT'S RIGHT.
BUT EVENTUALLY THEY'LL FIND SOME-THING.
LISTEN. AS SOON AS WE FIND THE EVIL-BLOODED, WE KILL HER.
JUST LIKE THE BOSS ORDERED!!

CHAPTER 140: I'M HERE!

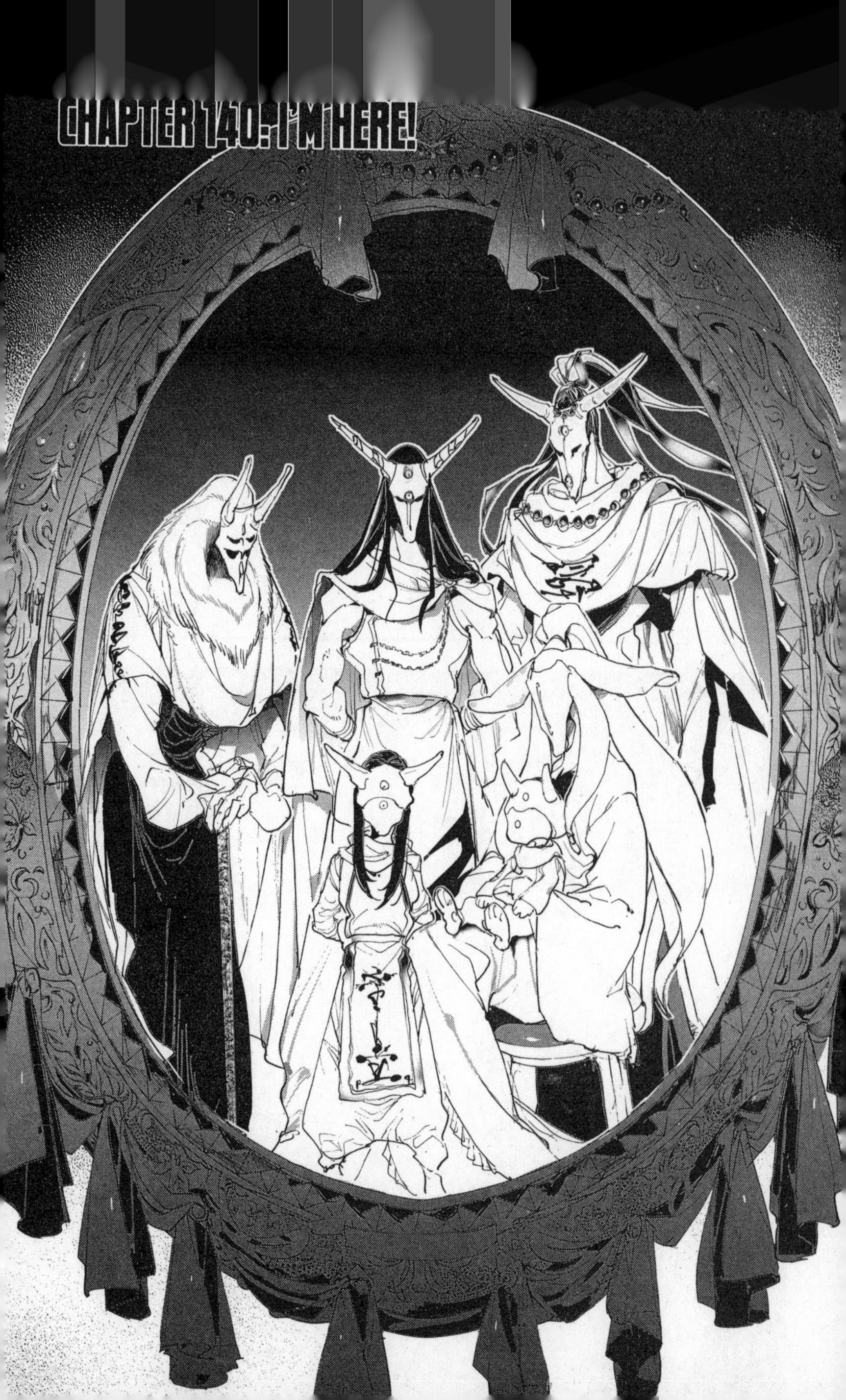

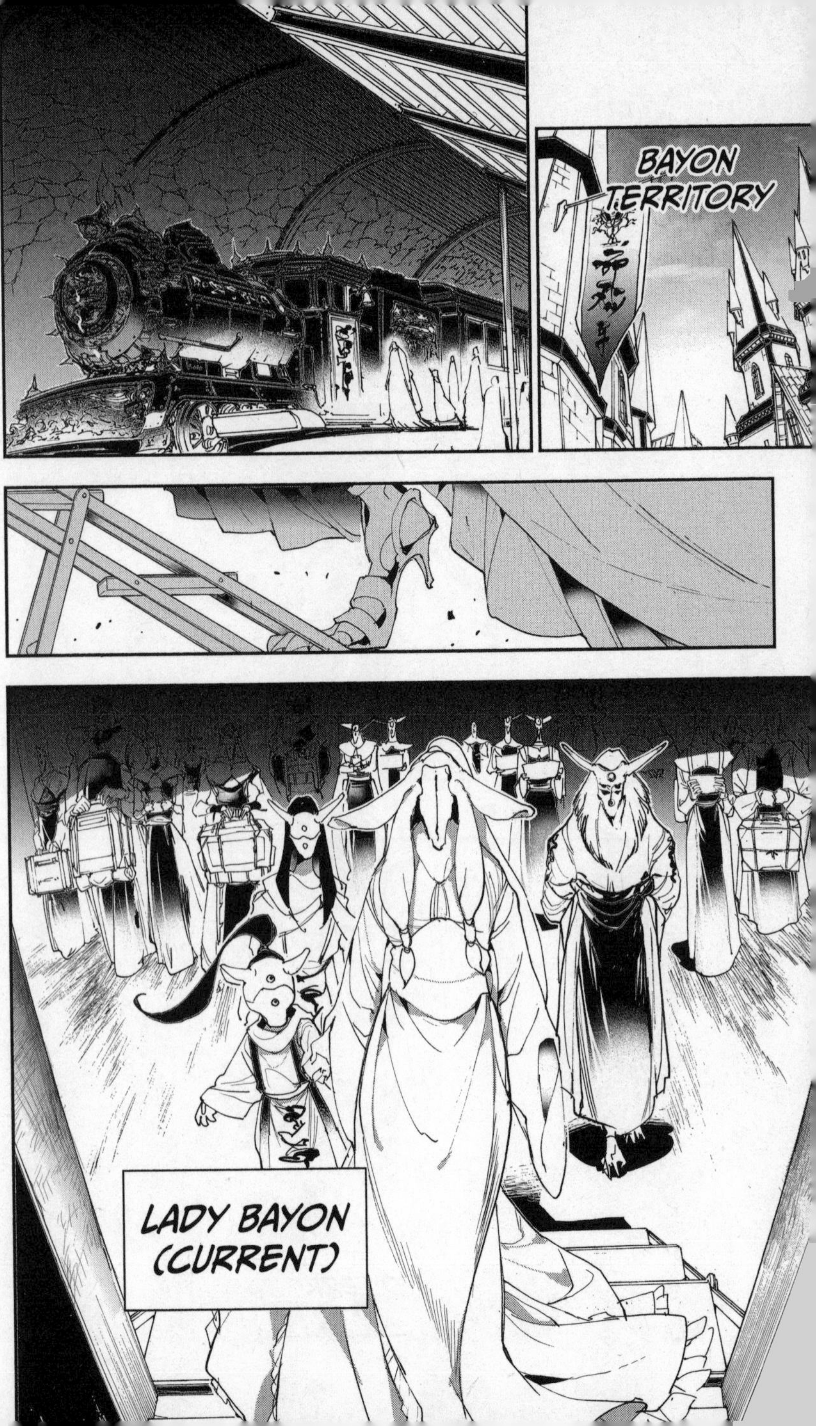
BAYON TERRITORY
LADY BAYON (CURRENT)

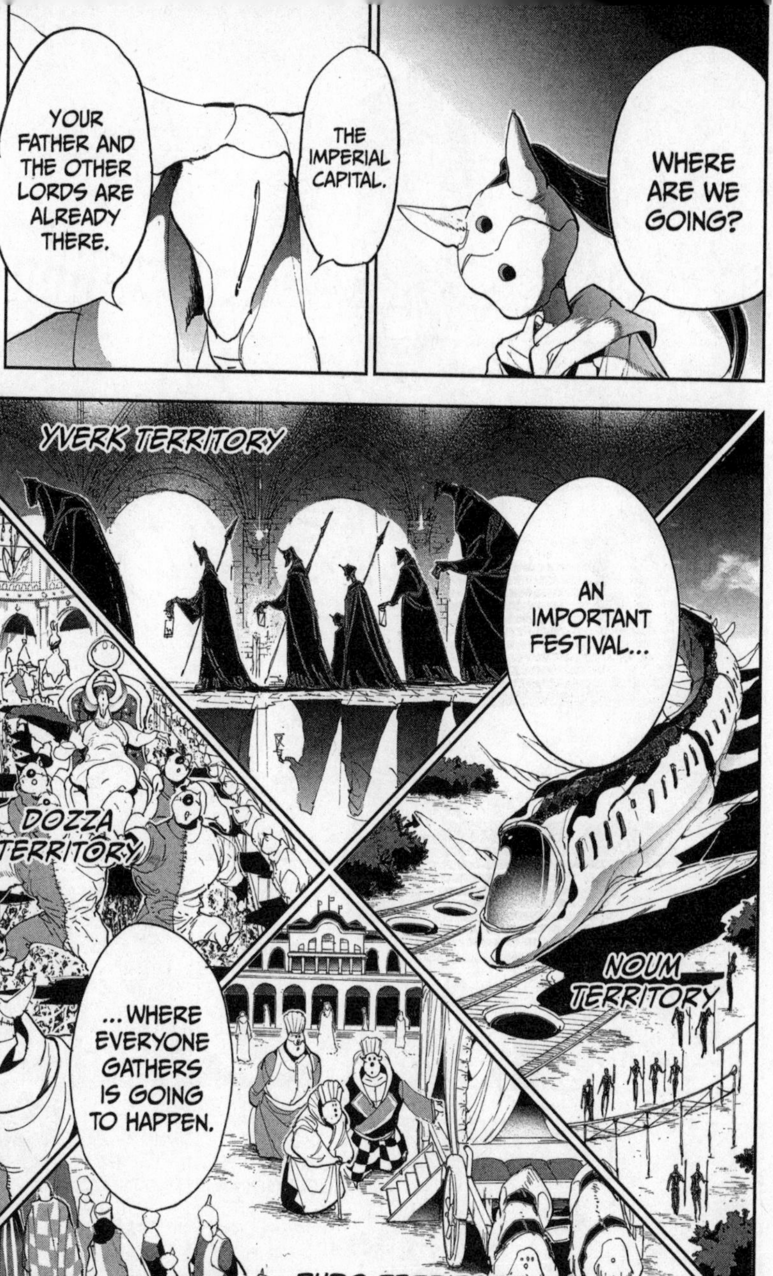
WHERE ARE WE GOING?
THE IMPERIAL CAPITAL.
YOUR FATHER AND THE OTHER LORDS ARE ALREADY THERE.
YVERK TERRITORY
AN IMPORTANT FESTIVAL...
NOUM TERRITORY
DOZZA TERRITORY
...WHERE EVERYONE GATHERS IS GOING TO HAPPEN.
PUPO TERRITORY

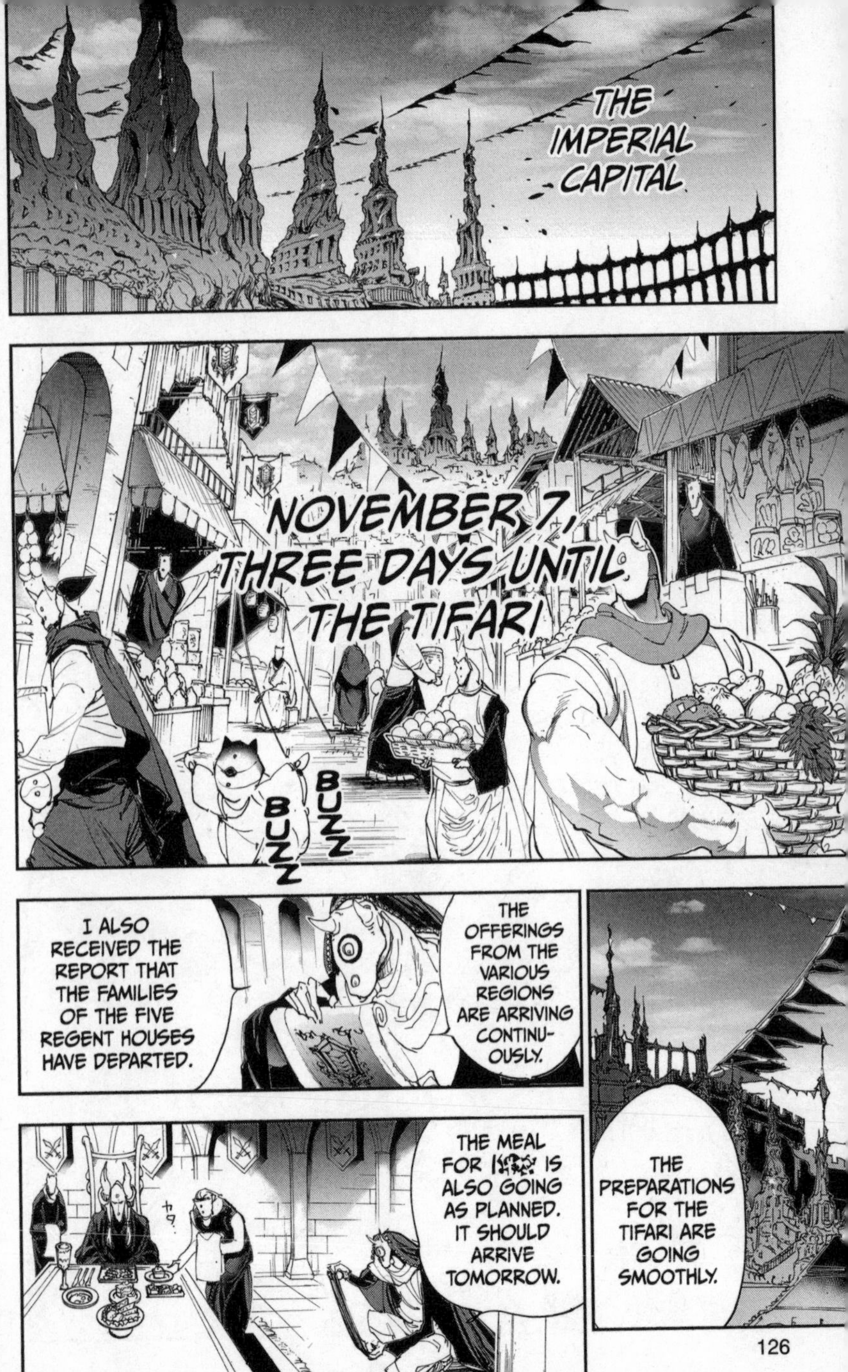
THE IMPERIAL CAPITAL
NOVEMBER 7, THREE DAYS UNTIL THE TIFARI
BUZZ
BUZZ
THE PREPARATIONS FOR THE TIFARI ARE GOING SMOOTHLY.
THE OFFERINGS FROM THE VARIOUS REGIONS ARE ARRIVING CONTINUOUSLY.
I ALSO RECEIVED THE REPORT THAT THE FAMILIES OF THE FIVE REGENT HOUSES HAVE DEPARTED.
THE MEAL FOR IS ALSO GOING AS PLANNED. IT SHOULD ARRIVE TOMORROW.

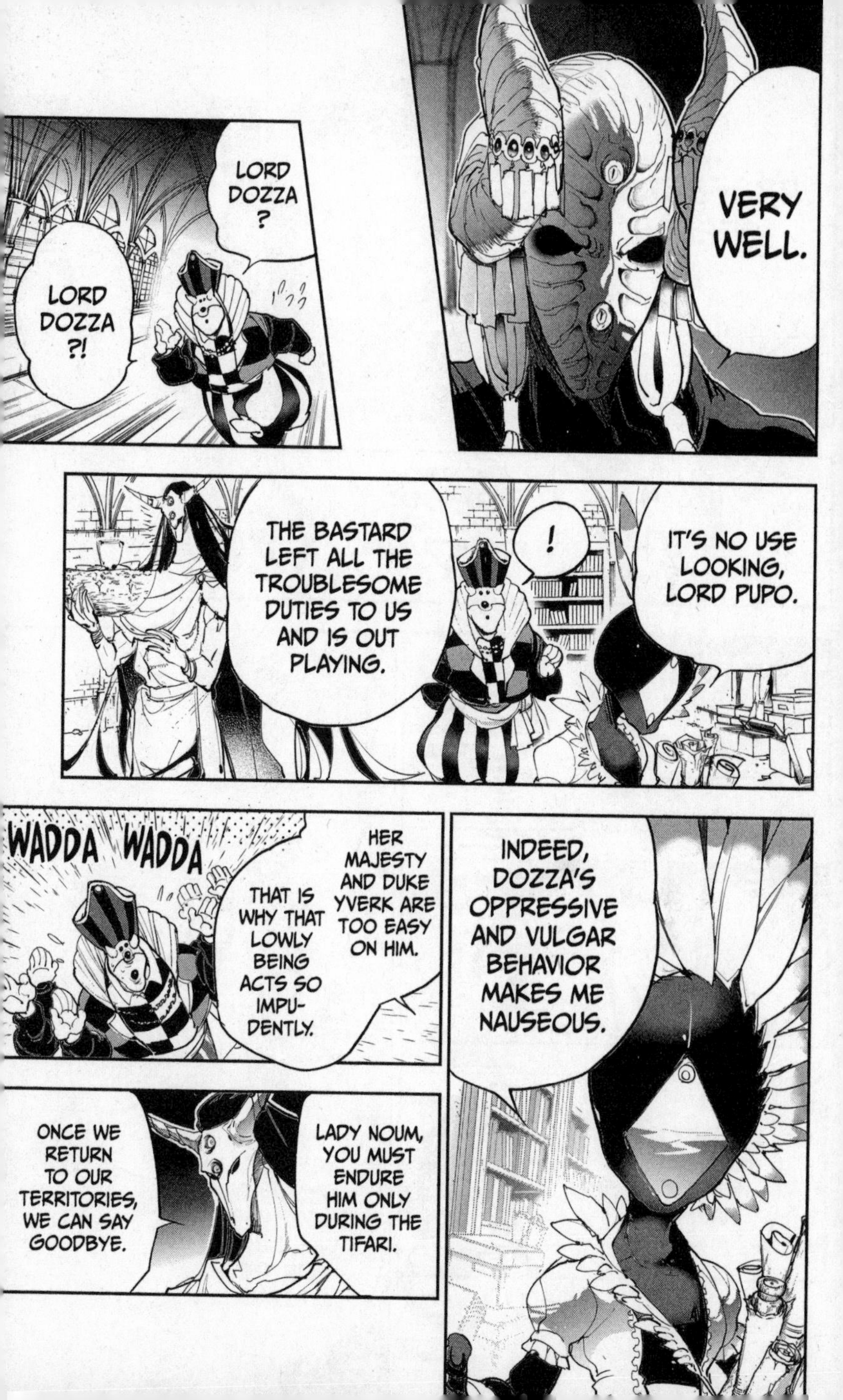
VERY WELL.
LORD DOZZA ?
LORD DOZZA ?!
IT'S NO USE LOOKING, LORD PUPO.
!
THE BASTARD LEFT ALL THE TROUBLESOME DUTIES TO US AND IS OUT PLAYING.
INDEED, DOZZA'S OPPRESSIVE AND VULGAR BEHAVIOR MAKES ME NAUSEOUS.
HER MAJESTY AND DUKE YVERK ARE TOO EASY ON HIM.
THAT IS WHY THAT LOWLY BEING ACTS SO IMPU- DENTLY.
WADDA WADDA
LADY NOUM, YOU MUST ENDURE HIM ONLY DURING THE TIFARI.
ONCE WE RETURN TO OUR TERRITORIES, WE CAN SAY GOODBYE.

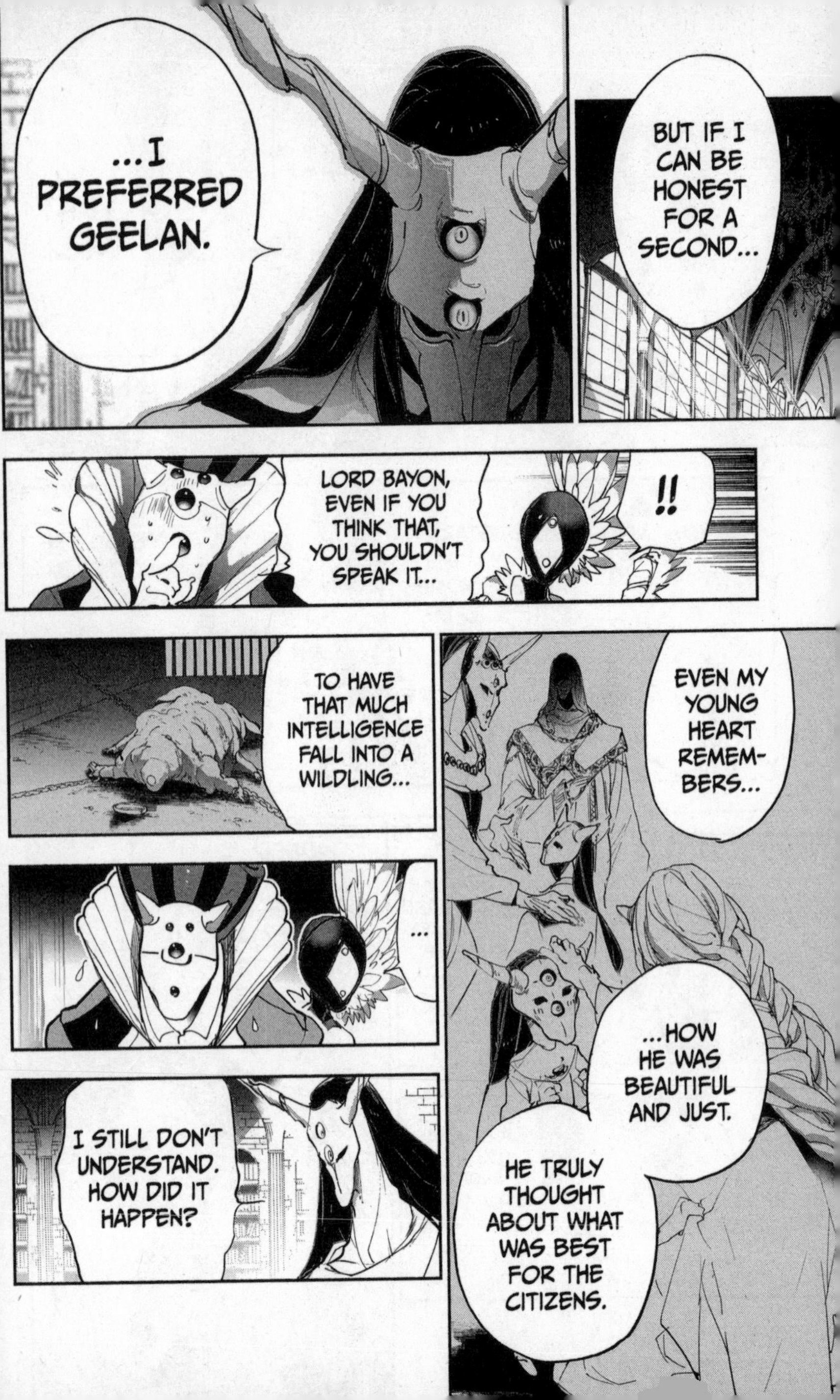
BUT IF I CAN BE HONEST FOR A SECOND...
...I PREFERRED GEELAN.
!!
LORD BAYON, EVEN IF YOU THINK THAT, YOU SHOULDN'T SPEAK IT...
EVEN MY YOUNG HEART REMEMBERS...
...HOW HE WAS BEAUTIFUL AND JUST.
HE TRULY THOUGHT ABOUT WHAT WAS BEST FOR THE CITIZENS.
TO HAVE THAT MUCH INTELLIGENCE FALL INTO A WILDLING...
...
I STILL DON'T UNDERSTAND. HOW DID IT HAPPEN?

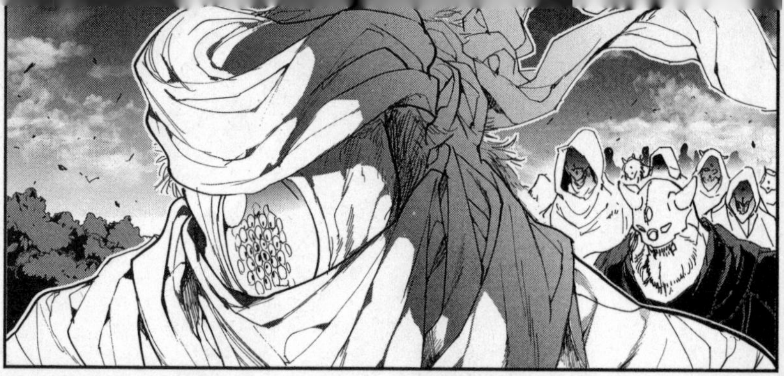
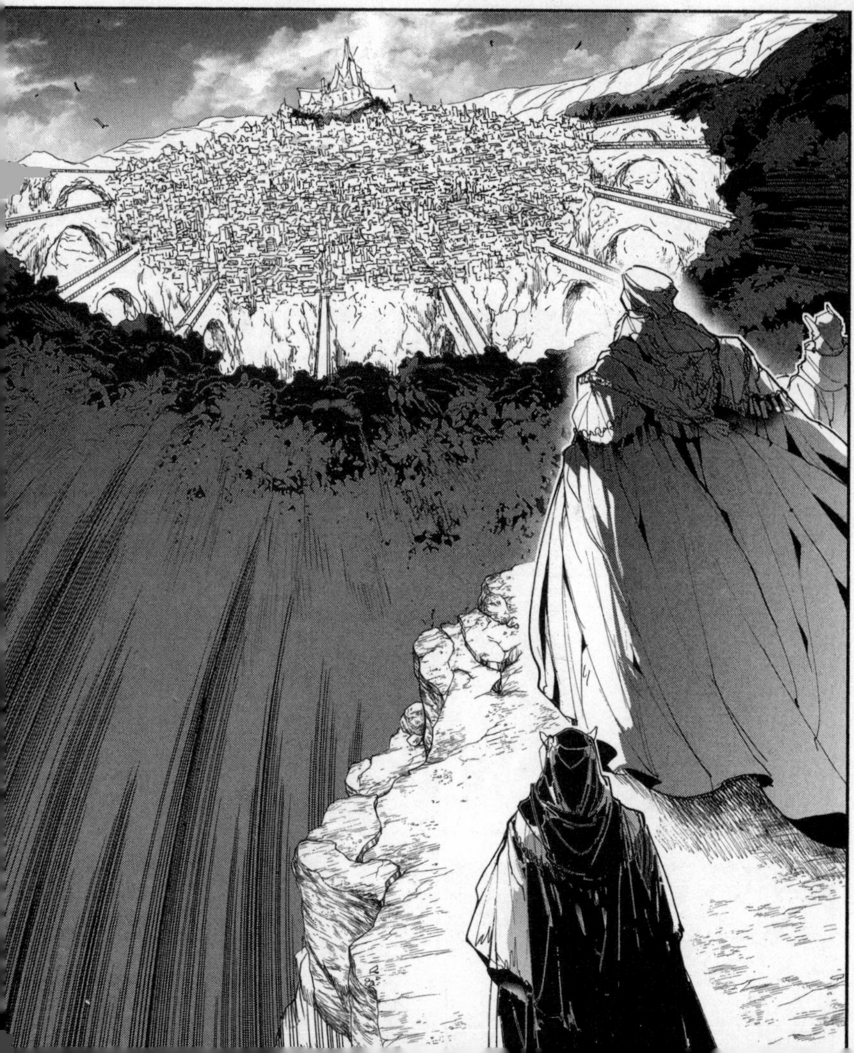

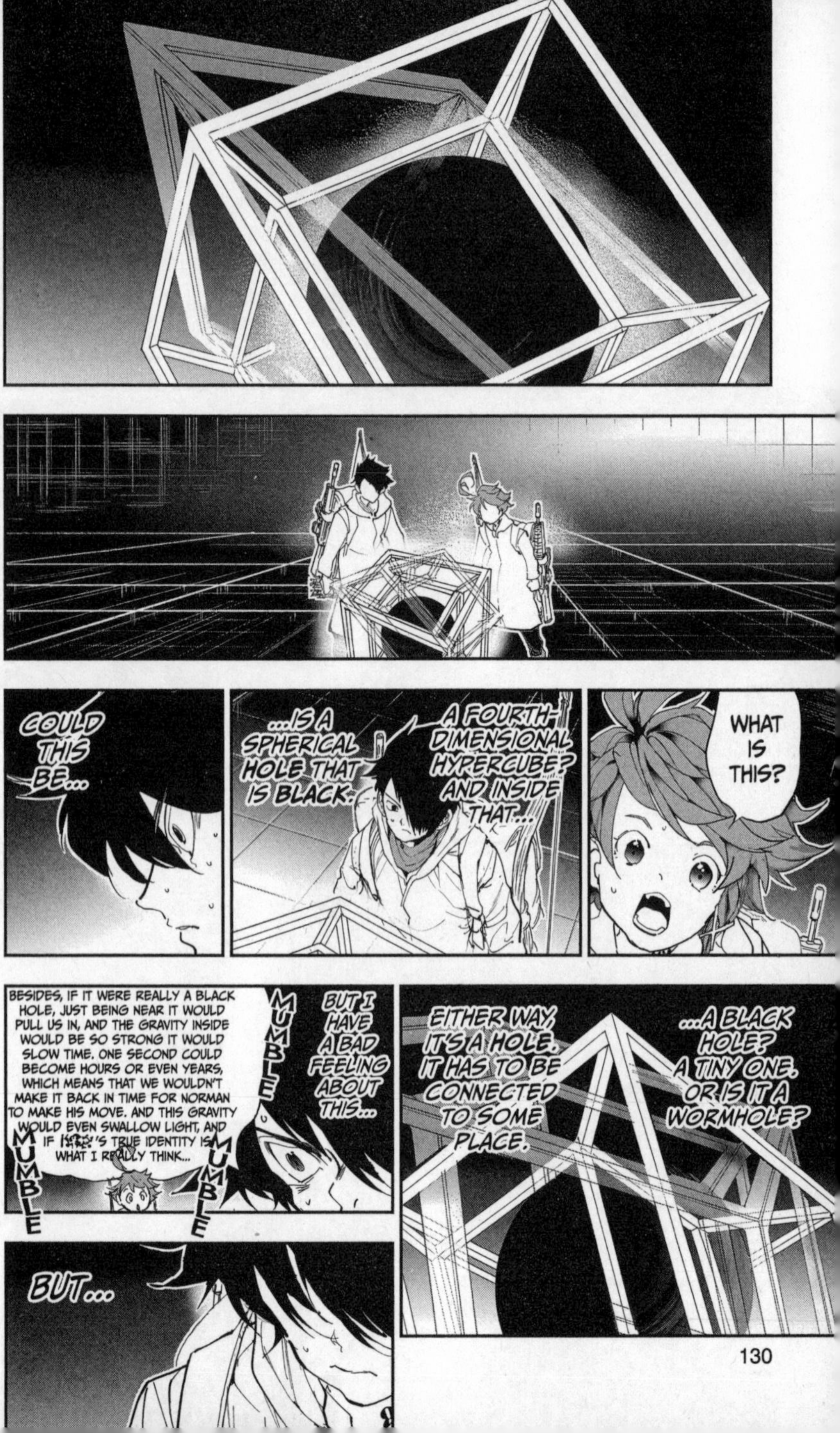
WHAT IS THIS?
A FOURTH-DIMENSIONAL HYPERCUBE? AND INSIDE THAT...
...IS A SPHERICAL HOLE THAT IS BLACK.
COULD THIS BE...
...A BLACK HOLE? A TINY ONE. OR IS IT A WORMHOLE?
EITHER WAY, IT'S A HOLE. IT HAS TO BE CONNECTED TO SOME PLACE.
BUT I HAVE A BAD FEELING ABOUT THIS...
MUMBLE
BESIDES, IF IT WERE REALLY A BLACK HOLE, JUST BEING NEAR IT WOULD PULL US IN, AND THE GRAVITY INSIDE WOULD BE SO STRONG IT WOULD SLOW TIME. ONE SECOND COULD BECOME HOURS OR EVEN YEARS, WHICH MEANS THAT WE WOULDN'T MAKE IT BACK IN TIME FOR NORMAN TO MAKE HIS MOVE. AND THIS GRAVITY WOULD EVEN SWALLOW LIGHT, AND IF 'S TRUE IDENTITY IS WHAT I REALLY THINK...
MUMBLE
MUMBLE
BUT...

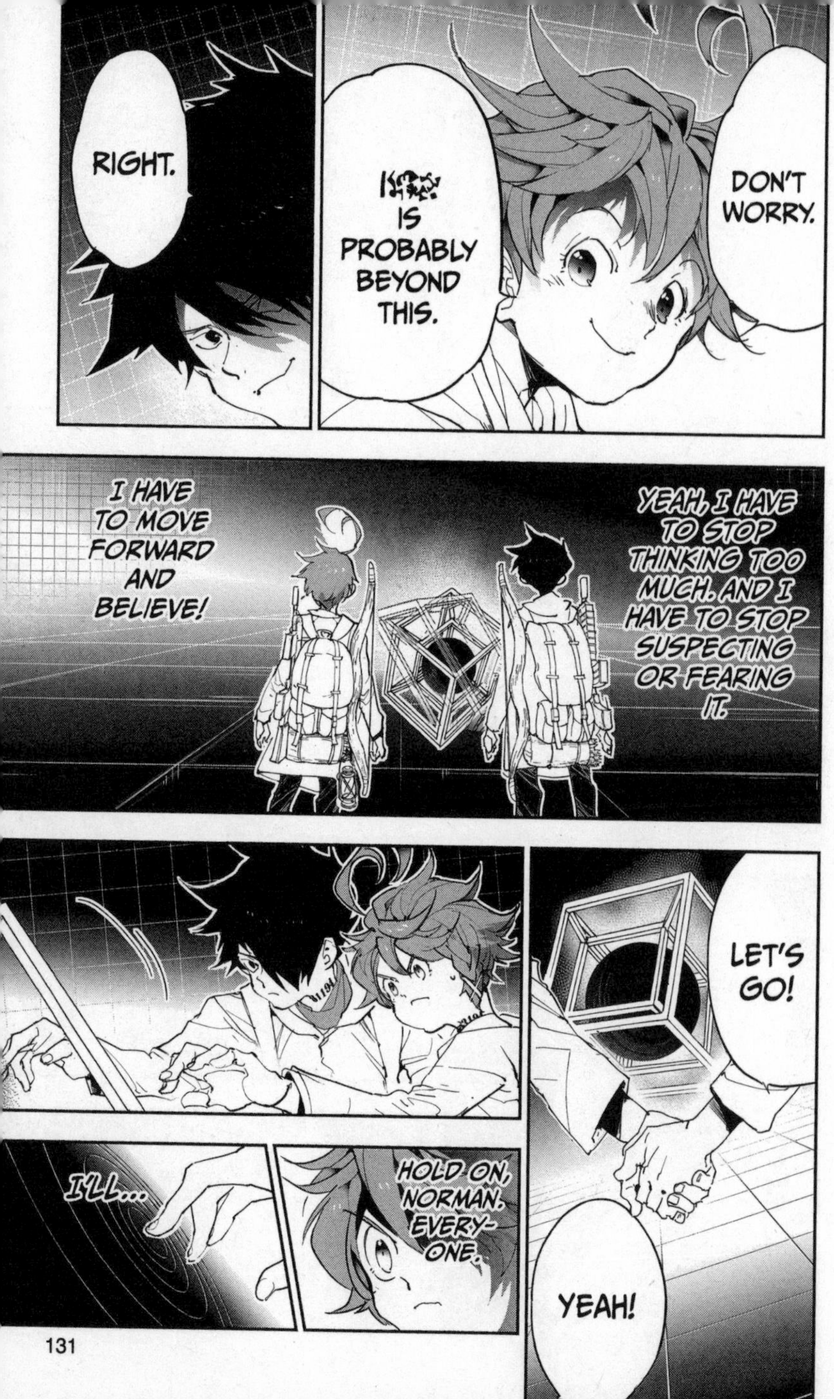

DON'T WORRY.
IS PROBABLY BEYOND THIS.
RIGHT.
YEAH, I HAVE TO STOP THINKING TOO MUCH. AND I HAVE TO STOP SUSPECTING OR FEARING IT.
I HAVE TO MOVE FORWARD AND BELIEVE!
LET'S GO!
YEAH!
HOLD ON, NORMAN. EVERY-ONE.
I'LL...

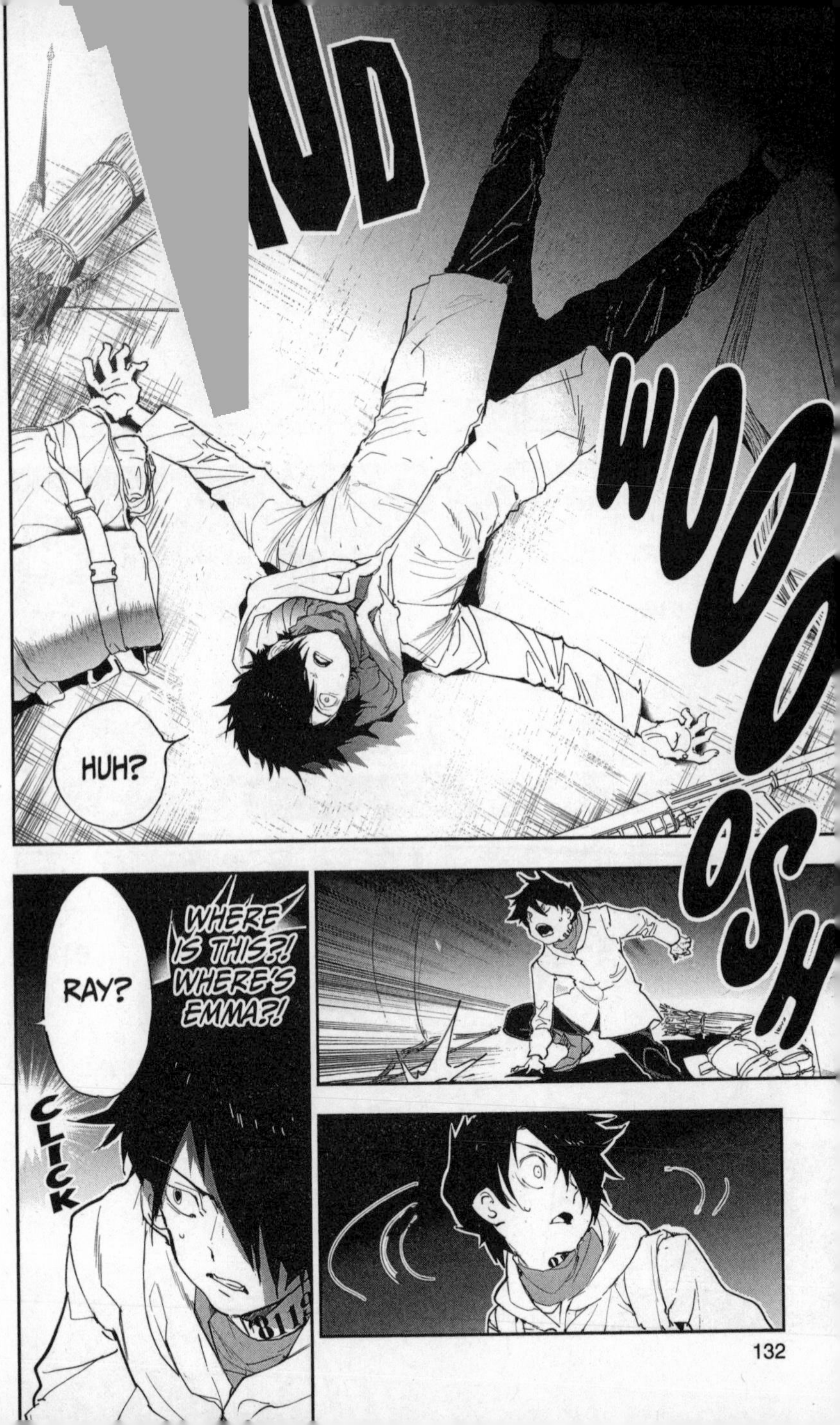
WOOOOOSH
HUH?
WHERE IS THIS?! WHERE'S EMMA?!
RAY?
CLICK

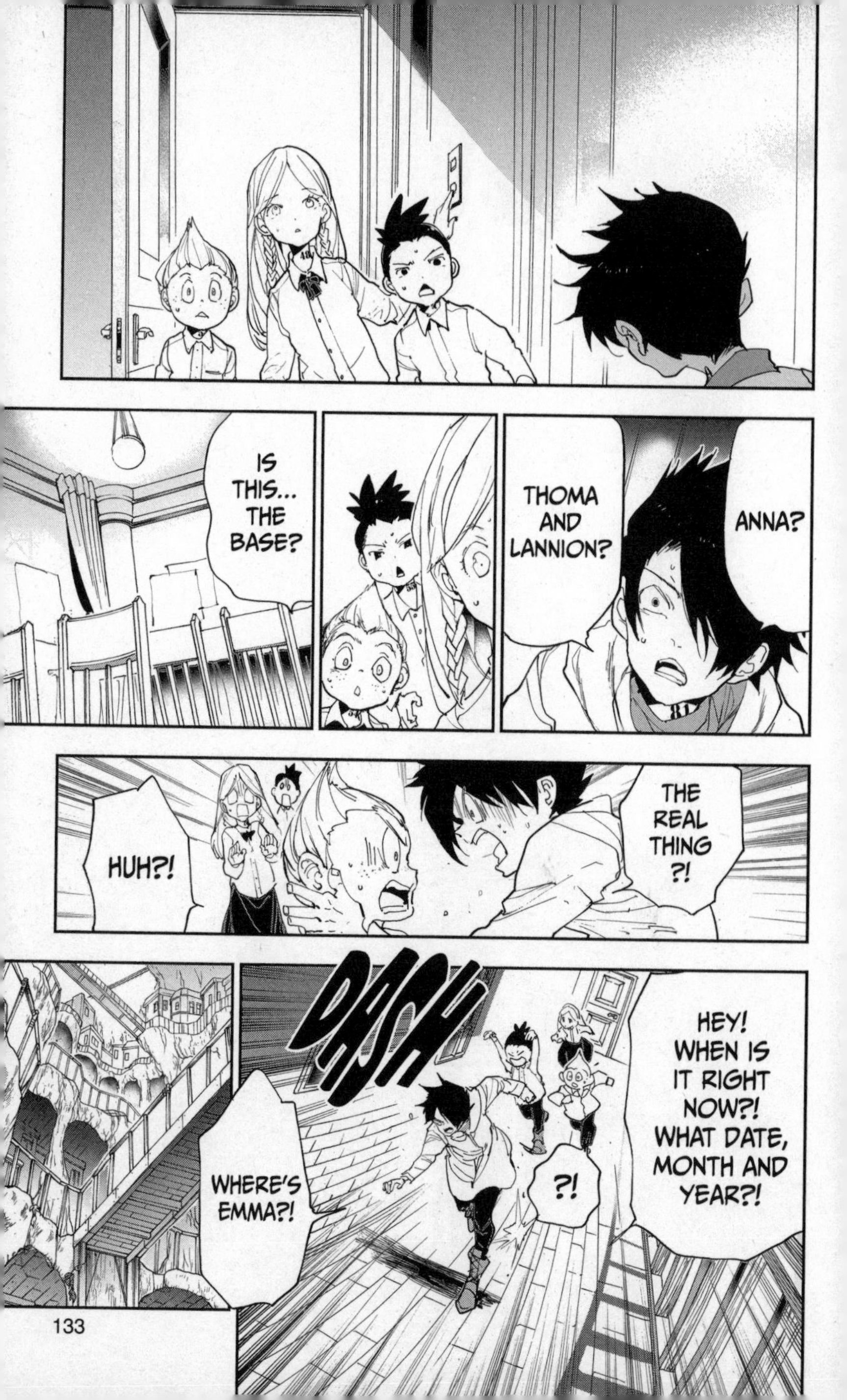
ANNA?
THOMA AND LANNION?
IS THIS... THE BASE?
THE REAL THING?!
HUH?!
HEY! WHEN IS IT RIGHT NOW?! WHAT DATE, MONTH AND YEAR?!
DASH
?!
WHERE'S EMMA?!

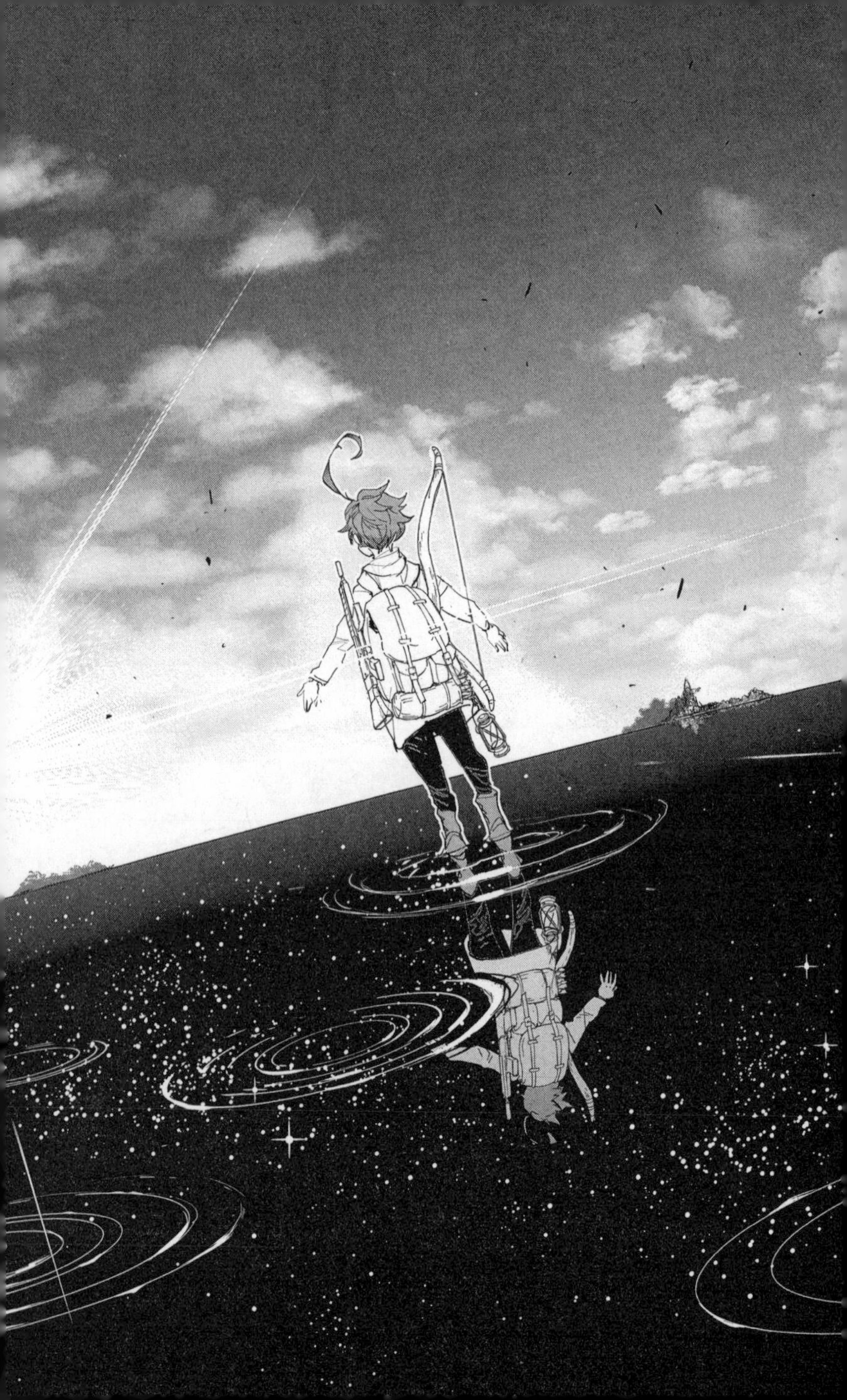

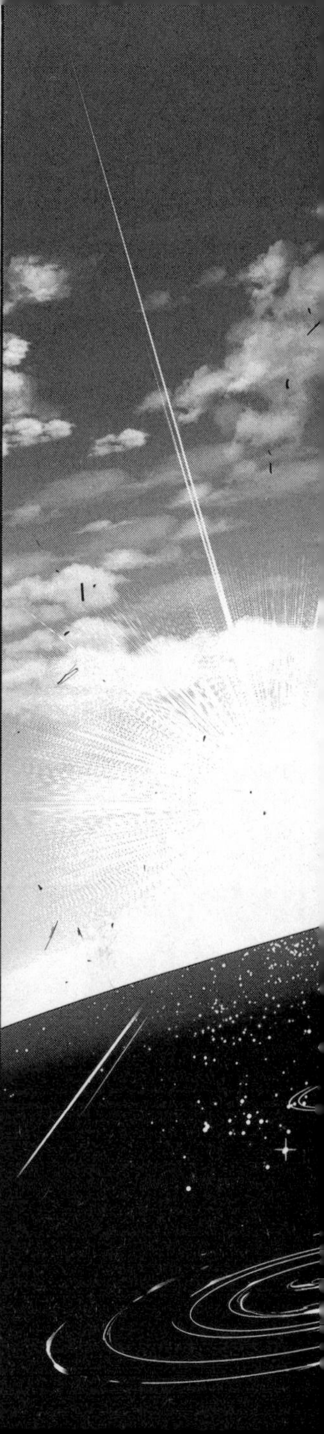

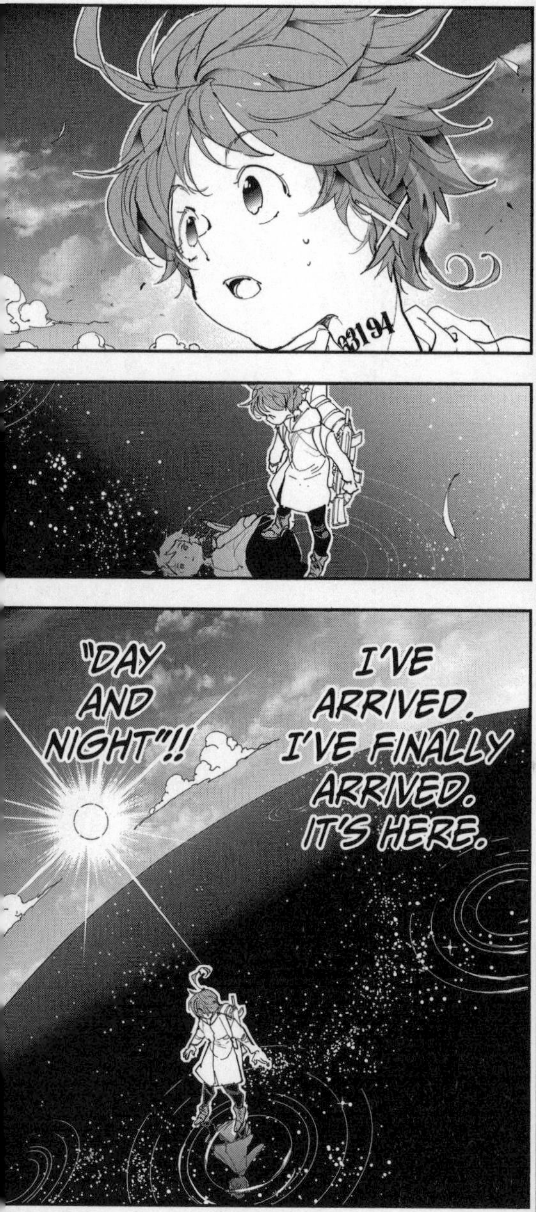
I'VE ARRIVED. I'VE FINALLY ARRIVED. IT'S HERE.
"DAY AND NIGHT"!!

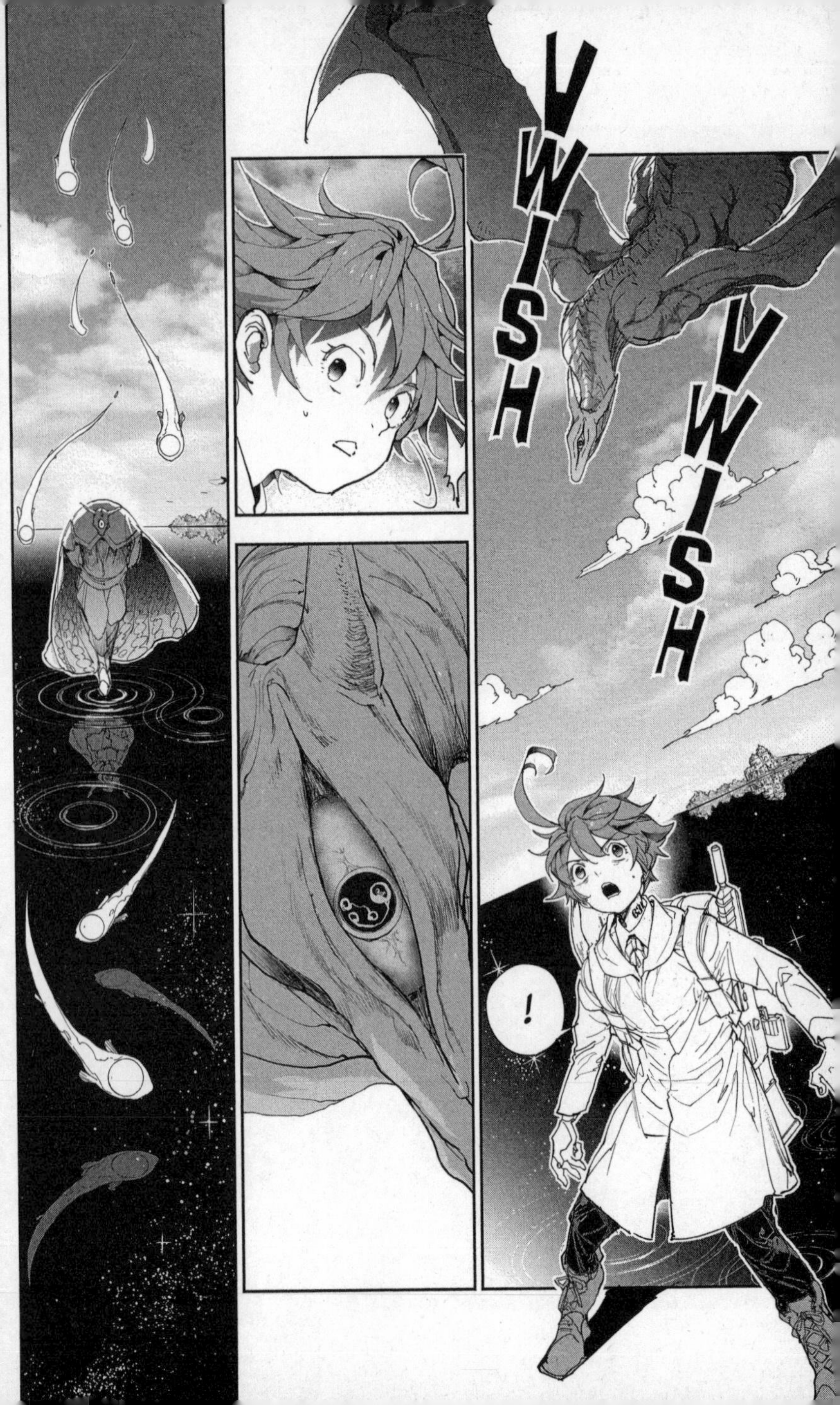
VWISH
VWISH
!

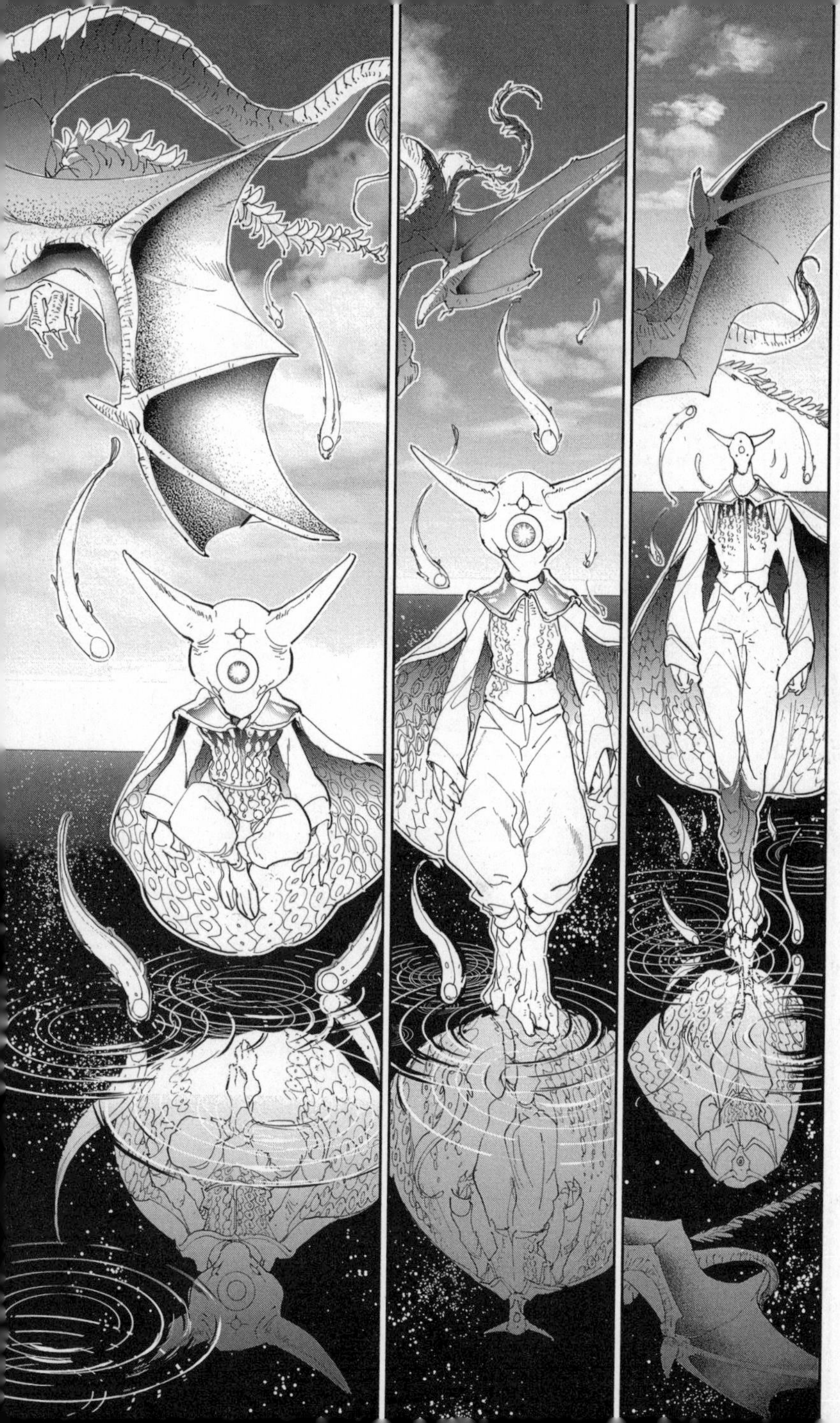

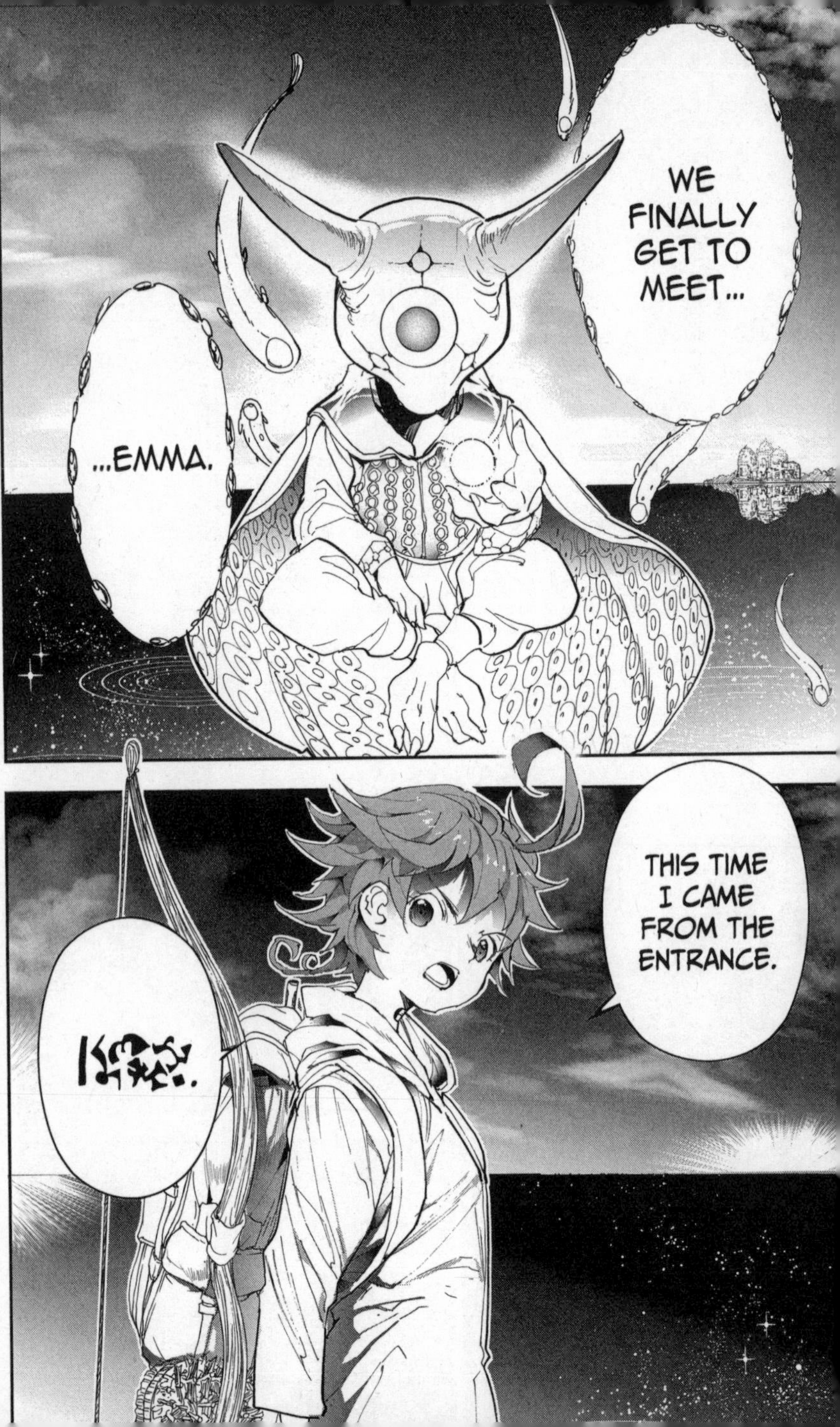
WE FINALLY GET TO MEET...
...EMMA.
THIS TIME I CAME FROM THE ENTRANCE.

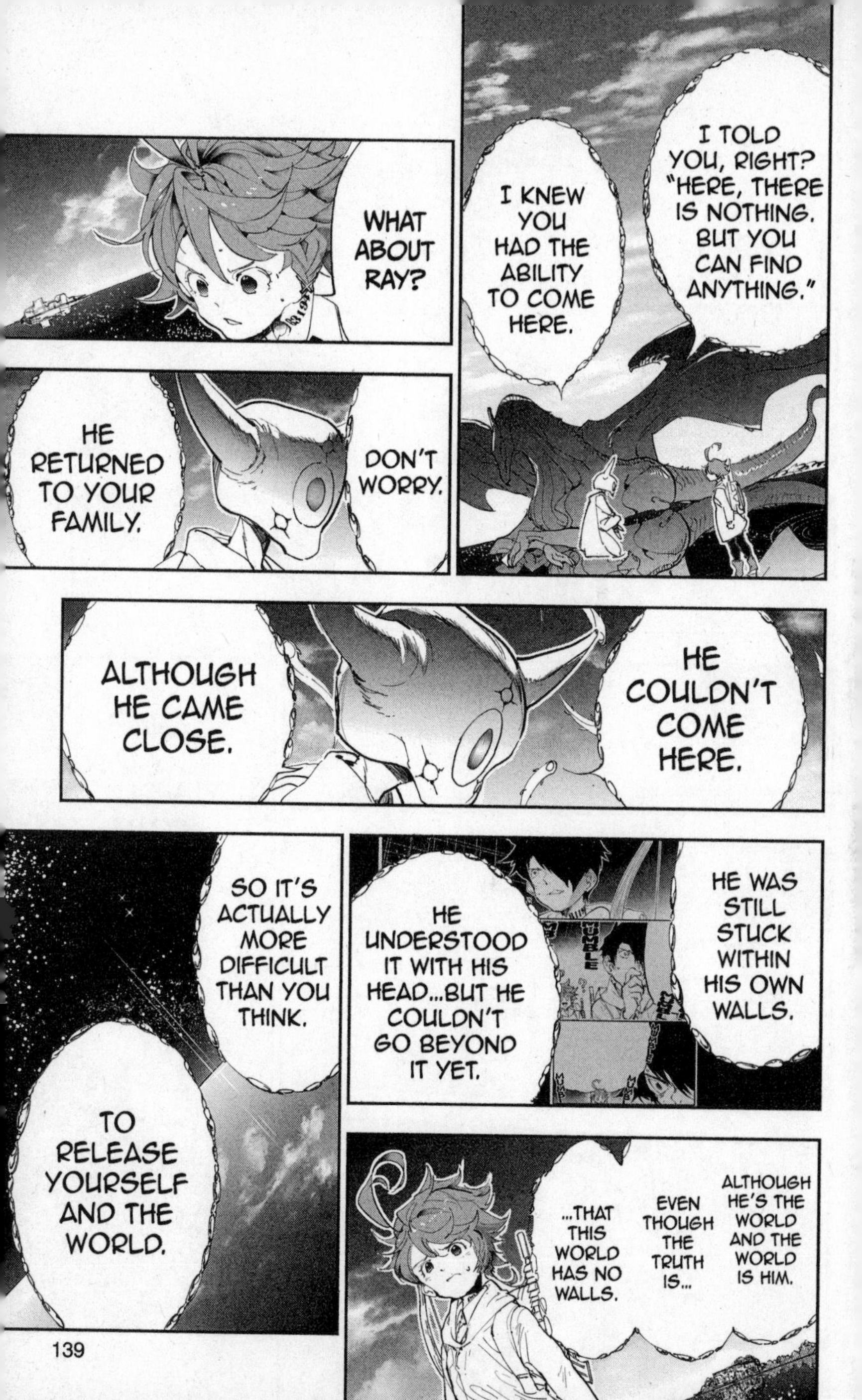
I TOLD YOU, RIGHT? "HERE, THERE IS NOTHING. BUT YOU CAN FIND ANYTHING."
I KNEW YOU HAD THE ABILITY TO COME HERE.
WHAT ABOUT RAY?
DON'T WORRY.
HE RETURNED TO YOUR FAMILY.
HE COULDN'T COME HERE.
ALTHOUGH HE CAME CLOSE.
HE WAS STILL STUCK WITHIN HIS OWN WALLS.
HE UNDERSTOOD IT WITH HIS HEAD...BUT HE COULDN'T GO BEYOND IT YET.
MUMBLE
ALTHOUGH HE'S THE WORLD AND THE WORLD IS HIM.
EVEN THOUGH THE TRUTH IS...
...THAT THIS WORLD HAS NO WALLS.
SO IT'S ACTUALLY MORE DIFFICULT THAN YOU THINK.
TO RELEASE YOURSELF AND THE WORLD.

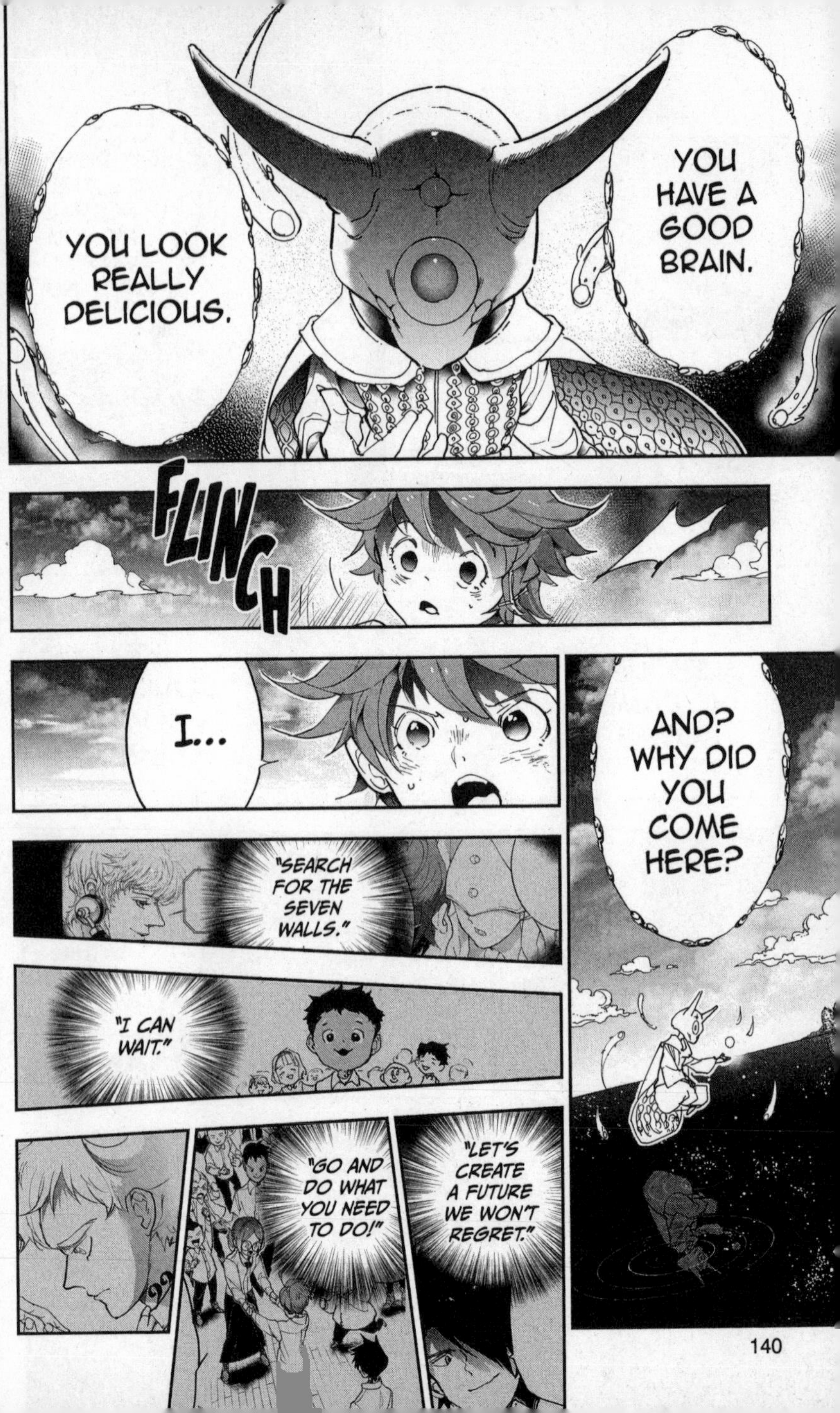
YOU HAVE A GOOD BRAIN.
YOU LOOK REALLY DELICIOUS.
FLINCH
AND? WHY DID YOU COME HERE?
I...
"SEARCH FOR THE SEVEN WALLS."
"I CAN WAIT."
"LET'S CREATE A FUTURE WE WON'T REGRET."
"GO AND DO WHAT YOU NEED TO DO!"

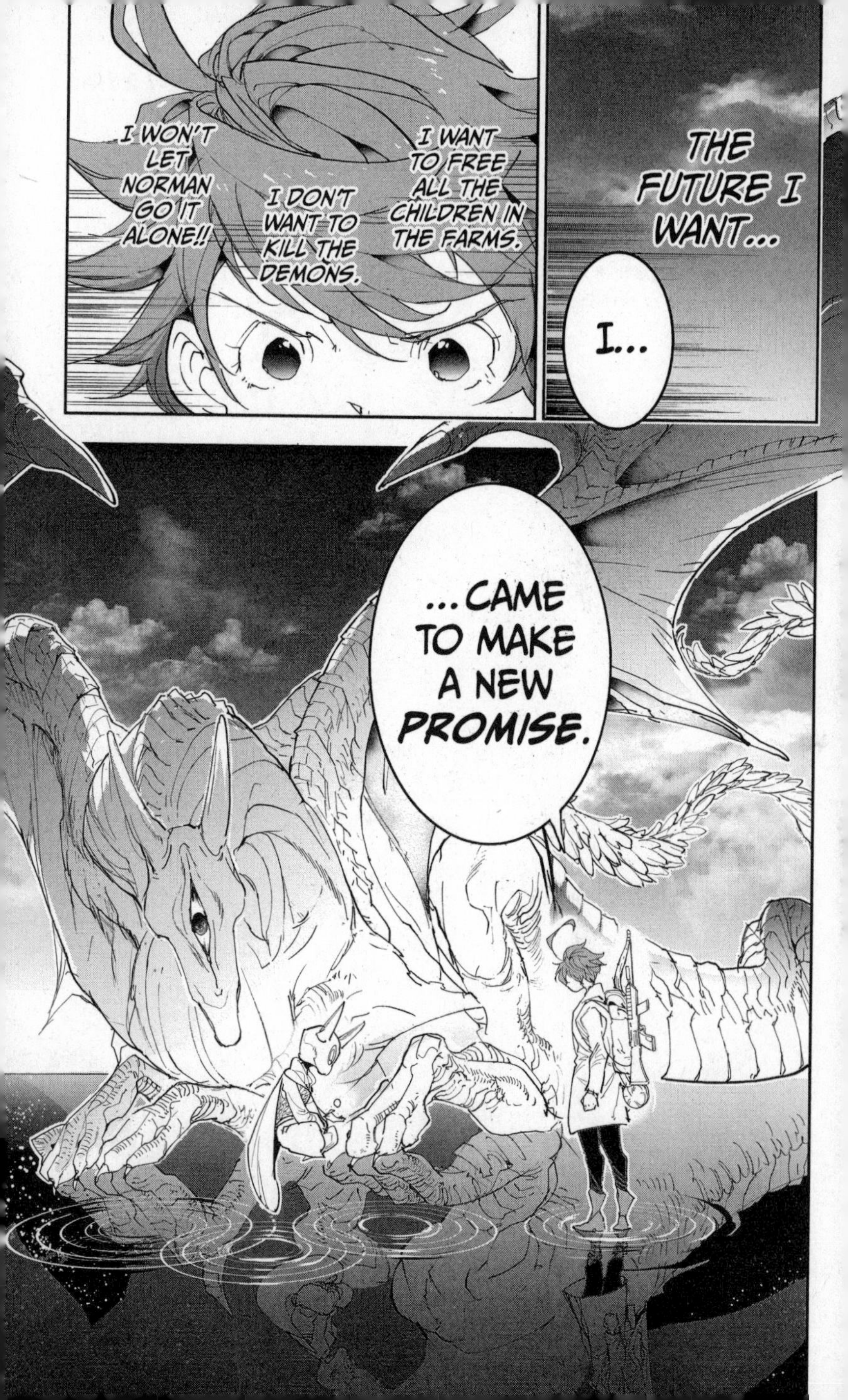
THE FUTURE I WANT...
I...
I WANT TO FREE ALL THE CHILDREN IN THE FARMS.
I DON'T WANT TO KILL THE DEMONS.
I WON'T LET NORMAN GO IT ALONE!!
...CAME TO MAKE A NEW PROMISE.

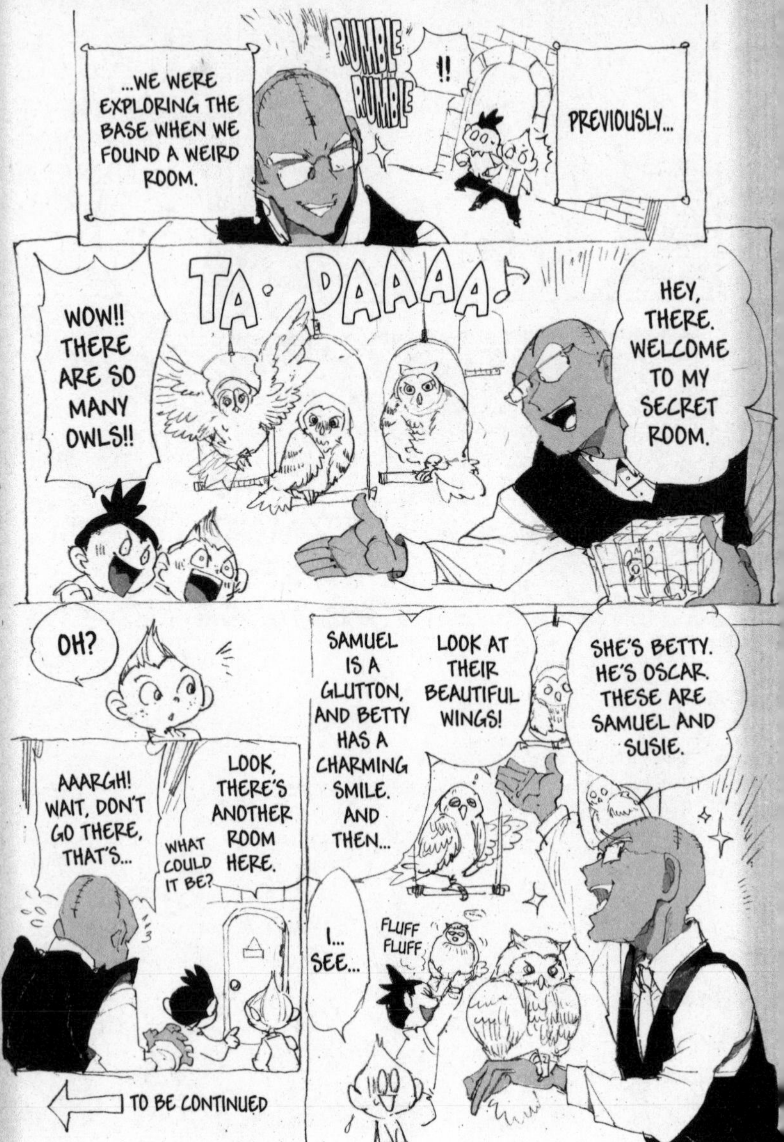
PREVIOUSLY...
RUMBLE RUMBLE
!!
...WE WERE EXPLORING THE BASE WHEN WE FOUND A WEIRD ROOM.
HEY, THERE. WELCOME TO MY SECRET ROOM.
TA-DAAAA♪
WOW!! THERE ARE SO MANY OWLS!!
SHE'S BETTY. HE'S OSCAR. THESE ARE SAMUEL AND SUSIE.
LOOK AT THEIR BEAUTIFUL WINGS!
SAMUEL IS A GLUTTON, AND BETTY HAS A CHARMING SMILE. AND THEN...
I... SEE...
FLUFF FLUFF
OH?
LOOK, THERE'S ANOTHER ROOM HERE.
WHAT COULD IT BE?
AAARGH! WAIT, DON'T GO THERE, THAT'S...
TO BE CONTINUED

TO BE CONTINUED IN A SPECIAL EXTRA PART 2, CHAPTER 3

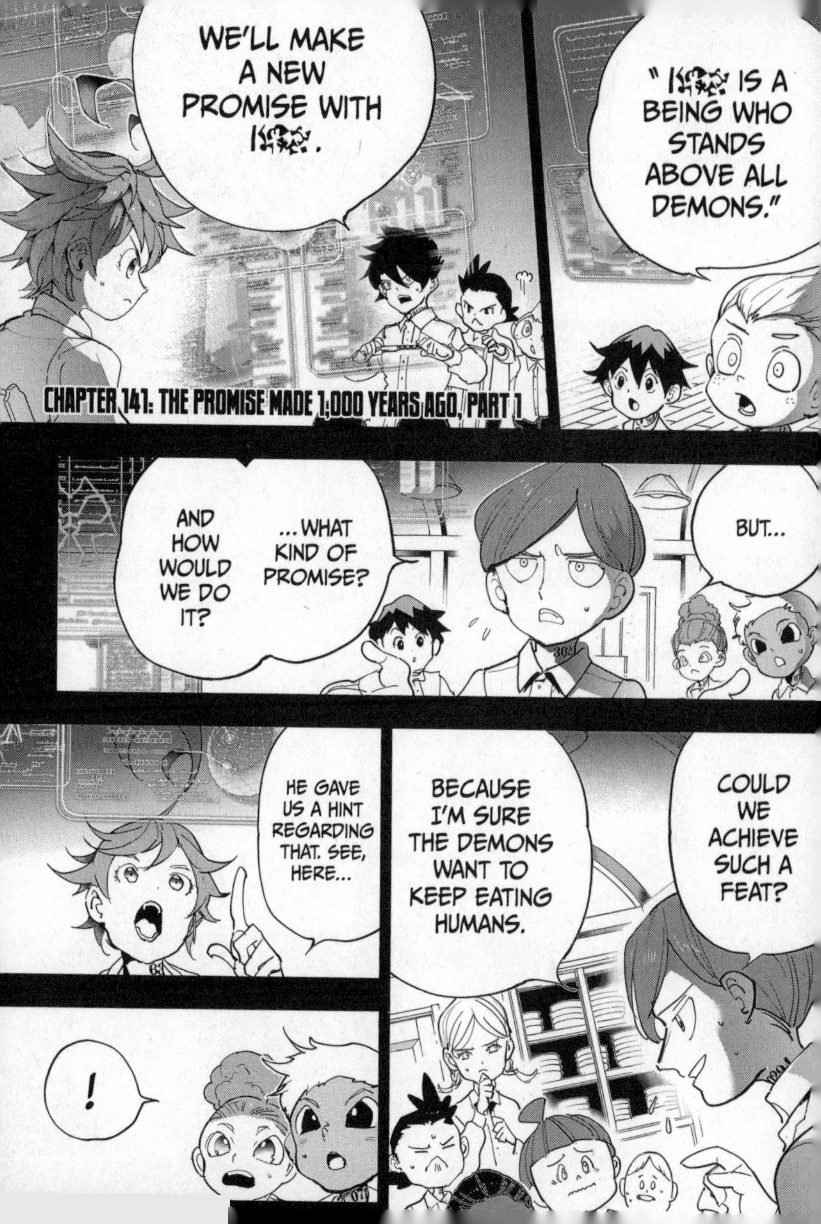
" IS A BEING WHO STANDS ABOVE ALL DEMONS."
WE'LL MAKE A NEW PROMISE WITH .
CHAPTER 141: THE PROMISE MADE 1,000 YEARS AGO, PART 1
BUT...
...WHAT KIND OF PROMISE?
AND HOW WOULD WE DO IT?
COULD WE ACHIEVE SUCH A FEAT?
BECAUSE I'M SURE THE DEMONS WANT TO KEEP EATING HUMANS.
HE GAVE US A HINT REGARDING THAT. SEE, HERE...
!

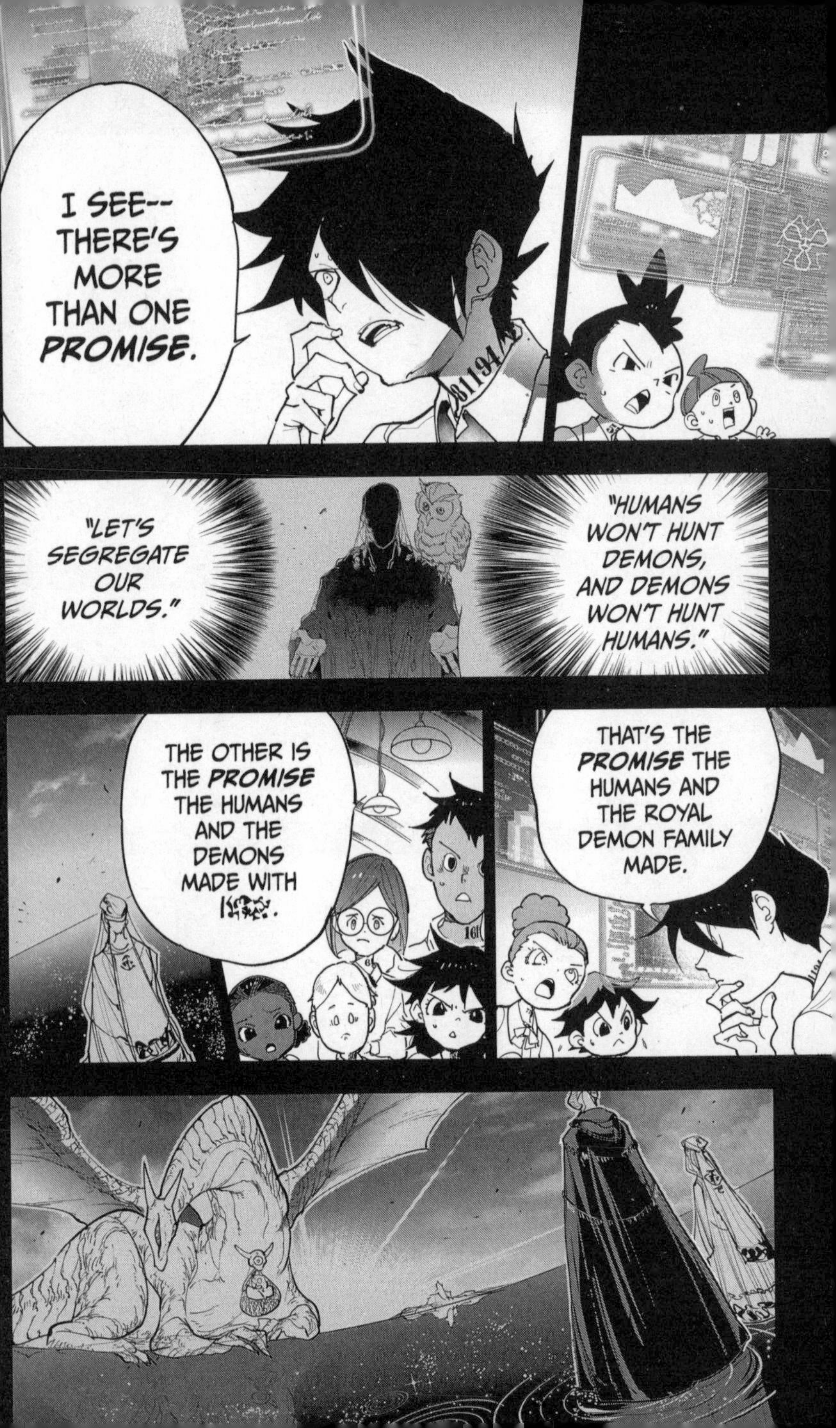
I SEE-- THERE'S MORE THAN ONE *PROMISE*.
"HUMANS WON'T HUNT DEMONS, AND DEMONS WON'T HUNT HUMANS."
"LET'S SEGREGATE OUR WORLDS."
THAT'S THE *PROMISE* THE HUMANS AND THE ROYAL DEMON FAMILY MADE.
THE OTHER IS THE *PROMISE* THE HUMANS AND THE DEMONS MADE WITH

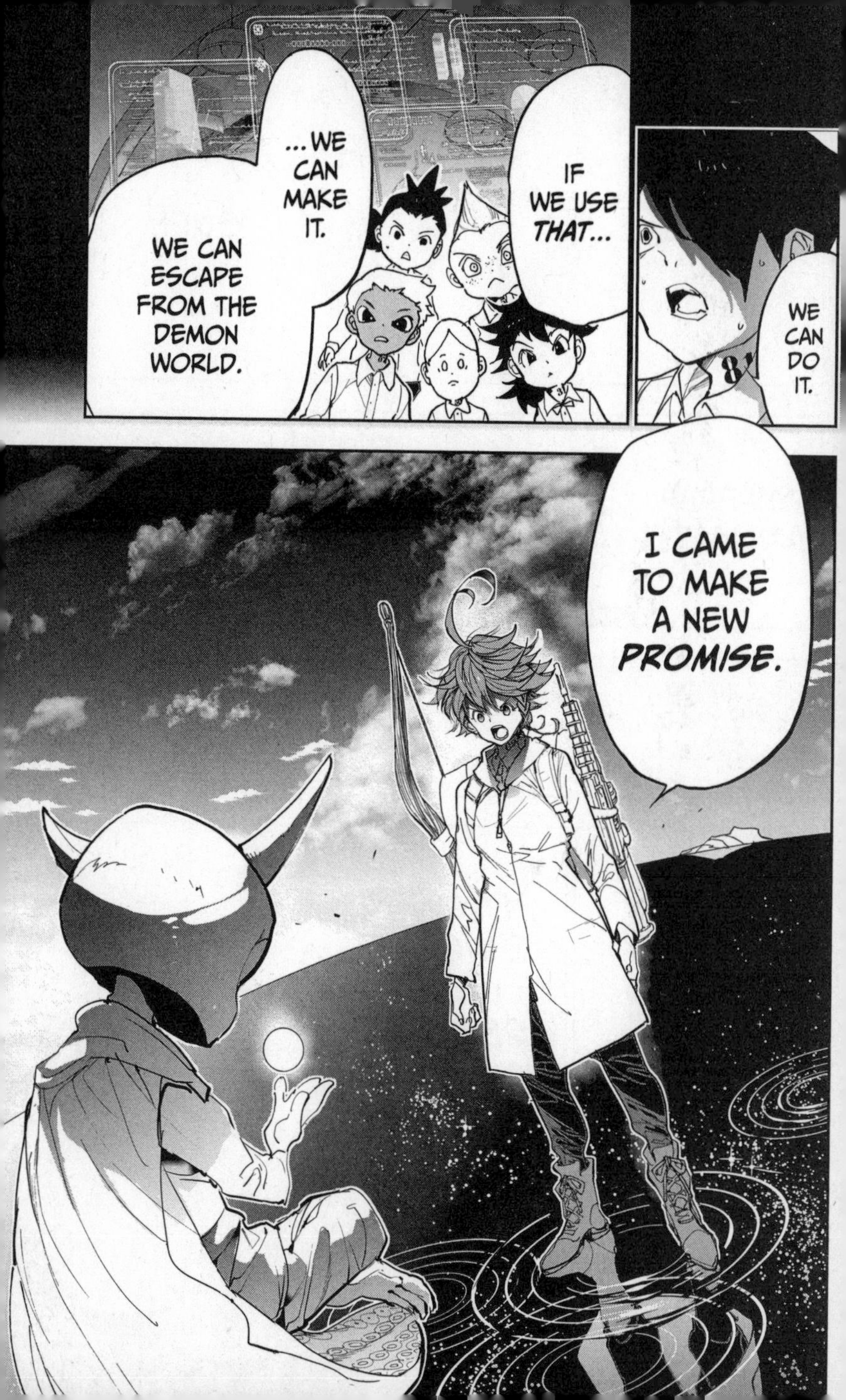
WE CAN DO IT.
IF WE USE *THAT*...
...WE CAN MAKE IT.
WE CAN ESCAPE FROM THE DEMON WORLD.
I CAME TO MAKE A NEW ***PROMISE***.

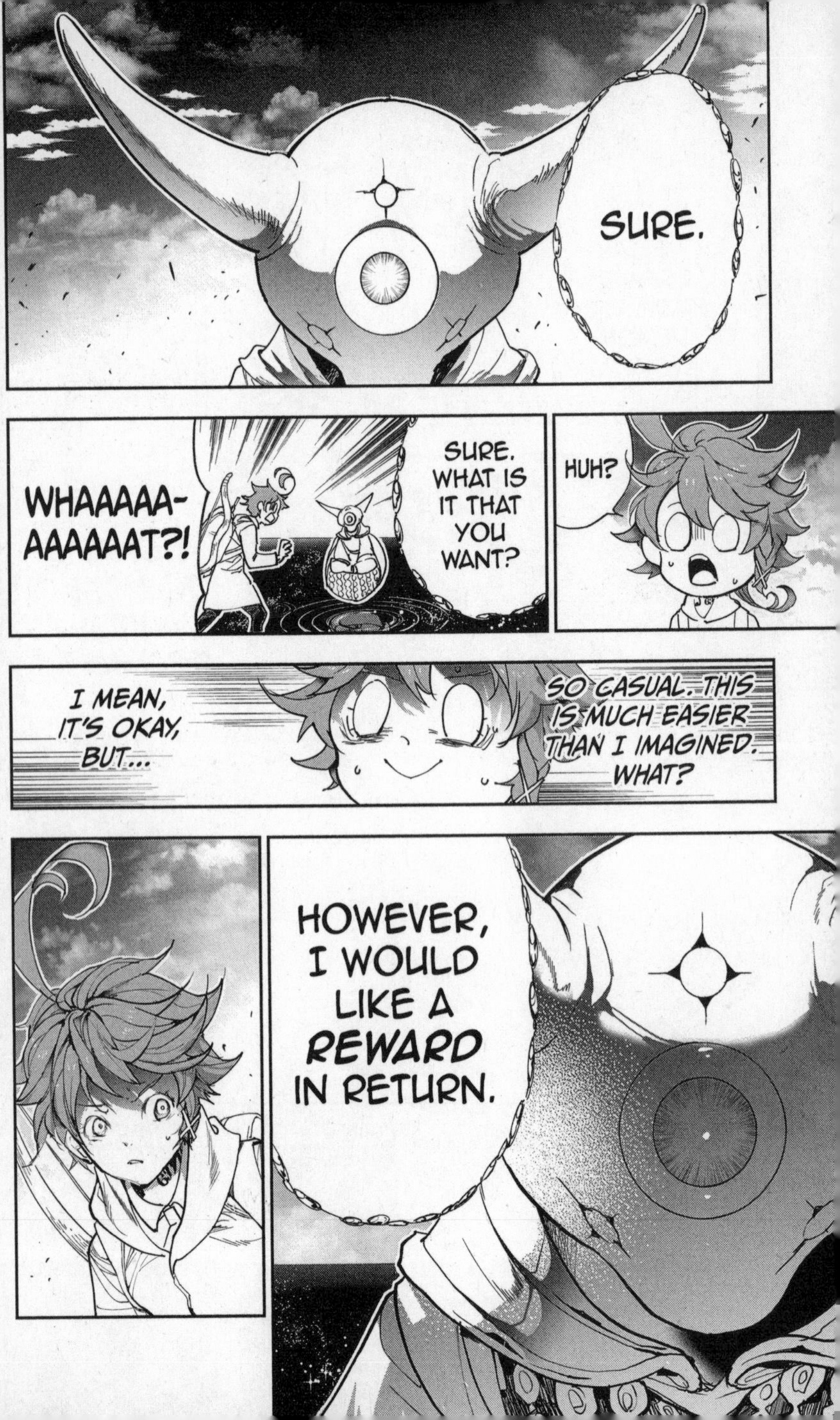
SURE.
HUH?
SURE. WHAT IS IT THAT YOU WANT?
WHAAAAA-AAAAAAT?!
SO CASUAL. THIS IS MUCH EASIER THAN I IMAGINED. WHAT?
I MEAN, IT'S OKAY, BUT...
HOWEVER, I WOULD LIKE A *REWARD* IN RETURN.

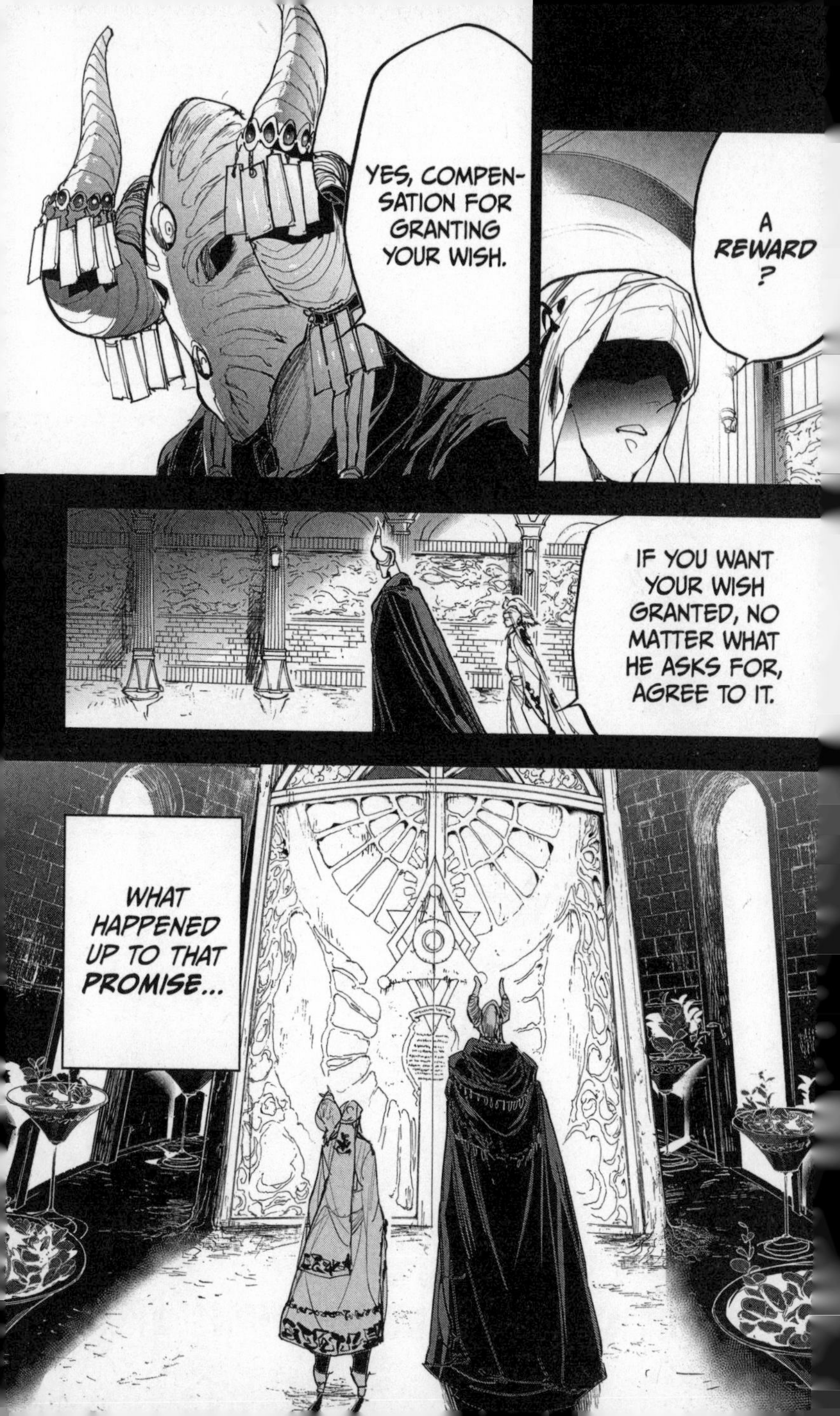
A REWARD?
YES, COMPENSATION FOR GRANTING YOUR WISH.
IF YOU WANT YOUR WISH GRANTED, NO MATTER WHAT HE ASKS FOR, AGREE TO IT.
WHAT HAPPENED UP TO THAT PROMISE...

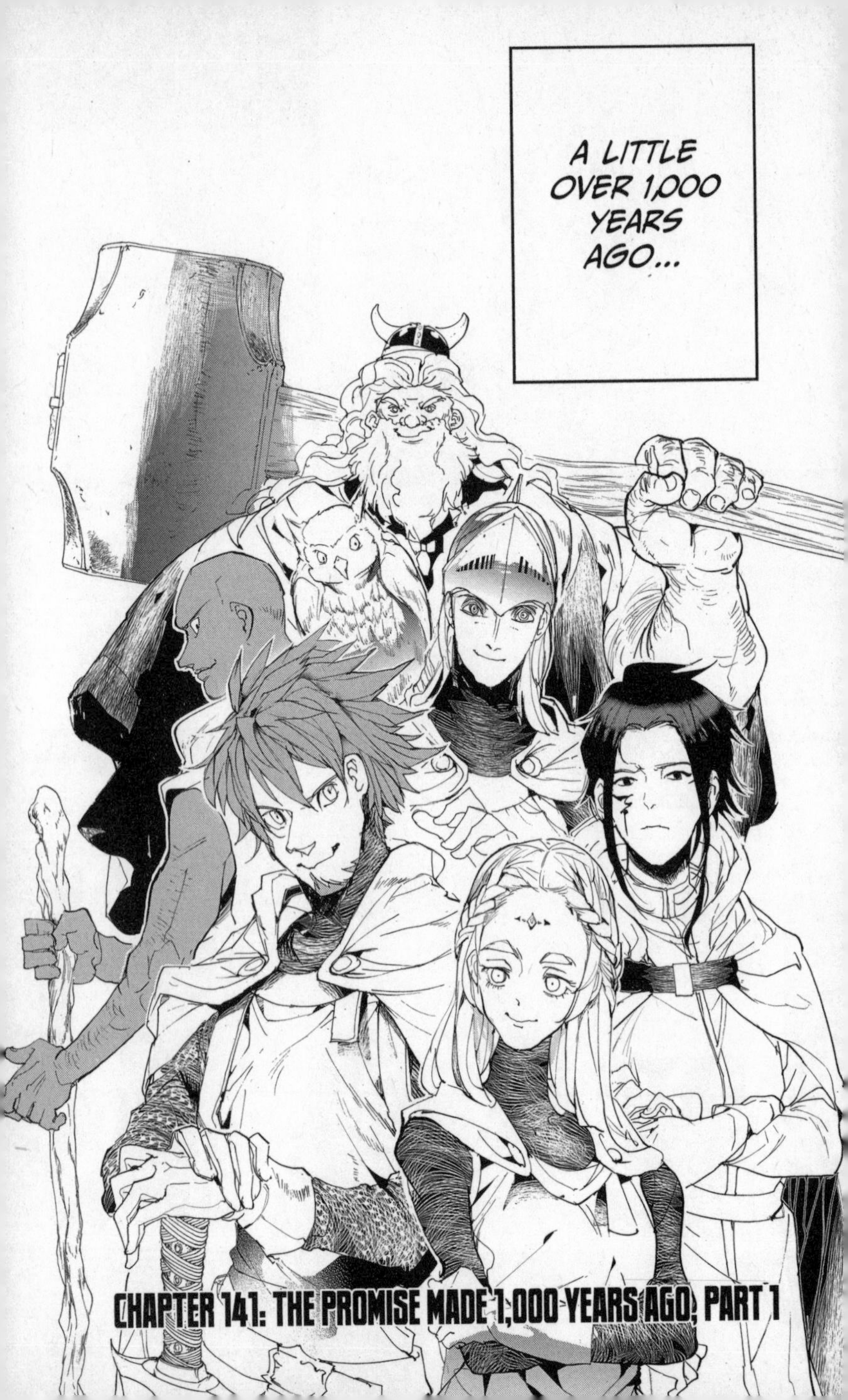
A LITTLE OVER 1,000 YEARS AGO...
CHAPTER 141: THE PROMISE MADE 1,000 YEARS AGO, PART 1

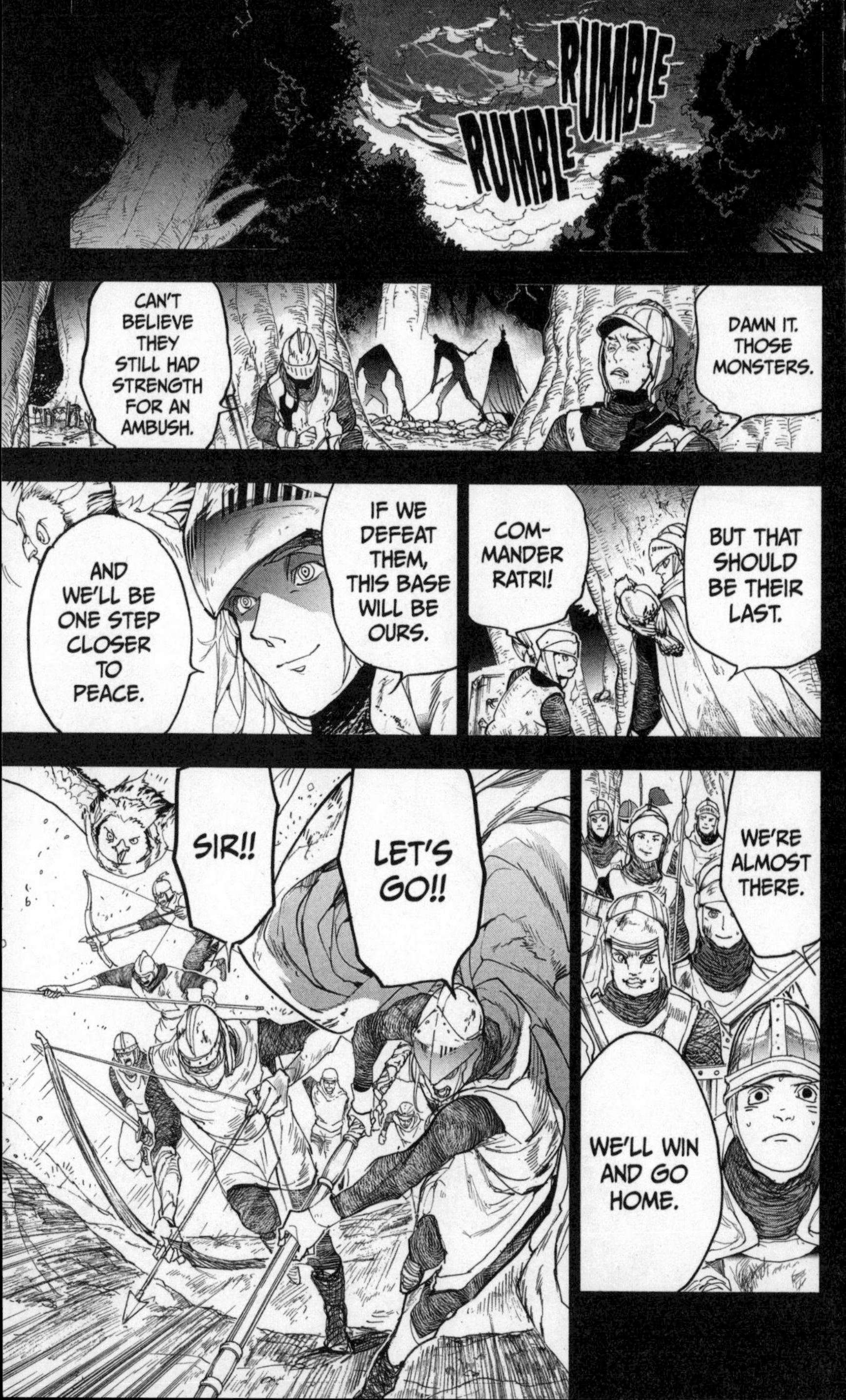
RUMBLE RUMBLE
DAMN IT. THOSE MONSTERS.
CAN'T BELIEVE THEY STILL HAD STRENGTH FOR AN AMBUSH.
BUT THAT SHOULD BE THEIR LAST.
COM-MANDER RATRI!
IF WE DEFEAT THEM, THIS BASE WILL BE OURS.
AND WE'LL BE ONE STEP CLOSER TO PEACE.
WE'RE ALMOST THERE.
WE'LL WIN AND GO HOME.
LET'S GO!!
SIR!!

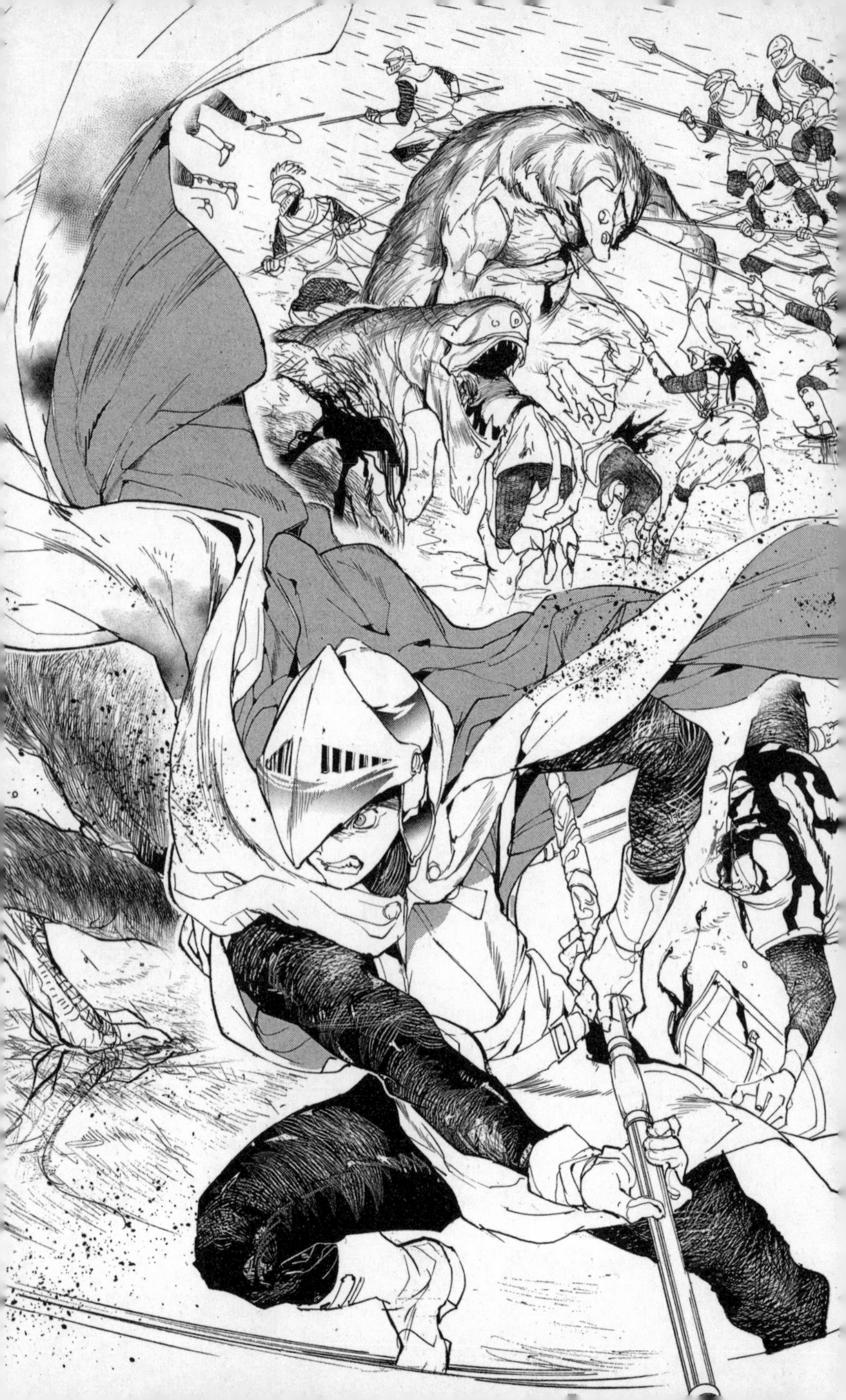

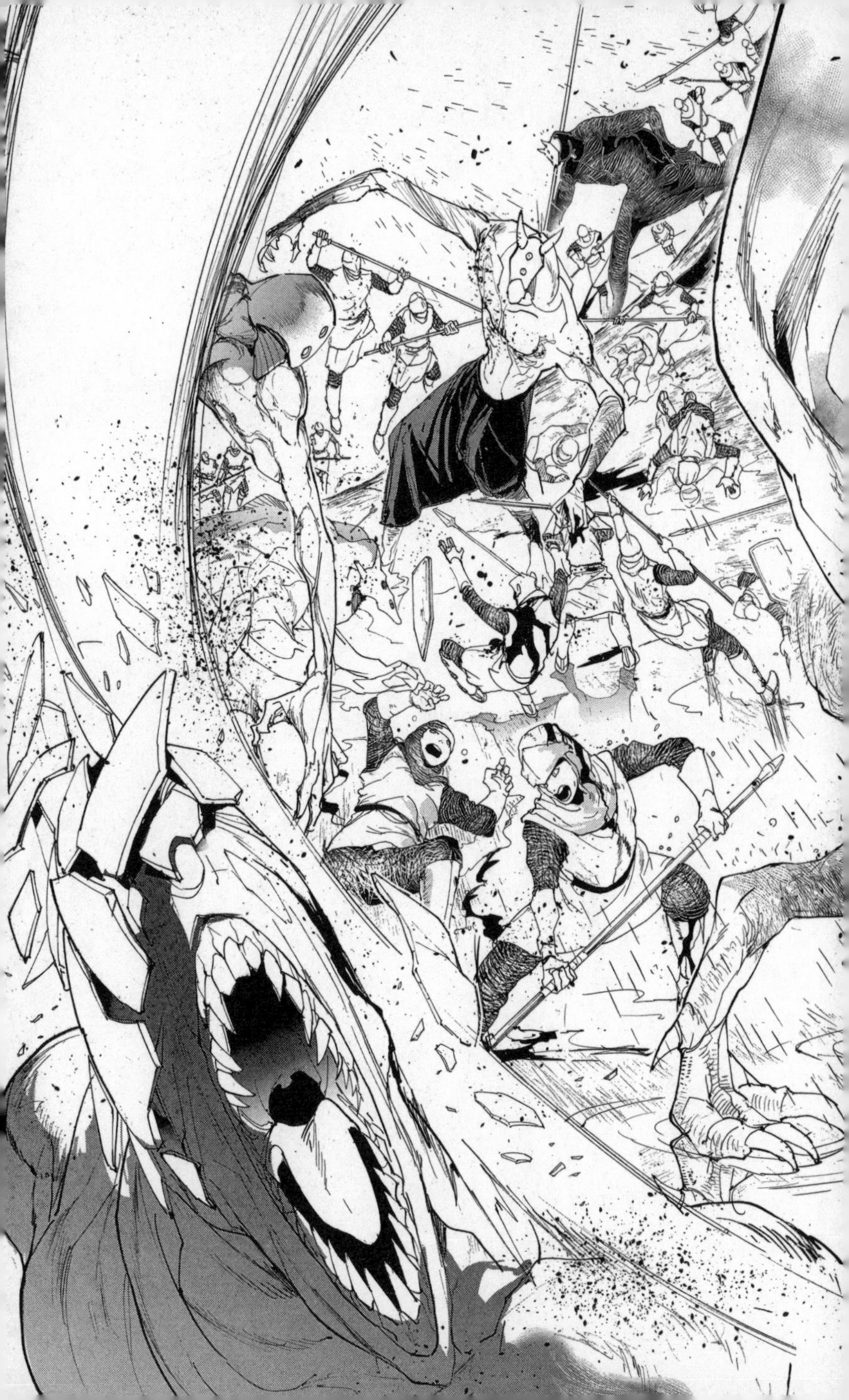

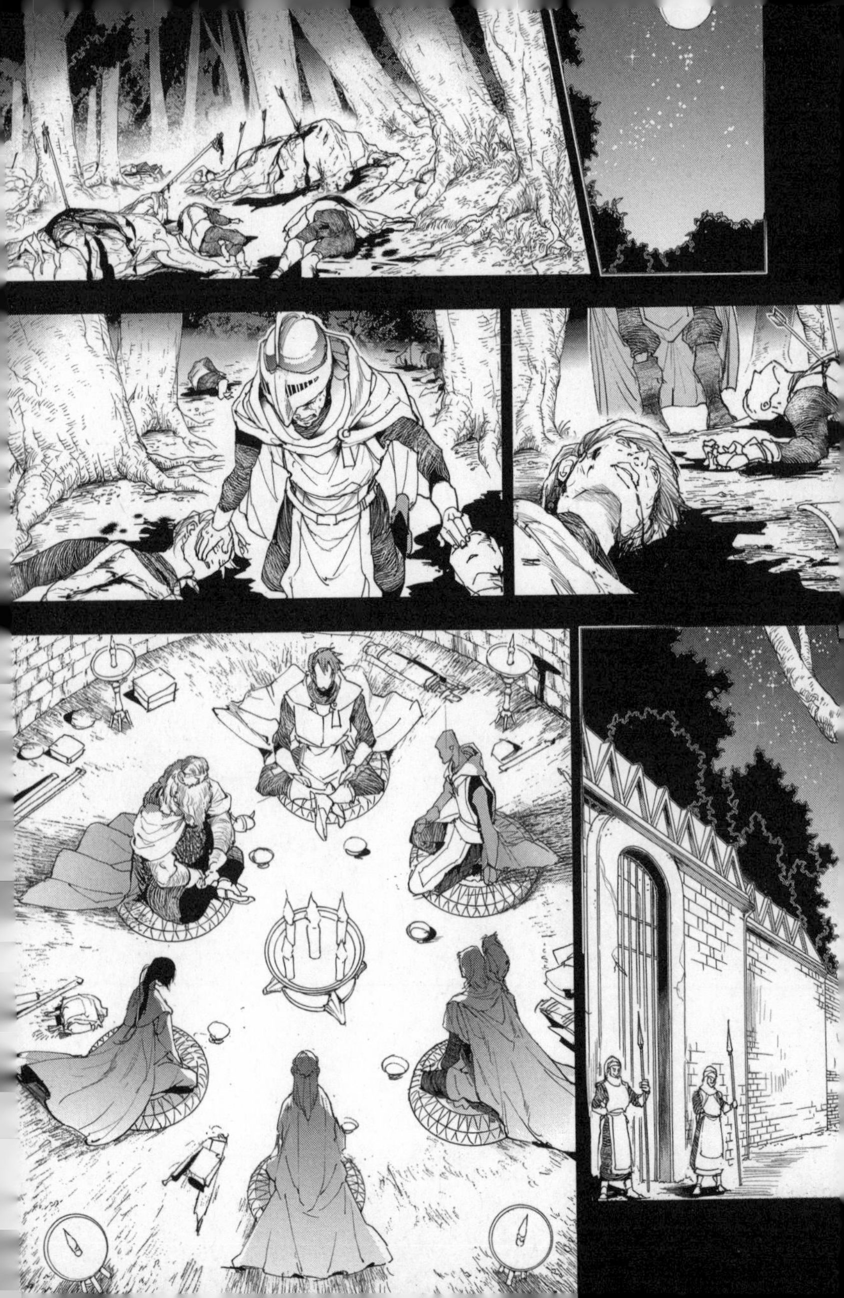

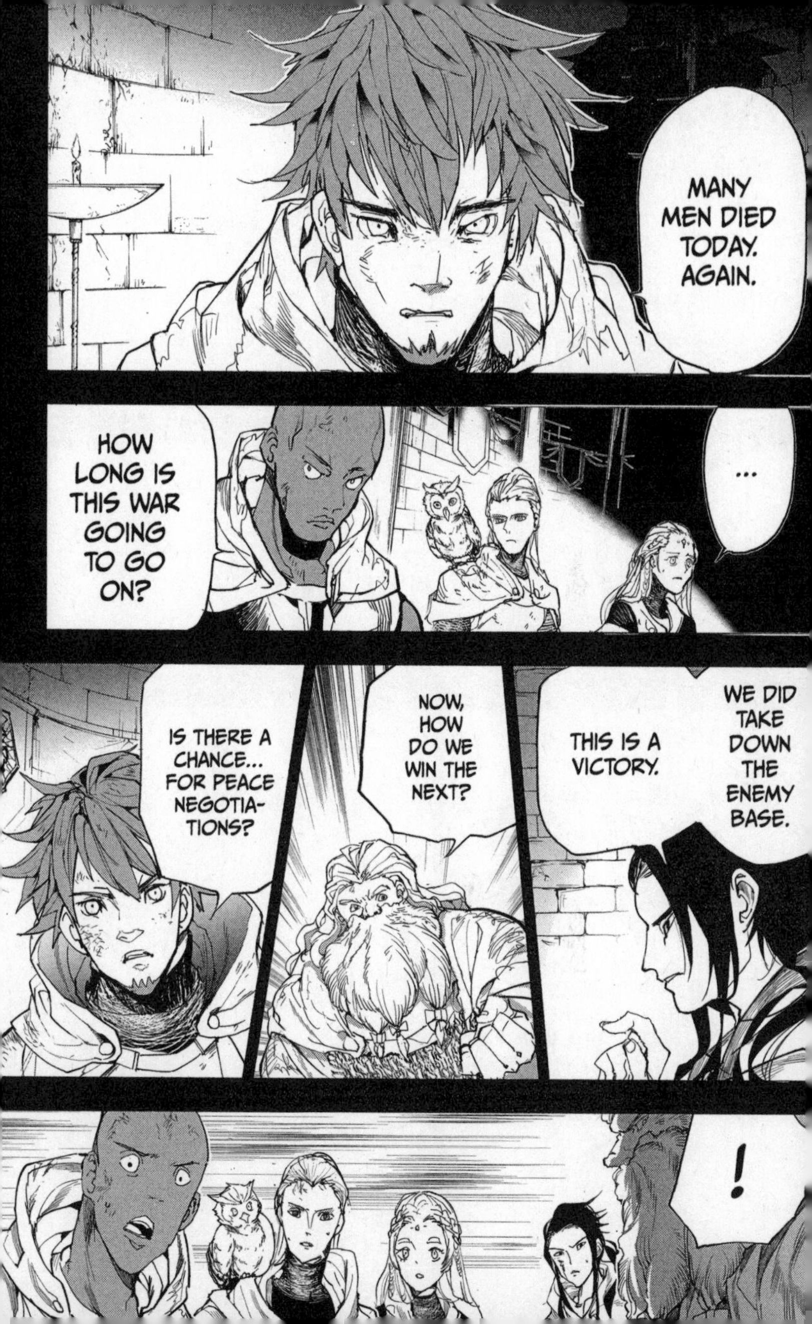
MANY MEN DIED TODAY. AGAIN.
...
HOW LONG IS THIS WAR GOING TO GO ON?
WE DID TAKE DOWN THE ENEMY BASE.
THIS IS A VICTORY.
NOW, HOW DO WE WIN THE NEXT?
IS THERE A CHANCE... FOR PEACE NEGOTIA- TIONS?
!

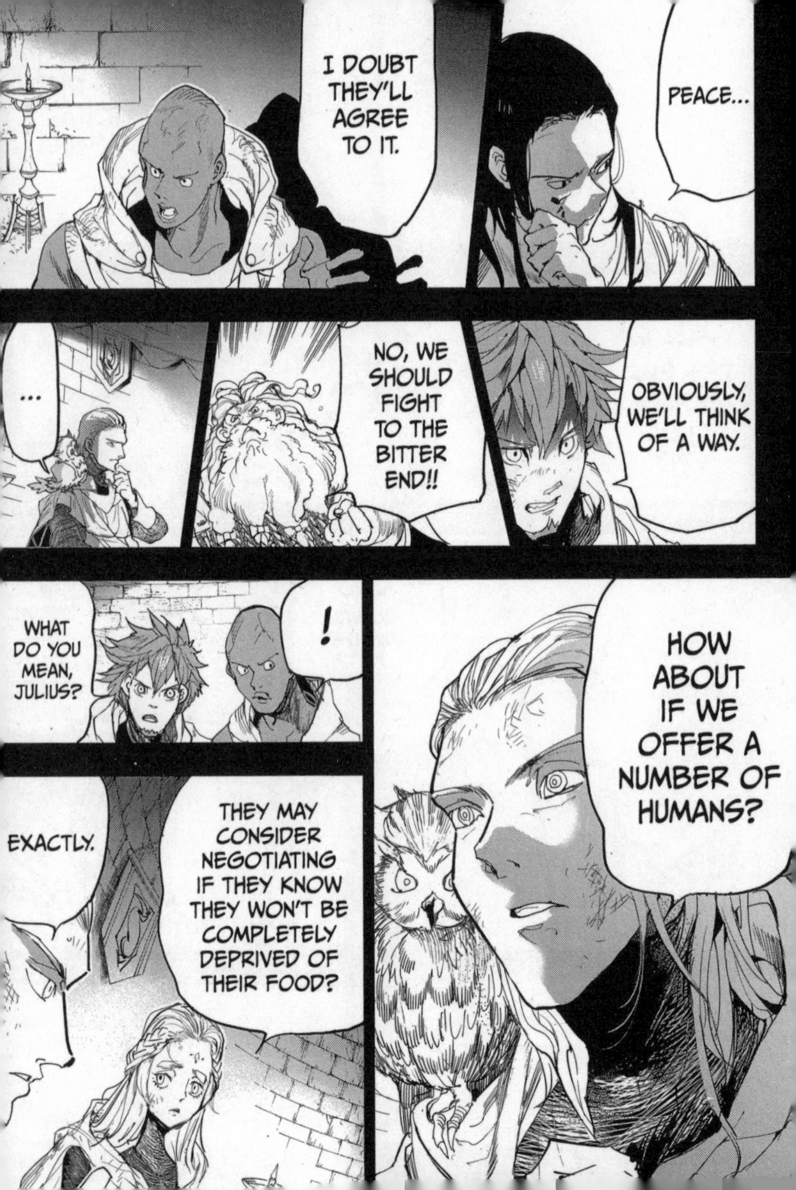
PEACE...
I DOUBT THEY'LL AGREE TO IT.
OBVIOUSLY, WE'LL THINK OF A WAY.
NO, WE SHOULD FIGHT TO THE BITTER END!!
...
HOW ABOUT IF WE OFFER A NUMBER OF HUMANS?
!
WHAT DO YOU MEAN, JULIUS?
THEY MAY CONSIDER NEGOTIATING IF THEY KNOW THEY WON'T BE COMPLETELY DEPRIVED OF THEIR FOOD?
EXACTLY.

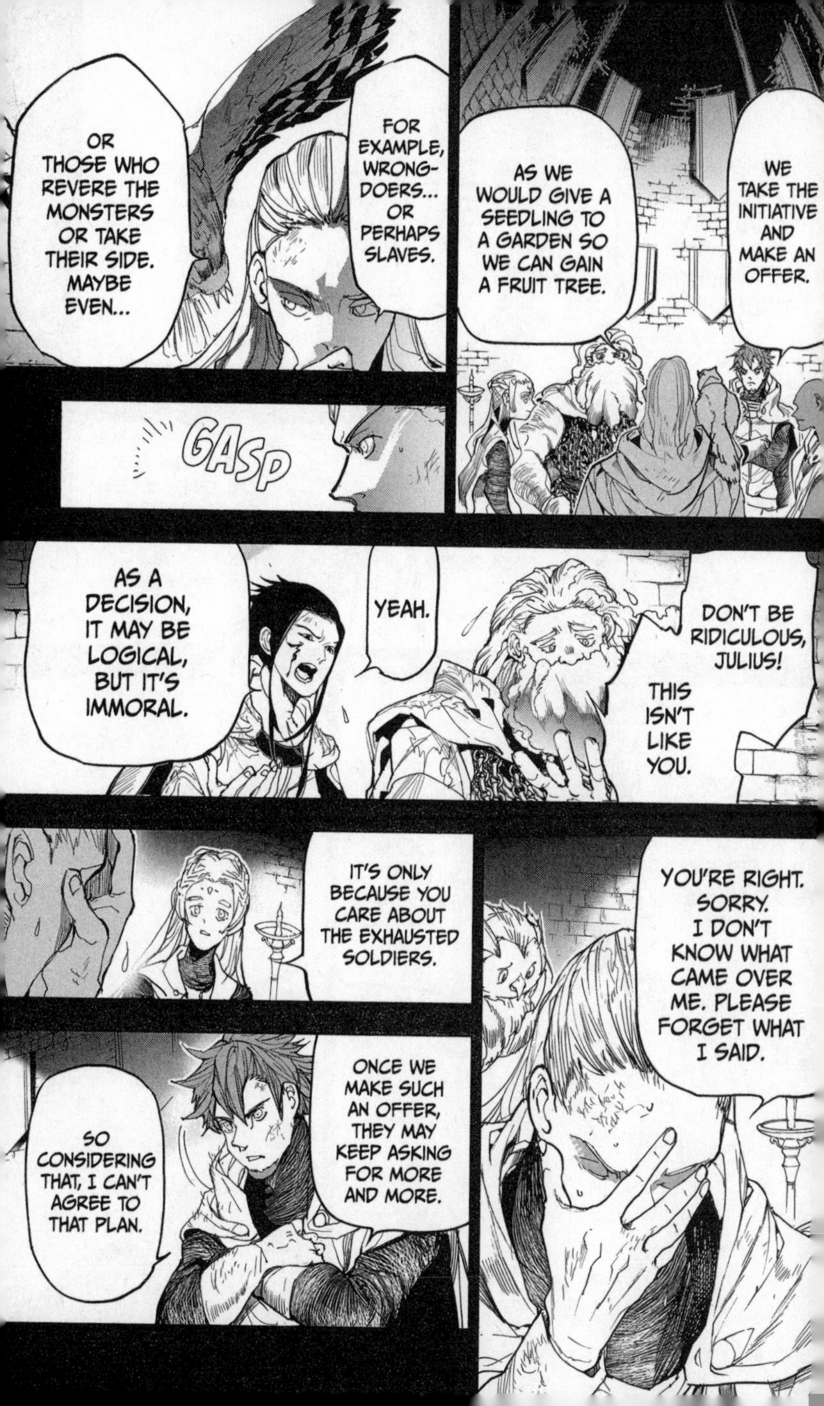
WE TAKE THE INITIATIVE AND MAKE AN OFFER.
AS WE WOULD GIVE A SEEDLING TO A GARDEN SO WE CAN GAIN A FRUIT TREE.
FOR EXAMPLE, WRONG-DOERS... OR PERHAPS SLAVES.
OR THOSE WHO REVERE THE MONSTERS OR TAKE THEIR SIDE. MAYBE EVEN...
GASP
DON'T BE RIDICULOUS, JULIUS!
THIS ISN'T LIKE YOU.
YEAH.
AS A DECISION, IT MAY BE LOGICAL, BUT IT'S IMMORAL.
YOU'RE RIGHT. SORRY. I DON'T KNOW WHAT CAME OVER ME. PLEASE FORGET WHAT I SAID.
IT'S ONLY BECAUSE YOU CARE ABOUT THE EXHAUSTED SOLDIERS.
ONCE WE MAKE SUCH AN OFFER, THEY MAY KEEP ASKING FOR MORE AND MORE.
SO CONSIDERING THAT, I CAN'T AGREE TO THAT PLAN.

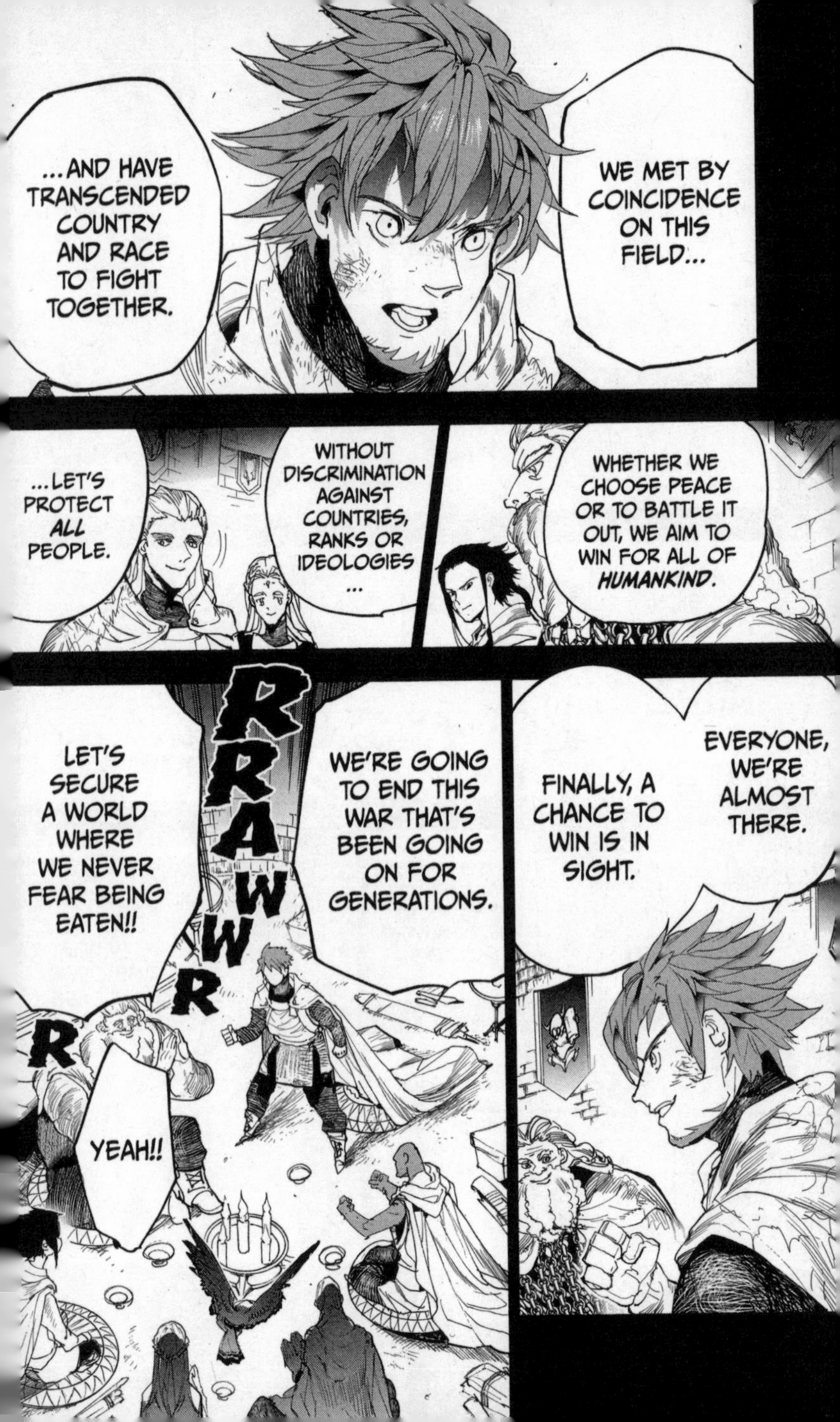
WE MET BY COINCIDENCE ON THIS FIELD...
...AND HAVE TRANSCENDED COUNTRY AND RACE TO FIGHT TOGETHER.
WHETHER WE CHOOSE PEACE OR TO BATTLE IT OUT, WE AIM TO WIN FOR ALL OF *HUMANKIND*.
WITHOUT DISCRIMINATION AGAINST COUNTRIES, RANKS OR IDEOLOGIES...
...LET'S PROTECT *ALL* PEOPLE.
EVERYONE, WE'RE ALMOST THERE.
FINALLY, A CHANCE TO WIN IS IN SIGHT.
WE'RE GOING TO END THIS WAR THAT'S BEEN GOING ON FOR GENERATIONS.
LET'S SECURE A WORLD WHERE WE NEVER FEAR BEING EATEN!!
RRAWWRR
YEAH!!

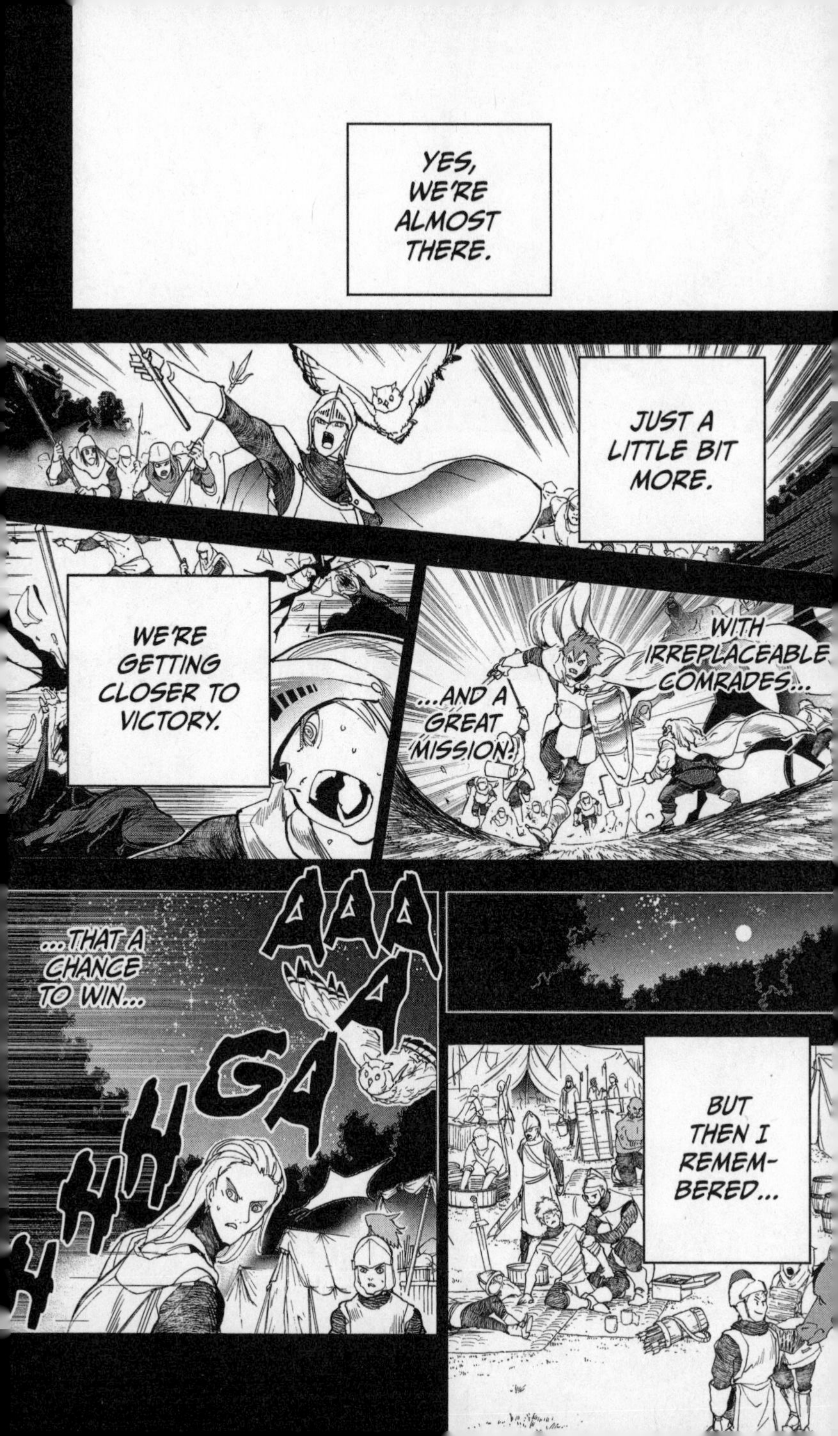
YES, WE'RE ALMOST THERE.
JUST A LITTLE BIT MORE.
WITH IRREPLACEABLE COMRADES...
...AND A GREAT MISSION!
WE'RE GETTING CLOSER TO VICTORY.
BUT THEN I REMEMBERED...
...THAT A CHANCE TO WIN...
AAAA
GA
HHH

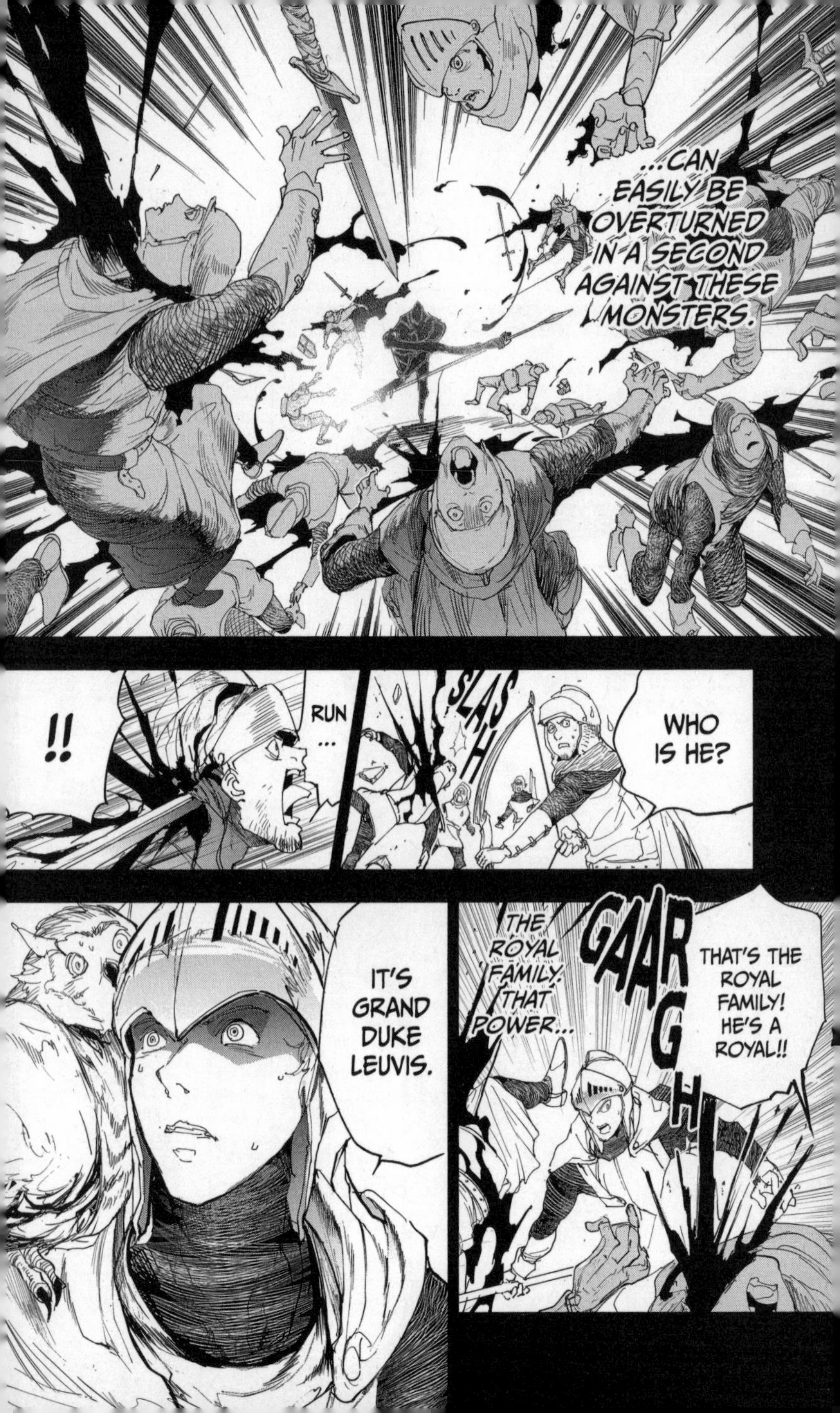
...CAN EASILY BE OVERTURNED IN A SECOND AGAINST THESE MONSTERS.
WHO IS HE?
SLASH
RUN ...
!!
THAT'S THE ROYAL FAMILY! HE'S A ROYAL!!
GAARGH
THE ROYAL FAMILY. THAT POWER...
IT'S GRAND DUKE LEUVIS.

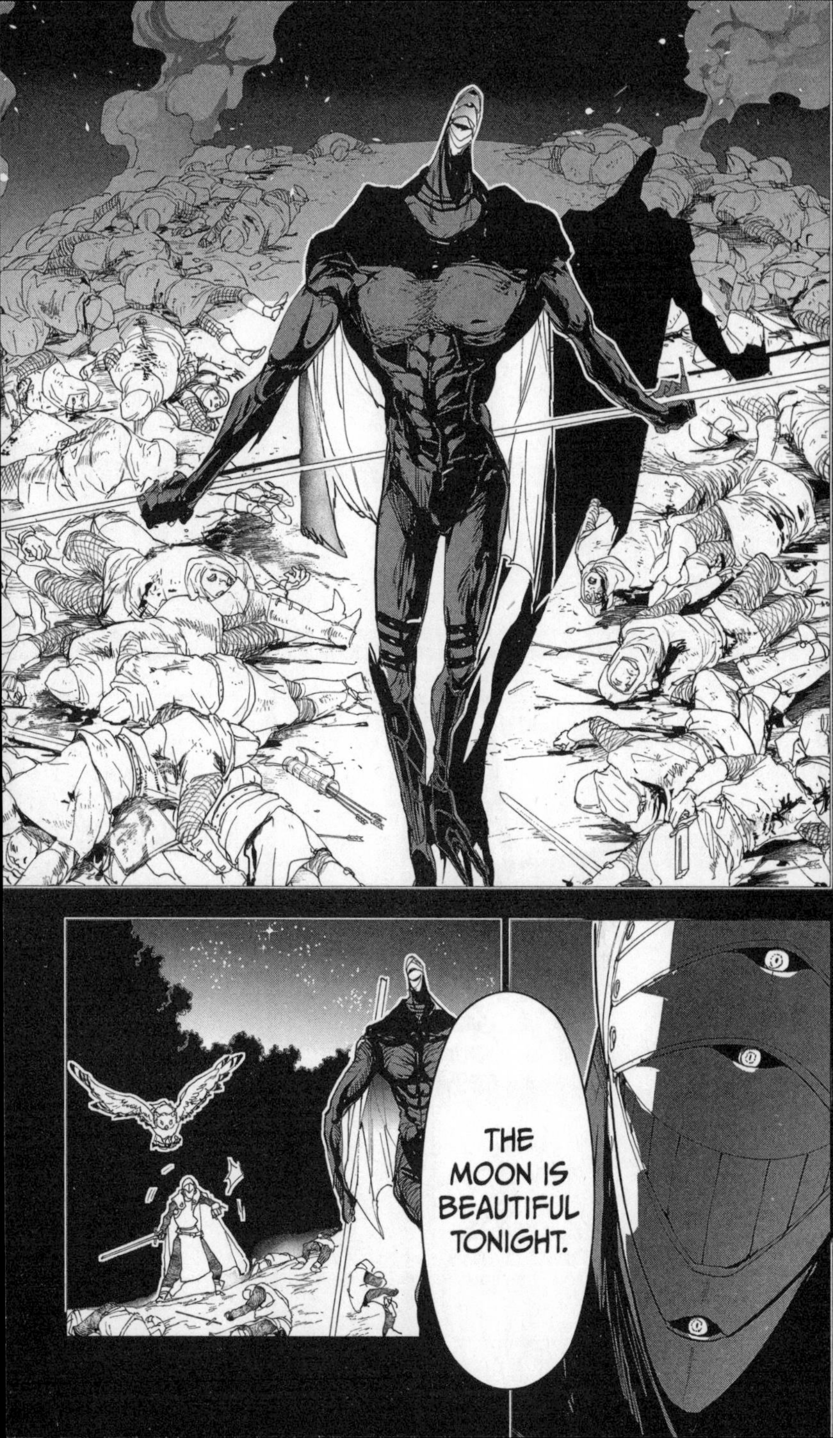
THE MOON IS BEAUTIFUL TONIGHT.

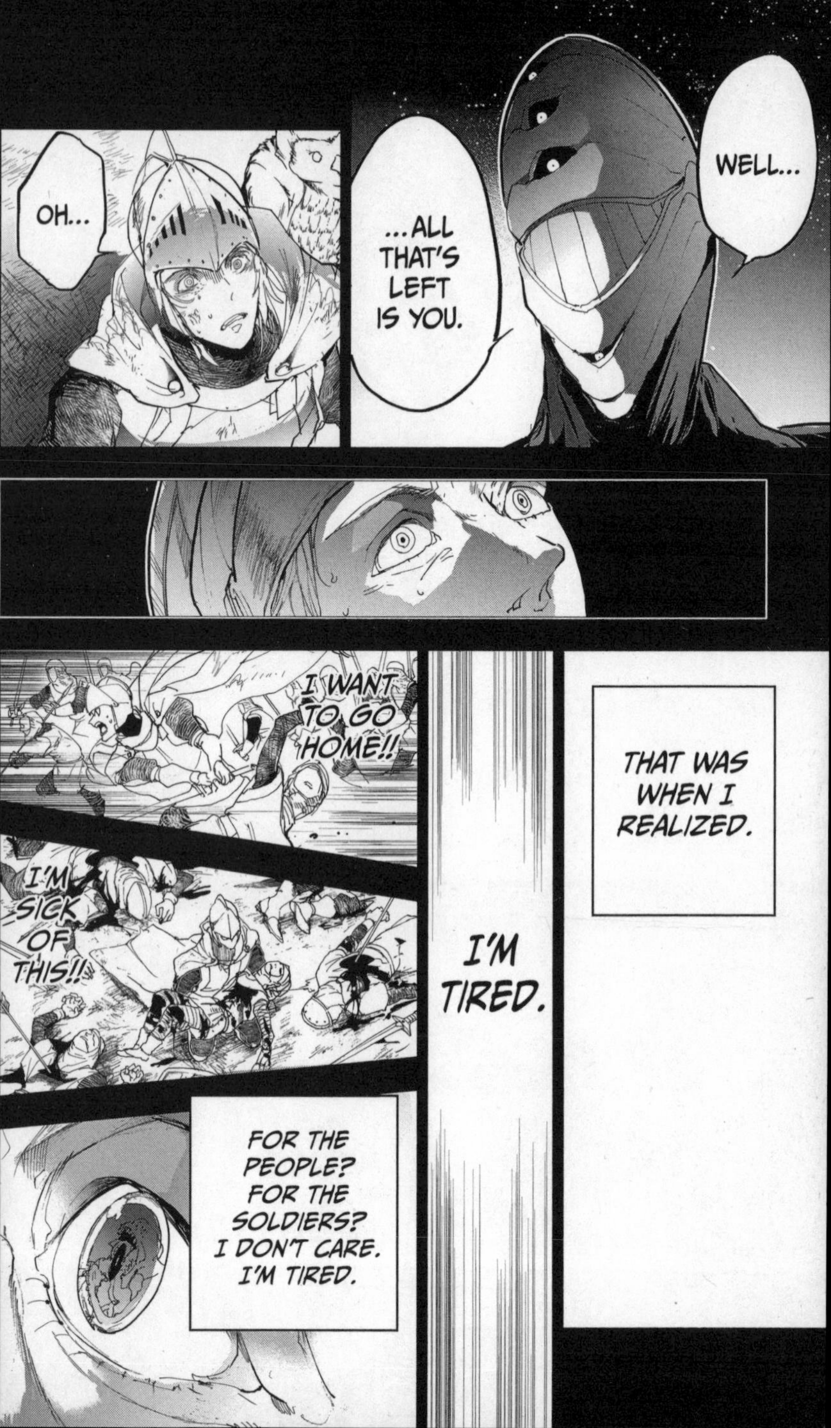
WELL...
...ALL THAT'S LEFT IS YOU.
OH...
THAT WAS WHEN I REALIZED.
I'M TIRED.
I WANT TO GO HOME!!
I'M SICK OF THIS!!
FOR THE PEOPLE? FOR THE SOLDIERS? I DON'T CARE. I'M TIRED.

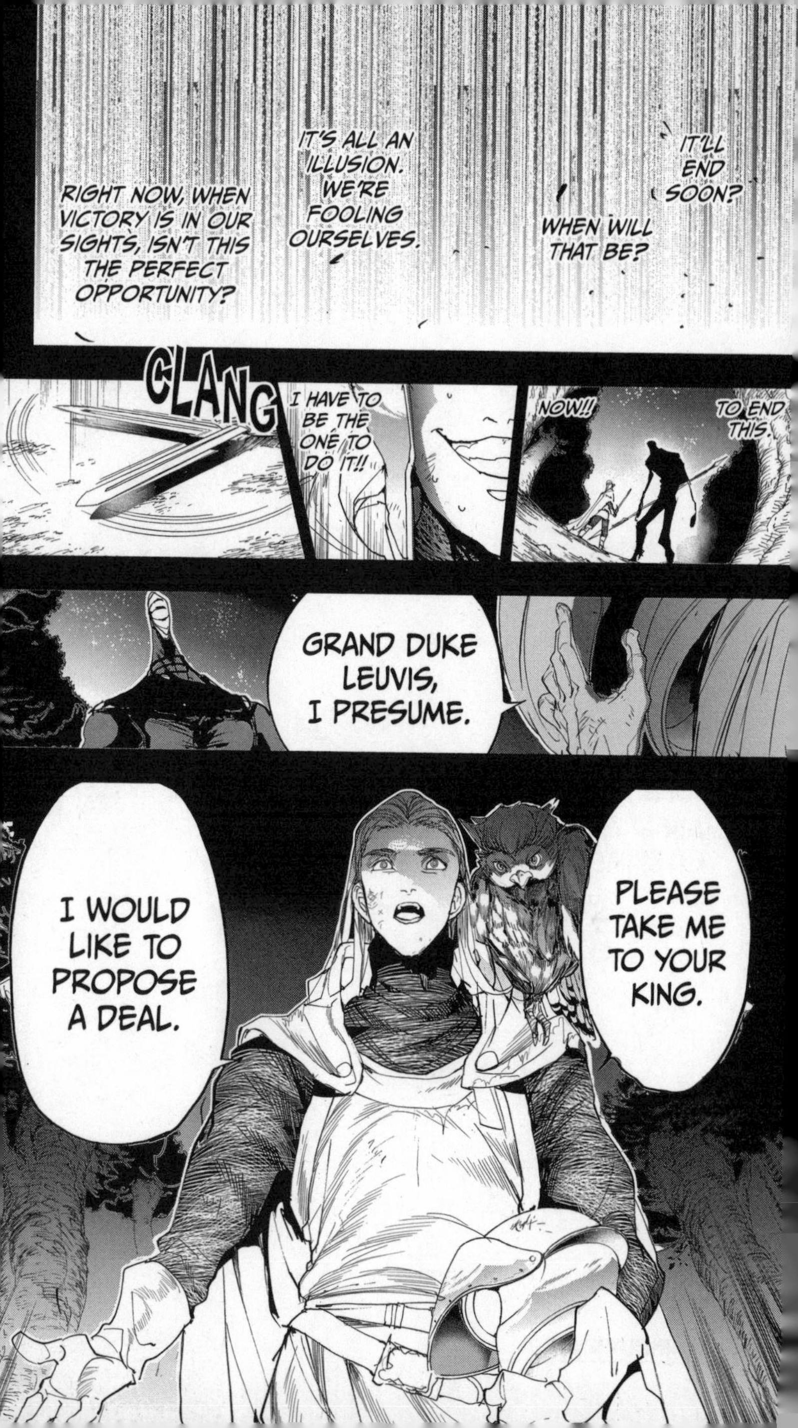
IT'LL END SOON?
WHEN WILL THAT BE?
IT'S ALL AN ILLUSION. WE'RE FOOLING OURSELVES.
RIGHT NOW, WHEN VICTORY IS IN OUR SIGHTS, ISN'T THIS THE PERFECT OPPORTUNITY?
TO END THIS.
NOW!!
I HAVE TO BE THE ONE TO DO IT!!
CLANG
GRAND DUKE LEUVIS, I PRESUME.
PLEASE TAKE ME TO YOUR KING.
I WOULD LIKE TO PROPOSE A DEAL.

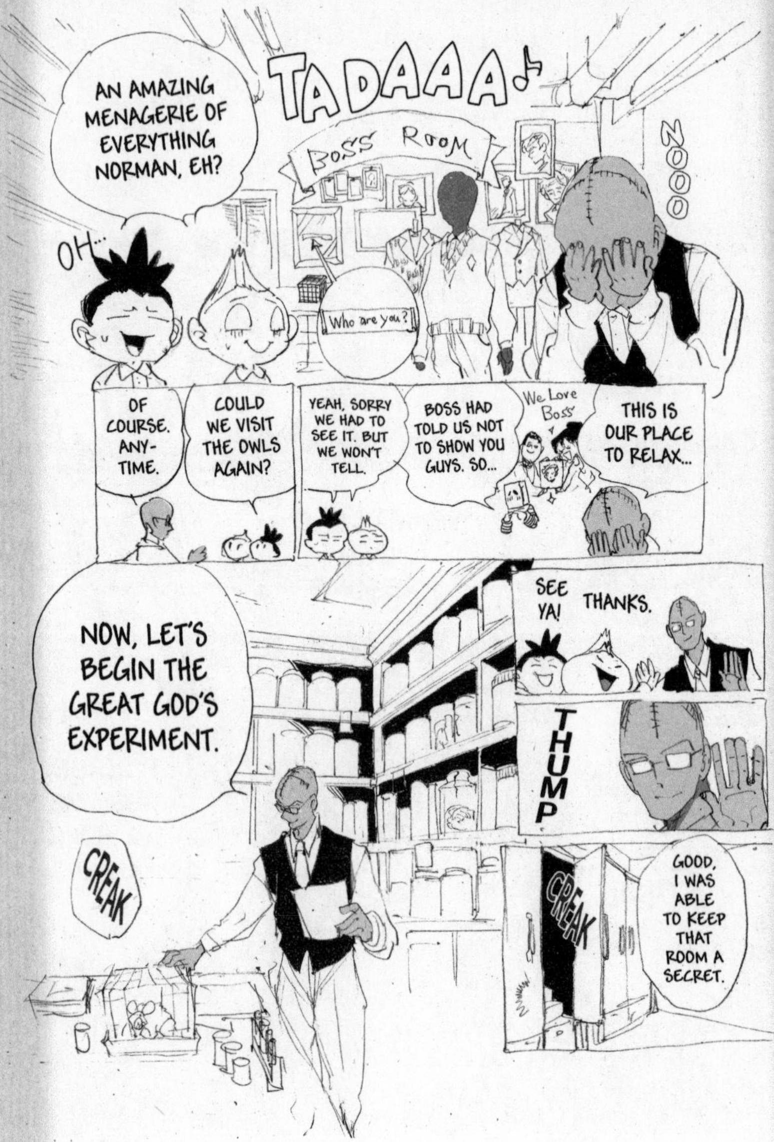
NOOO
TADAAA♪
BOSS ROOM
AN AMAZING MENAGERIE OF EVERYTHING NORMAN, EH?
OH...
Who are you?
THIS IS OUR PLACE TO RELAX...
We Love Boss
BOSS HAD TOLD US NOT TO SHOW YOU GUYS. SO...
YEAH, SORRY WE HAD TO SEE IT. BUT WE WON'T TELL.
COULD WE VISIT THE OWLS AGAIN?
OF COURSE. ANY-TIME.
THANKS.
SEE YA!
THUMP
GOOD, I WAS ABLE TO KEEP THAT ROOM A SECRET.
CREAK
NOW, LET'S BEGIN THE GREAT GOD'S EXPERIMENT.
CREAK

A SPECIAL EXTRA PART 2...FIN

CHAPTER 142: THE PROMISE MADE 1,000 YEARS AGO, PART 2

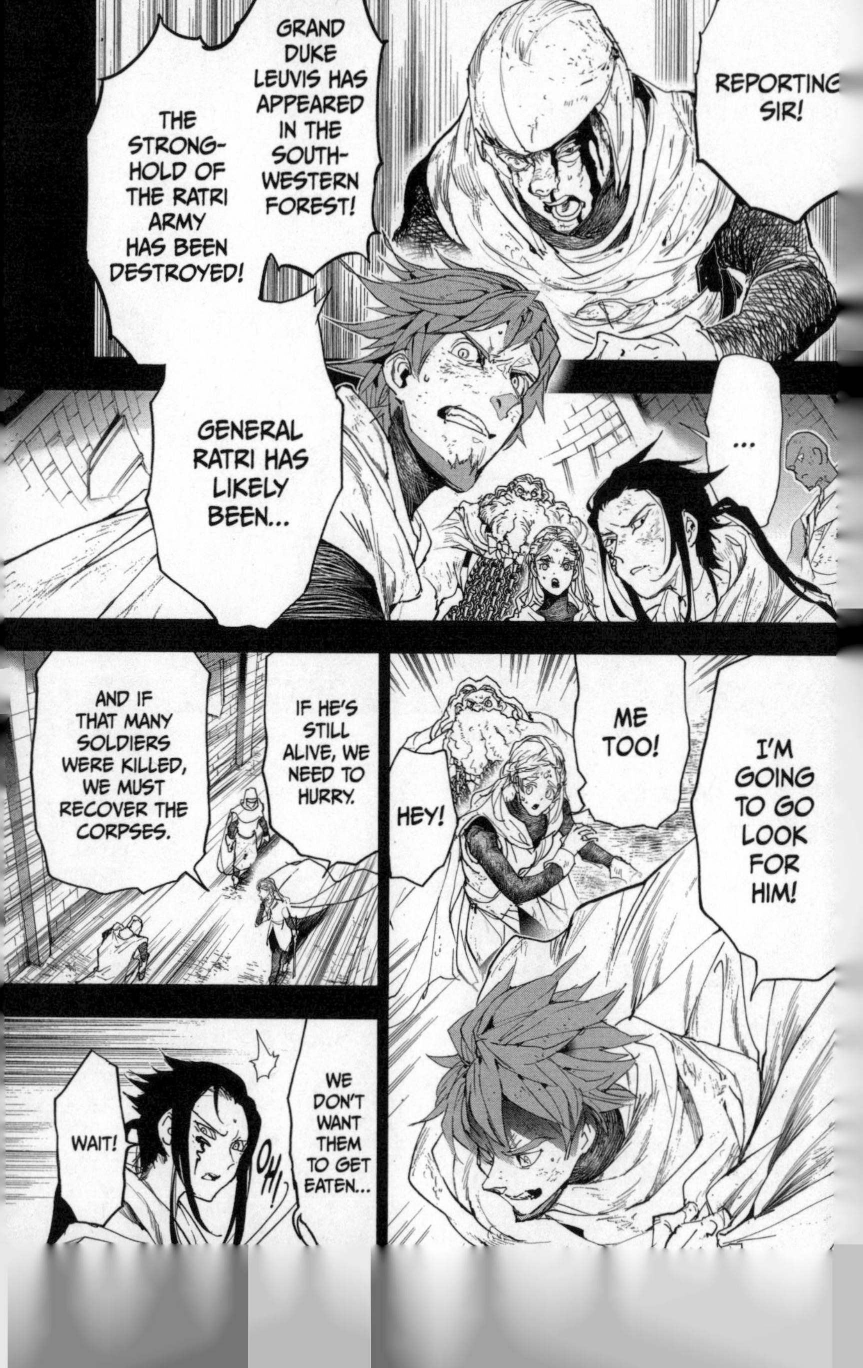
REPORTING SIR!
GRAND DUKE LEUVIS HAS APPEARED IN THE SOUTH-WESTERN FOREST!
THE STRONG-HOLD OF THE RATRI ARMY HAS BEEN DESTROYED!
...
GENERAL RATRI HAS LIKELY BEEN...
I'M GOING TO GO LOOK FOR HIM!
ME TOO!
HEY!
IF HE'S STILL ALIVE, WE NEED TO HURRY.
AND IF THAT MANY SOLDIERS WERE KILLED, WE MUST RECOVER THE CORPSES.
WE DON'T WANT THEM TO GET EATEN...
OH!
WAIT!

I NEED TO TALK TO ALL OF YOU, IMMEDIATELY.

ARE YOU HURT?!

THANK GOODNESS!

JULIUS!!

SORRY TO MAKE YOU WORRY.

BUT FORGET THAT.

CHAPTER 142: THE PROMISE MADE 1,000 YEARS AGO, PART 2

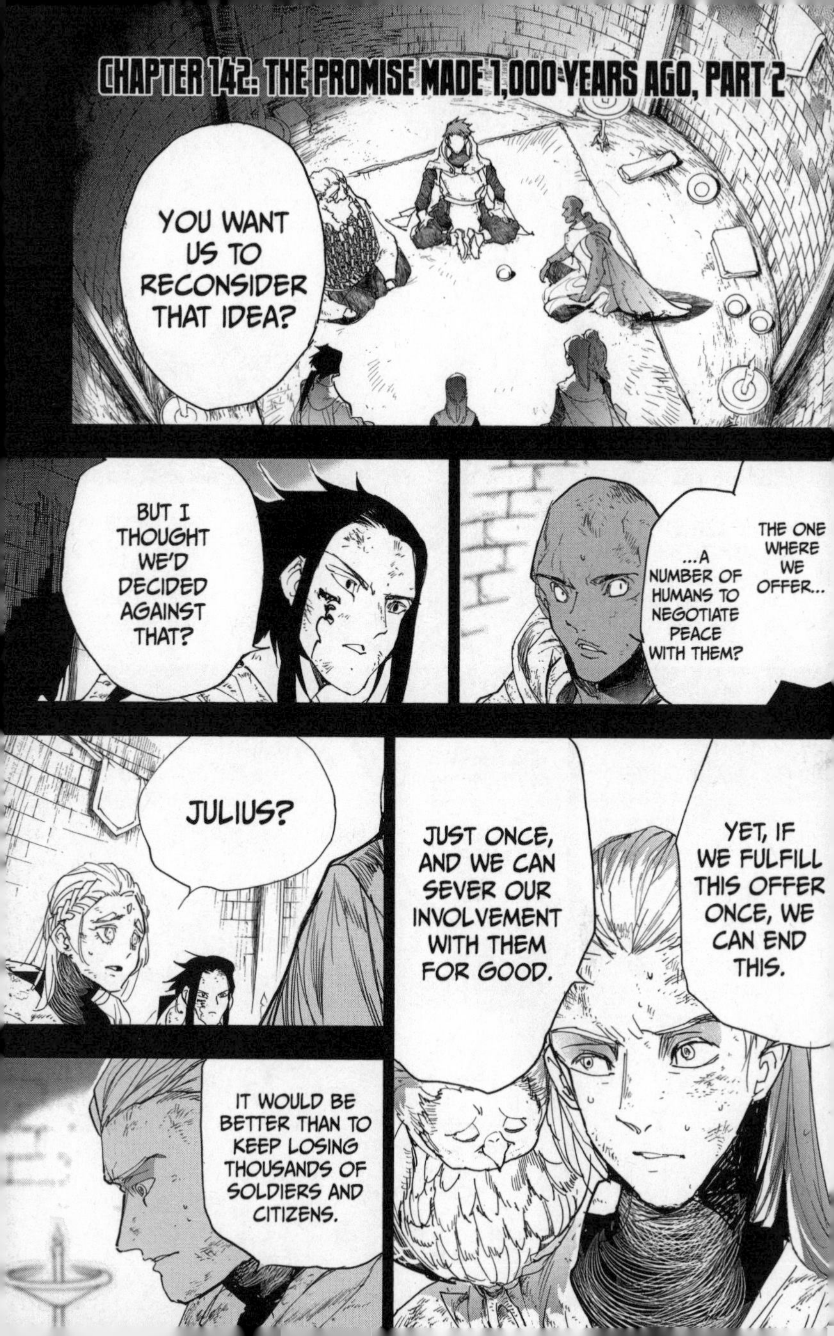
YOU WANT US TO RECONSIDER THAT IDEA?
THE ONE WHERE WE OFFER...
...A NUMBER OF HUMANS TO NEGOTIATE PEACE WITH THEM?
BUT I THOUGHT WE'D DECIDED AGAINST THAT?
YET, IF WE FULFILL THIS OFFER ONCE, WE CAN END THIS.
JUST ONCE, AND WE CAN SEVER OUR INVOLVEMENT WITH THEM FOR GOOD.
JULIUS?
IT WOULD BE BETTER THAN TO KEEP LOSING THOUSANDS OF SOLDIERS AND CITIZENS.

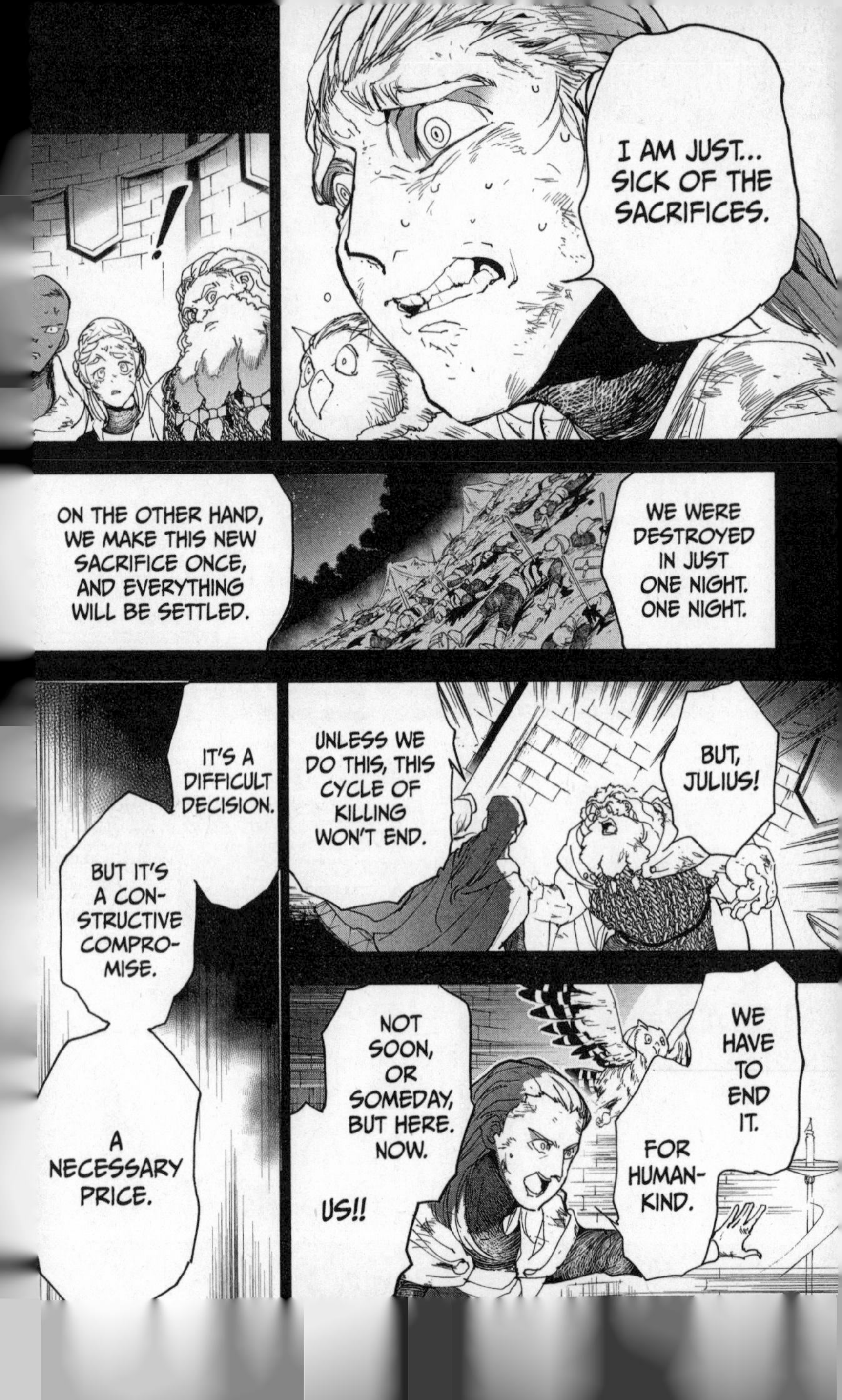
I AM JUST... SICK OF THE SACRIFICES.
!
WE WERE DESTROYED IN JUST ONE NIGHT. ONE NIGHT.
ON THE OTHER HAND, WE MAKE THIS NEW SACRIFICE ONCE, AND EVERYTHING WILL BE SETTLED.
BUT, JULIUS!
UNLESS WE DO THIS, THIS CYCLE OF KILLING WON'T END.
WE HAVE TO END IT.
FOR HUMAN-KIND.
NOT SOON, OR SOMEDAY, BUT HERE. NOW.
US!!
IT'S A DIFFICULT DECISION.
BUT IT'S A CON-STRUCTIVE COMPRO-MISE.
A NECESSARY PRICE.

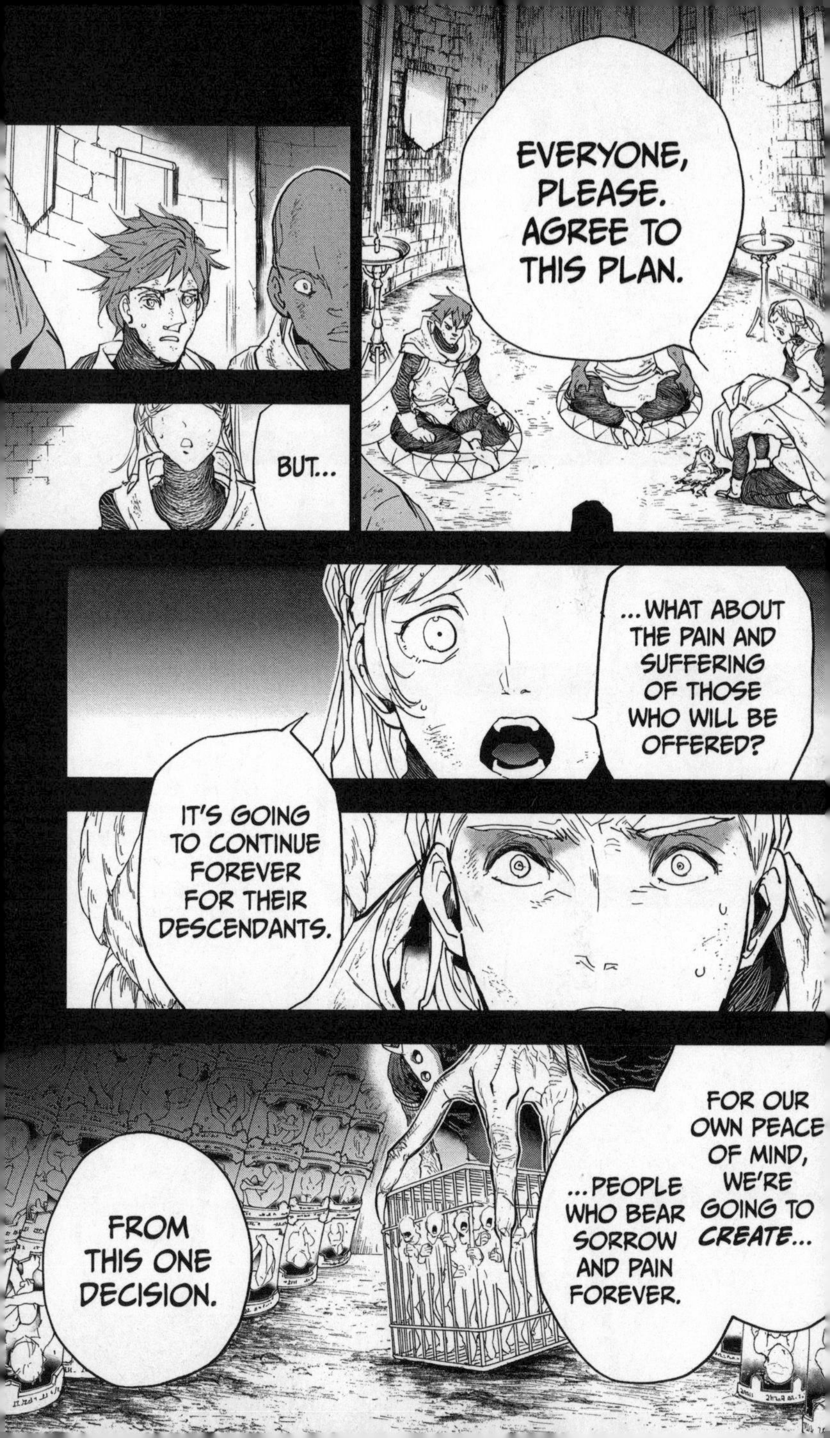
EVERYONE, PLEASE. AGREE TO THIS PLAN.
BUT...
...WHAT ABOUT THE PAIN AND SUFFERING OF THOSE WHO WILL BE OFFERED?
IT'S GOING TO CONTINUE FOREVER FOR THEIR DESCENDANTS.
FOR OUR OWN PEACE OF MIND, WE'RE GOING TO *CREATE*...
...PEOPLE WHO BEAR SORROW AND PAIN FOREVER.
FROM THIS ONE DECISION.

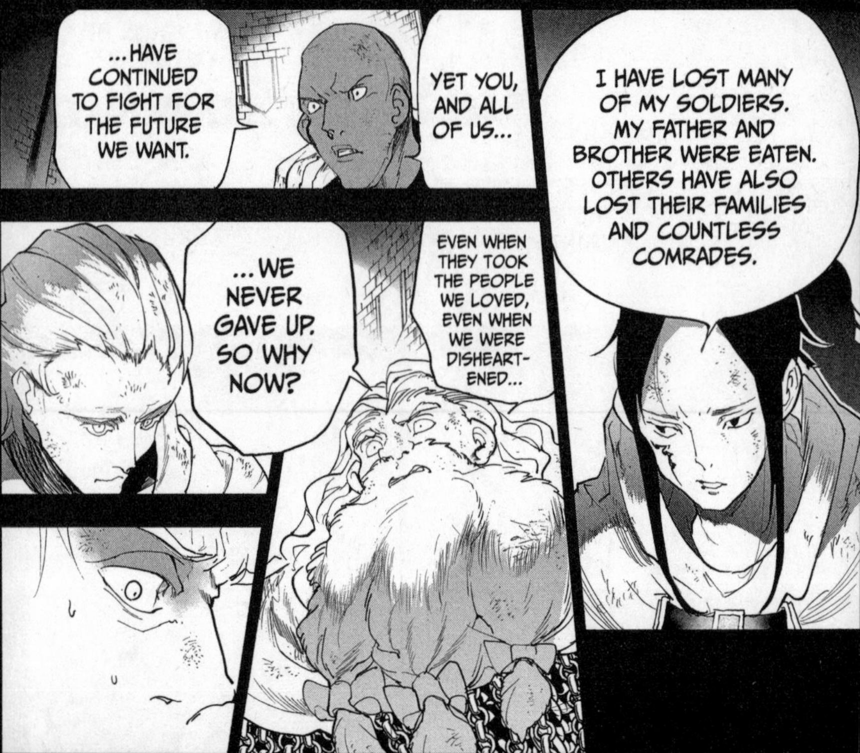
I HAVE LOST MANY OF MY SOLDIERS. MY FATHER AND BROTHER WERE EATEN. OTHERS HAVE ALSO LOST THEIR FAMILIES AND COUNTLESS COMRADES.
YET YOU, AND ALL OF US...
...HAVE CONTINUED TO FIGHT FOR THE FUTURE WE WANT.
EVEN WHEN THEY TOOK THE PEOPLE WE LOVED, EVEN WHEN WE WERE DISHEART-ENED...
...WE NEVER GAVE UP. SO WHY NOW?

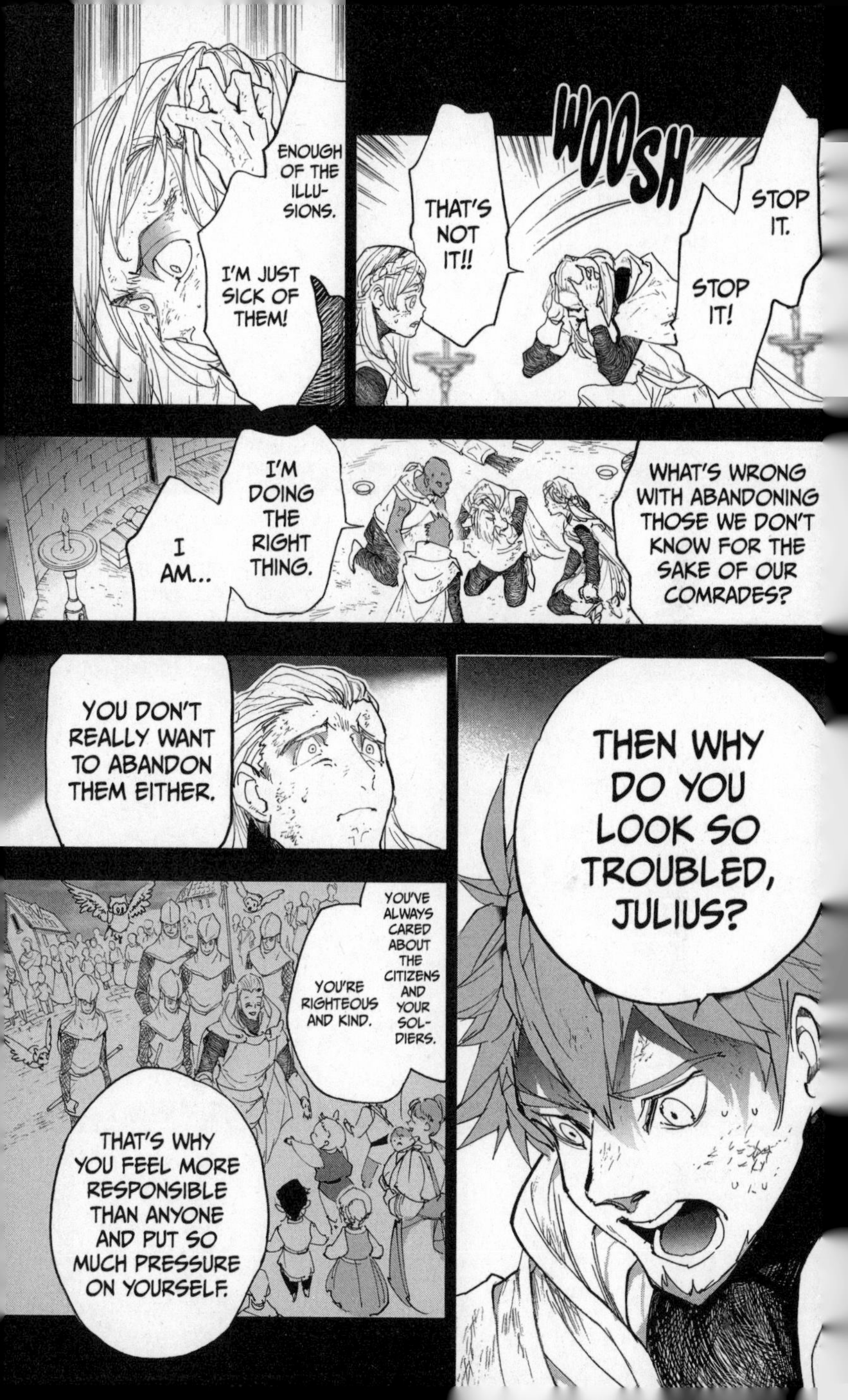
STOP IT.
WOOSH
THAT'S NOT IT!!
STOP IT!
ENOUGH OF THE ILLU- SIONS.
I'M JUST SICK OF THEM!
WHAT'S WRONG WITH ABANDONING THOSE WE DON'T KNOW FOR THE SAKE OF OUR COMRADES?
I'M DOING THE RIGHT THING.
I AM...
THEN WHY DO YOU LOOK SO TROUBLED, JULIUS?
YOU DON'T REALLY WANT TO ABANDON THEM EITHER.
YOU'VE ALWAYS CARED ABOUT THE CITIZENS AND YOUR SOL- DIERS.
YOU'RE RIGHTEOUS AND KIND.
THAT'S WHY YOU FEEL MORE RESPONSIBLE THAN ANYONE AND PUT SO MUCH PRESSURE ON YOURSELF.

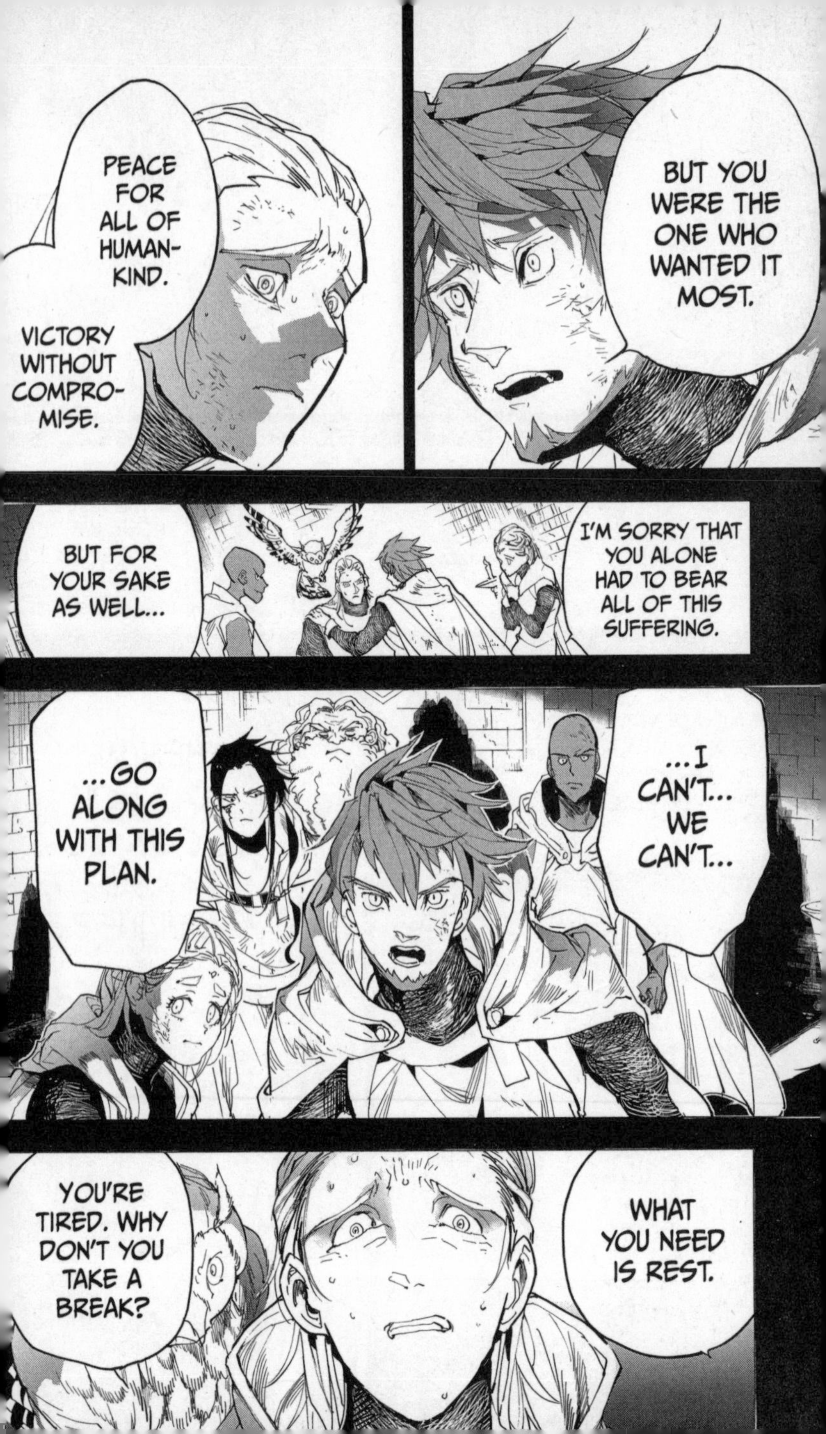
BUT YOU WERE THE ONE WHO WANTED IT MOST.
PEACE FOR ALL OF HUMAN-KIND.
VICTORY WITHOUT COMPRO-MISE.
I'M SORRY THAT YOU ALONE HAD TO BEAR ALL OF THIS SUFFERING.
BUT FOR YOUR SAKE AS WELL...
...I CAN'T... WE CAN'T...
...GO ALONG WITH THIS PLAN.
WHAT YOU NEED IS REST.
YOU'RE TIRED. WHY DON'T YOU TAKE A BREAK?

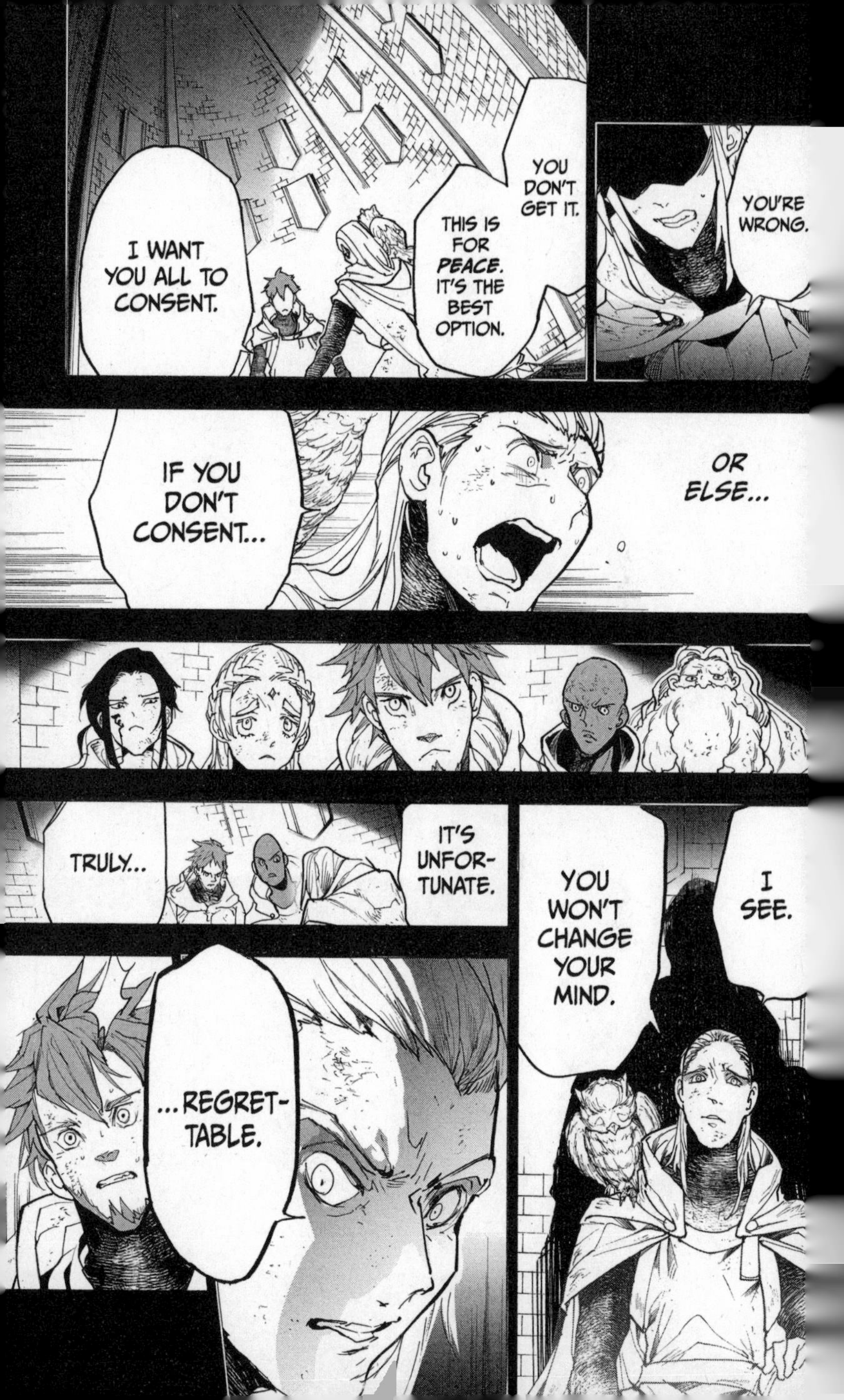
YOU'RE WRONG.
YOU DON'T GET IT.
THIS IS FOR *PEACE*. IT'S THE BEST OPTION.
I WANT YOU ALL TO CONSENT.
OR ELSE...
IF YOU DON'T CONSENT...
I SEE.
YOU WON'T CHANGE YOUR MIND.
IT'S UNFORTUNATE.
TRULY...
...REGRETTABLE.

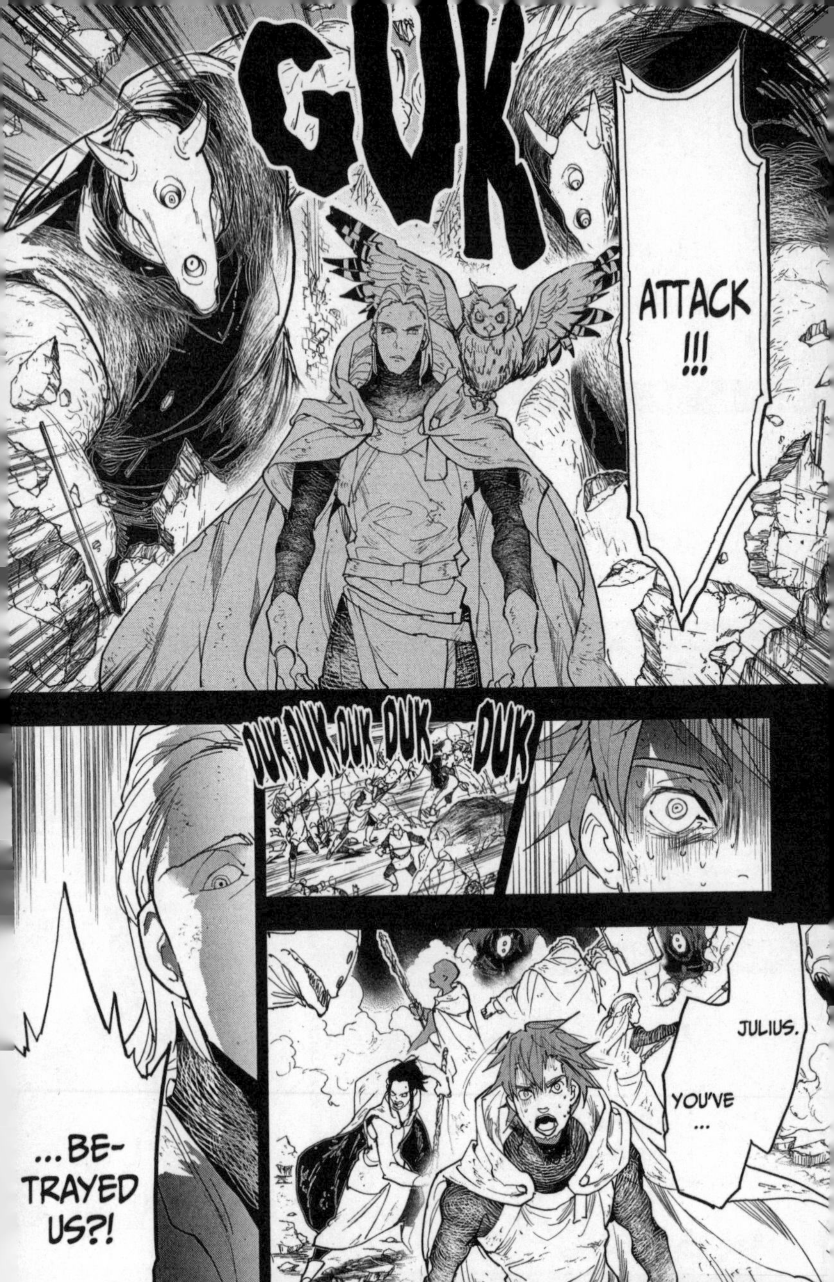
GUK
ATTACK!!!
DUK DUK DUK DUK DUK
JULIUS.
YOU'VE ...
...BE-TRAYED US?!

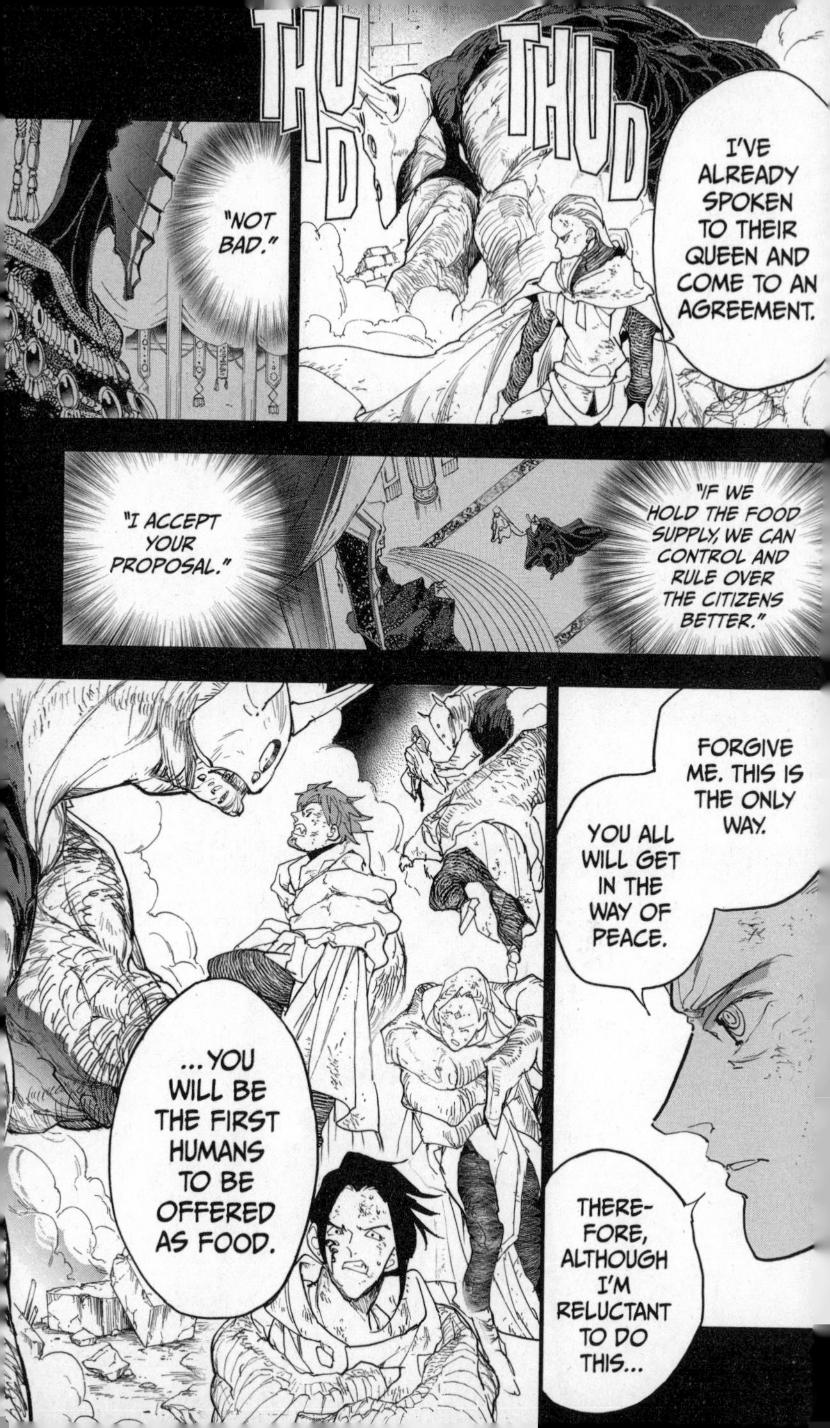
THUD THUD
I'VE ALREADY SPOKEN TO THEIR QUEEN AND COME TO AN AGREEMENT.
"NOT BAD."
"IF WE HOLD THE FOOD SUPPLY, WE CAN CONTROL AND RULE OVER THE CITIZENS BETTER."
"I ACCEPT YOUR PROPOSAL."
FORGIVE ME. THIS IS THE ONLY WAY.
YOU ALL WILL GET IN THE WAY OF PEACE.
THERE-FORE, ALTHOUGH I'M RELUCTANT TO DO THIS...
...YOU WILL BE THE FIRST HUMANS TO BE OFFERED AS FOOD.

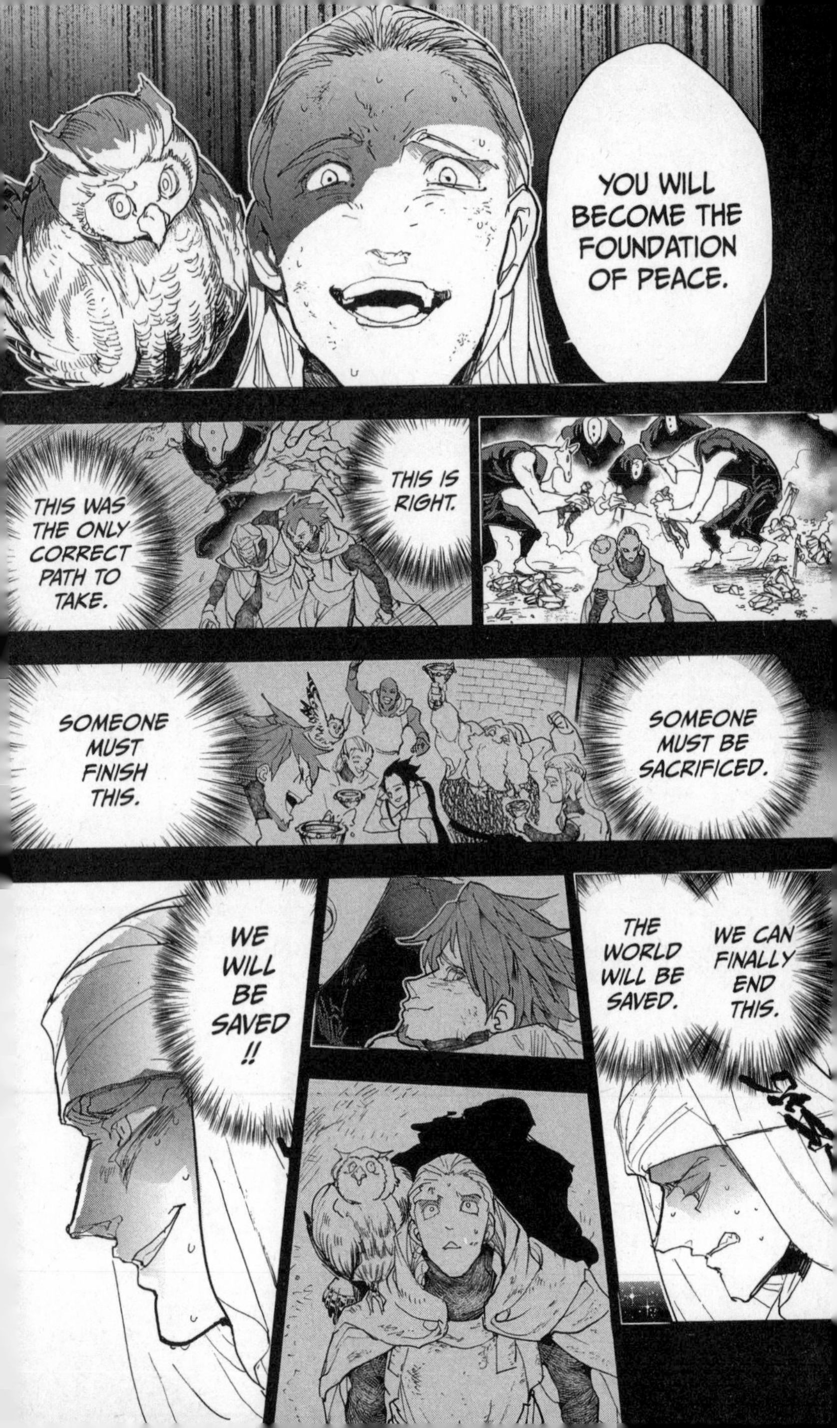
YOU WILL BECOME THE FOUNDATION OF PEACE.
THIS IS RIGHT.
THIS WAS THE ONLY CORRECT PATH TO TAKE.
SOMEONE MUST BE SACRIFICED.
SOMEONE MUST FINISH THIS.
WE CAN FINALLY END THIS.
THE WORLD WILL BE SAVED.
WE WILL BE SAVED!!

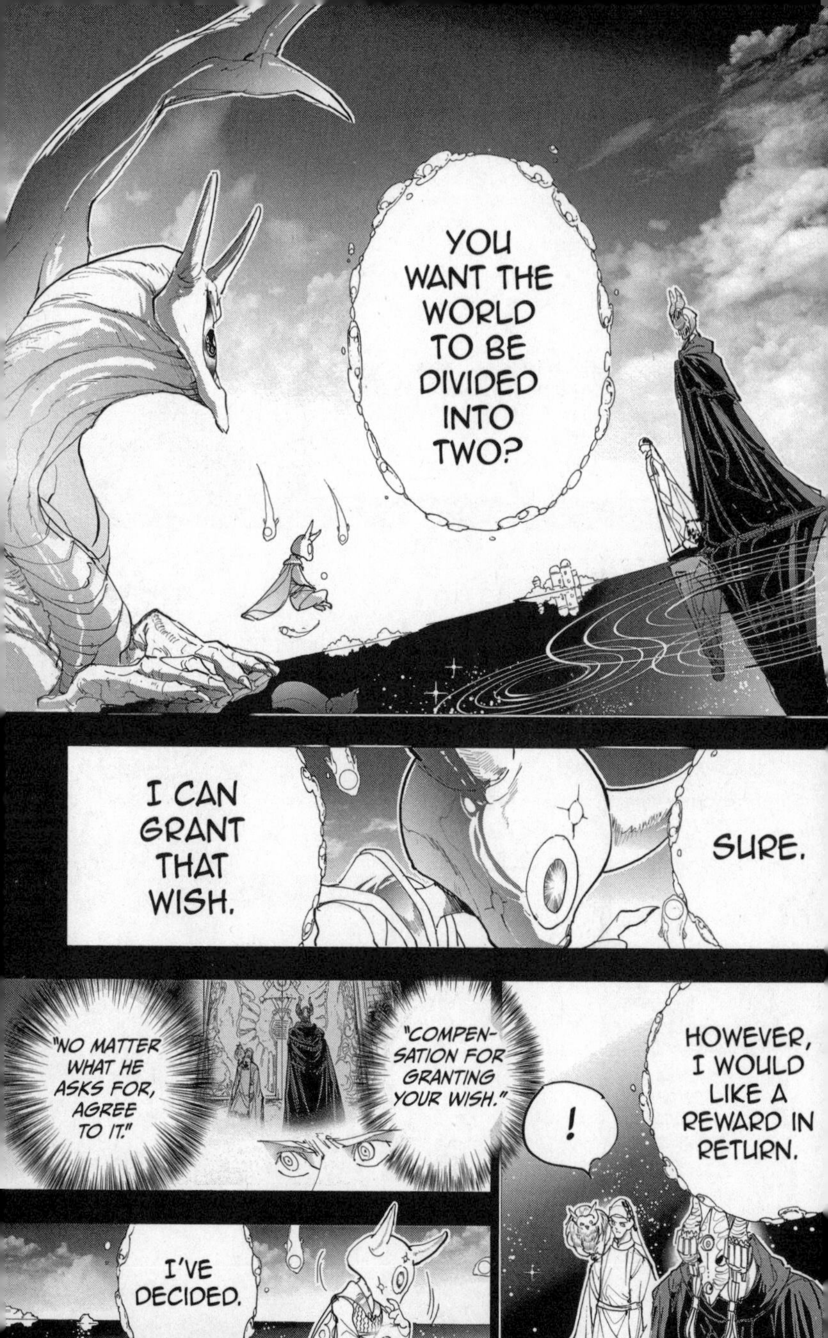
YOU WANT THE WORLD TO BE DIVIDED INTO TWO?
SURE.
I CAN GRANT THAT WISH.
HOWEVER, I WOULD LIKE A REWARD IN RETURN.
!
"COMPENSATION FOR GRANTING YOUR WISH."
"NO MATTER WHAT HE ASKS FOR, AGREE TO IT."
I'VE DECIDED.

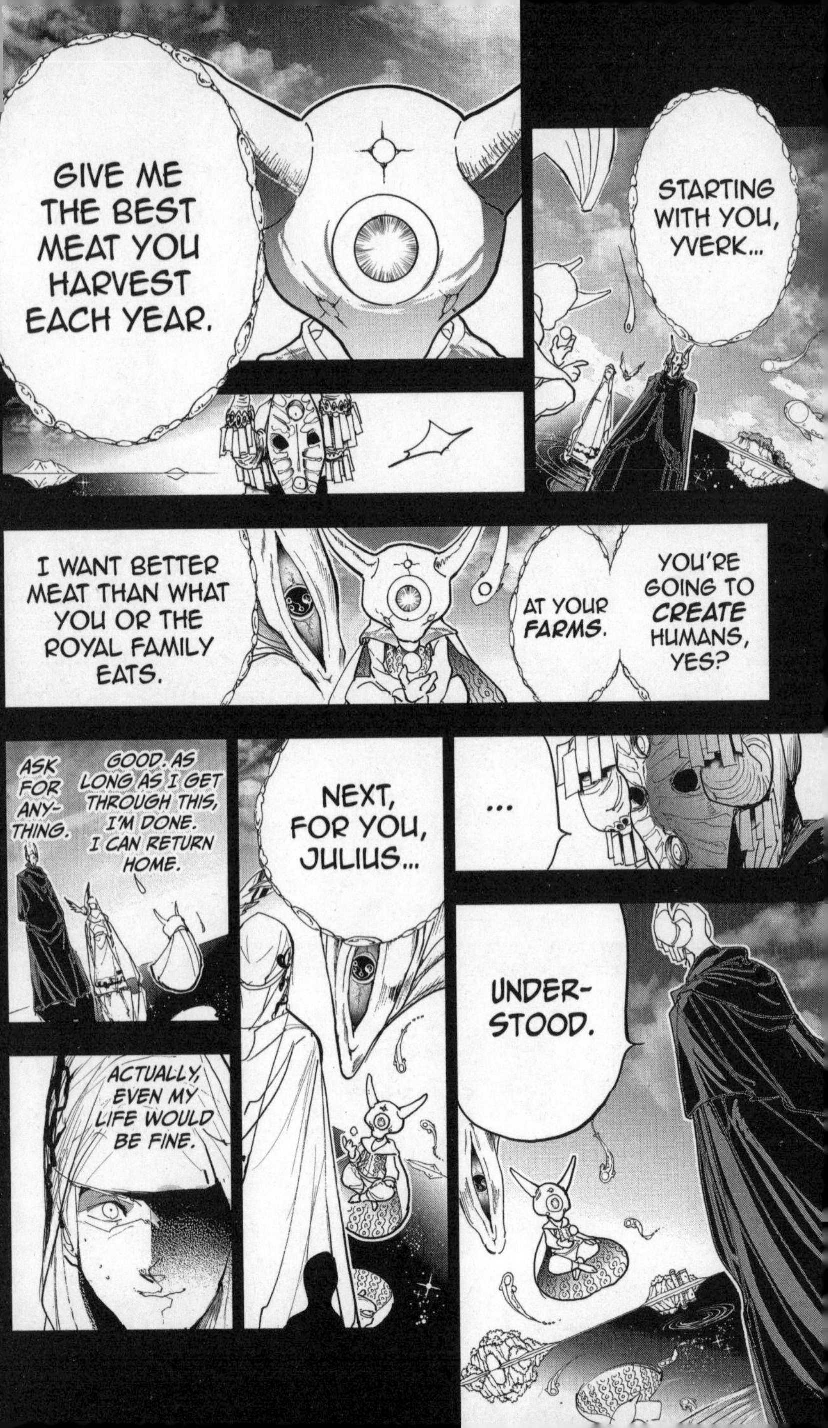
STARTING WITH YOU, YVERK...
GIVE ME THE BEST MEAT YOU HARVEST EACH YEAR.
YOU'RE GOING TO CREATE HUMANS, YES?
AT YOUR FARMS.
I WANT BETTER MEAT THAN WHAT YOU OR THE ROYAL FAMILY EATS.
...
UNDER-STOOD.
NEXT, FOR YOU, JULIUS...
GOOD. AS LONG AS I GET THROUGH THIS, I'M DONE. I CAN RETURN HOME.
ASK FOR ANY-THING.
ACTUALLY, EVEN MY LIFE WOULD BE FINE.

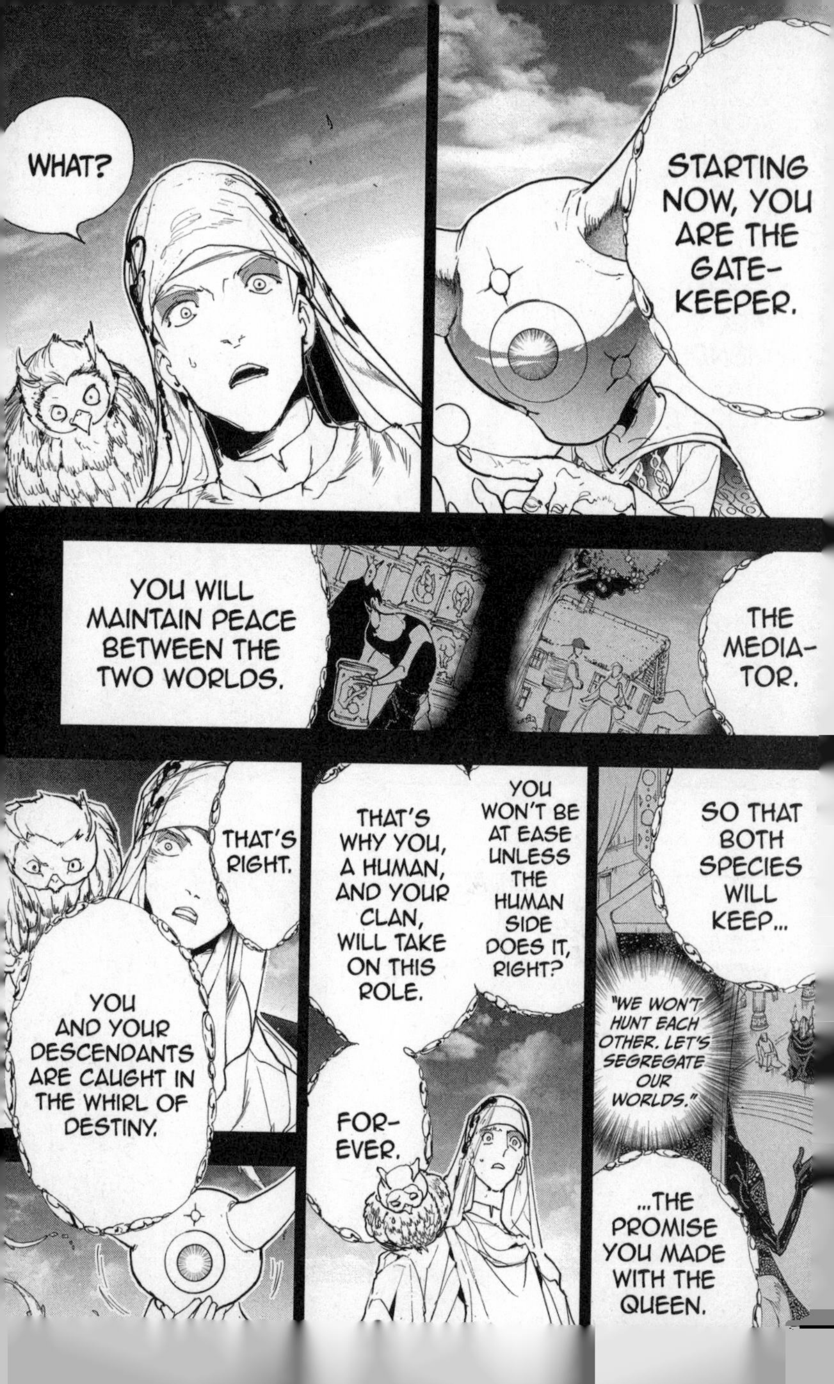
STARTING NOW, YOU ARE THE GATE-KEEPER.
WHAT?
THE MEDIATOR.
YOU WILL MAINTAIN PEACE BETWEEN THE TWO WORLDS.
SO THAT BOTH SPECIES WILL KEEP...
"WE WON'T HUNT EACH OTHER. LET'S SEGREGATE OUR WORLDS."
...THE PROMISE YOU MADE WITH THE QUEEN.
YOU WON'T BE AT EASE UNLESS THE HUMAN SIDE DOES IT, RIGHT?
THAT'S WHY YOU, A HUMAN, AND YOUR CLAN, WILL TAKE ON THIS ROLE.
FOR-EVER.
THAT'S RIGHT.
YOU AND YOUR DESCENDANTS ARE CAUGHT IN THE WHIRL OF DESTINY.

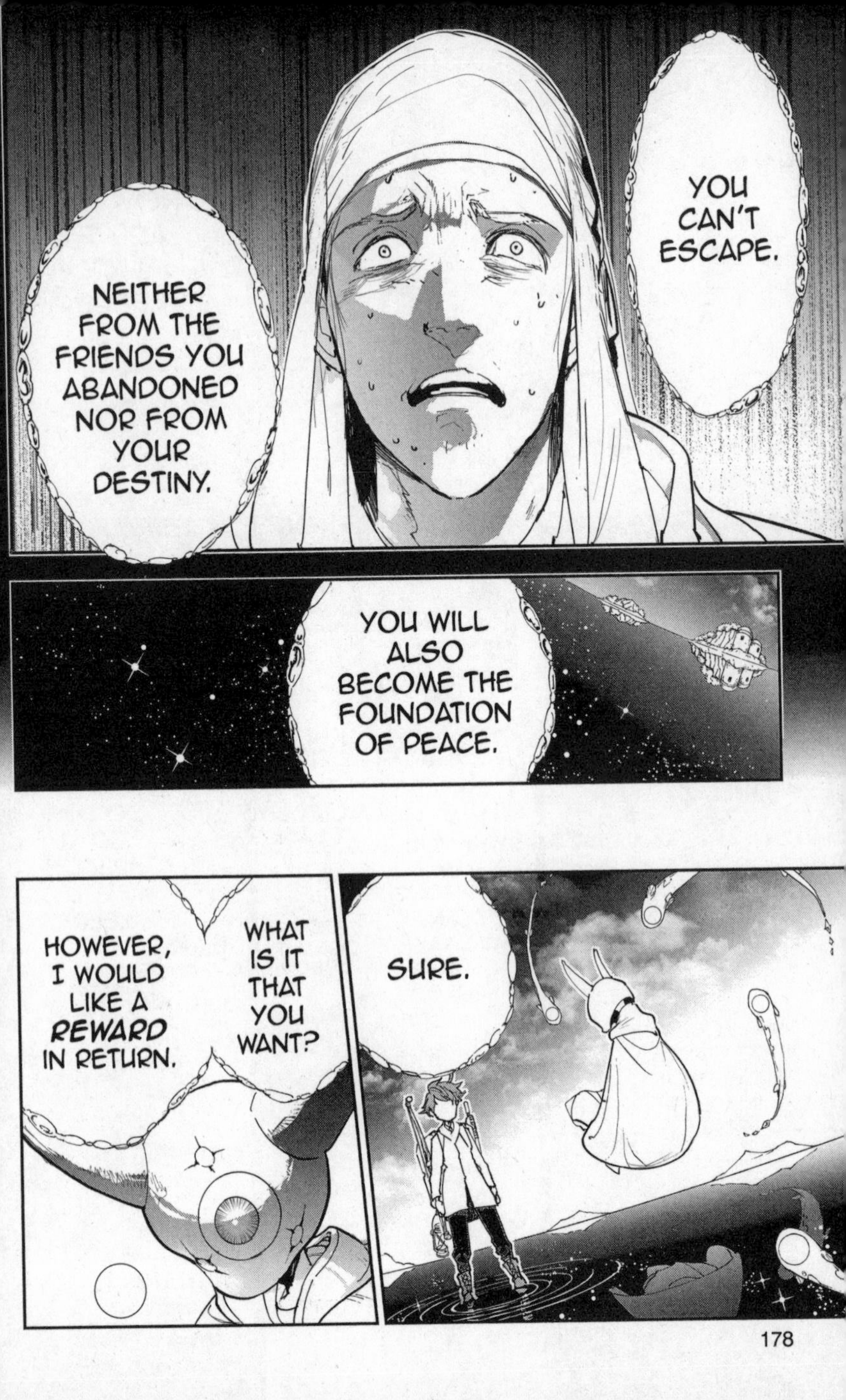
YOU CAN'T ESCAPE.
NEITHER FROM THE FRIENDS YOU ABANDONED NOR FROM YOUR DESTINY.
YOU WILL ALSO BECOME THE FOUNDATION OF PEACE.
SURE.
HOWEVER, I WOULD LIKE A *REWARD* IN RETURN.
WHAT IS IT THAT YOU WANT?

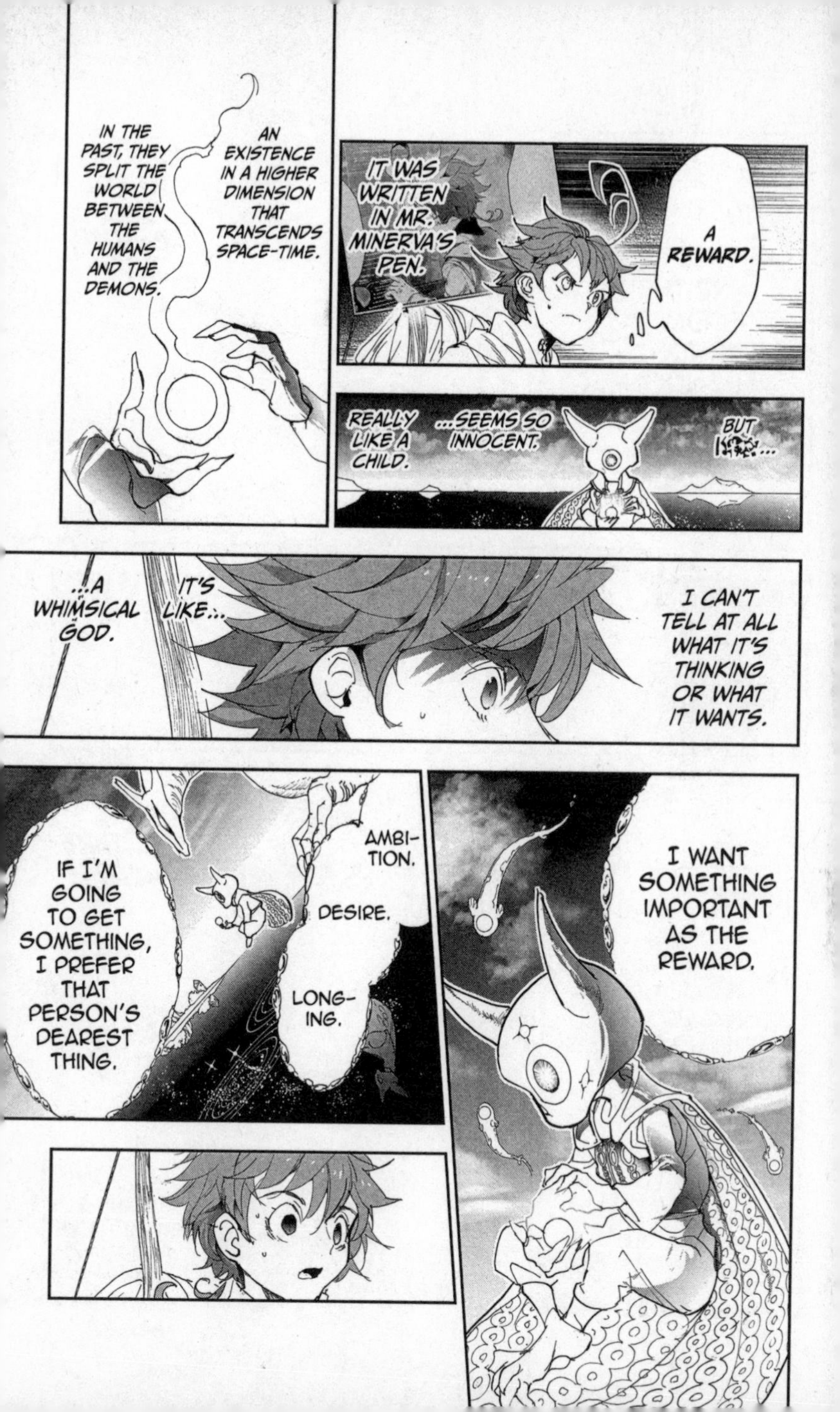
A REWARD.
IT WAS WRITTEN IN MR. MINERVA'S PEN.
BUT
...SEEMS SO INNOCENT.
REALLY LIKE A CHILD.
AN EXISTENCE IN A HIGHER DIMENSION THAT TRANSCENDS SPACE-TIME.
IN THE PAST, THEY SPLIT THE WORLD BETWEEN THE HUMANS AND THE DEMONS.
I CAN'T TELL AT ALL WHAT IT'S THINKING OR WHAT IT WANTS.
IT'S LIKE...
...A WHIMSICAL GOD.
I WANT SOMETHING IMPORTANT AS THE REWARD.
AMBITION.
DESIRE.
LONGING.
IF I'M GOING TO GET SOMETHING, I PREFER THAT PERSON'S DEAREST THING.

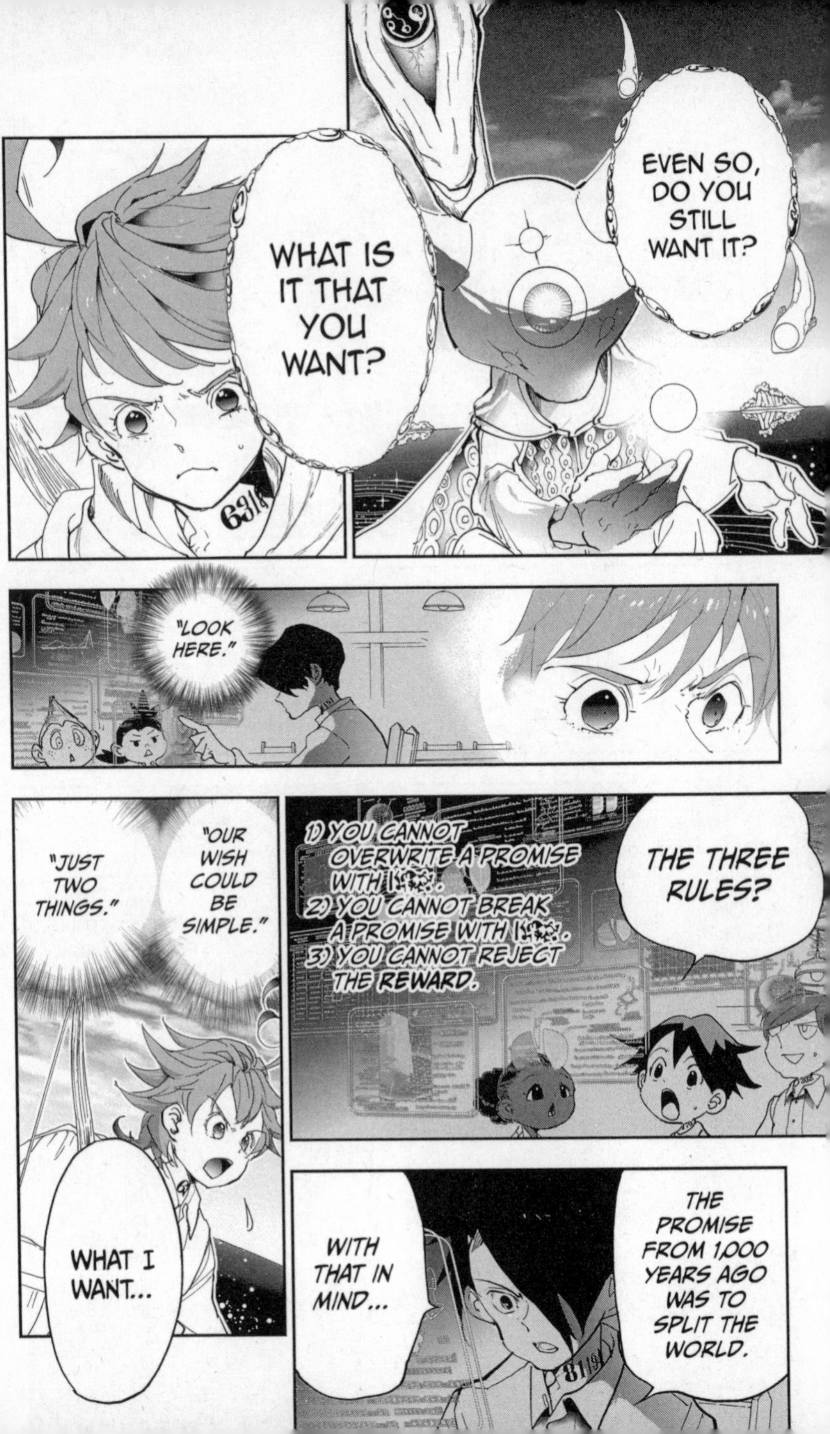
EVEN SO, DO YOU STILL WANT IT?
WHAT IS IT THAT YOU WANT?
"LOOK HERE."
THE THREE RULES?
1) YOU CANNOT OVERWRITE A PROMISE WITH
2) YOU CANNOT BREAK A PROMISE WITH
3) YOU CANNOT REJECT THE REWARD.
THE PROMISE FROM 1,000 YEARS AGO WAS TO SPLIT THE WORLD.
WITH THAT IN MIND...
"OUR WISH COULD BE SIMPLE."
"JUST TWO THINGS."
WHAT I WANT...

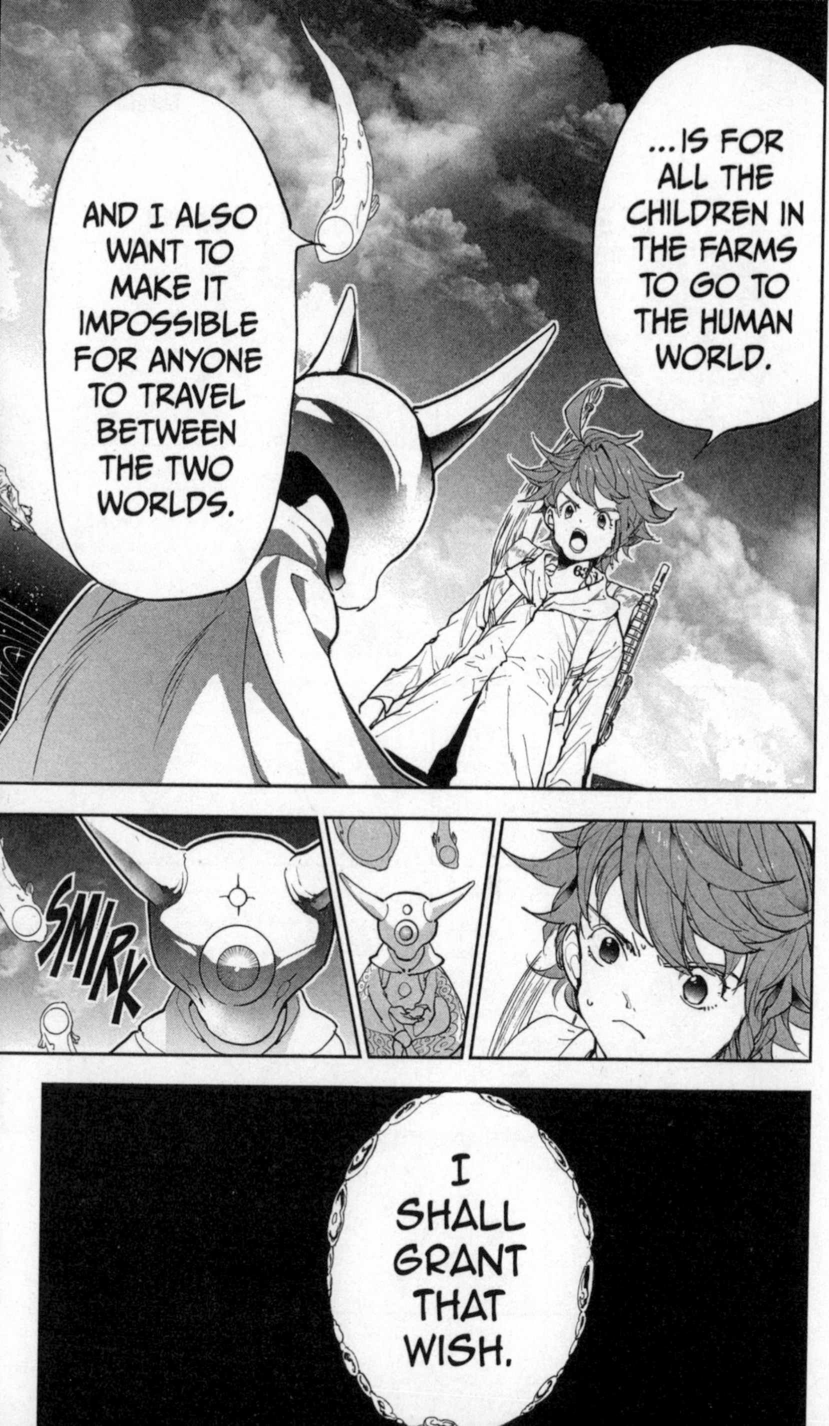
...IS FOR ALL THE CHILDREN IN THE FARMS TO GO TO THE HUMAN WORLD.
AND I ALSO WANT TO MAKE IT IMPOSSIBLE FOR ANYONE TO TRAVEL BETWEEN THE TWO WORLDS.
SMIRK
I SHALL GRANT THAT WISH.

SIDE STORY 14

ALL GOOD BECAUSE IT'S SUMMER

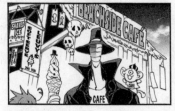

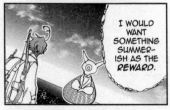

I WOULD WANT SOMETHING SUMMERISH AS THE *REWARD*.
FIREWORKS.
EDAMAME.
A BEER GARDEN.
I KNOW.
GLOW
!!
I WANT LEUVY'S SOFT SERVE.
BEACHSIDE CAFÉ
SHAVED ICE
SOFT SERVE
LEUVY'S
350 YEN
CAFE
CAFE
WAFER
CHOCOLATES
THAT'LL BE 350 YEN.
...
AND WHAT ABOUT THE *REWARD?*
OH...
HUH?! WHAT THE HECK?! WHAT IS IT? YOU'RE KILLING ME!!
SCURRY SCURRY
SCURRY

SIDE STORY 14...FIN

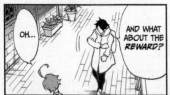

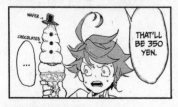

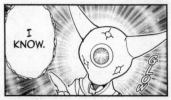

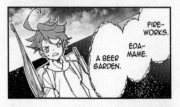

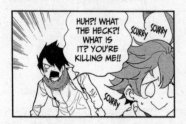

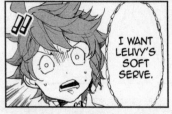

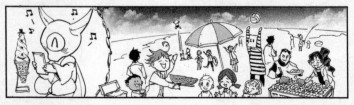

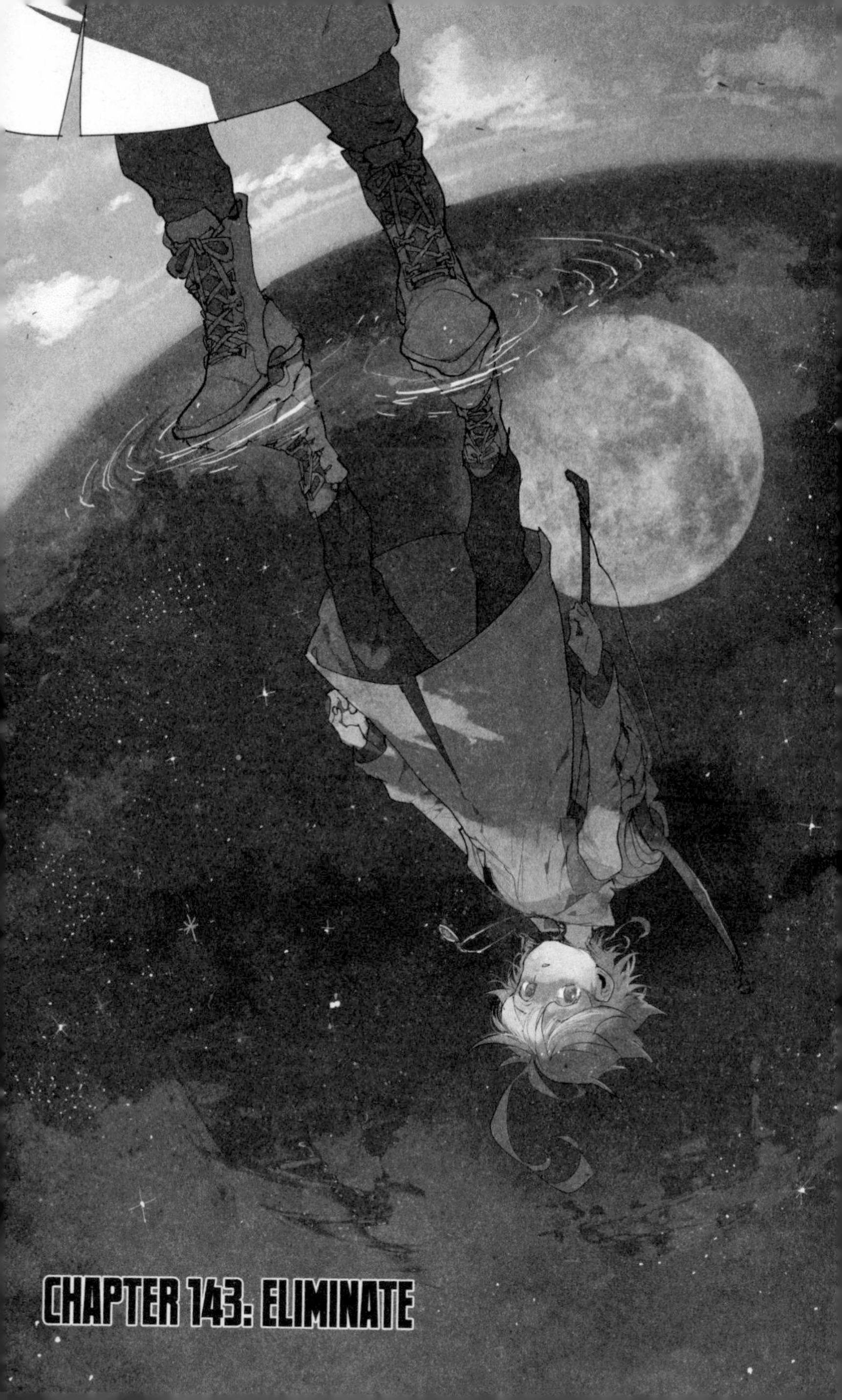

CHAPTER 143: ELIMINATE

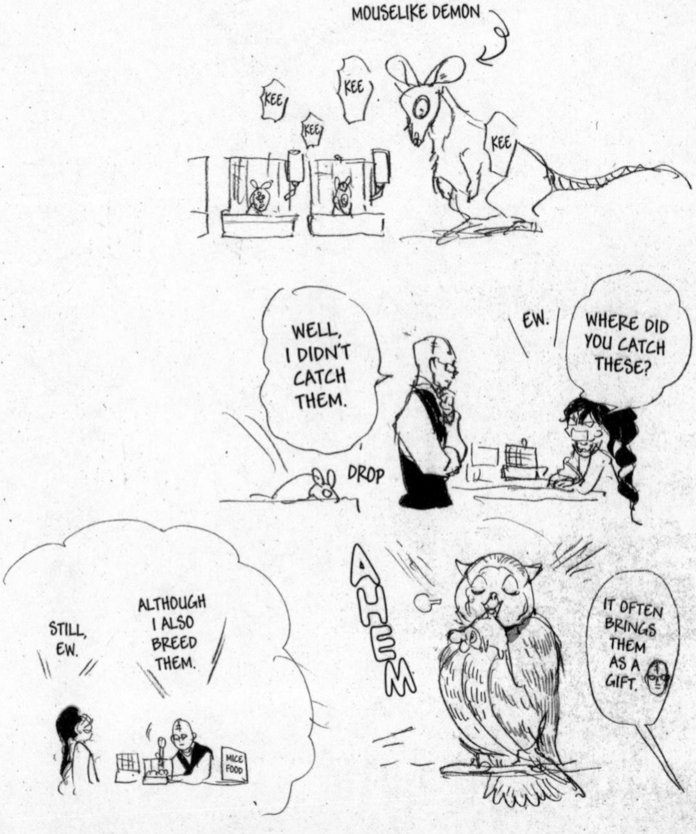

MOUSELIKE DEMON
KEE
KEE
KEE
KEE
WHERE DID YOU CATCH THESE?
EW.
WELL, I DIDN'T CATCH THEM.
DROP
IT OFTEN BRINGS THEM AS A GIFT.
AHEM
ALTHOUGH I ALSO BREED THEM.
STILL, EW.
MICE FOOD

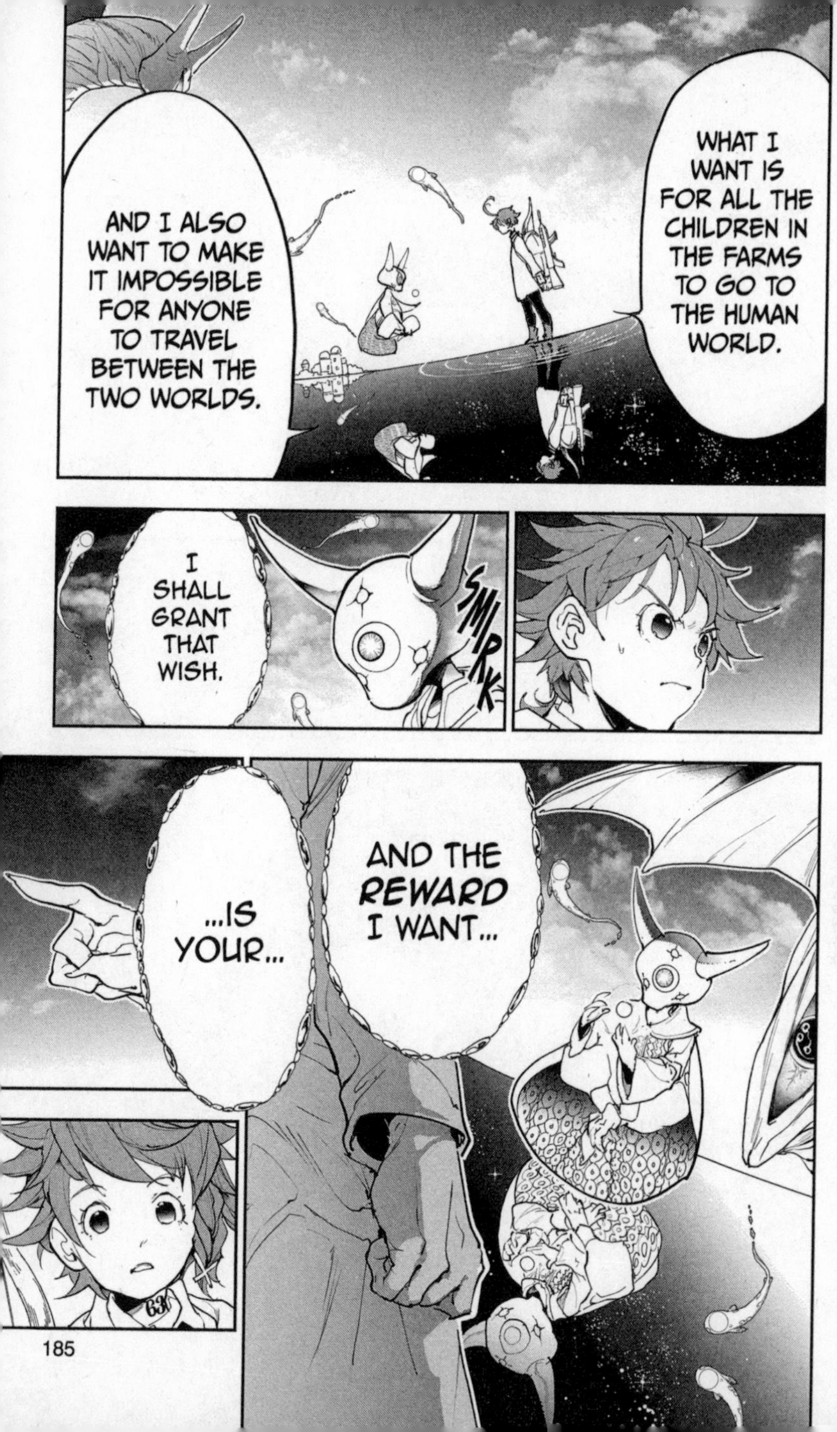

WHAT I WANT IS FOR ALL THE CHILDREN IN THE FARMS TO GO TO THE HUMAN WORLD.
AND I ALSO WANT TO MAKE IT IMPOSSIBLE FOR ANYONE TO TRAVEL BETWEEN THE TWO WORLDS.
I SHALL GRANT THAT WISH.
SMIRK
AND THE *REWARD* I WANT...
...IS YOUR...

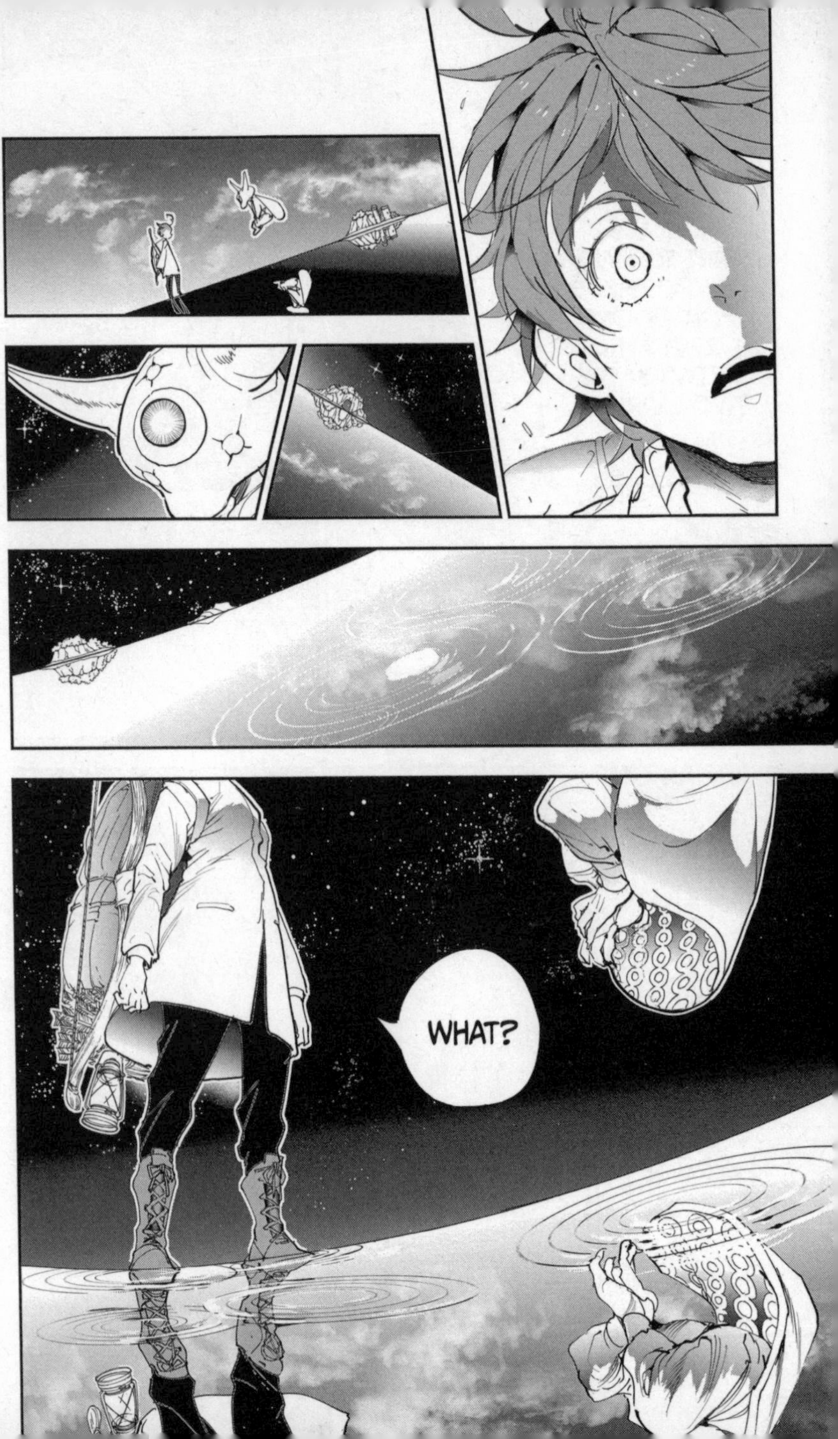
WHAT?

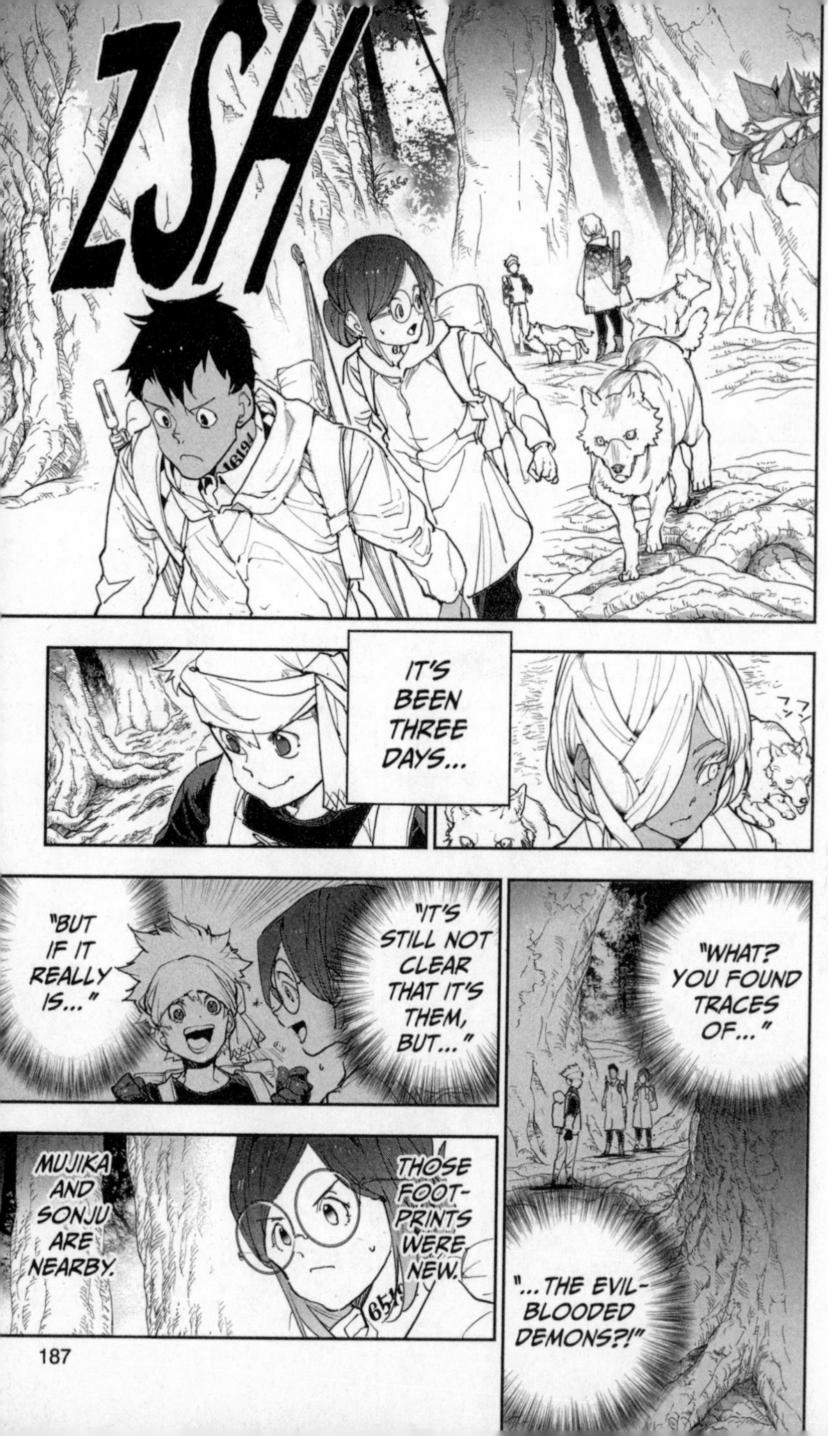
ZSH
IT'S BEEN THREE DAYS...
"WHAT? YOU FOUND TRACES OF..."
"...THE EVIL-BLOODED DEMONS?!"
"IT'S STILL NOT CLEAR THAT IT'S THEM, BUT..."
"BUT IF IT REALLY IS..."
THOSE FOOT-PRINTS WERE NEW.
MUJIKA AND SONJU ARE NEARBY.

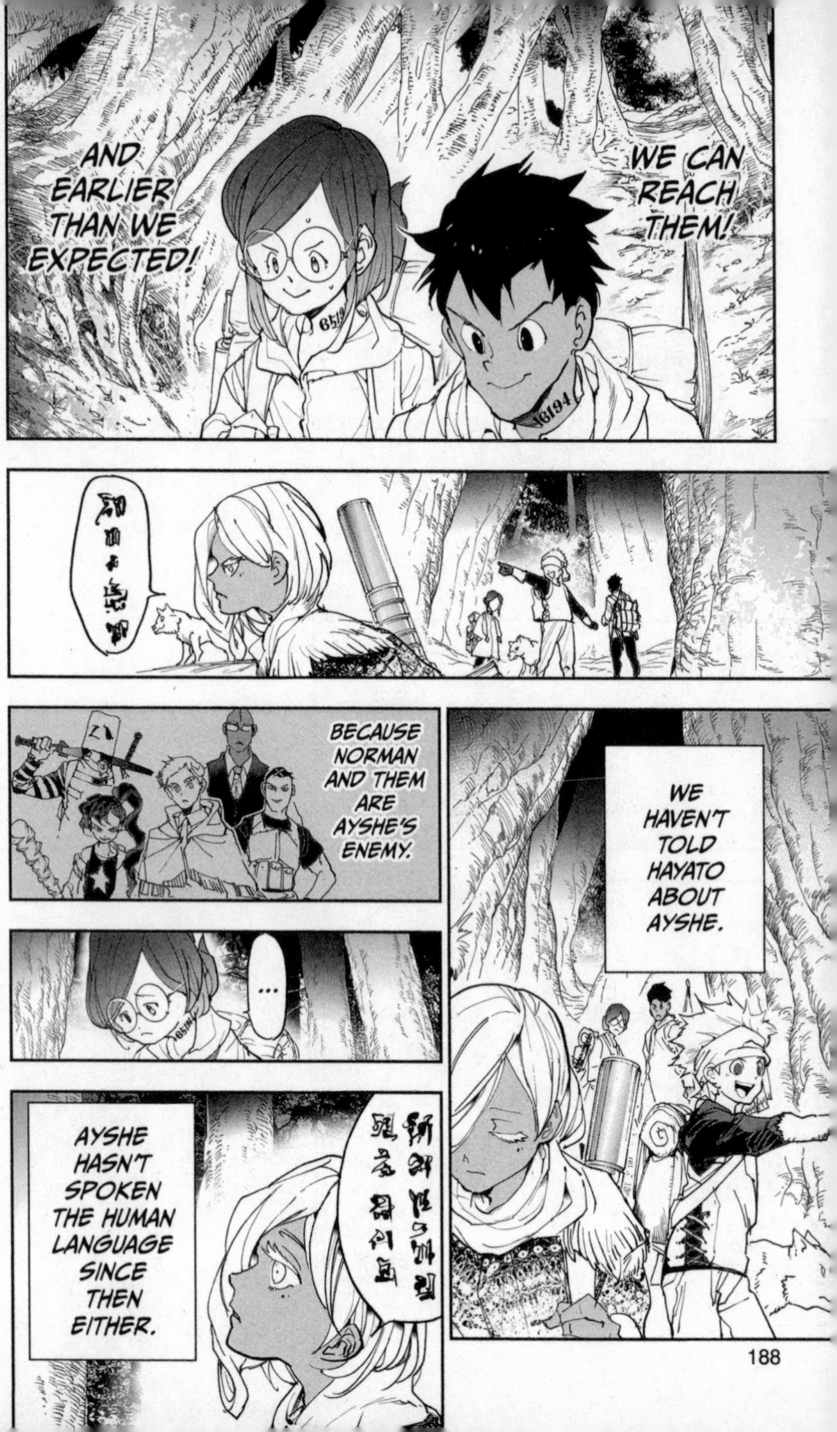
WE CAN REACH THEM!
AND EARLIER THAN WE EXPECTED!
WE HAVEN'T TOLD HAYATO ABOUT AYSHE.
BECAUSE NORMAN AND THEM ARE AYSHE'S ENEMY.
...
AYSHE HASN'T SPOKEN THE HUMAN LANGUAGE SINCE THEN EITHER.

DON! GILDA! WHAT ABOUT THESE FOOT-PRINTS?!

SNIFF SNIFF

IT MEANS THAT MUJIKA AND SONJU ARE THAT GOOD AT HIDING.

THESE CLUES ARE REALLY HARD TO FIND, EH?

IT'S NOT THEM.

SORRY...

IT'S FINE. WE'RE GOING IN THE RIGHT DIRECTION.

EVEN ON NORMAN'S MAP...

YES. THEY'VE DISAPPEARED EVER SINCE WE FOUND THOSE FOOTPRINTS THREE DAYS AGO.

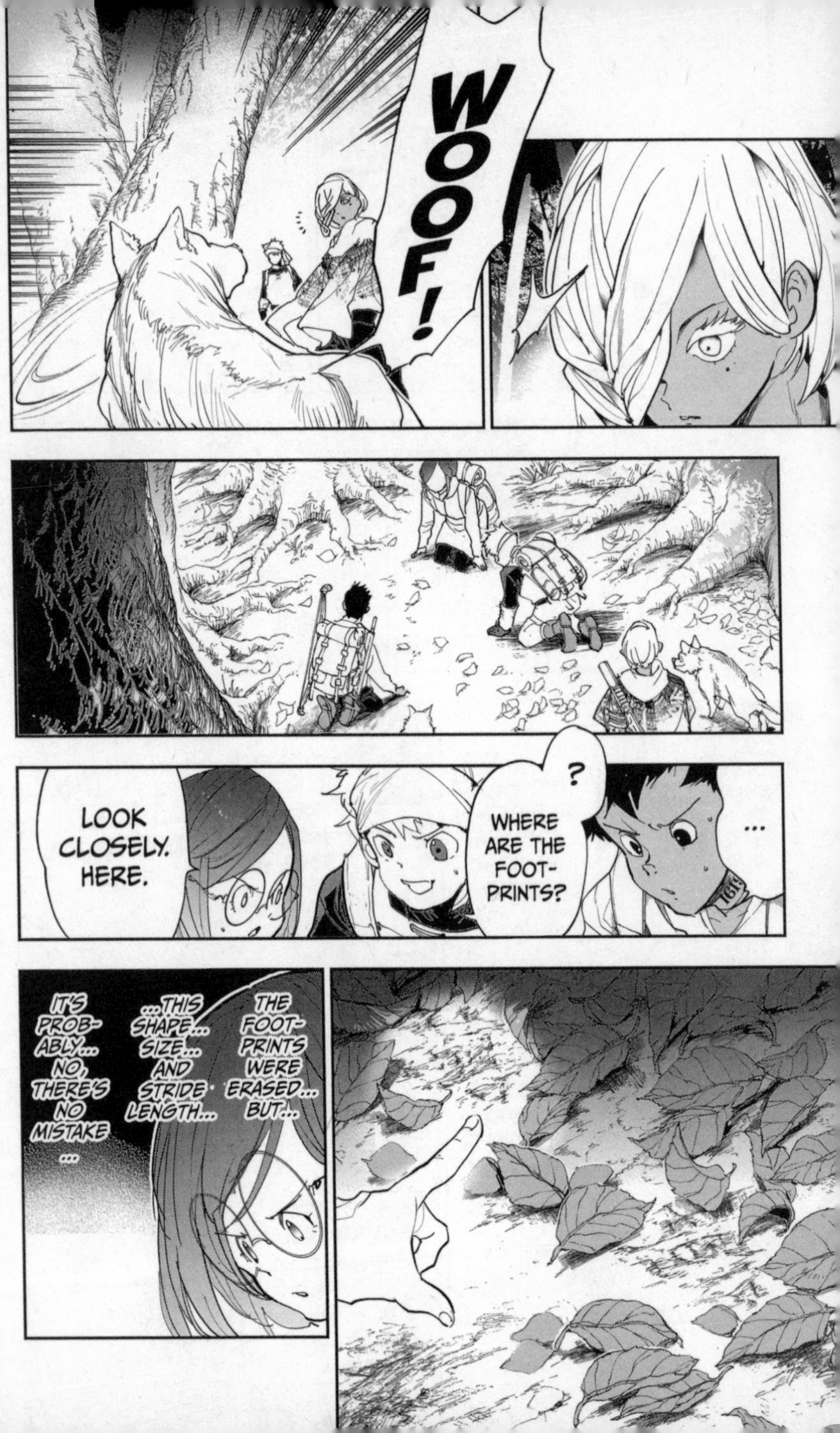
WOOF!
...
?
WHERE ARE THE FOOT-PRINTS?
LOOK CLOSELY. HERE.
THE FOOT-PRINTS WERE ERASED... BUT...
...THIS SHAPE... SIZE... AND STRIDE LENGTH...
IT'S PROBABLY... NO, THERE'S NO MISTAKE...

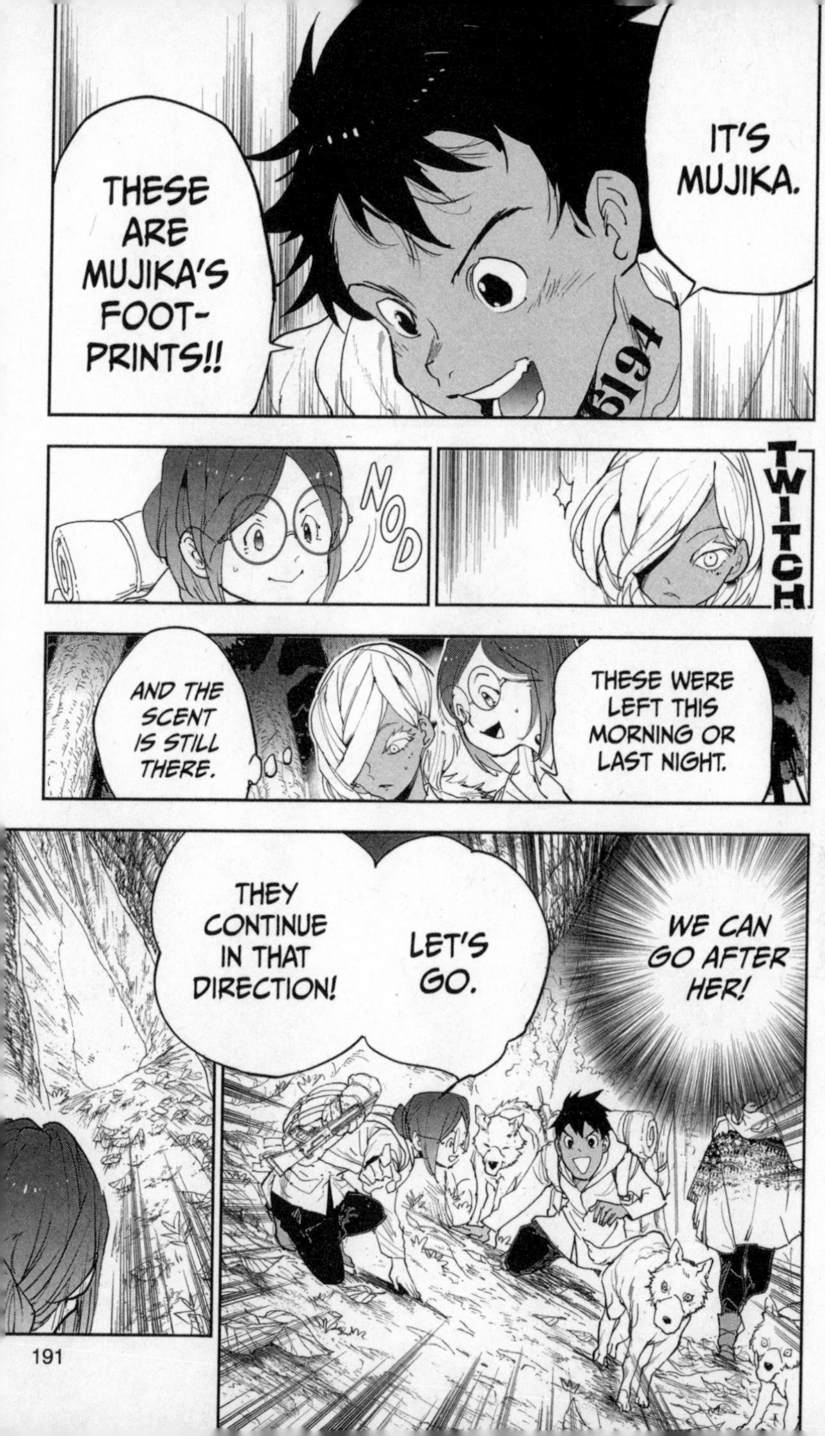
IT'S MUJIKA.
THESE ARE MUJIKA'S FOOT-PRINTS!!
6194
TWITCH
NOD
THESE WERE LEFT THIS MORNING OR LAST NIGHT.
AND THE SCENT IS STILL THERE.
WE CAN GO AFTER HER!
LET'S GO.
THEY CONTINUE IN THAT DIRECTION!

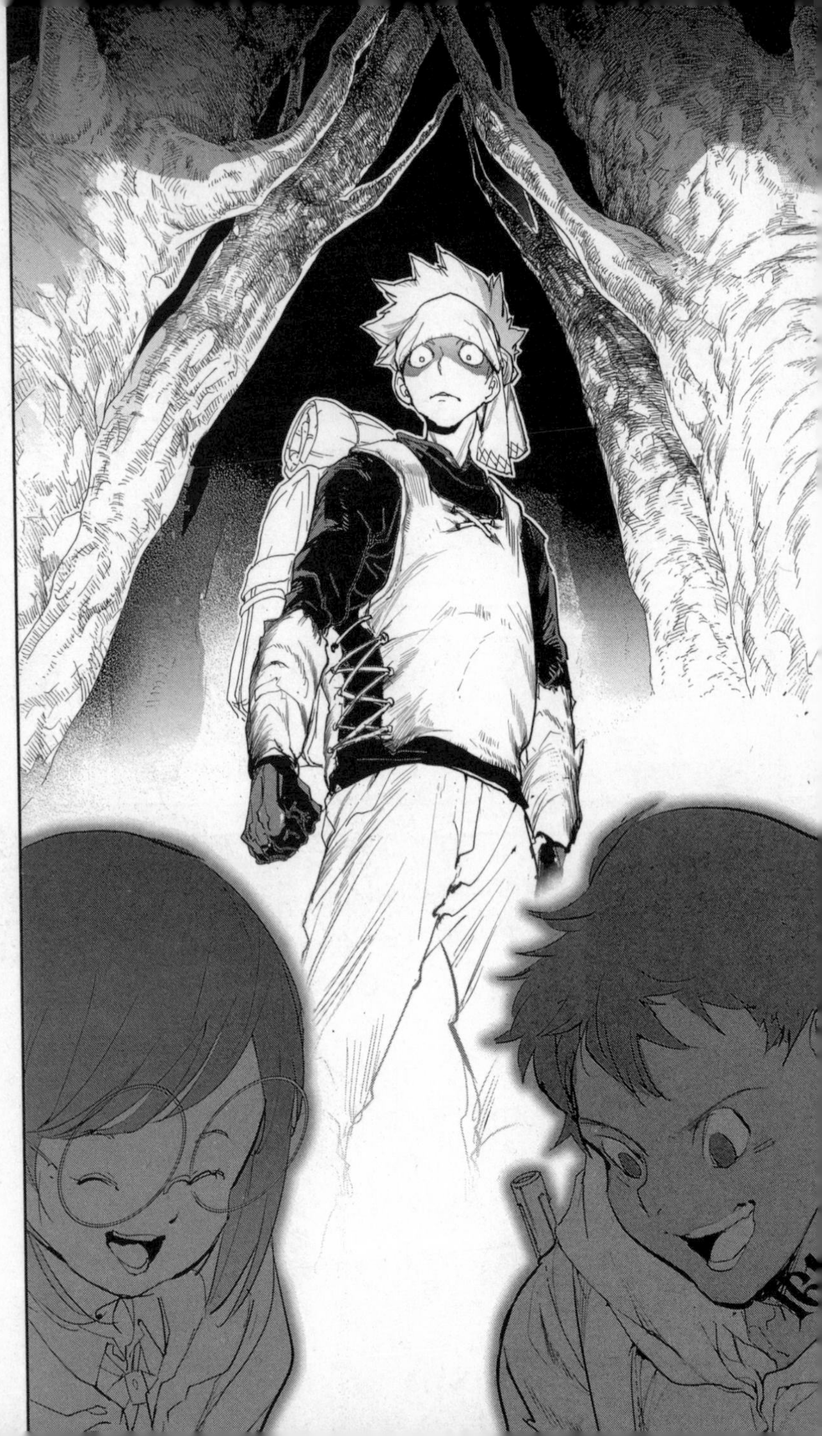

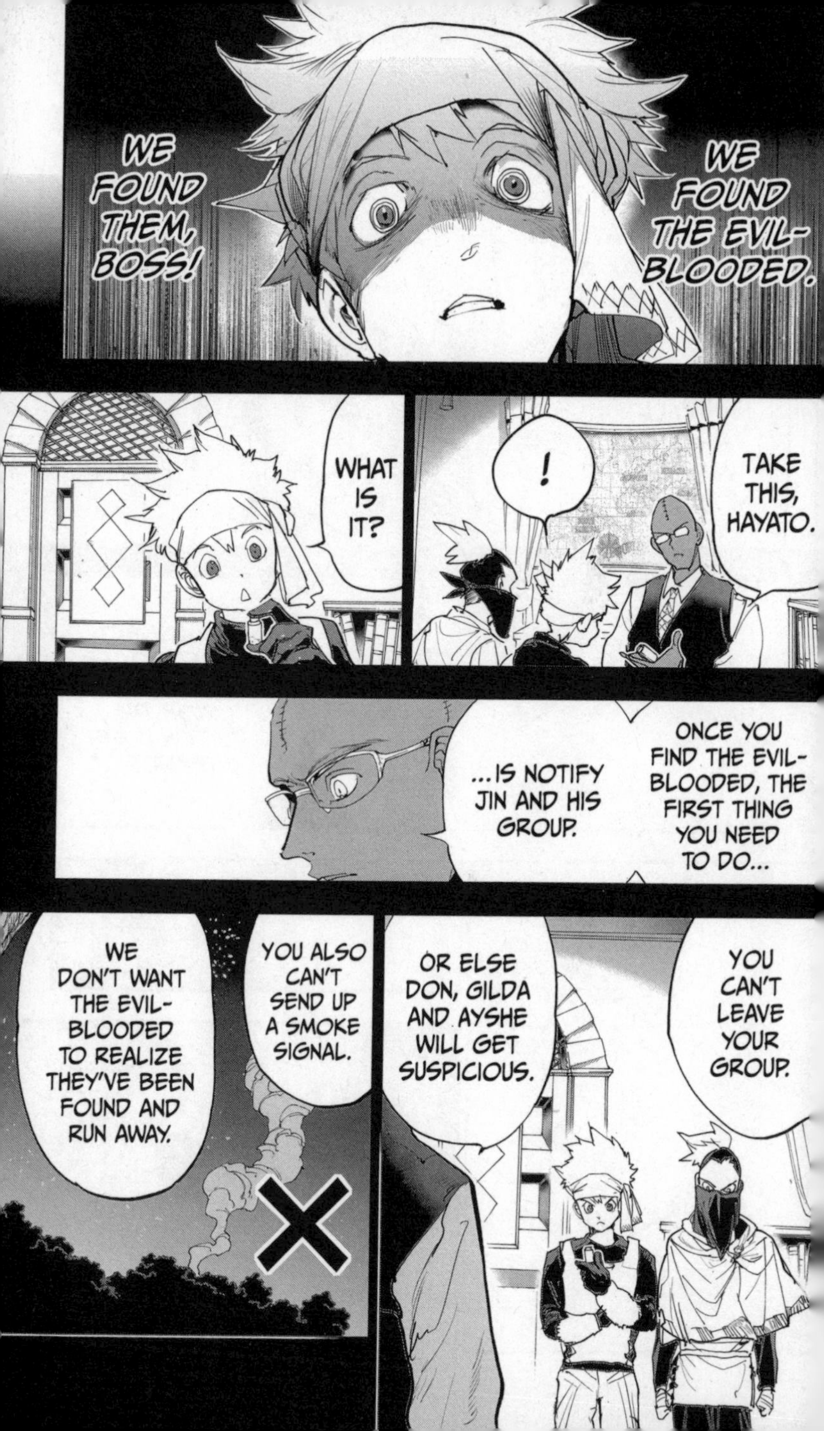
WE FOUND THE EVIL-BLOODED.
WE FOUND THEM, BOSS!
TAKE THIS, HAYATO.
!
WHAT IS IT?
ONCE YOU FIND THE EVIL-BLOODED, THE FIRST THING YOU NEED TO DO...
...IS NOTIFY JIN AND HIS GROUP.
YOU CAN'T LEAVE YOUR GROUP.
OR ELSE DON, GILDA AND AYSHE WILL GET SUSPICIOUS.
YOU ALSO CAN'T SEND UP A SMOKE SIGNAL.
WE DON'T WANT THE EVIL-BLOODED TO REALIZE THEY'VE BEEN FOUND AND RUN AWAY.

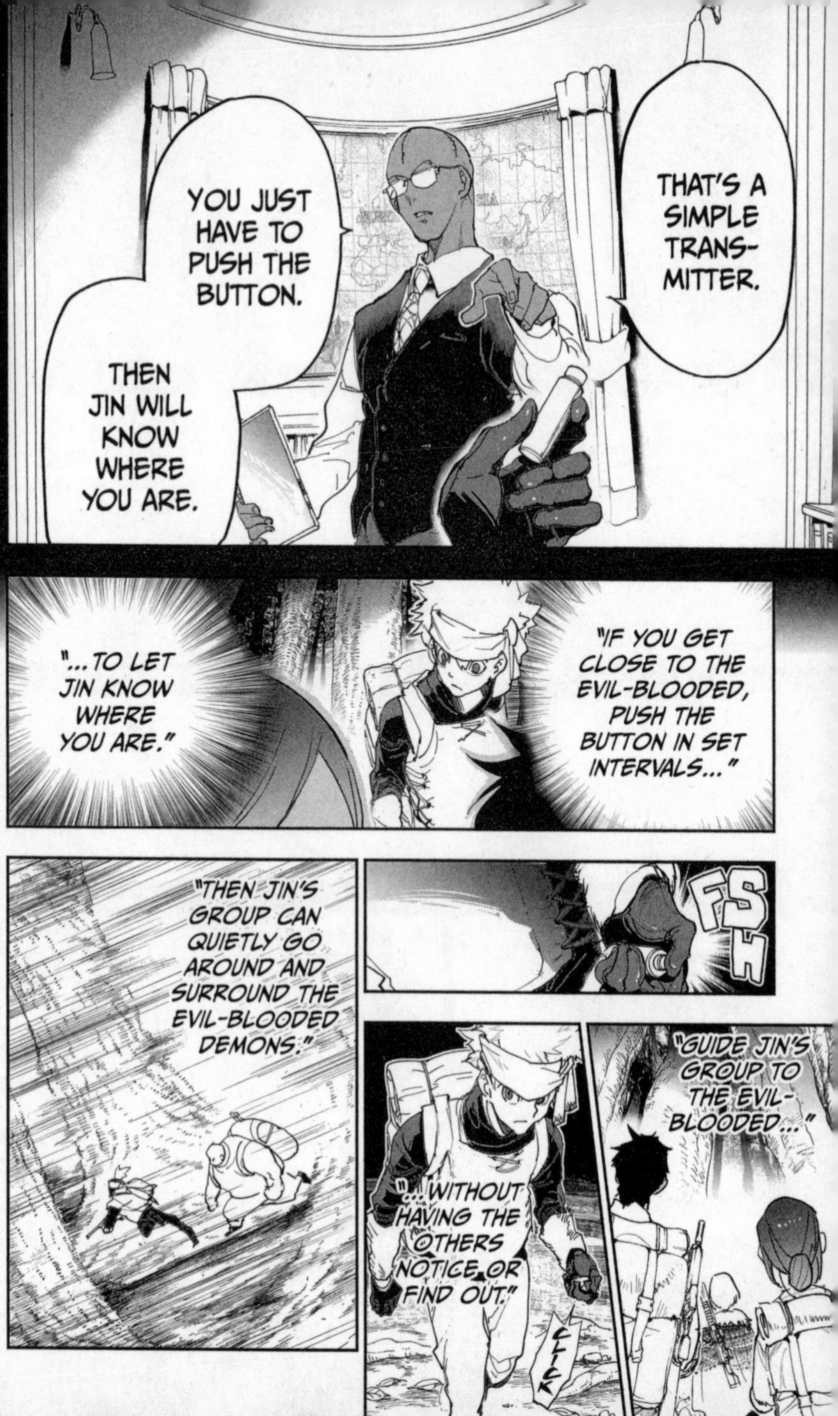
THAT'S A SIMPLE TRANS-MITTER.
YOU JUST HAVE TO PUSH THE BUTTON.
THEN JIN WILL KNOW WHERE YOU ARE.
"IF YOU GET CLOSE TO THE EVIL-BLOODED, PUSH THE BUTTON IN SET INTERVALS..."
"...TO LET JIN KNOW WHERE YOU ARE."
FSH
"GUIDE JIN'S GROUP TO THE EVIL-BLOODED..."
"...WITHOUT HAVING THE OTHERS NOTICE OR FIND OUT."
CLICK
"THEN JIN'S GROUP CAN QUIETLY GO AROUND AND SURROUND THE EVIL-BLOODED DEMONS."

"THE STRENGTH OF LAMBDA WILL LAY THE EVIL-BLOODED TO REST."

"THERE'S NO FLAW IN BOSS'S PLAN."

DON, GILDA, AYSHE AND HER DOGS HAVEN'T NOTICED.

I'M DOING GOOD.

WE HAVE TO KILL THE EVIL-BLOODED!!

IT'S AN ORDER FROM BOSS.

I DECEIVED BOTH OF YOU.

I'M SORRY, GILDA, DON.

AND FOR ALL OF OUR FUTURES.

BUT THIS IS FOR US, FARM CHILDREN.

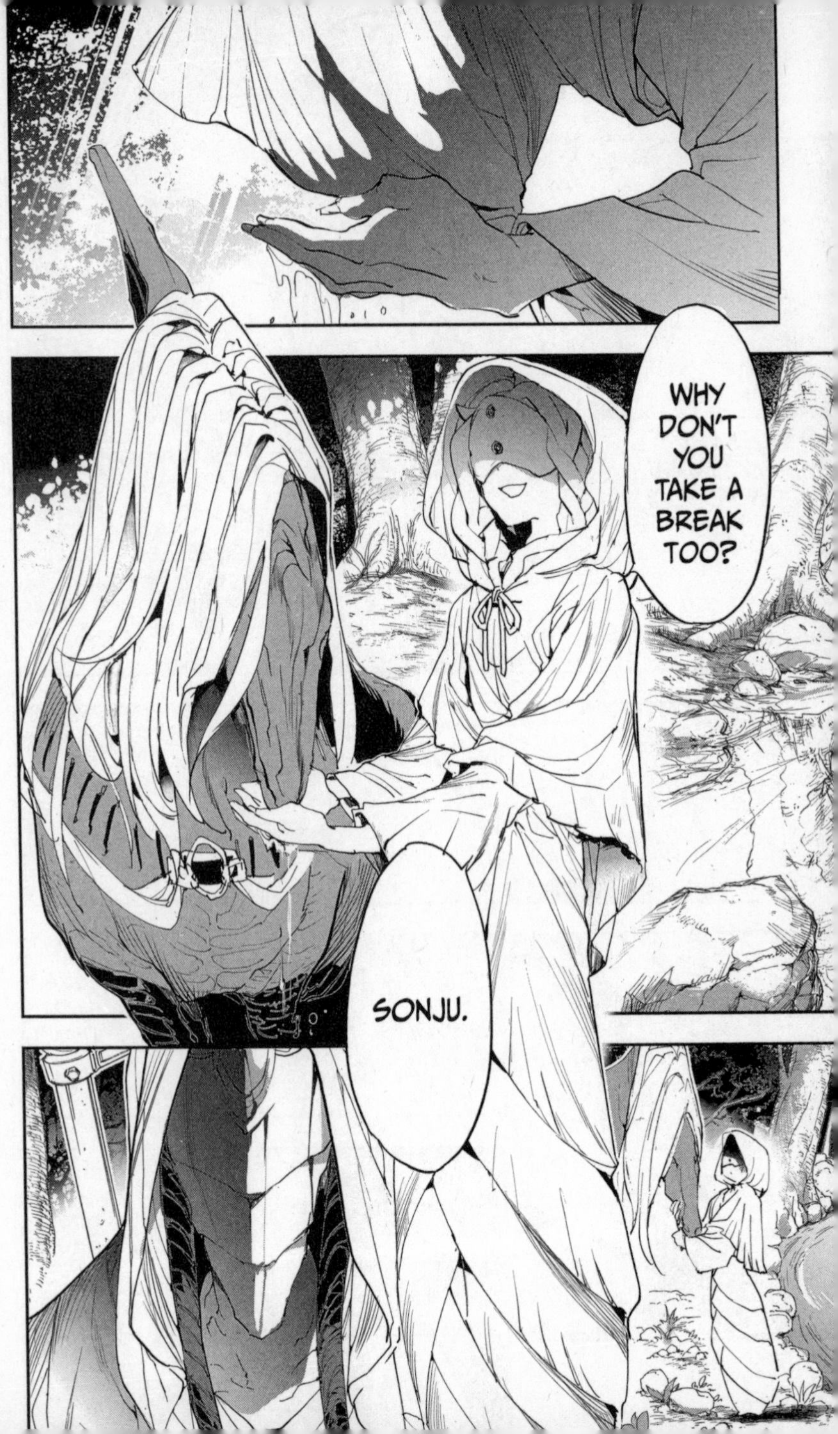
WHY DON'T YOU TAKE A BREAK TOO?
SONJU.

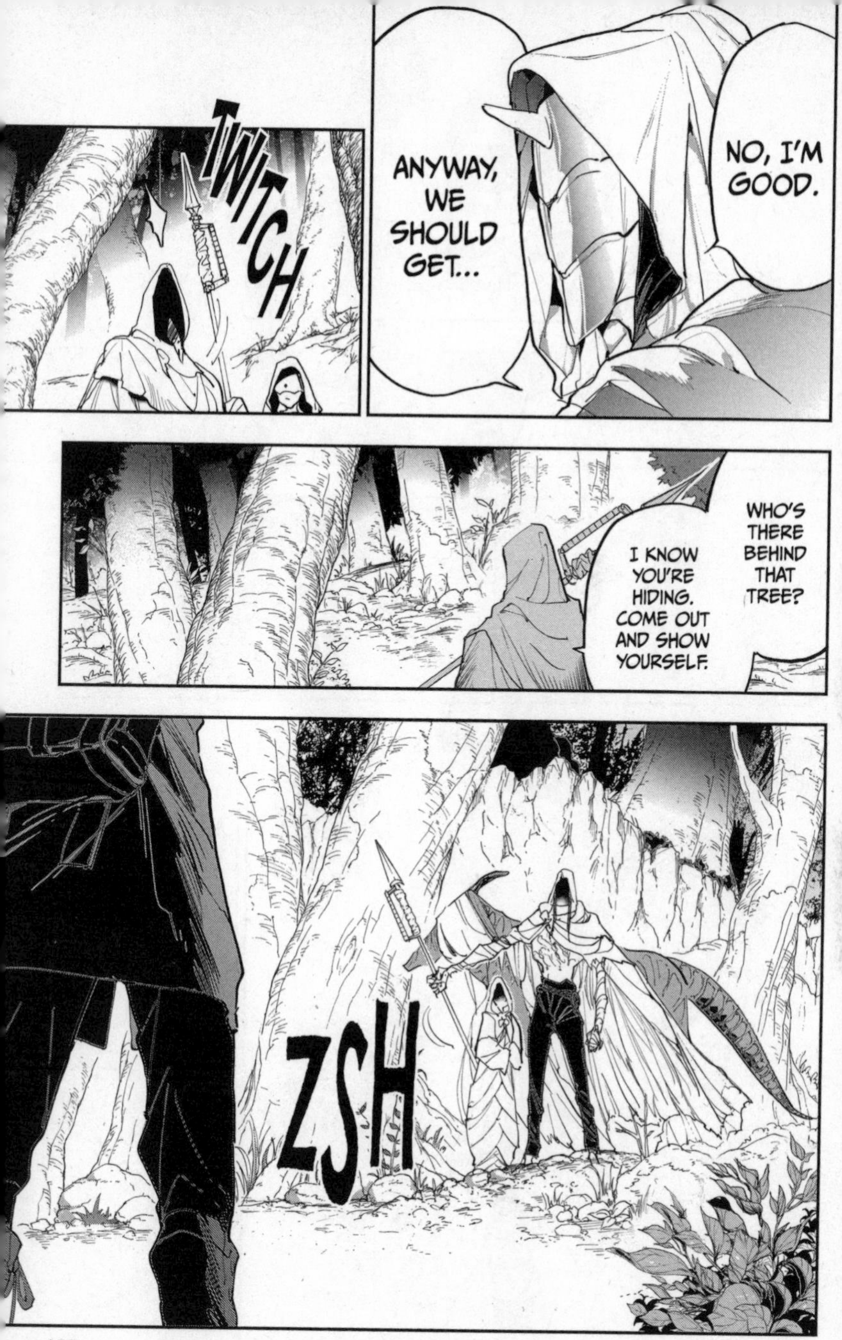
NO, I'M GOOD.
ANYWAY, WE SHOULD GET...
TWITCH
WHO'S THERE BEHIND THAT TREE?
I KNOW YOU'RE HIDING. COME OUT AND SHOW YOURSELF.
ZSH

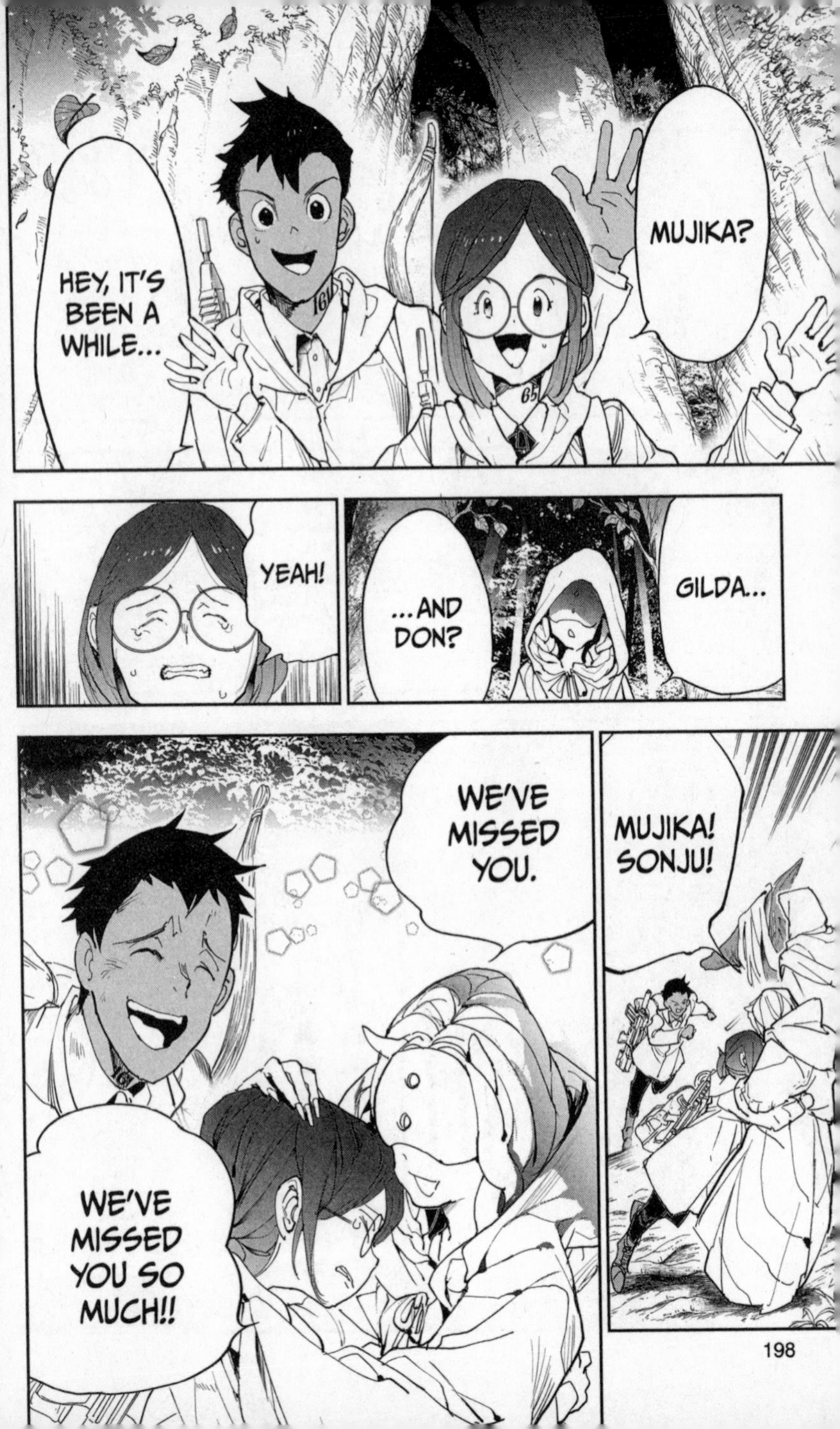
MUJIKA?
HEY, IT'S BEEN A WHILE...
GILDA...
...AND DON?
YEAH!
MUJIKA! SONJU!
WE'VE MISSED YOU.
WE'VE MISSED YOU SO MUCH!!

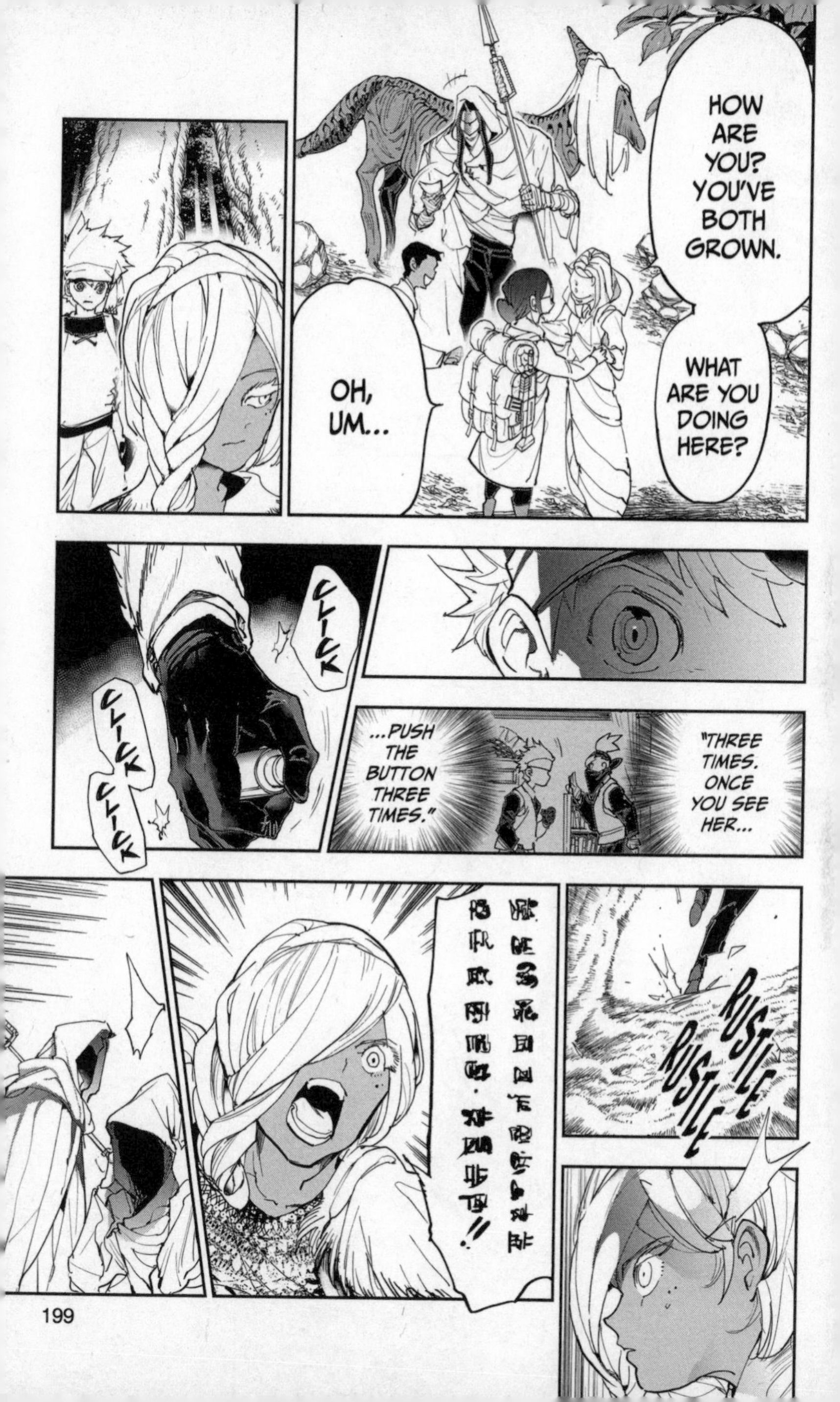

HOW ARE YOU? YOU'VE BOTH GROWN.
WHAT ARE YOU DOING HERE?
OH, UM...
"THREE TIMES. ONCE YOU SEE HER...
...PUSH THE BUTTON THREE TIMES."
CLICK
CLICK
CLICK
RUSTLE
RUSTLE

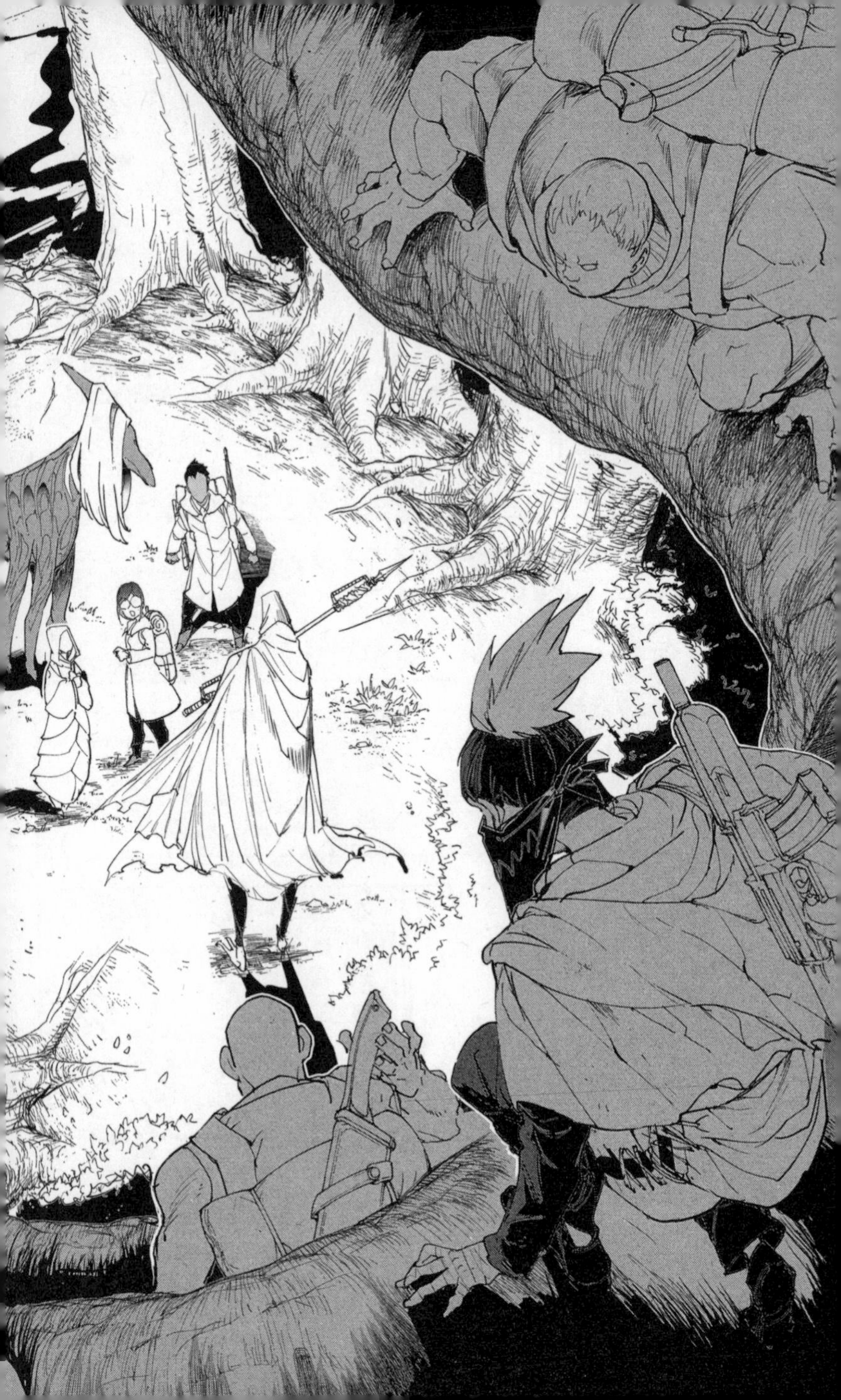

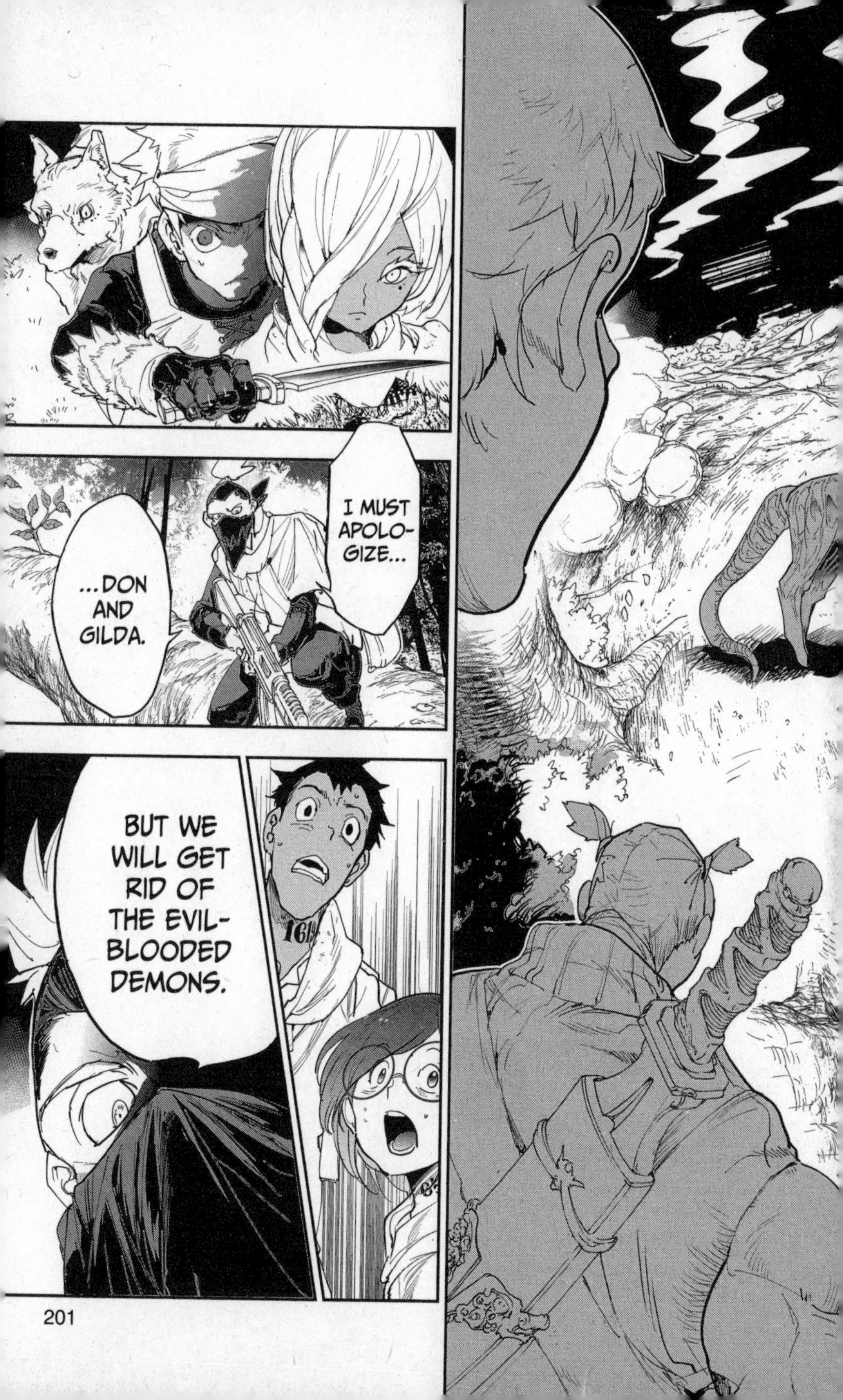
I MUST APOLOGIZE...
...DON AND GILDA.
BUT WE WILL GET RID OF THE EVIL-BLOODED DEMONS.

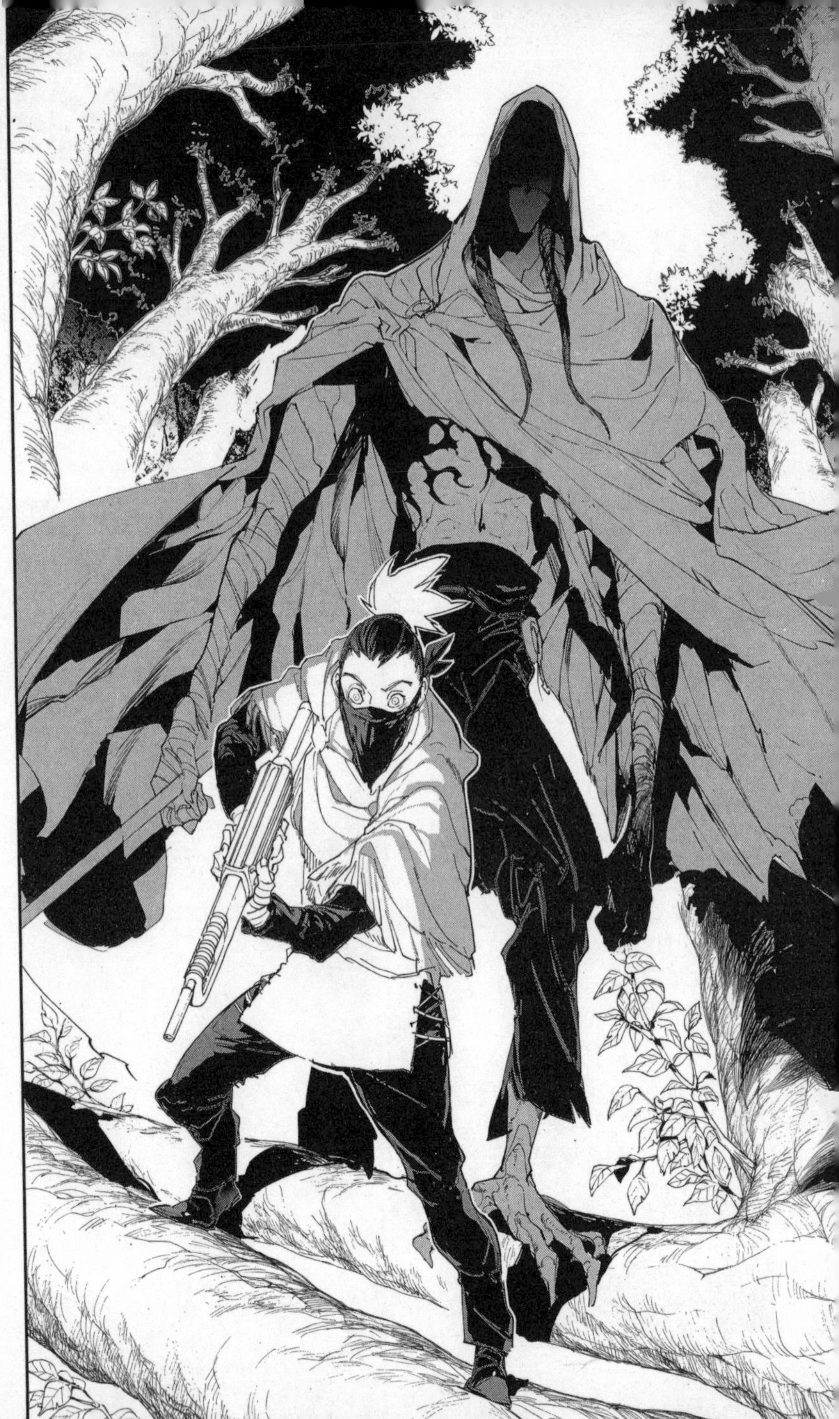

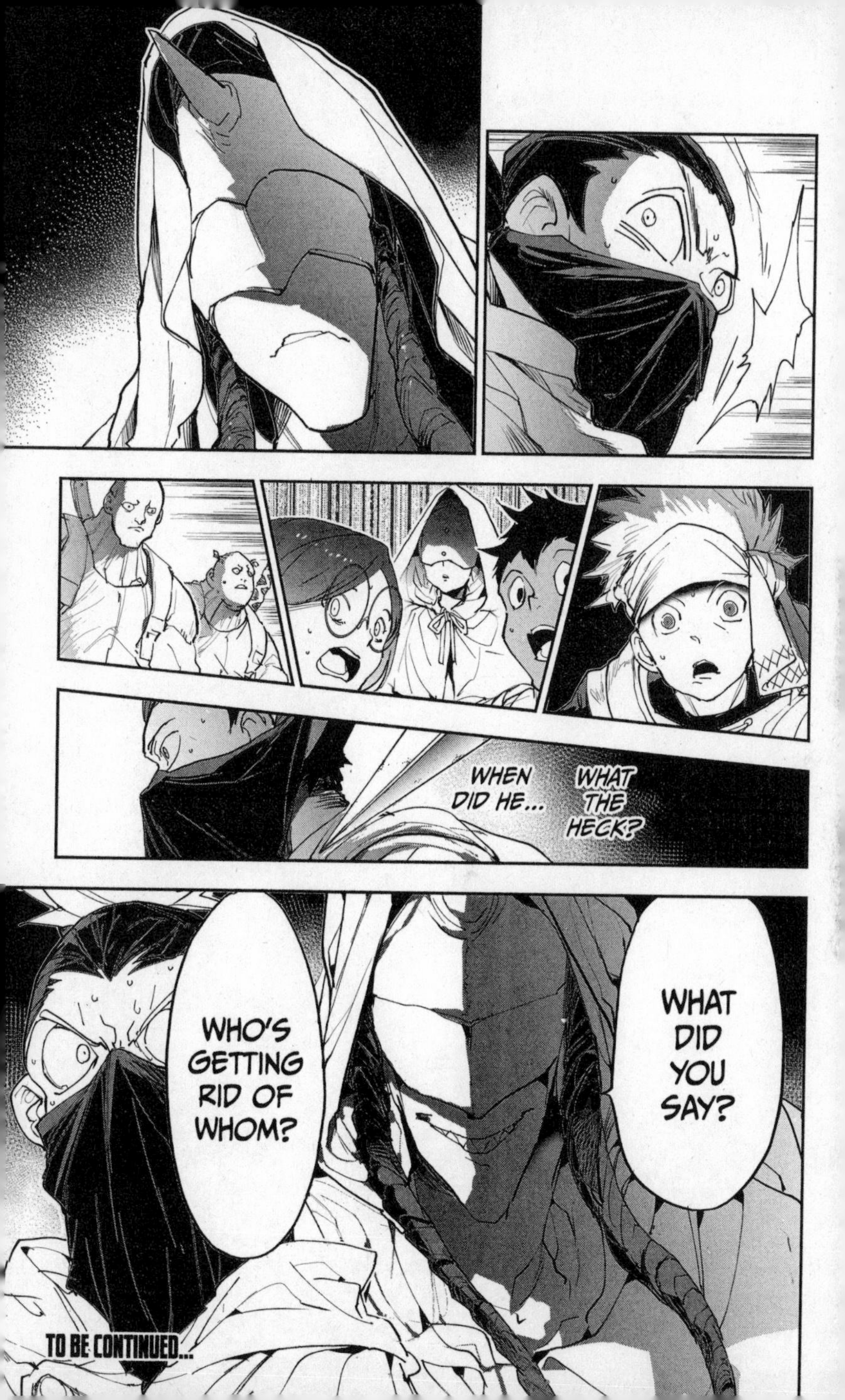
WHAT THE HECK?
WHEN DID HE...
WHAT DID YOU SAY?
WHO'S GETTING RID OF WHOM?
TO BE CONTINUED...

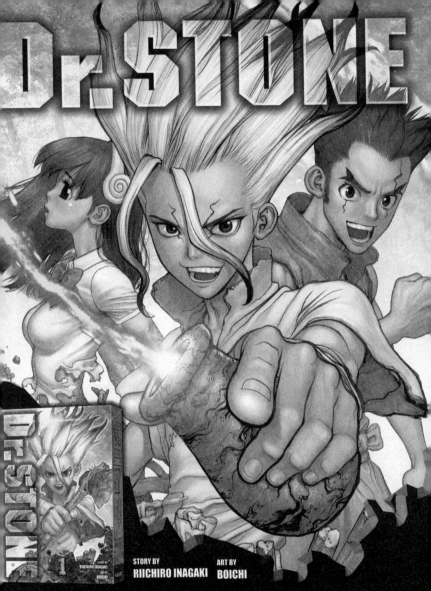

Dr.STONE

STORY BY
RIICHIRO INAGAKI

ART BY
BOICHI

One fateful day, all of humanity turned to stone. Many millennia later, Taiju frees himself from petrification and finds himself surrounded by statues. The situation looks grim—until he runs into his science-loving friend Senku! Together they plan to restart

Story and Art by
KOYOHARU GOTOUGE

In Taisho-era Japan, kindhearted Tanjiro Kamado makes a living selling charcoal. But his peaceful life is shattered when a demon slaughters his entire family. His little sister Nezuko is the only survivor, but she has been transformed into a demon herself! Tanjiro sets out on a dangerous journey to find a way to return his sister to normal and destroy the demon who ruined his life.

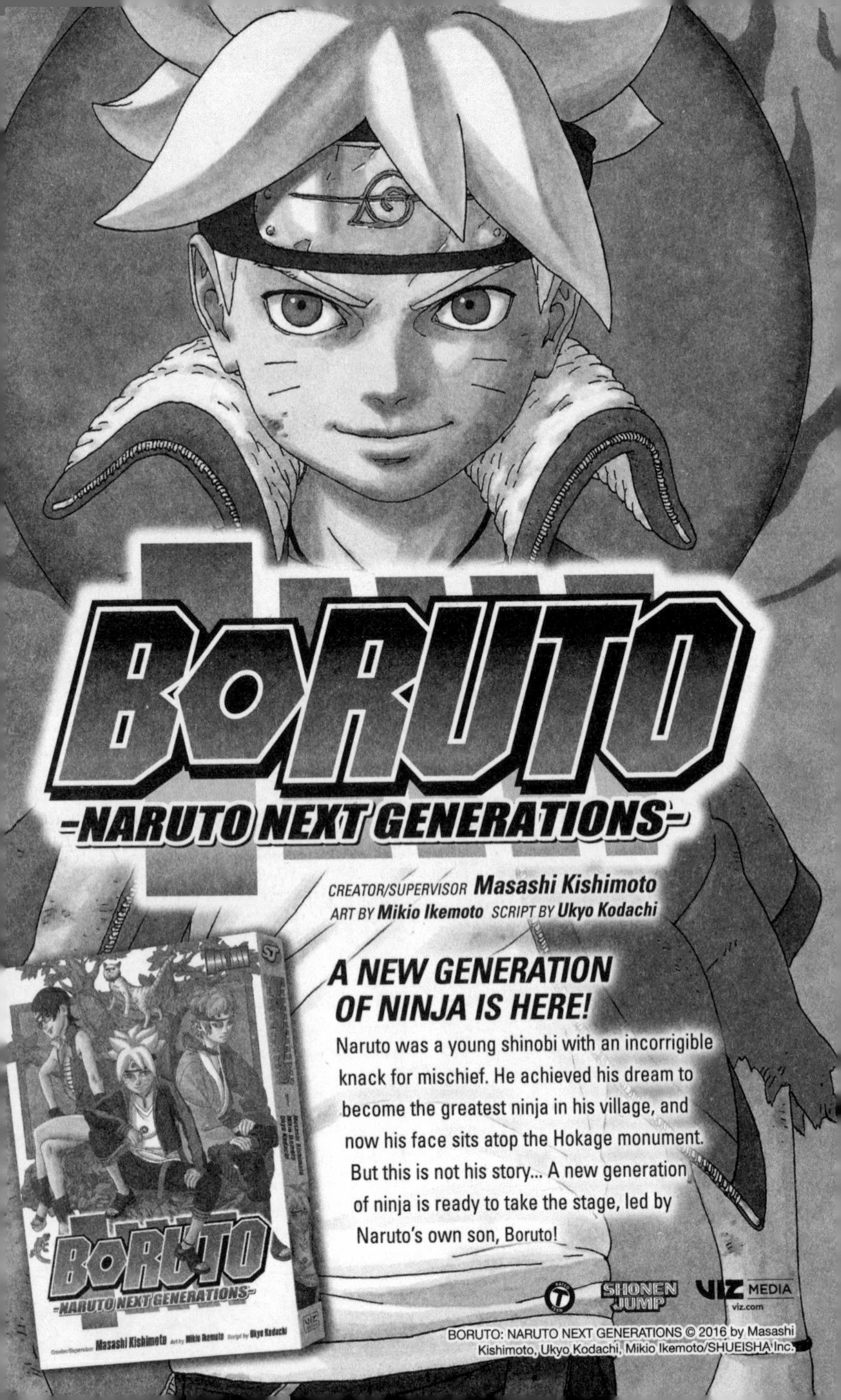
BORUTO
-NARUTO NEXT GENERATIONS-
CREATOR/SUPERVISOR Masashi Kishimoto
ART BY Mikio Ikemoto SCRIPT BY Ukyo Kodachi
A NEW GENERATION OF NINJA IS HERE!
Naruto was a young shinobi with an incorrigible knack for mischief. He achieved his dream to become the greatest ninja in his village, and now his face sits atop the Hokage monument. But this is not his story... A new generation of ninja is ready to take the stage, led by Naruto's own son, Boruto!
BORUTO
-NARUTO NEXT GENERATIONS-
Masashi Kishimoto
SHONEN JUMP
VIZ MEDIA
viz.com
BORUTO: NARUTO NEXT GENERATIONS © 2016 by Masashi Kishimoto, Ukyo Kodachi, Mikio Ikemoto/SHUEISHA Inc.

YOU'RE READING THE **WRONG WAY!**

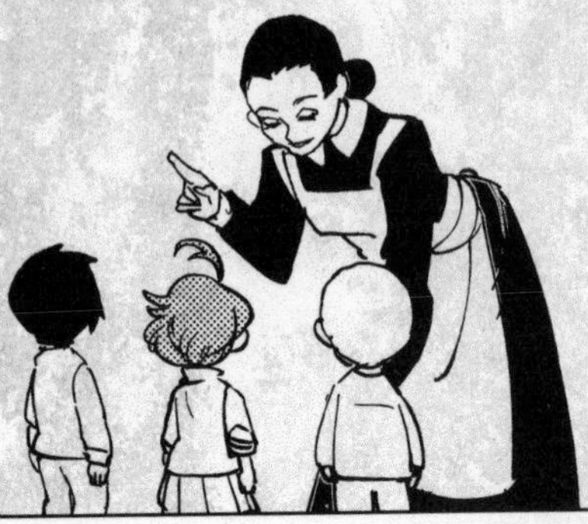

The Promised Neverland **reads from right to left, starting in the upper-right corner. Japanese is read from right to left, meaning that action, sound effects and word-balloon order are completely reversed from English order.**

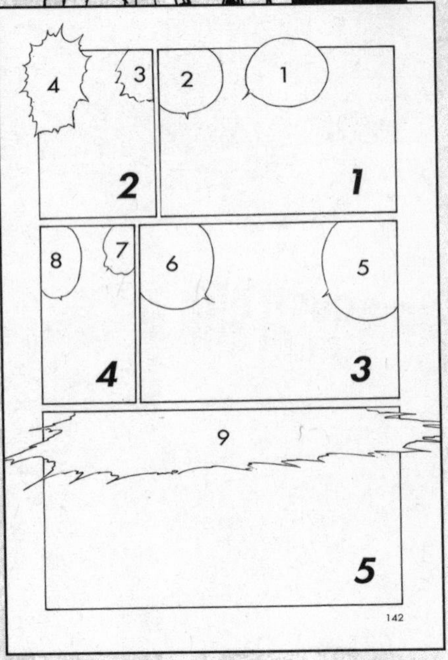

1
2
1
3
4
2
5
6
3
7
8
4
9
5
142